Harald Zieger's story is those who have lost sight and are naive enough to believe it can't happen here." His firsthand account of life under the thumb of communist oppression and flight to America is inspiring, tempered only by his insightful (and chilling) observations about the erosion of the freedom he and his family risked their lives seeking.

—Brian Thomas
Talk Radio Show Host at WKRC

John Adams stated, "But a constitution of government, once changed from freedom, can never be restored. Liberty once lost is lost forever."

In this incredible book, Harald shares his life story of growing up under the tyranny of Communist East Germany. Having escaped communism then socialism in Austria, he makes his home now in America, the land of the free. However, what he sees is a land heading down the same paths of destruction from which he left. Every citizen should heed his wake-up call and do whatever they can to keep America "one nation under God."

—Dr. Michael T. George
Nationally Acclaimed Speaker and Author

FREEDOM'S NIGHTMARE

HARALD ZIEGER

FREEDOM'S NIGHTMARE

TATE PUBLISHING
AND ENTERPRISES, LLC

Published by Tate Publishing & Enterprises, LLC
127 E. Trade Center Terrace | Mustang, Oklahoma 73064 USA
1.888.361.9473 | www.tatepublishing.com

Tate Publishing is committed to excellence in the publishing industry. The company reflects the philosophy established by the founders, based on Psalm 68:11,
"The Lord gave the word and great was the company of those who published it."

Book design copyright © 2015 by Tate Publishing, LLC. All rights reserved.
Cover design by Allen Jomoc
Interior design by Caypeeline Casas

Published in the United States of America

ISBN: 978-1-62994-428-9
Biography & Autobiography / Personal Memoirs
15.10.02

In the train in the wrong direction

DEDICATION

From a thankful heart,
I dedicate this book to my
Lord and Savior Jesus Christ
For the glory of our Father in Heaven

To Ashley

from

Harold

ACKNOWLEDGMENTS

My deepest thanks are going to my wife. Thank you for rescuing me from a path of eternal destruction, and for your loving and faithful support in difficult times, as well as your patience and endurance for the hours I spent in writing and not with you.

CONTENTS

THE SEVEN MIRACLES OF SOCIALISM

1st   Everyone had a job

2nd   Although everyone had a job, in reality nobody worked

3rd   Although nobody really worked, all business plans were fulfilled 100 percent

4th   Despite fulfilling all plans shelves remained empty in stores

5th   In spite of empty stores all had what they needed

6th   Although everyone had all they needed, everyone stole

7th   Although everybody stole nobody lacked anything

Although trials failed multiple times during the last century, there are people who still believe it works out just fine if they'd be in control, and this is actually a miracle in itself.

Berlin Wall on the way to the embassy

PROLOGUE

Why Empty Streets Can
Indicate a Shock in the Morning

I T HIT ME like that soccer ball in the middle of my face many years ago. How could I've been so stupid? The clarity came over me like a flashlight in the middle of the night. Focused on the visit at the embassy and with that feeling that we had done it so many times without having any trouble, I had totally neglected the explosive political situation in East Germany. One factor probably was that even the East German media did not mention it.

Thousands of East German citizens were able to enter the West German embassies all over East Europe. Nearly every country of the communistic block, including Poland, Czechoslovakia, and Hungary were occupied by masses of East Germans who demanded to be released into West Germany. Because of the inability of East Germany to block the western media from reaching them many people were informed about this situation, including us.

I saw two men from the state security police walking towards my family and me, and I realized how empty the street was. Unusual empty! And these two men hadn't been there before either. I was sure that when we had entered the street two minutes ago there was nobody, the street was empty, zero, nothing. Yet, that should have warned me that something was wrong here in the first place. From both ends of the street where the Austrian embassy was nearly in the center, these two men of the state security police walked towards us. They walked faster and faster, and my fear that they could outrun us increased with every step. I hesitated but I had to take the risk to....

One eventful year later, an almost ten-year-long fight for freedom was over and we could leave one of the largest prisons on earth. The communists named it *the paradise of the working class*, a misnomer if there ever was one. It was a country you could only leave in two ways: either you became old or sick enough to retire, or you risked your life. And so many—actually several thousand—were killed trying to escape that paradise.

Life was a permanent struggle with the aftermath of the dictatorship of the Socialist United Party (SED), with all the appearances of central, micromanaged economy where a politically correct attitude was higher ranked than knowledge and ingenuity. All we wanted was freedom and nothing more than to leave this worker's paradise and put behind us the most horrible part of our life. The decision to go this road was made years ago.

East and West Germn Flag SW

THE RESULT OF
TWELVE YEARS:
THOUSAND-YEAR REICH

The Outcome of the Thousand-Year Reich or Why Two Germanys Are Not Always Better

To UNDERSTAND THE totally different situations between East Germany and West Germany after the end of the Third Reich and the horrifying World War II, it is necessary to get a small "lecture" in German contemporary history. Many times when I talked to Americans about Germany I am surprised to learn how many have actually served in the armed forces and have been stationed in Germany. But at the same time, I am surprised at how marginal the knowledge is about the situation behind the Iron Curtain, as well as why Germany ended in a divided nation, let alone an understanding of what happened after the Cold War started in Germany, which became the Russian Military Occupational zone, or the Soviet Zone for short. Let's go back in history for a moment and look how it was when the weapons finally turned silent.

At the Yalta Conference held in February 1945, the Western Allies and the Soviet Union agreed on the division of Germany into occupation zones. Estimating the territory that the converging armies of the Western Allies and the Soviet Union would overrun, the Yalta Conference determined the demarcation line for the respective areas of occupation. The demarcation line between the Russian zone and the American and United Kingdom zone later set the border between East and West Germany.

Following Germany's surrender, an Allied Control Council was found. The United States, Britain, France, and the Soviet Union assumed governmental power in their zones in postwar Germany. Economic demilitarization, especially the stripping of industrial equipment, was the responsibility of each one of the occupational powers individually.

You may remember the scene in the movie about the great General Patton when he met the Russian commander and was asked to toast to Stalin and the great Soviet Union but he refused to do so. This scene was related to the conjunction of Russian and American troops at the Elbe River near the town Torgau, on April 25, 1945.

Because the Russians put so much value on the encirclement and capture of Berlin, they totally neglected the advancement of the Western Allied Troops into the German Southeast Territory. In fact the symbolism of hoisting the Soviet flag on top of the Reichstag, the building where the German parliamentary democracy was slowly but certainly moved towards the National Socialism dictatorship under Adolf Hitler, had a higher priority for Stalin.

He ordered the largest concentration of armed forces in history to the battle for Berlin. Roughly 1 million German soldiers with approximately 800 tanks and less than 100 aircraft were confronted by a total of 2.5 million troops, 6,250 tanks, and 7,500 aircraft of three Russian armies. It is said that the Russians had so much artillery that every 5 meters was a cannon when they started the assault on Berlin. When it was over, Berlin was a debris field with additional 250,000 Germans and 100,000 Russians dead.

The conference of Potsdam was delayed three times because the Soviet Union had to create the facts that in the east of the Oder-Neisse line not more than two million Germans lived because they would leave that territory to the newly built Polish Nation. This was mainly because of the 1939 robbed Polish Territory in the east as agreed with the Hitler-Stalin Pact, and she had already integrated this former part of Poland in its own territory. Since Churchill had refused to make more than five million Germans refugees, the Soviets tried to accomplish facts by allowing and supporting the Polish government to dislodge the Germans in great numbers. The western allies eventually agreed to a so-called territorial administration by the Polish government, which ultimately ended in a total displacement of all Germans from those former German territories.

Winston Churchill, who had denied the Soviets' requirements from the earliest appearance of the so-called "*question of the eastern territories,* was furious about that development, but he was powerless. The British parliamentary elections and the results interrupted the conference on July 25, 1945, and when it started on July 28th, Churchill wasn't a part of it anymore. The Soviets had an easy game with the new British leader, Clement Attlee. Even though that Truman objected to the Soviet's *solution* of the eastern territory problem, the loss of Winston Churchill in the middle of the poker game for the future spheres of influence was tremendous. The Soviets were the clear winner. Although it was agreed to clarify the *German Eastern Territory question* on a separate Freedom Conference, the ethnical cleaning and dislodging activities continued. The beginning of the Cold War prevented even the Freedom Conference from becoming reality. It is at this time that some historians attribute the statement *we slaughtered the wrong pick* to Winston Churchill, while others say it was General Patton who said it. I remember the scene in the movie about Patton where he denied saluting the Russian dictator Stalin, and I can't stop myself from leaning more to the version that Patton said it.

At the conference of Potsdam in 1945, configuration of the occupational zones was confirmed, and the jurisdiction of the Soviet Military Administration took place east of the demarcation line. Berlin was also divided in to four occupation zones. With the reconfirmation of the agreements of Tehran and Yalta, the Allied troops had to withdraw from the southeastern German territory and to move back behind the demarcation line. This was again a shock for the population in those areas because it was another charter for plunder, robbery and rape through the Russian troops. Each occupation force started to rule in its zone by June 1945.

The powers originally pursued a common German policy. This would be focused on the removal of the members of the *Nationalsozialistische Arbeiterpartei* (National Socialist German Workers Party,

NSDAP) from all public services and total demilitarization in preparation for the restoration of a democratic German nation-state. While the western allies took that seriously and started to rebuild a democratic public administration, the Soviet occupational troops started a series of plunder, robbery and rape excesses which in some parts of the Soviet military occupational zone lasted for three days and very rarely, if at all, got punished.

The Soviet occupation sought to extract the $10 billion from its occupation zone in eastern Germany, in addition to the trophy removals; an estimated $10 billion was to have been transferred in material form by the early 1950s, including in 1945 and 1946 over seventeen thousand factories, amounting to a third of the productive capital of the eastern occupation zone. Military industries and those owned by the state, by Nazi activists, and by war criminals were confiscated by the Soviet occupation authority. These industries amounted to approximately 60 percent of total industrial production in the Soviet zone. Most heavy industry approximately 20 percent of total production was claimed by the Soviet Union as reparations, and Soviet joint stock companies were formed. The remaining confiscated industrial property was nationalized, leaving 20 percent of total industrial production to private enterprises.

Contrary to the release of German POWs from American or British captivity, the Russians transported all of their POWs to Russia. Keeping them with hard labor for almost ten years, the last German POWs were released in 1955. East Germany faced a lack of qualified workers, which had devastating effects on the reconstruction of the public life. Yet before the war was over, the Soviet Union began to build up the human resourses they needed to make their occupational zone a vassal. Therefore the Soviet communist party ordered the Soviet Army to fly the German communist leaders Walter Ulbricht and Wilhelm Pieck into the conquered area and to provide them with everything necessary to secure the public power to the German Communist Party (KPD).

One of the first steps of the military administration was to establish civil administration by placing noncommunists in the leadership position of the civil administrative organs throughout the Soviet military zone. With the order number two of the military administration in 1945 an additional two political parties were newly founded within the Soviet zone. The Liberal-Democratic Party (LDPD) and the Christ-Democratic Party (CDU) were parties which agreed on the important points necessary to solve in the aftermath of WWII, but not totally. They had to agree to work only within the limitation of the so-called *Democratic Block of the Antifascist Power* and were used by the communists to camouflage their activities. This was done to avoid the impression that the hated Soviet Union would use the German communists to establish a Soviet State. Because of the German propaganda during all the years the NSDAP was in power, and more so during the final development of the Second World War, the Soviet system was the allegory of unimaginable terror against individuals. It was considered worse than the Gestapo terror. By placing unsuspected former liberal or national moderate politicians in front of the civil administration, they could build up the real power apparatus behind that camouflage. Walter Ulbricht, the head of the communists by mercy of the Soviets, was quoted, "It has to look democratic, but we must have control!"

But as early as in fall of 1945, they recognized that the German communists could not gain enough support within the population and so they decided to change the strategy. The social democrats were forced to work together within the build-up process of power towards the communist party. But there was resistance to the power grab by the communists in using the social democrats of the Soviet Zone, and that resistance increased, much larger than the Soviets would have dreamed of.

What followed was brutalized elimination of the political dissidents, almost always former members of the internal resistance organization during the Nazi time in the underground, most often survivors of the Nazi concentration camps. They had fought an unequal fight against the Terror State secret police Gestapo and barely survived the concentration camps only to be thrown into the same camps they just had escaped a year or so ago. Approximately fifty thousand people died in reopened concentration camps between 1945 and 1949. These camps were controlled by the Soviet KGB and their 1949 official newly founded East German brotherhood *Staatssicherheit* (*Ministry of State Security*. STASI). The first usage was to detain all the Nazi criminals. But soon it also became a chosen place for political dissidents.

The *Entnazifizierung* (denazification) was absolutely single handed by the communists and was part of the strategy to establish the so-called Central Administration. This administration built by the Soviets was the basis for the later executed seizure of power by the communists. The East German communists used this enormous possibility, covered by Russian military commanders, to decide who was to be kept in his position and who was to be removed. With that they were able to build the structure in all decisive parts of the civil administration.

With the unitization of the communist and social-democrat parties they had all their people in place. And as so often in history, the system of the denazification would be used by one neighbor to smear the other. Because when they got sentenced and very often disappeared forever, the shamus was rewarded to take possession of their properties.

Under the influence of this pressure and several other political circumstances, the social-democrats finally agreed to unite with the communists and in April 1946 the *Sozialistische Einheitspartei Deutschlands* (Socialist United Party of Germany [SED]) was born. and in fall of 1946 general elections were hold.

Beside all restrictions and obstructions the communistic party was unable to gain the expected number of votes and the SED answered with intensified propaganda, decrial and a new wave of denunciation of uncomfortable political dissidents, which most likely disappeared by night only to be never seen again. With the increased restrictions and based on the massive presence of the Russian army whenever necessary the power of the SED increased continuously, accompanied by the decline of any kind of opposition. In 1947 met the first People's Congress, initiated by the Soviets, and the result was the formation of the German People's Council. Beside all efforts to get the other political parties in line with their demand for absolute power and the total claim for leadership, the resistance inside those parties became stronger and stronger.

To be able to gain the necessary power to enforce her objectives, the SED conspired to form two new parties. Both parties, the *Demokratische Bauernpartei Deutschlands* (Democratic Farmer's Party [DBD]) and the *National Demokratische Partei Deutschlands* (National-Democratic Party Germany [NDPD]) were founded by renegade former members of the other parties and paid off by the SED and were highly supportive for the intentions of the communists. Together with the admission of the FDGB, the communistic controlled union organization, the SED had gained the absolute majority of the votes for the People's Council. The only job of this council was to create a constitution, which was presented in 1949 to the voters together with the vote for the second People's Congress. Although the people denied the constitution to a large majority, with the absolute majority of the votes for the SED, using the newly formed DBD and LDPD votes, the People's Congress accepted the constitution. The second People's Congress also elected a new People's Council which declared the founding of the German Democratic Republic (GDR) on October 7, 1949, as a counteraction to the founding of the Federal Republic of Germany (FRG) to which the East German administration zone had been invited but harshly declined by the Soviet controlled and powerful Socialist United Party (SED) and their allied block parties LDPD and DBD. This was the locking up of the division of Germany, and it would endure for the next forty years with devastating impacts on the life of more than seventeen million Germans caught behind the demarcation line between East and West, later called the *Iron Curtain*.

FREEDOM'S NIGHTMARE

The communist United Socialist Party achieved the absolute power in East Germany and started to form a type of Russian communistic society, yet with the difference that they allowed several other political parties to exist. But they only did this to keep up the appearance that it was a democratic republic. Following the road map of the *Great Brother* Soviet Union towards totalitarian power and control of the complete life and to ensure that even the faintest idea of doubt in the right of the United Socialist Party to have the absolute power over life and death, the Ministry of State Security (German: Staatssicherheit, abbreviation: STASI) was officially placed into operation. And since the precursor was carefully built over the years by the Russian KGB, within a few months this cancer-like organization gained control in all institutions of the public and private life.

Another very decisive role in the grasp at and the securing of the power of the SED was played by the union organization. It was actually the second official confirmed organization in East Germany by the Russian Military Commandant in 1945. On June 15, 1945, the communists in East Germany placed the appeal for a national congress to form free unions. In February 1946 congress of the *Freier Deutscher GewerkschaftsBund* (Free German Federation of Trade Unions [FDGB]) was founded. With that, one of the most important instruments of the enforcement of the claim to power for the East German communists was created. The exploitation of this organization by the SED throughout her existence was one of the most powerful tactics ever used in protection of a dictatorship. For any kind of propaganda for the purpose of mass manipulation the FDGB was the perfect instrument. The organization itself was formed to contravene the requirement to enforce the claim for leadership of the SED and the protection of her government power as well as the representation of the interests of the working class. The balancing act to represent both the interests of the employer and the employee was doomed to failure. And so it ended up being another very powerful instrument to do exactly what is was founded for—keeping a finger on the pulse of the working masses. The main focus of the activities was the mediation of the communistic ideology, the mobilization of the workers force and ethic and the education of the functionaries, the appointment of the members of the jury and was hence used for the interests of the SED and the socialistic government.

The FDGB pushed in contrary to the majority of its members the implementation of a mandatory three shift system in all manufacturing companies and with that the all-embracing children-support service by nursery schools, solemnly controlled by the Socialist United Party. Because the education of the professional Kindergarten teachers was one hundred percent in the hand of the Socialist United Party, the communistic infiltration, manipulation and brainwashing from the cradle to the grave was perfect, so to speak.

With the delegation of the execution of the social welfare system to the FDGB and the involvement of the FDGB in the subsidized housing program, the overarching back-breaking control, and monitoring power of the Socialist United Party was limitless. Virtually none of the life of the people was private and protected from the influence of the all-encompassing idea of a collectivized life. The Union received the exclusive authority to regulate sectors such as workers' rights, salary, culture and sport, work safety regulations, supply of food and the appointment of factory canteens, the socialistic education of the children, the social security insurance, as well as the organization and assignment of desired, and highly subsidized company vacation spots in one of the company-owned vacation homes. This was a very powerful instrument to correct deviant behavior. Because of the permanent divergence between supply and demand—and this was valid for nearly everything—the only way to get a vacation place at the desired places in summer on the coast and in winter in the hills was either you enjoyed a good reputation with the companies' union organization leaders, or you knew somebody who knew somebody who lived in those areas and had been able to convert the grandfather's chicken barn into a vacation home, and of course you had to have enough money. Often times, it was necessary to have a part of that in Deutsch Mark, and of course you were willing to spend that money because that was the price you had to pay to be not part of the socialistic power game.

The Shield and Sword of the Communist Party

STASI logo

The Ministry for State Security (STASI) was the secret police force, secret intelligence service, and organ for criminal investigations, primarily in political criminal cases. It was virtually directed and controlled by the head of the SED only. The Ministry for State Security was the most important instrument used by the leadership of the SED to secure its dictatorship. It was accordingly designated the *shield and sword of the party*. Even though it was a *ministry*, it was not under the control of the chairperson of the Council of Ministers, but from 1960 and on, it was under the control of the chairperson of the National Defense Council, who was at the same time secretary-general of the SED.

From the 1970's on, important issues with regard to the State Security Service were discussed directly between the SED Secretary-General Erich Honecker and Minister Erich Mielke. The singular position of the STASI was also clear from the fact that it was responsible for monitoring both of the other security ministries, the Ministry of the Interior and the Ministry for National Defense. In addition, it exerted significant influence not only on the Ministry for Justice since it participated in the decision on the employment and promotion of public prosecutors but deep into the industry and in the public life by drafting the basic reports which had significant influence by the appointment of leaders in industry, financial, and health care institutions.

The total STASI budget was secret in the GDR and was also in collusion vis-à-vis the pseudo-parliament, People's Chamber, and even the Council of Ministers. The last known numbers from 1989 indicate that the total budget was actually higher than that of the police forces and reached roughly €500–€600 million. This was the second-largest budget of the armed forces right behind the National People's Army.

There are some rumors around today that East Germany collapsed because of the costs for the armed forces, which is not true. Although the armed forces had a large part in it, the total collapse of the East German economy, which created the tumescent protest and finally ended in the collapse of the totalitarian regime their role, was negligible.

The real reason for the economic collapse of the system was the disability of the total centralized control of the manufacturing processes to produce the wealth which was necessary to keep up with the social programs, such as subsidized house building, food, schooling, etc. In the era of Honecker, the GDR lived socio-politically well above its means.

In the GDR, the investigative organs of the STASI had the authority of police offices of investigation. They were authorized to open preliminary criminal proceedings and to carry out investigative operations, such as arrests, searches, detentions as well as interrogations and to conduct all required investigations up to the final report to the judicial authorities. The preliminary proceedings in the GDR, however, were *de jure* under the administration of the public prosecutor, who had decisional authority in relation to the investigative authority within this framework. *De facto*, however, since the STASI approval report was of vital importance for the appointment of the prosecutors, the organization made sure that prosecutors followed their leads. The legal foundations of the STASI's work as an investigative organ changed in the course of the 40-year of GDR history, without an essential change to the basic structures. The Russian term *sledstvennyj organ* (investigative organ) is of Soviet origin. It gradually replaced the traditional term of investigative authority in the Soviet Occupation Zone (SBZ) or GDR, and of the justice system in the course of the Sovietization of the police apparatus. In addition the term *investigative organ* from the 1960s and the nearly synonymous term *justice administration authority* are also used in connection with the STASI. The Ministry for State Security was the most important instrument of the SED leadership to secure its dictatorship. This was extremely amplified with the construction of the *Berlin Wall*.

In comparison to the situation in workshops or in normal civil administrations, the SED party organization in the STASI was shaped by special conditions. With the STASI the SED created a watchdog to monitor opposition throughout the whole public and private life, and to do so they had to give that watchdog total control over any other institutional organization, even the police. But at the same time they needed to ensure that the watchdog did not begins to gain control over their master. To avoid any kind of complications in this direction, the party organization inside the STASI was over proportionally large and had an overwhelming educational function to hammer the inferior position of the STASI under the SED. Many times I heard reasoning among communists and even non-party members that the STASI was a state within the state and had control over the party and when a party leader didn't play according to the rule, he just disappeared. Just the opposite was true. The heads of the STASI always reported to the heads of the communist party. The communist party had made sure as early as 1946 that their absolute ruling wasn't in danger. Whereas the highest party body in the headquarter of the STASI in Berlin was directly under the control of the central committee of the Socialist United Party, the absolute leadership and decisive organ of the party, all regional STASI party organizations were under the control of the regional party leadership.

In the early years, this was not the case; until September 1953 there was still a uniform party organization in the STASI. The rebellion of the workers throughout East Germany in 1953 was a hard-learned lesson and changed everything. One part of *lesson learned* in the national uprising in 1953 was that the total control was only possible with the implementation of total monitoring of each and every suspicious people or movement, even if it was absolutely inconsiderable and seemed insane at the beginning. With this awareness, the STASI overlaid East Germany with a network of informants which was second to none worldwide. From the beginning of the STASI, there were approximately 250,000 persons who worked officially at the STASI, of which approximately 100,000 were direct employees, including the "Felix Dzierzynski" guard regiment, back-up units, and some small other special units. On October 31, 1989, 91,015 official employees were employed at the STASI, including guard regiments, etc., and among these, 13,073 were regulars.

There were also roughly six hundred thousand of so-called informal employees (IM) which may have been over the years 1949-1989. With the end of the STASI in 1990, there were 174,000 informal employees and societal employees (GMS with a kind of leadership functionality) registered and working for the STASI collecting information about peers, colleagues, friends, and family members. Most were rewarded with blood money of a couple of hundred GDR Marks. They ruined careers, friendships, and complete families.

In contrast to many other societal areas, the Ministry for State Security hid its activities in the National People's Army and the border patrols far less. The STASI was officially represented by an employee right at the physical examination of a draftee. In the troop units and facilities themselves, the talk was all about *Administration 2000*, the internal army designation for the STASI Division 1 about their VO liaison officers, and occasionally about their military defense. The liaison officers wore the uniform of the troop unit that they had to process. In this way, they were able to move unhindered and inconspicuously. The concentration of informal employees was quite high in the border troops. If someone was scheduled for employment in the so-called special troops and services as well as in the border troops, as a professional military trainee or as construction soldier, the STASI prepared a detailed security analysis.

In particular, construction soldiers were the object of the army-integrated STASI investigation. Construction soldiers were men who denied serving with weapon because of their religious orientation. It had to be ensured that they were not just trying to avoid the eighteen months of service in the armed forces, and they had to serve twenty-four months as construction soldiers. To make it worse for these young men who denied taking a weapon in their hand for a hated regime, they were often deployed to build or repair the border security systems along the border with West Germany or West Berlin.

The State Security and the People's Police were supposed to work together to guarantee the internal security in the GDR. The SED leadership wished for a smooth collaboration in the different key activities of both organizations. The secret police and People's Police followed the specifications of the party in anticipatory obedience, which resulted in an aligned action. The party head defined the aims and decided on the distribution of scarce resources, such as personnel, whereby the STASI apparatus was allowed in a leading position. The so-called *political-operative cooperation* applied to coordination in questions of principle and procedure based on a division of labor in relation to citizens. The cooperation of both apparatuses was useful; State Security had IM and GMS in the highest management levels of the People's Police at their disposal. These contacts with individual employees were kept secret and served primarily for the surveillance of colleagues. The Mielke apparatus pushed for the advancement of its IM (informal employee) and GMS (societal employee) in the ranks of the People's Police and left incapable directors at their posts, simply because they cooperated well with the secret police. However, not all IM *functioned* smoothly—many ran *out of the rudder*, limited the dissemination of information to what was absolutely necessary or were uncovered by their colleagues. Indeed, leaky positions were expected within the People's Police, but it was not known for the most part who the individual informers were.

The State Security Service indirectly influenced the control operations of superior administrative offices of the People's Police and of the security division of the SED. When the administrative offices of the People's Police were checked locally for functional efficiency and management problems, the State Security was already aware of the methodical as well as the short-term inspections through its IM network and was able to intervene accordingly. State Security, in the process of vetting, had to approve, or were able to refuse, when the People's Police wanted to employ someone, promote employees into leading positions, or send someone for professional training. For this purpose, the STASI apparatus also investigated family members and friends of those concerned, for political, character, familial, or other elements of uncertainty. In this way, the State Security Service significantly contributed to the fact that loyalty to the party line had priority over professional qualifications in the People's Police. The secret police were responsible for the surveillance of the People's Police with regard to morality and world view.

The dominance of the STASI apparatus, the partial overlapping of the spheres of action, led to tensions, conflicts, and defensive reactions from time to time. The STASI was represented at the points of entry with the passport control units of the so-called Line Sixth of the Ministry for State Security. The main functions of the passport control units were the control of travel documents, search measures, and the gathering of information of interest to the intelligence service. However, several institutions with different functions were employed at the points of entry. Those were the border troops of the *Nationale Volksarmee*, German term for National People's Army (NVA) for military protection of the border, and also included the People's Police, part of the Ministry of the Interior, which was responsible for the pre-control before the border crossing and the customs control, part of the customs authority, which was subordinate to the Ministry for Foreign Trade. The STASI members were not used directly in customs control, but the State Security monitored their colleagues through unofficial employees.

The director of the customs authority from 1963 to 1989 was a Stasi officer on special assignment (OibE). These were special educated and trained STASI officers who were undercover assigned to the job. Not even their direct supervisor had the faintest idea that this officer was a cuckoo's egg from the STASI. The other institutions named above were also monitored with the assistance of unofficial employees.

Murder plots of the STASI are preserved separately. Here are two exemplary cases listed. First, the sergeant of the National People's Army, Rudi Thurow, who had fled from border duty and second, the murder attempt on the escape agent, Wolfgang Welsch, and his family by means of poison that has been proven. For obvious reasons, orders for murder and their execution were not put into writing. Internal training records for the task forces of the STASI murder specialists from the '70s and '80s document that attempted murders were to be carried out in compliance with a high concealment potential. Methods such as simulated suicides and accidents, simulated criminal acts of violence, and alleged terrorist attacks of violent leftwing powers were to be used for execution. For these reasons, there is still a question of participation by the STASI with some deaths, as with that of the soccer player Lutz Eigendorf, who fled from the GDR.

The most striking is the particular size of the STASI in the international scale, as measured by the population. The mere unbelievable ratio from 1 official STASI employee, not to mention the unofficial or informal employees, to 180 GDR citizens was not even approximately achieved by the KGB which had a ration from 1: 595. On the other hand it doesn't really mean much regarding the effectiveness of their work. However, this does not say much about the brutality of the repression carried out. In contrast to the GDR, the Communist intelligence services in most other countries were not independent ministries but were integrated in the interior ministries. The head of the intelligence service usually had the rank of a deputy minister of the interior. This is in my opinion again a confirmation of the sheer incredible effectiveness of the organizational talent of Germans. The most horrifying combination in the world is a dictatorship together with the German addiction towards perfection. In any kind of a reasonable, decent society the law is above the political interests even of the vast majority of the people's interests. Not so in a socialistic or communistic dictatorship, and especially not in combination with Germany.

In the GDR the law was subordinate to the policy determined by the Socialistic United Party. The STASI employees had to adhere to the law only so far as it served the interest of the SED. Even so that the SED had the absolute control over the STASI, the SED control apparatus did not have insight into all concrete secrets and intelligent service activities. Further, the total integration of the foreign intelligence and the internal secret security authority combined with the investigative and executive power in one single organization was a powerful way to suppress any kind of resistance against the unlimited leadership entitlement of the SED. The absence of any kind of legal political opposition or independent media made it impossible to openly discuss the unlimited authority of the STASI apparatus. Since the STASI was extensively formed under strict instruction of the Russian KGB its influence never really ceased even though the number of the liaison officers has been reduced over the years. Since the master of the STASI, the SED, was directed in any aspect of the political orientation, it is obvious that the STASI followed the same addiction. Every officer who would like to exceed the rank of a captain had to successfully complete the University of the KGB in Moscow. The additional deepened indoctrination of the policy of the Russian communist party ensured that the leading officer corps of the STASI was always on track.

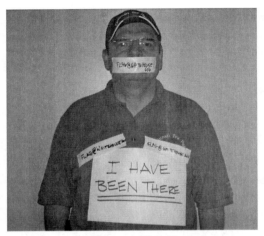

Report your Neighbor

The Elite Hotbed of the Communist Party, or Why Brown Shirts Equal Blue-Shirts

The *Freie Deutsche Jugend*, also known as the Free German Youth (FDJ), was the official socialist youth organization of the GDR and the Socialist United Party of Germany. The organization was meant for young people, both male and female, between the ages of 14-25 and comprised about 75 percent of the young population of former East Germany. After being a member of the *Thälmann* Pioneers, named after the leader of the German Communist Party which was killed by the Hitler SS in 1944 at the concentration camp Buchenwald, which was for schoolchildren ages 6-14, East German youths would usually join the FDJ. The FDJ was intended to be the reliable assistant and fighting reserve of the Worker's Party, or Socialist United Party of East Germany. She had representatives in the People's Chamber. The political and ideological goal of the FDJ was to influence every aspect of life of young people in the GDR, distribution of Marxism-Leninism, the deepening of the friendship with the Soviet Union and the indoctrination of socialist behavior.

Membership in the FDJ was nominally voluntary, but those who did not join lost access to organized holidays, and found it more difficult to be admitted to universities, pursue chosen careers, etc. The majority of youths who refused to join did so for religious reasons. While the movement was intended to indoctrinate East Germany's young people in Marxism-Leninism, it did not concentrate on this to the exclusion of other activities. Although the organization officially did not appear violent, the sheer masses and the intrusiveness of their presence at any place where the Socialist United Party needed them dispersed bare fear. Especially during the first years of their existence and the brutal and ruthless seizure of power by the communists, the youth organization FDJ was the real fighting reserve of the party of the working class. The members of that organization were always the core of any newly formed organization the SED needed to secure their total power.

As early as 1952, members of the FDJ formed, initially local in the nationalized companies in order of the central committee of the SED, the so-called Fighting Units of the workers class. The "army in blue" it was called first because the uniforms were just reworked work clothing. Later it was replaced by field grey uniforms with a sleeve pad showing the red flag crossed by an AK 47. This paramilitary organization under the command of the local youth organization leader was initially trained and armed by the barracked people's police, later with the formation of the NVA by officers of the NVA. They were to play a bloody role during the national uprising on June 17, 1953, and again by securing the workers building the Berlin Wall on August 13, 1961.

However, the performance of the Worker's Fighter Units during the national uprising on June 16th and at its high point June 17th was everything but excellent. Several of the members of those units which actually should have been in front of the headquarters of the Socialist United Party and secure the party leaders from the people's rage deserted. And only after the Russian military command ordered the deployment of Russian troupes and tanks, some of the Workers Fighter Units got organized and brave enough to march out and build barricades in front of the valuable buildings. Following are two examples of the most impressive actions these fighting units participated in to secure the absolute power of the Socialist United Party of East Germany.

The power of the SED until this time was based only on the Russian Military power. The population had not really accepted the domination of the communists up to this time. The whole system was standing on feet of clay. The internal weakness of the system and the restrain of the Russians to invest in the Military 10 percent of the GDP, combined with the reparations East Germany had to pay to the Russians at 16 percent of the GDP, the economic situation got worse day by day and reached a critical level in 1953. The Communists tried to compensate this by reducing investments in the reconstruction of the industry, apartment buildings and the increase of taxes. By that, the standard of living, already far lower than in the Western German area, had been reduced dramatically by 1953.

At the end of 1952 the production of consumer goods in East Germany was fallen to a level of the time before WWII. This was the situation when the requested increase of the work standards for the same salary was insisted to become law. The SED used one of their front organizations, the central-controlled FDGB, to paint that law as a request of the workers. On June 16th an article appeared in the FDGB newspaper that categorical demanded that the working class had to follow the leading party and fulfill the demanded new standards. This was the straw that broke the camel's back.

All hell broke loose, and within hours, strike committees appeared all over East Germany. More than ten thousand workers marched to the SED's headquarter in Berlin and demanded free and secret elections, freedom of speech and the release of all political prisoners. Hundred of thousands were on the streets all over East Germany, and the early demands for retraction of the increase of the work standards changed into political demands. The answer of the communists, fearing for their power, was brutal and bloody. Martial law was declared and the Russians sent 167 tanks into the city of East Berlin. More than two thousand cities and villages were put under martial law, and the loyal armed Workers Fighting Units marched side by side with the Russian Soldiers to squash the revolt. The massacre lasted till June 20, 1953, and the exact number of the killed people remains unknown. Approximately one hundred insurgents were killed during the revolt, approximately 50-80 were shot according to martial law and more than fifteen thousand ended up in jail for years. A result of that national uprising was the immediate removal of the head of the STASI because of their inability to see that coming. Also, the Workers Fighter Units were better equipped and trained by experienced military professionals.

This would pay off when the SED finally decided to close the last way into freedom. Contrary to the famous line from the speech of Walter Ulbricht, the General Secretary of SED gave a few days before the regime worked hard on a secret event that would shake the world and incarcerate the East-German citizens for many years. He said, "Nobody is planning on building a wall in Berlin. The building labor has enough to do building homes for our families." Just few days later on August 13, 1961, when the residents of Berlin woke up to go to work, for many of them that way to work did not exist any longer. It was closed by a wall, barbed wires and the paramilitary troops of the Workers Fighter Units. The wall was set approximately 50-100 yards back from the original border of the Russian Zone with those of the American, British and France to have enough room for further fortification wherever that was possible. Sometimes it was in the middle of a street and families who were normally just crossing the street to see each other were suddenly separated. And although the picture of that young soldier who threw his weapon away jumped over the barbed wire rolls into freedom was going around the world, many people were critically injured or died doing the same as he but just from an apartment window down to the other side of a growing wall.

Without the strength and the masses of the political reorganized and indoctrinated power of the Worker Fighter Units it would have been impossible for the SED communists to encircle the combined sectors of the Western Allies of West Berlin at night and close any way in or out of West Berlin for over twenty-eight years.

A very important role had the FDJ by the founding and formation of another paramilitary unit, the so-called *Gesellschaft fuer Sport und Technik* (Association for Sport and Technique [GST]). It is inevitable to draw parallels between the Hitler youth and the structural appearance of the youth organizations of the GDR. Contrary to the workers class Fighting Units, the GST was oriented towards the youth. While the workers class Fighting Units were build out of the party loyal workers, the GST was at first initiated and presented as the association to allow the East German youth to practice all kind of technical sport disciplines, such as target shooting, sky diving, soaring and so on. But it was actually just the first step into another paramilitary organization. What began as a voluntary organization of enthusiastic young people who liked to be together, have fun, and to go in for sports ended in yet another mandatory paramilitary organization to prepare the youth for the general conscription.

The Early Bird or Why Sport Does Not Always Equal Sport

Because the broad public did not appreciate strong political organized structures after the second world war, the communistic youth organization had begun very early to establish sport clubs as the way to encourage the youth to become a member. Since any kind of sport activity was dependent on the reliability of equipment and training resources, and the communists controlled all of those, there was virtually no other way.

Beside all these influences the FDJ was not able to grow the sport activities under their umbrella according to the requirements of the Socialist United Party. Independent sport clubs initiated by private people and enthusiasts grew much faster than the political leaders liked and became more and more attractive for the East German youth.

The situation escalated so far that the leader of the FDJ, Erich Honecker, who would years later become the leader of the Socialist United Party, nearly lost his power and influence. Only because of the protective hand of Walter Ulbricht, the leader at that time, the position and with that the political future of Erich Honnecker was saved. As early as 1952 the central committee ordered that all technical-oriented sport activities had to be inferior to the FDJ, and that included the newly founded (actually renamed) sport clubs now the GST.

In the aftermath of the people's uprising in 1953 the party took direct control over the GST and ordered the focus on the implementation as well as the improvement of the military usable field events. More and more the GST degenerated to a basic and pre-military training organization for the National People's Army. With the dead of Walter Ulbricht and the enthronement of Erich Honecker as his successor a new era began.

Many people in East Germany believed that it was a change to the better, but actually only for those who had decided to arrange their life as best as possible to the circumstances they could not change. But the ambitions to secure the absolute power were unbowed. One important part was the mandatory institution of the pre-military training of the youth. Every man and woman was obligated at the end of the high school to serve for two weeks in a paramilitary GST camp. All young men were trained in all kind of military skills. Those who were members of the GST before because of the interest in a certain special discipline, such as radio transmission, were further trained and educated in their discipline. All others get special training like infantry soldiers of a regular army. That included theoretical education in battlefield tactics, weaponry knowledge about the weapons of the Warsaw Pact and the enemy, the NATO.

But the main focus was on physical battlefield training, storming hills throughout the day till the instructors were satisfied, trench fight trainings, and hand-to-hand fighting techniques. All that with a special version of the AK47 standard rifle of the Warsaw Pact what we called the mini AK or KK47. It was a.22LR caliber and we had blank cartridges for storming hills and cleaning trenches and real cartridges for the training at the shooting range. And those guns were really good at what they were designed for. It was even possible to fire automatic with these little guns. At least as long as the quality of the ammunition was good enough. Often enough it wasn't and then the cartridges jammed and you needed to clean the mess, which was also the case with the active battlefield exercise because the more blanks you ran through that gun the worse was the cleaning.

Since the instructors were regular sergeants from the army, sometimes from special units, they gave these young men a hard time to be on top of the requirement when the conclusion maneuver demanded a twenty-four hour exercise, which included a nearly sixteen-mile march totally equipped with gear such as the KK47 with eight magazines fully loaded with blanks, and everything in the backpack you'd need to camp overnight outside. It finally culminated in the capture of the enemy's trenches up on the hill where they were trained during the two weeks. That happened during the first two years during your education after high school.

And since everybody in East Germany had to go into that education cycle, no matter what grade his high school degree had, everybody went through those two weeks. And those of the alumni who indicated that they were able to fulfill a leadership function, not only in military aspects of that training program but foremost from the political point of view, were separately billeted a week longer and got special training and education in leadership, strategy, and tactics on the battlefield including tuition about the findings of the NATO tactic in battlefield.

For the next year they were called in a week before the first-time train-ees and all the knowledge was refreshed in intensive training sections. And then these men were promoted to leadership positions like group leader, platoon leader, and sometimes up to company leaders. Usually they were on the way to an army academy to become an officer of the regular army after they finished the normal education cycle.

The women had a different education, but it was also strictly military oriented. They were trained as the paramedics and had actually a very sim-ilar physical training in the battlefield, and at least twice during the train-ing camp week, sometimes more often, they were included in the men's training to storm the hills and had to practice the treatment of wounded soldiers. For that the instructors of the fighters declared some of them wounded and the instructor of the paramedics simulated different wounds on those men.

All things considered it was a very realistic training with very realistic exercises and weapons infrastructure, equipment, paramedics, and com-mand structures. In case of an emergency, which meant in this specific case a conventional war between the Warsaw Pact and the NATO, the GST—remember it was founded and named as the *Association for Sport and Technique*—would have been a more perfect copy of the Hitler youth in World War II.

The only difference might have been that they were not as fanatic as the Hitler Youth has been, because even this organization, the *Association for Sport and Technique*, was a mirror of the division of the people of East Germany. One third were one hundred percent politically motivated and would follow any directive of their leaders. Another third were just will-ingly followers because they would not risk their professional career. They had adapted themselves to the system to make the best out of it for them-selves. The next third was against all that crap, but too afraid to say any-thing so they kept a low profile and becoming invisible was their highest priority. And then there was that ten percent of people who happened to be brave enough to protest against the militarization of the youth, which was so devastating for Germany not so many years ago. Those were prob-ably backed by a strong home and openly disagreed with the usage of the GST as the *Talent Hotbed* for the National People's Army. These guys were usually extremely harassed and ordered to perform the filthiest jobs during that time.

But anyhow, all of the training focused on using these potential paramilitary units as a kind of underground guerilla in case that Eastern Germany territory would be conquered by NATO troupes. With both organizations sponsored by the FDJ, the official youth organization and Talent Hotbed of the dictatorial ruling Socialist United Party (SED), the FDJ was able to indoctrinate and suppress any kind of resistance against the absolute power of the Socialist United Party. She used these powerful instruments whenever necessary, be it to force the farmers into the collectivistic organization *Landwirtschaftliche Produktionsgenossenschaft*, German for Agricultural Production Cooperative, or to disseize the last piece of entrepreneurial owners of manufacturing companies at the beginning of the 1970s. The modality to virtually dispossess of both the farmers and the small business owners was one of the ugliest chapters in the history of the communistic youth organization. The illustrated results were destroyed families, ruined existences, suicides, and often enough, whole families were betaken oneself to flee the country. The economical situation in the early years of the dictatorship was exactly that scenario where this communistic youth organization had its best practical test.

A real devastating effect was caused by control over the agricultural production. Under the cloak of the assurance of the food supply for the population and to avoid black marketeering, every farm was put under regulation with rigorous control. They had to produce what was required, not what was normally grown in a specific area. If you could not fulfill the requirements, it was often punished as sabotage and many farmers just disappeared forever.

Farmers Are Enemies of Freedom or Peaceful Protest Sometimes Doesn't Gives You Peace

The collectivization of private and state-owned agricultural land in East Germany was the progression of communistic policy at the expense of large scale farmers. It began in the years of Soviet occupation (1945-48) as part of the need to govern resources in the Soviet Sector. The agrarian reform expropriated all land belonging to former Nazis and generally limited ownership to approximately 247 acres. Some 500 estates were converted into state farms mostly operated by the former agricultural laborers. More than 7.4 million acres were distributed among 500,000 peasant farmer and refugee families. The land was redistributed in small pieces to incoming landless refugees driven off lost German Territory to the east.

A territory of approximately the same size as the Russian occupation zone itself spit out its residents into a land which was already filled with homeless people and lay in ruins. Nearly 70 percent of all housing estates where destroyed by the air raids during the war. The destiny of those refugees from the former eastern territory was often driven by the bottomless hate of the succeeding polish people as revenge for the cruel experience during the German occupation.

Between 1945 and 1948 nearly 3.5 million Germans had to leave their homeland. The Russians took over a huge part of western White Russia, which came to Poland after the First World War. Poland was compensated by getting all the former east provinces of Germany such as East Prussia, Pomerania, Silesia, and parts of the German core land itself. These new farmers were given limited ownership rights to the land, meaning that they kept it as long as they worked it. The vast majority had no experience with farming at all and the result was accordingly bad. Many of the remaining experienced farmers with largish holdings of 125 to 165 acres were effectively driven out of business through means such as denying access to pooled machinery and by setting production targets that rose exponentially with amount of land owned to levels that were impossible to meet or to grow crops that were not domestic at this area.

The grandfather of my wife, as an example, was imprisoned for a couple of weeks because he was not able to deliver the required amount of tobacco. Now, one has to know that the northeastern part of East Germany, just for fun called "South Sweden," has not the weather or soil you need to grow a decent kind of tobacco. And the greatest problem was getting it dried without to it starting to grow mold. Christiane's grandfather had the misfortune that it happened. With that he could not fulfill the required standard and was put in jail for a couple of weeks under suspicion of sabotage while the STASI executed its investigation. Even though he was considered a *big farmer*, he owned twenty-one hectares a little short of 52 acres and he had a high reputation by the people in his village because of both of his sons were fallen during the World War II. The local communists, who always hated him since he was a devoted Christian, expropriated the maximum possible of his sixty hectares in 1945. So the STASI wasn't really able to confirm the accusation of sabotage and finally had to let him go home.

However, from the late 1950s to early 1960s, pressure mounted on remaining independent farmers to join the agricultural production cooperative German LPG. To make that happen the communists used any possible dirty trick. First of all they used the voluntary youth organization, which camped in large groups around the farmers' property and constrained their ability to work. Since there was no way to buy tools or machines on the free market, and most of the farmers had been ripped off all their belongings by the Russians as reparation, the farmers relied on exchanging their remaining tools and machines among each other to get the work done. Again a very smart maneuver of the communists educated by their Russian friends on how to take total control. After the plunder and otherwise justified confiscation of nearly every single tool, machine or any kind of equipment by the Russian soldiers right after the German capitulation, production equipment in the Russian occupational zone was almost not existent.

And the communists used that to implement another of the manipulation tactics. The brotherly, helpful Russian communist party and the Russian people to whom we bad Germans did so much harm are the greatest Samaritans and helped the East German to rebuild their infrastructure, companies, and agricultural production. And they shipped Russian machines, which were most of the time, although newly manufactured, old technology. Most likely it was stolen German technology from before the First World War. Now this incredibly generous gesture was not ascertained towards those evil *big farmers*, who still wanted to belief that there was a new dawn raised in Germany, the communists had the power. All those machines, tools, and equipment were given to newly founded *Maschinen Traktoren Stationen* (German for Machines Tractor Stations). Of course these kinds of a machinery rental stations were owned by the Socialist United Party the SED and the comrades decided who was worthy to get the machines and for what price rented. And of course you could bet on it that the New Farmers, full of gratefulness towards the Socialist United Party that they got the land to live from had a first priority and the lowest possible price to pay. Since they had often not the faintest idea what to do and how to work on the field, they needed the machines much longer than normally. It nearly automatically led to the situation that the evil Big Farmers got the machines too late to prepare the fields in spring and too late for harvest in fall. But anyhow, they were used to doing their job; they had the knowledge and the desire to earn their livelihood.

And they were sparing with their money as real farmers always have been, so over a few years they begin to have machines and horses, though no tractors for sure because those were restricted. Step by step they got back to the situation where it became clear to the communists, that they were a threat to the idea of the total collectivization of the agricultural production. It could not be what should not be, and so the Socialist United Party decided it was time to fight the last battle with the evil Big Farmers.

With the decision of the Socialist United Party to collectivize agriculture completely in the shortest possible time, the actions of the FDJ became violent. Personal assaults and attacks on animals and property were daily. I remember narratives about that time by the farmer where we lived for many years in a part of his house, because I do not have strong memories since I was just six when it was over. He said at the end he finally gave in and signed the accession document. At this time he had twelve dogs running on long leashes along the border of his backyard property, he had memorized all of their songs and chanting, and he wasn't able to sleep any night more than two hours because of the noise the FDJ made in front and actually around his property twenty-four hours a day.

When he had to leave the barnyard to go to the fields he had his kids to open the gateway each on one side at the same time and then he had to force the hoses to gallop through the three to four row deep staggered youth in that way that they had to jump out of the way. When he first moved at normal speed they just blocked the way and the horses stopped. He lost an average of two dogs a month by poisoned baits, but without the dogs these guys, with no respect for anything, just moved with their tents into his backyard and camped on his grassland. They sparked campfires around his property and anybody who wanted to enter his property, no matter if it was just a visitor, relatives or other evil Big Farmers, became targets of direct or indirect offenses.

The leaders of those activities carefully watched that nobody got really injured or harmed, because they called that peaceful persuasion about the unimaginable gratefulness of the communistic agricultural future. The teams were paid by the FDJ organization and they were mostly recruited at the nationalized heavy industry companies. They did not understand the real reason for those activities and they believed that it was necessary to do that for the greater good of the society. But it wasn't always that peaceful, and when the project leader got too much pressure from his bosses then it happened, and actually quite often, that the activities turned violent. Towards the end of the fifties a downright competition broke out between the different administrative districts and their political leaders. It became all about who had the highest success rate of the collectivization of the evil Big Farmers in his district.

Every week the central newspaper of the Socialist United Party and the local offspring reported the improvement, named extremely successful districts and gave room for interviews and reports for the most success-ful project leaders and their bosses. This was a very important part for the outcome of one's career. If they made it into the central newspaper of the FDJ the *Junge Welt* (German for Young World) or one of the regional party newspapers it was a success, and if they made it into the central paper of the SED *Neues Deutschland* (German for New Germany) they could secure a lift into the highest possible ranks of the party hierarchy. One of the most famous methods was arson. Those evil farmers who were steadfast till the end of the season had to watch their barns being lighted and the whole crop burst into flames.

FREEDOM'S NIGHTMARE

A very popular method of arson was the use of electrical power. Usually when the farmers had their straw and/or hay in the barn, filled up under the roof, they disconnected the main fuse for the light in the barn to avoid accidentally ignite a fire by turning on the lights when the lamps couldn't be seen because they were totally covered with straw. The FDJ provocateurs would break into the barn in night and replace the fuses and switch on the light and then sit outside and sing till the fire broke through the roof. Only a few members of the propaganda teams would be involved in such criminal activities, and the vast majority of the team would have no clue why that happened. All would jump into action to help to extinguish the fire. To make things worse, the government then sued the farmers for not fulfilling their target because they could not deliver what they were ordered or worse for involuntarily destroying valuable goods. In ninety-nine percent of those incidents that was the point when even the hardened evil Big Farmers would capitulate in sheer desperation. Most of them just signed the documents and became members of the cooperatives, some flew by night and not so few just committed suicide. Many of the farmers who surrendered were broken forever and could never really get over it. Those who flew to West Germany—through the loophole West Berlin—leaving behind everything, were not really welcome. Since the Cold War between East and West was speeding up, both sides used those poor families as propaganda tool. The losers were always the families and especially the kids. They were ripped from their natural environment, friends, and relatives.

The West German Government tried at least to disburden by the payment of a compensation for the lost goods, but there is not really a compensation for the loss of the basis of your life. Some of these families went through that situation twice within less than fifteen years. The process to nationalize the whole manufacturing industry and to collectivize the agricultural sector was finally accomplished just before the wall was built. With that action on August 13, 1961, the communists closed the last loophole into freedom and gained total control over the life of nearly seventeen million people.

HARALD ZIEGER

The End of the Unsustainable Antagonism, or How to Erase the Last Piece of Effective Manufacturing

The situation for the owners of small business was equal to the situation of the whole country. Nearly ninety-five percent of the country lay in ruins when the weapons eventually turned silent. And after the plunder and otherwise justified confiscation of nearly every single tool, machine, or any kind of equipment by the Russian soldiers right after the German capitulation, the production equipment in the Russian occupational zone was almost nonexistent. When the small business owners began to restart the manufacturing, they needed money to buy equipment, material and tools. The only way to get money was to get a loan from a bank. And the bank asked for collateral to secure the credit.

Since the banking industry—blamed to be the financier of the Nazis and the Second World War—had been expropriated right at the end of the war, it had been nationalized and handed over to the communists. Every single small business owner who needed a loan to reestablish his business had to agree to secure that loan by handing over a percentage of their company in nonvoting shares to the bank, and with that to the SED. Most of those loan agreements were made in this way so that the loan actually never was paid off. As it always is around the world, when entrepreneurial desire combined with good products and a demanding market begin to work it is most likely a recipe for success. And so it was in East Germany. Owner-led companies had their finger on the market, understood what the customers liked and tried to produce exactly that. With that a blooming small industry was developed and many of these manufacturers were able to export their products to West Germany beside the strong competition. There were certain industries which were well-known for their excellence and quality, such as the shoe industry, textile industry, watches from Glasshuette, hunting weapons from Suhl, handcrafted glass goods from the Lausitz, and so on.

With the increase of the demand and the restructuring of the Eastern German economy after the uprising in 1953 accompanied by several social programs, remaining private manufacturing companies were still allowed to acquire additional loans but with more and more strings attached. This was mainly caused by a sudden change of the conditions for those companies. Such changed conditions were in example suddenly increased taxes together with high additional claims or suddenly increased supply prices for merchandise and raw materials. The fantasy to get the remained private industry in trouble was limitless. Even though the FDJ was meagerly represented in these companies, it had enough opportunities to create additional problems, be it by arson in material depots, denunciation, or assertion without substance. Since all these incidences were considered white-collar crime, the STASI was automatically involved. That ensured that the truth never really was the objective of the investigation and ended mostly with the conviction of the owner. To pay for the economic damage they needed a loan, and to get those loans, the owner had to agree to a public partnership. And yes, actually sometimes they needed a loan just for the modernization of the manufacturing equipment. The SED enabled the owners of those companies to get loans only by agreeing to a new form of company, the corporation with public participation. With that agreement they lost the control of purchase and distribution. They got connected to one of the nationally-owned corporations, and every purchase and distribution was channeled through those ineffective giants of the communist economic system.

It wouldn't take long for the East German communists to confiscate the rest of the private industry and transfer whilom blooming small private manufacturing industries into money-wasting state-owned companies producing useless products with bad quality and never enough quantity to supply the demand. Another very effective way to get them into the hands of the workers class and end the capitalist ownership was the in the power of the Central Planning Commission. Since everything was centrally controlled it was easy to *forget* i.e. to plan the demand on leather for this evil capitalist shoe producer or to plan no wool or yarn for that other evil capitalist shirt manufacturer. But despite all their activities to make the life of the last few entrepreneurs as horrible as possible, they actually were successful to some degree. Their products had better quality, they were able to keep the promises they had agreed to in contracts and they came up with new developments and innovations which earned them great reputation even in the Western markets. These capitalists had the impertinence to ask to export their products to the West directly, where they could get better prices. Actually the SED became jealous of these small entrepreneurial business owners. In defiance of the rigor of the communistic command economy, and all the harassments of the communistic bureaucrats, they were successful. Many of the owners were able to live a lifestyle even most of the public corporation directors couldn't afford. They drove the newest cars, had weekend homes in the mountains and sometimes also at the sea. Their wives and children wore the finest, exquisite clothing that attracted the envy of many party officials, and the party leaders had to explain why there were still capitalist structures existing in the socialistic society.

Not only inside but also the brother parties of the other communistic countries under Russian control received derisive requests as to why the otherwise so extremely exemplary GDR (for German Democratic Republic) was not able or willing to end this unsustainable antagonism. How could that happen that they still existed? That wasn't allowed in the paradise of the workers class. The Nationalized industry under the leadership of the only authorized party of the workers class, which posses the absolute truth, had to be at the top of economic development. And after all, who did they think they were, those moldered, parasitic capitalists. They wouldn't exist without the generosity of the Party of the workers class. And that was right. At least for a part as always they said partly the truth and mixed it smartly with lies so that at the end the lie was the truth. And they used the same strategy as they had used with the farmers. The time to make an end to that farce—as the communistic East German propaganda named the success of the small business—was at the beginning of the seventies.

After the central committee had decided to confiscate the remains of the rotten capitalisti exploiter order, they looked for a strategy to do it without to be upfront in that upcoming fight. As always the communists wanted to have somebody else to do the dirty work and be in the background waiting to see how it went and then jump on the bandwagon, fire the driver, take control, correct direction if necessary and own the movement. In this case they used the so-called Block-Parties here, especially the National Democratic Party of East Germany (NDPD). After the decision of the central committee of the SED, they met with the leader of the NDPD and demanded that the block parties where most of those owners were members had to do the convincing.

The SED "suggested" that the nationalization of the remaining capitalist companies would go off without a hitch. Shortly after this meeting with the heads of the SED, the party congress of the NDPD took place. Several line-toeing members held speeches saying they couldn't take it anymore to be the barrier on the way to the realization of the socialistic society and therefore they offer to bring their companies into the great socialistic public-owned industry. What a farce. The vast majority of the company owners were caught by surprise. Only a few of the owners of companies with public participation were really interested in the complete nationalization of their companies. And they were most likely those whose companies were already over indebted, so for them it was the only way to get out of the situation with at least a kind of a golden handshake.

But there were many of them whose complete family life was in jeopardy and it has been reported that many of them had tears in their eyes when they realized that it was over. Decades of hard work after WWII ended and very often centuries of family traditions would be erased. That couldn't be. Resistance germinated but that was exactly what the SED needed to start the campaign. A sheer hell of defamation broke loose. Not one day passed by without the mass media reporting how these bloodsuckers betrayed the workers class. Denunciation about dislocation of goods to West Germany, defalcation and falsification of balance sheets filled the otherwise boring socialistic news papers. The daily occurrence, real and made-up stories about criminal investigations against owners of small businesses, often in the hands of families for generations, prepared the situation for the communists to bring it home.

In the entire incidence the hand of the STASI was clearly noticeable. The systematic activation of all their potentials to gather information wherever possible was the basic. They had learned their lesson from 1953 and didn't want to be surprised again. All available informal employees were instructed to collect every single piece of information of the Private owners. Banks were ordered to register strictly all account movements by the company owners and report these regularly to the appropriate contacts. The custom authority was instructed to collect all information and report even the smallest irregularity from the past and update the reporting weekly. All regional and local STASI offices were instructed and brought to a higher alarm level. But the uproar they hoped for to show that they were ready this time didn't happen.

The whole action to nationalize the last capitalist hope in East Germany took a little more than six months. There are a lot of reasons for this. The international situation had seriously changed during the years since 1968. The chairman of the council of the ministers of East Germany met with the chancellor of West Germany. West Germany had acknowledged the Inner-German border and most of the people believed it couldn't take that long for West Germany to acknowledge the GDR. The hope of the private owners of industrial production were overwhelmed by the back-crushing power of the SED, and few had the vision to think of a free society in a not too far future. Together with the overall daily problems the small business owners had to fight with, many of them just gave up and several committed suicide. Sick and tired of fighting with logical arguments and facts against irrationality and an inhuman and unjust ideology, the last bastion of a whilom blooming private industry was destroyed.

Working on a thesis in the subject of material science during my graduate study at the Institute of Technology at Goerlitz, I actually met the widow of the former owner of the largest brewery in that area. She was the librarian at the technical documentation center of the contact manufacturing company which had asked the Institute for help with a very specific problem. I had the opportunity to research that problem and write a thesis about my findings with the result that I did not have to go through the test and certification stress.

Since I spent many hours at the documentation center and there wasn't much public traffic, we had time to talk, and she told me her story, after we had built some kind of trust over several days approaching each other's political opinions. She was a small woman, almost a head shorter than I and very slim, but not skinny. And she spoke with a soft, very quiet voice. When we discovered that we both were believers in Christ, she began to speak. Every day I'd get a part of the story. I had to ask questions, she would never start by herself.

"What did you do before you started working here?" I asked her.

She looked at me with a questioning expression in her eyes and her turned head, looking out of the window before she answered. "I grow up in this town, not far from here. My parents owned a bakery, and I loved to bring the ordered bread to the small restaurant down the street before they opened in the evening. The owner had two children, a boy just two years ahead of me and a daughter my age." She paused and looked again at me with this questioning expression in her eyes, which she always had. It was as if she wanted to say, "Are you really interested in the story of an old woman?"

Then she would go ahead, "Since we all had to help our parents after school at the business, we mostly would just sit down at the backyard and talk about what we would do differently when we would be grown up. Karl, that was the name of the boy, and Angelika, his sister, but everybody called her Angie…"

She fell silent, and when I looked up from my work, I saw that she was looking out of the window and seemed totally lost in remembrances. She might have felt that I looked at her; she turned around and said, "He was a dreamer. He dreamed about founding a brewery and brewing beer that really deserved the name beer, not the watered-down yellowish swill, he used to say.

"We married two weeks before he got his conscription, and I would not see him for about seven years—that was when he came back from captivity." Again she stopped and walked away to write several more labels to stick on the binders.

It was as if she needed a few minutes to collect herself. I focused back onto my work, analyzing the microscopic pictures I had made the other day of some contact-alloys, when I suddenly felt her standing beside me. I looked up and there she was, asking me, "Do you want to hear more about it?"

Since I was so concentrated on my work, she probably saw a disinterest in my reaction and walked away. I immediately realized that she was disappointed. I did not bother her that day with more questions, yet had a very good start two days later.

While I was looking for a specific article from a West German journal about relay contact alloys and couldn't find it, she was suddenly on my side, grabbed one of the binders and said, "Things would often be much easier in life if people would have the courage to ask questions."

Now I was warned. Suddenly I thought, *What if she is not whom I think she is? If she is an IM for the STASI, I would be in big trouble. I would be immediately expelled from the Institute and would never again have a chance to go to grad school.* For her it was different. She was almost at the age of retirement. "What do you mean by that?" I asked her, trying to hide my surprise.

She answered, "I know you're looking for that article, which requires a specific approval because it is in a West German journal. And I know that you don't have that," she said with a smile on her face.

She handed me the binder, and while I carried it to my table, I asked, "What did you do when your husband came back from war? Görlitz wasn't really much damaged, right?"

"No," she said, "it was so late in April that even the worst fanatics saw their safety in getting as far west as possible, and with that the city wasn't defended." Again she was carried away in her thoughts to the past, and when she went on after a while, she said, "He was so filled with enthusiasm about building his own brewery that I wondered where he had been all those years."

"Did he tell you about the war?" I asked.

"No, not really. He would lose a word here and there, but he never really told me much about it. He would say, 'Better you don't know.' On his way back home, he had seen a totally bombed brewery about thirty kilometers to the west, and he knew that there was usable equipment. He borrowed a horse carriage, and we went there and got what we needed to start brewing beer. It took us several years to get everything in order as he wanted it, and our beer became famous."

The remembrance on that time seemed to bring the joy back into her, because she had such a smile on her face.

"We were so happy," she said, going on in her description, "although we worked hard and twelve-hour, seven-day weeks were normal. At the end of the sixties, we were the largest privately owned brewery in the district."

I had to look up at her because when she went on, her voice had changed.

"Then everything changed virtually overnight." Anger was now noticeable in her voice. "A new law required us to accept a paid union leader in our company, who would represent the workers. We had to provide an office and all the material he needed. Our workers actually didn't like that person, but by law, he was their representative before the 'capitalist owners' as he preferred to name me and my husband. Once a week he would call all the employees together and would tell them that they did not have to keep silent. He began to insist on being at our meetings and presenting the concerns of the employees about paying not enough yet making profit. It didn't take long before we had the first strike, and my husband was arrested and questioned by the STASI."

I could definitely hear that she was now emotional and could barely hold her tears.

"When he came back two days later, he was a different man. He was embittered and wouldn't talk much. We were forced to accept an investigation by a control commission, which was composed of the union, the SED, and people from the finance department. Their findings resulted in a fine of almost all of our savings and the loss of fifty percent, plus one vote of our ownership. The substantiation basically accused us of stealing from the employees." It took her several minutes to finish the last sentence: "Two days later I found my husband hanging at the drying loft."

Now she was in tears but was not done yet.

"After we had buried him, I found a new kind of power within myself and thought now even more, *I will fight for what we worked so hard for so many years,*" she said, suppressing a sob. "I called our oldest brew master in the office—he was with us at the beginning—and asked him if he would stand with me to bring the company back on its feet. But he was too scared. He said he would not risk his young family against the powers to be, and we had to accept that they had the power now."

She stood there at my desk for a while, saying nothing but looking out the window, and when she finally walked back to her desk, she said, "I was alone—nobody wanted to stay on my side. I had already read about all the other privately owned companies being nationalized under more or less the same circumstances when the monsters who destroyed my life offered me a payout. It wasn't much, and the biggest thing was probably the ten boxes of beer per month. They may have thought I'd drink myself into insanity. I did not, and honestly, the beer they started to brew after a while wasn't even worth drinking."

That was the story of the ruined life of one family, and there were thousands. Maybe somebody will write a book about that, or maybe it's already written.

The Communist Version of the First Amendment or Scissors in the Head

Here are just a few words about the communistic version of the First Amendment. I remember very well the statement Erich Honecker gave once a when a western journalist asked him about the freedom of opinions.

The reporter wondered, "Is there really any worth in media reporting when it's controlled by the absolute ruling party?" And going on, he said, "That would actually be considered censorship in any free country."

"Well, the constitution of the GDR guarantees the freedom of speech and opinion," Erich Honnecker replied.

However, what he did not say was that the wording itself restricted this freedom to the framework of the constitution which at the very first place stipulated the top ranking of the SED. He also said that the media in East Germany is free to report whatever they believed was worthy to report and however they believed to say what they had to say. This was a very bold statement because it was a typical communistic way to counter the truth. It wasn't wrong and it wasn't right. It was communistic.

Now what's that all about? Here is the explanation. East German media was one hundred percent under control of the Socialist United Party, the party in power. Not a single newspaper, Journal, magazine, radiobroadcast, television show, book or whatever kind of printed or broadcasted message to the public was unmonitored by the party. Actually East Germany had a high concentration of periodicals and daily newspapers because it was considered a highly important propaganda instrument of the Socialist United Party. To insure that the reader get only what the party wanted him to read they used two easy instruments. First of all the national mail service had the exclusive delivery rights. With that it was ensured that any disagreeable message could be stopped by just taking the undesirable magazine or newspaper off the list. Even in case of accidentally misplaced or misspoken information it was possible to suppress the delivery in the last minute. One example of this kind of reaction was the central yearly calendar of the GST organization.

In 1953, they had to recall the calendar and to annihilate it because there was no picture of Walter Ulbricht, the party leader at this time, and no reference to his speech of the last party conference in it. This was an affront against the party and I'm sure that the responsible persons at least lost their jobs. Another example is the disappearance of a very popular Russian magazine *Sputnik*. It was a satire magazine and was known for taking the excrescences of the communistic misgovernment to lampoon. Especially after the restructuring of the Soviet system began by Michael Gorbatchov, the *Sputnik* felt free enough to criticizes the stupidity of the communistic bureaucrats. This was too much for the East German party leaders and so the *Sputnik* just disappeared from the list of available magazines. Secondly there was no free choice to become a journalist, official yes, but not in reality.

To become a journalist you had to be a perfect party soldier throughout your whole life. You had to have a spotless personal file and family background. Which meant membership in children and youth organizations with leadership positions in them was essential. Since the acceptance on any of the East German Universities required at least two recommendations it was nearly impossible to get inscribed without a strong partisan opinion. And there was only one university where it was possible to get a degree in journalism. Everything concerning media and freedom of speech and reporting the truth was taken care of because the communists were in power there too, and the general on all Universities obligatory and mandatory courses in Marxism-Leninism over the whole length of the time was extended to the extreme. That made sure that journalists knew what they had to write or say or report without to offend the Socialist United Party. They called it the *Scissors in the Head*.

And as the very last security there was always the criminal code with the very powerful and endless expandable paragraph 106. It punished every expression which deglorified the all-encompassing and historically-proven power of the Socialist United Party as the exclusive representative of the workers class. That would be considered as *Staatsfeindliche Hetze* (German for subversive agitation). Another favorite method to silence a dissentient newspaper, magazine, or journal was to cut the paper allowance. No paper, no newspaper.

Under those circumstances, it was no wonder that the average newspaper reported with monotonous stupidity the fight with the elements.

FREEDOM'S NIGHTMARE

In spring and in fall the workers at the agricultural cooperatives with the inconvenience of the groundless rain-soaked farmland to bring the last seed into the earth in spring or harvest the last acre of crop or potatoes in fall. Day by day the readers were bored by endless reports about the heroes of the clod of the earth.

And winter time opened another frontline. The mine workers became the heroes. Because energy production East Germany relayed to nearly 90 percent on the open mines with brown coal, which led to problematic situations nearly every winter. Mostly because of the bad quality and the high level of non-burning minerals it contained, it was a horrible load for the environment. Those huge open mines often several square miles became soaked by the rain in fall and when the winter hit the areas everything froze and the equipment wasn't able to work. Additional to the low heating value, which caused a permanent deficit between demand and supply, was the liability to defects of the equipment. This was the reason for the neverending dramatization of the fulfillment of the requirements of the SED to secure enough combustibles supply for the people. It was so boring that most of the people just stopped watching or reading it.

And there was a special propaganda broadcasting every Monday. It was named the *Der Schwarze Kanal* (German of *Black Channel)* in consideration that to watch the TV broadcastings from Western Germany was called black watching. And there was a joke told in these days. Kids were asked in school who is hosting the TV broadcast on Monday night and Fritzchen (German for the little Fritz) who happened to be the major person in jokes with kids answered, it's Karl-Eduard von *Klack.* Now for those who are younger than 40 years old you may not know that there was a time when you had to stand up from the sofa and physically shut off the TV with the main switch, and this *Klack* was exactly the noise made by the main switch.

The real name of the host of that TV show was Karl-Eduard von Schnitzler. He was the black sheep of a very wealthy West German family, but because he wasn't able to be up to the moral standards of his family, he decided to stand with the communists in East Germany. And actually it was beneficial for both. The communists had a very fine propaganda tool. They would say, see, even the noblemen, when they use their brain and are realistic, acknowledged the leading role of the workers party. And he became the well-paid Goebbels of the communists of East Germany. And this came not as a surprise. He had an unbeatable talent to pull statements of western journalists or politicians out of context and re-assemble these fragments so that it became the opposite of what these guys originally said. There were hundreds of incidences where he virtually turned the statement of a western Presidents or Prime Ministers into the pure opposite. I remember one incidence where I had seen the original interview, then three days later the mutilated version of Karl Eduard and on the next weekend the horrified politician in West Germany when he had to defend himself because Karl-Eduard was so successful with his perversion of the facts that his own peers believed what they got reported from their assistants about the East German statement by Karl-Eduard von *Klack*, pardon, Schnitzler.

A very good indication about his character quality was the fact that he was four times married, even though that was by law impossible in East Germany, you could only be married three times, he got a special allowance by the general secretary of the SED, Erich Honecker.

In general the news was brought to the people in a stoical manner. Not only were the content of the news messages almost always formulated in a way that you had to read between the lines, but the reader, you would today call him probably the anchor, was ordered to read it as neutrally as humanly possible. Many of the East Germans had learned that especially that what wasn't said was the interesting news. As an example when foreign leaders would visit the GDR and it wasn't one of the communistic bloc nations, it began usually with the announcement of a growing international interest for the achievements of the great socialistic German Democratic Republic, although it was neither democratic, nor a republic and for sure it wasn't about the growing interest of the achievements because there were none.

It was mainly because of the fact that the East German communist leaders had the ear of the Russian communists in a way no other communist leader in the Warsaw Pact had. Another reason was that the GDR was constantly short in convertible currency and needed at least some of that to pay for the obligations they had. For that the communists would sell everything for any price they could get for inconvertible currency. Even though they had established foreign branches of some of the more developed industries in several different countries, the money coming in from those businesses wasn't really much. To the contrary, it was often just to camouflage the activities of the *Stashiva*—Russian for espionage—within those countries. And it can be expensive to bribe people to betray their own country.

The news broadcast, which was called the *Aktuelle Kamera* (German for Current Camera) was broadcasted every night from 7:30 p.m. till 8:00 p.m. As said before, it wasn't really something you'd consider a news broadcast; it was more like a brainwashing propaganda message, but since we had learned to read between the lines and considered what wasn't said, we got a pretty good feeling what was going on.

Especially those who were still able to use their brain and were curious enough to questioning everything they were told. For a large part of the youth, mainly those with parents who were deeply integrated into the political life, that wasn't the case. They did not have had the possibility to ask questions outside the norm. And when you lived in an area where the receiving of western TV broadcasts was almost impossible and radio stations were only receivable on very expensive, high-quality radios, you had nothing to compare and ended up with believing the lies thrown at you day in day out.

Now, when such an international guest was visiting the GDR to admire the great achievements of the socialistic society a standard verbiage in the evening news was "The Leaders discussed points of mutual interest." Then they showed some seconds of the "Leaders" marching through a manufacturing plant—what for sure was prepped up before for several months—some smiles and handshakes and that was it. All you were actually listening to was where the visiting statesman was from and what position he or she held in his or her country. And the most important part was where the visitors had been during the visit. The manufacturing facilities and the cities they had visited were the best indication of what you had to buy next before those goods produced at those facilities and cities became as rare as gold nuggets.

And then there were the endless reports about the great brother Soviet Union, which was on the brink of passing the might and power of the capitalistic world with rocket speed. For several years they used the slogan: *Überholen ohne Einzuholen* (German for *Passing Without Catching Up*). But it never happened.

There was a joke related to some of the slogans like this one which went like this: Fritzchen at school during his "political economy of socialism class" (yeah, we really had special education with that name) can't get his mind around what the teacher tried to explain. So he asks the teacher, "If I get that right, Teacher, last week you taught us the rotten parasitic capitalism is currently at the edge of a precipice, now you're telling us that we socialists, are always one step ahead of them capitalists, does that explain why we can't buy what we need, because we're already over the cliff?"

One of the two main news anchors had once the chutzpa to say both slogans at the end of a news broadcast like this: "We all, my dear audience, know that the rotten and parasitic capitalism is at the edge of a precipice. And we also know that the winning socialism is always one step ahead. Now you know where we are. Good Night!" Two days later this news anchor was seen working on a shipyard removing rust from steel plates in a zebra uniform. It happened actually twice. Only because of his huge popularity among those who regularly watched the broadcast he was paroled within a few months and appeared on TV again. Some years later I had the opportunity to see the same news anchor walking down the road of that same shipyard, where I was working at that time. He was within a group of inmates of the local jail. That time he was sentenced because one night when he was done with reading all those lies and half truths he *blew air* and said, "Now you know the news and what it is worth".

Finally at Home

EVENTUALLY A HOME

HARALD ZIEGER

A Sudden Awareness
or How I Crushed a Party Meeting

ERE I WAS. Sitting among all those brown-noses, apple-lickers, and would-be revolutionaries and could barely hold my breath. I could not take it anymore. I just couldn't. How could it happen that I had come so far? What had made my life so complicated that I sat here and thought about risking everything, my job, my family, my freedom, even my life? I was about to do it, and the only reason why I hesitated was the thought of my young family, my wife and two little children. What brought me to a point in life where I had to decide whether walk further down the path of self-denial or just stand up and say, "I'm done."

And I started to let my mind wander back in time. Because it was not only me, it was the question about the country also. Actually it was a two-fold question, what brought this country into a situation that the citizens tried everything, and I mean really—everything up to risking their very life by crossing a deathly border—to leave that country, and how came I so far to risk that everything myself? Crossing that deathly border which had eaten away so many lives, mostly young people who died through mine explosions or under the fire of the AK 47, the standard weapon of the border guards. And those who had their finger on the trigger were often still teens. A thought flashed through my mind and before I could really develop it, it was gone. Something like why do they have to kill those who even won't to be part of the victorious workers' paradise? Let them go, because they aren't really assets to the system. In the contrary, they did everything they could not to be a positive part of the system.

For so many years I had first tried to do what I had debated with excitement with my literature teacher, what I called *changing the system from within*. And she tried to convince me, a senior at high school, that it wasn't going to work. The system would not allow me to be changed from within. Then, after I realized how true that was, I just tried to become invisible, and that didn't work either. The communist party just did not accept inactivity and invisibility.

Here I was sitting in a meeting of the smallest unit of the party in power as a member, yet miles away from agreement with the ideology and

68

doctrine, the doctrine of the absolute power of the party of the workers class which was led by people who actually for the most part didn't even knew what work was. It was a party which controlled every single aspect of one's life, virtually into the bedrooms of the citizens.

Freedom—what was that? There was no freedom.

I wasn't in jail. Wasn't I? When the area you are allowed to move around is encircled with a fifteen-feet-high fence, crowned with barbed wires, secured by anti-personal mines and spring-guns—sounds like jail, or not? When the *power to be* dictates every phase of your life such as what you're able to buy, what you can earn, what profession you can learn, and which study direction you're not allowed to choose, how you have to raise your children, and what to watch on TV—sounds like prison, or not?

Although it was a large prison, a little larger than 41,700 square miles, somewhat larger than Ohio, I felt locked-up. And even if many did not dare to say or express it in any kind, thousands felt the same way. This feeling was especially intensified when we were able to receive the West German TV transmission. Seeing that there was no shortage on all the products needed for a decent life, understanding that they could go wherever they wanted to go, and knowing the only way they got killed when they left West Germany was by car accidents—it made all the phrases and ideological indoctrination a farce, downright ridiculous. Follow me on my way through a childhood full of fear, a life with permanent awareness of danger into freedom, and understand why I feel like heading back in time.

Parents, Siblings, an Accident, a One-Way Trip in the Wrong Direction and Years of Horror

My mother was the second child out of seven children my grandparents had. She was born in a small village in East Prussia—today a part of Poland. My grandfather was an officer in the German Army. Her mother died due to postpartum at the birth of her youngest brother Harry. And only the Almighty God knew at this time that he would play an important role later in my life. When my grandmother died in 1935, all children were separated and given to foster parents, but my Uncle Harry, the youngest, was adopted by his uncle, a brother of my grandfather who lived in southern Germany.

My mother was given to a childless couple in a small town in that region where she got a decent education because they were nicely situated and owned a dairy. That was at least what she told me. But the idyll of a well-protected childhood did not last long. The Second World War started in 1939 and ended with a catastrophe. With the breakthrough of the Russian Army through the German lines in January 1945, the town my mother lived in with her foster parents was overrun before they were able to leave. Her foster parents were killed by Polish marauders. She hid in a barn during that three days of plunder and when the marauders moved on, she flew out of the town, and after a couple of days she caught a trek from another town. These people tried to reach the German core land but had been overrun by the front line too and were now shifted towards the southern border of Poland. My mother never really talked about that time. She was fifteen years old, and she went through hell on earth. Just from reading books about the German retreat and the revengefulness of the Polish civilians as well as the Russian soldiers, I got a foggy notion about what she may have gone through in those months. In constant danger of being raped or killed, nothing to eat beside that what was found in deserted or destroyed farms, and often enough they had been attacked by machine-gun fire from Russian fighter aircrafts which came back from the frontline. Thousands were killed through those attacks.

Finally at the end of the war in May 1945, my mother found herself detained in a refugee camp in Czechoslovakia. For two years she had to work twelve hours a day in a textile factory. She was fifteen years old. Eventually in 1947 she was relieved and with a train organized by the Red Cross she came to Germany. She finished her school and met my father in 1949. That was her story as she told it to me, but till today, I'm not sure how much of that is really true.

My father was an Austrian citizen or probably an American, but at the time my mother and my father met, he did not know that. Why? It's another unbelievable story. My grandfather, on my father's side, my mother told me was a silversmith, but he was really a sought-after chef at a German restaurant in the Bronx between the world wars. Just recently I was able to discover some unknown details about my ancestors on my father's side. My grandfather and his brother immigrated to the United States around 1913, but for sure before the First World War. Born in 1897, he would have been drafted in to the Austrian army, and for that reason he and his brother moved to the United States. My grandfather was a professional chef and since the Austrian cooking tradition was, and I believe still is, among the best in the world, he had no trouble being hired in New York. According to my second grade cousin both my father and his brother traveled several times back and forth between Austria and the United States after the war. Both earned good incomes and were able to support their family over there. In 1921 it happened that a young girl from Allentown, PA, was visiting her relatives in Austria living in the same village as my grandfather's relatives. They met and fell in love with each other.

My grandmother got pregnant, so they had to marry before she could go back to the United States, because at that time, it was considered scandalous to be pregnant and not married, especially in Austria, which was ninety percent Catholic

My grandfather and my grandmother got married in a small village in Austria. The strange thing is that she, my grandmother on my father's side, was born in Allentown, PA, in the US, which I did not know till fall 2010, when I began to look into the history of that part of my family. I found my second grade cousin in Allentown, who happens to be the son of my grandfather's brother. Although he did not know much about my grandfather and his life, he was the estate executor for my grandfather when he died in 1984. Here is what I found since that contact.

My father was born in 1922 in Austria. A passengers list from September 28, 1923, lists my grandfather together with my father on board of the vessel *Aquitania*, so I knew for sure they left Austria after his birth. The next document I found was the census for the city of New York from 1930 in which my grandfather was listed with his family, my grandmother, my father, and one sister Irene, born in 1925 in New York. My aunt Helen was born in 1930 right after the census, which was the reason that she wasn't listed.

Sometime in the mid 1930s my grandmother traveled with all three children to Austria There are two possible reasons for that. First she was sick, some kind of woman sickness and Austrian doctors were well renowned at that time as specialists for women sicknesses. A second reason was the economica situation. During the depression there wasn't much to earn with a high-end German-style restaurant, and the relatives in Austria were farmers and had food enough to feed the family. My grandfather stayed in New York, and when my grandmother died towards the end of the 1930s and he got message that the children were taken care of by the family, he signed the application for naturalization as an American citizen. Since my father was still there at the time Austria became a part of the Third Reich, and he was considered an Austrian citizen and old enough, he was automatically drafted to the German army. He made it through the whole war and ended 1945 in American captivity.

My grandfather died sometime in 1984 in Allentown, PA. I'm pretty sure that there are relatives I don't know much about. I really do not know so much about my family on my father's side. One reason is that we did not spend much time together and the other is that when we met, we talk mostly about the time after the war. In 2010, I did find one of my cousins, daughter of my aunt Irene, who lives in New Mexico. But since her mother did not know much about her American citizenship and because she married a German, she had to apply for naturalization when she came back to the states, and so did my cousin.

And I found a passenger list notice that my aunt Helen arrived at the United States in 1946 with a US passport issued by the American embassy in Vienna. In that passenger list she declared that she left the US before the war in 1934. Since I do not know the maiden name of my grandmother and could not find Aunt Helen or her family yet, that part of my family is still a dark area.

But let's go back to the timeline. From the day of my birth, my life appears as crazy as many years should follow. It was like permanently swimming against the stream of the surrounding life with the constant fear that any of the oncoming waves would drown me. It took till I got married for my life to be stabilized and started to be a little more normal, but not really. I was born in a little town in West Germany. This town was well-known for its large number of small and middle-sized furniture manufacturing companies. I was the third child of a connection between my mother and my father and I was born in 1954. My oldest brother Peter was born in 1950 and my sister Connie in 1952. My father was still married to another woman with whom he had another three children. Eventually in November 1954 they married and I was legalized as his son by the decision of the family court in our town. I actually have seen that enrollment in the family register. This was the most important action he did for me. It will become clear later why. Our family was about to grow again. In 1955, my mother was pregnant with my younger brother when a horrible accident happened.

I was just over a year and I have no remembrance on that but my older sister told me about it. It was at this time when the refrigerators had no magnetic band to hold them closed and instead there was a normal door handle. Connie and my brother Peter played hide-and-seek. Peter was tall enough to open the fridge to hide himself with the door falling into its lock after him. But my sister was too small to open the door and he asphyxiated before any help was available. Connie suffered her whole life under the load of that accident. I don't know where my mother was when it happened and as so many things in our family, it was an issue off-limits.

My younger brother, Michael, was born in December, just a few months after that horrible accident. Many years later, I think it was in 1996 or 1997; I used the opportunity to combine a business trip with a visit to my native city. The whilom flourishing furniture industry was gone. Only a few family-owned, small manufacturers survived the downgrade of the appreciation of German craftsmanship. Cheap mass-produced furniture from the former communistic block countries had replaced the proudly produced masterpieces. I could not find anything that would help me to identify the place where we lived in these years and my mother just said she can't remember. I went to the church on Sunday and thought the Pastor might be able to help me to find the enrollment of my baptismal in the register, but he had no time that day.

In 1956, we left West Germany and moved to East Germany, better known as the Russian occupancy zone. What a strange move! Why did that happen? Actually everybody who would have publicly said that he would do this at this time would be declared mentally ill and maybe ended in an asylum. At this time the frontier between West and East Germany was closed, and the only way to move from one part into the other was through West Berlin-East Berlin.

Thousands of people and whole families crossed the open border between the Russian part and the Allied part of Berlin day by day going westwards. Consider the situation of those people who lived at this time in East Germany. The horror of the Nazi dictatorship was still fresh in the mind of the vast majority of the Germans, and yet the communists had already created a new one. The motto "Who is not with us, is against us" and the fallout of this motto turned into day by day politics and threatened a whole generation. Whose circumstance ever allowed to move left the Russian zone as most of the people who lived there still named the DDR, even years after the foundation of the state. It was neither Democratic nor a Republic it has been slowly but constantly developing into a communist dictatorship. Whosoever was not willing to accept the total control of the personal life and the complete elimination of freedom, escaped through the last open gate into the free world! That gate was the zone border between the Russian Military Occupation Zone of Berlin (East Berlin) and the three West-Allied Zones of Berlin (West Berlin), which still was able to be crossed.

Since you were only allowed to cross this line for daily life reasons, such as shopping, or work or visiting, people had to leave all their belonging behinds them. Everything! It was the second total loss of all possessions after they had already lost everything from the war. But they decided it was better to be free and start all over again than to stay and lose freedom. The escape of thousands of people and of whole families week by week was not only caused by the increasing pressure of the communistic system throughout the daily life. It was also caused by the growing discrepancy between the economical performances between both systems. On the east side the communist-controlled nationalized industry and agricultural production were led by the centralized decision-making bureaucrats who decided when where what had to be done down to the workbench of the blue-collar worker in the last small village hundreds of miles away. Bureaucrats who had never had their hands on a piece of wood or steel or walked behind the plow now decided when to put the seeds into the earth and when to put fertilizer on the fields and how much.

And on the other side the capitalistic system was open to the enthusiastic generation eager to forget the horrors of the war, to take the chance and build a new Germany under the guidance of a much younger nation but with a very strong basic understanding of freedom, individualism, and entrepreneurship to produce whatever the market was asking for and willing to pay the price necessary to make profit, which was able to feed the next innovation, feed the workers and their family, and share with the society that part which was needed to have the infrastructure, which made all that success possible. It wasn't a difficult decision for those who got the correct information and who understood that there was no change coming from somewhere to turn the situation around. And they decided to pay the price to live free. Others didn't and stayed, hoping for a change to the better and that it wouldn't be so bad—and this was the vast majority. I remember a neighbor who was an officer during the First World War saying "The Americans will come one day and we will be free. I'm not leaving my property and throwing it to those swine."

And then there were those who thought it a good thing to have the people owning the manufacturing facilities, the farms, and ranches. They thought that now social justice would win over capitalist greed, and everybody would participate on the prosperity of the creativeness of the German workers. And there were those who just used the new system to achieve their own personal advantages, no matter what it cost and no matter whom they had to sacrifice as long as they got what they wanted.

The daily loss of thousands of the most valuable minds, engineers, doctors, scientists, nurses, and highly experienced and qualified workers created a deep cut into the economic recovery plans of the communist government. The people voted with the feed. Leave this madhouse as long it is possible was the motto. And we moved eastwards, against the stream. How different my life could have been if that would not have happened, but then I'd have no story to write in this book.

Why in the world would somebody move in the opposite direction at this time? Swimming against the stream? As always when I asked my mother I got her versions of the story. And when I was able to ask my father many years later I got another story. To understand the insanity of our moving into the Russian Zone we needed to know a little about the German history as explained in chapter 1.

My mother's version explained that my father was a member of *Kommunistische Partei Deutschland* (Communistic Party of Germany [KPD]), newly founded after the war. To the contrary to the East German parties, the Communist Party and the Social Democratic Party of the American, British, and France military zones never united as they did in East Germany. Mainly because there wasn't any kind of backlash by the military powers in those zones as there was in the Russian zone. When the communists realized that their dream from a united und communistic control Germany like East Germany wasn't going to happen soon, they tried to overthrow the government of West Germany. The coup failed and the party was forbidden in 1956. According to my mother my father was a very active member of the Communist Party and had a leadership role in the area where we lived.

Now my mother said that my father was able at first to keep working for the party in the underground, but after a few months it became too dangerous and he flew to East Germany, fearing for his freedom. My mother with three little kids did not know what to do other than to follow him. Later they got divorced and he went back to West Germany because in the meantime the danger to be captured for his work for the German Communist Party did not longer exist. And that was the only version I knew for many years, and I had no reason not to believe it until I heard the other side of the story. And not only that, but got some pieces of information from the STASI evaluation of my Austrian citizenship and off her divorce paper as well as some photographs I found together with it.

FREEDOM'S NIGHTMARE

The other side of the story, told by my father when we met each other many years later in 1985 in Vienna, Austria, was different. Very different. He told me that one day when he came home from work his family was gone. He said he worked really hard because he had to feed a lot of yaps and at first he had no idea what was going on. The police took the data and that was it. That uncertainty did not last long. Just a few days later he got visitors and their questions were really strange to him. He thought that his wife was a caring mother of the three children. But what he learned during that visit changed everything. She was—at least that's what he told me— the party leader of the underground cell operating in that area, not just the town they lived in. It took him a while to realize that she was not just somewhere in the underground in another town, but out of the country.

Several days after the visit from the officers of the *Verfassungsschutz* (German for Federal Office for the Protection of the Constitution) he found a postcard in his mailbox which had no stamp, no text, no address, just the picture of a railway station. He jumped into the next train to West Berlin, crossed the zone border to East Berlin, and took the next train to that town where my mother had found shelter. He said that he tried to convince her to go back with him because as a mother of three little children she would never be thrown in jail, but she did not want to go back. So he decided to stay with the family and try to make the best out of the situation. There was no problem finding a job because he was qualified as a professional chemist and everything seemed to be fine. But he said it took only months for her to fall back into the old behavior—an irresistible urge to date other men. He locked the doors when he went to work his nightshifts, but she jumped out the window to go to dance and have fun.

Finally he said there was no other way than to get divorced, and since she had the better connection to the powerful people in town, she got the custody. That is actually confirmed by that what I read in the divorce papers many years later. A few weeks after the divorce he decided to leave East Germany—it was still possible to cross the border in Berlin—but he wanted to take me with him. He monitored the moving of my mother for a couple of days and when he felt he knew enough, he pulled me out of the stroller. But it does not turned out alright. My mother pulled all strings and alarmed all of her contacts in the local party. They forced the police to initiate a town wide manhunt. Within a few hours he was arrested. Now that was serious. Child abduction was the indictment and that meant up to eighteen years in the uranium underground mines in East Germany.

You need to know that the uranium produced from the underground mines in East Germany was very high concentrated at the core, and although the yield was very small, the Russians who took ownership of the mine in 1945 never allowed stopping extraction. And actually even though everybody knew about the incredible circumstances the prisoners had to work in there, nobody dared to talk about it.

But he could escape. The transporter, with which he was brought to the next larger city jail to wait for the transport with other inmates, had an accident and he could escape. He jumped on a coal train and buried himself under a layer of coal. He did not know where the train was headed but his first thought was to get as much distance between himself and the place of the accident as possible. The train stopped several times, and every time it came to a hold he dug himself in deeper. Sometimes he was close to drowning when he finally could go out and breathe fresh air when the train started to move again. Eventually the train came to a hold longer than before. It was much longer than it had stopped any time before, but he still felt unsecure about the situation. He also recognized that some of the wagons had been removed. At nightfall he dug out from the coal to look around and he decided to leave the train. At first he realized that it was a hump yard, and the next he realized was that he was in West Berlin. He was free.

Years later, he tried to contact my mother because of his citizenship, but she never answered. This contact letter conducted by his lawyer though was very important evidence many years later when I started to find out who I really was. They never met each other again even if it would have been possible after the reunion of Germany. I have many reasons to believe my father's version, mainly because when I knew both sides of the story, my father's version made more sense, more logical, and a lot of memories came into my mind. I remembered pictures of my mother marching at the frontline of a large crowd with communistic transparent requiring socialism for all Germans. I remembered so many lies I had been told over all the years. I asked myself time and again *why*? I did not get an answer.

Never! At that time I wasn't even able to be angry about my mother. All I felt was a total emptiness in that place where other people have their love for their parents. And that feeling won't go away. Even though years have gone by and my mother has had multiple opportunities to tell me the truth, when I ask her about certain events in her history or the history of our family, she keeps telling the same lies. Actually I think that she is at a point where she believes those lies herself. I have them forgiven both my mother and my father, but that's it.

I recall an occurrence in 2006; I was a guest of my aunt in Jacksonville, Florida, another long-missed part of the family on my mother's side, whom I first met in 2003. How? That is another part of this story I'll explain later in this book. We had bought several very nice picture post-cards to send greetings from Florida to our relatives in Europe When my aunt saw the card I had addressed to my mother, she said that a son ought to to write "in love" or "love you" or something like that. And the only answer I could give her was that I don't know what a son's love for his mother is, because I never felt a mother's love. And it still hurts when I see how children get hugged and kissed by their mothers because I can't remember even one time.

A Roof over Your Head and a Meal in Your Tummy Does Not Always Warm You

My early remembrance of the time before we finally settled down is more or less faded. Some remembrances are very clear and partly hurting still after all these years and some are just nebulous and fragmentary. I remember on living in a large building, kind of a barrack, and I'm sure it was a police barrack; because I remember that the men who lived there with us wore uniforms. It might be that it was the paramilitary police force that were so-called Billeted Peoples Police, which later became the cadre of the People's Army. I remember waking up one night to horrible noises coming from outside the separating blankets used to give us some kind of privacy. When I get up and looked out, I saw one of the police men throwing up. Later I learned that he died that night because of a ruptured appendix.

This was part of the rather restless lifestyle of my mother at that time, which caused a permanent change to where and with whom we lived. And perhaps it might be the reason why we ended up in an orphanage, actually at least two. One was the real hell on earth. It must have been large, because I remember that the refectory was large enough to feed at least 120-150 children at the same time. I remember that there were five or six tables each for twenty to twenty-five kids. And I know that I was there with my brother Michael. The food was meager and there was a strict discipline. I really can't recall any kind of laughter and I have still the picture before my eyes sitting on those tables and waiting for the command to eat that one slice of bread covered with a thin layer of cheap jam mixed together from 4 or 5 different fruits. We called it putty and it tasted like it. But it was at least sweet and it was the only sweet stuff we got for some years. And I still can see the paper buckets wherein it was delivered to the kitchen. The whole week was oriented towards the anticipation for the coming Sunday because on Sundays we got a slice of cake additionally to the bread.

One Sunday morning at the bathroom, I heard from Kurt, who was always a little more friendly, that this bully Dieter, who was sitting on the other side of my brother Michael, intended to take Michael's cake. Kurt went on to tell me, "Dieter says if you try to tell HER about it, that he will come over to your bed tonight and kill you." SHE was what we called the orphanage educator, who was more like a watchdog in a jail, complete with the appearance of what you might expect to see in your nightmares.

Dieter was the incarnation of evil in the body of a boy. He would not miss any opportunity to stir things up, or to find a reason to beat others, just for fun. With Kurt's warning in mind and my little brother's best interests at heart, my eyes narrowed as I carefully watched Dieter's every move. I slowly wrapped my hand around my fork. Dieter reached. I stabbed with all the force I could muster. Dieter squealed and a rather impressive display of red sprayed from his hand as the fork penetrated his hand.

I needed three days to be able to move my fingers and I couldn't sit or lay on my back for another couple of days and it might be that the pain I feel in one of the fingers on my right hand sometimes is related to the punishment I got for securing the cake for Michael. But at this time it did not matter much because I was in the *Darkroom* for five days. The room had no windows, no light at all, and was so small that it was impossible to lie down. You could only stay or sit in there. The longest punishment being arrested in that *Darkroom* was eight hours, so I had broken at least a record. Three times during the day a small slot in the door was opened and the food was pushed through. When I finally get out there, I needed several hours to be able to see on a normal level and a couple of days to fall asleep at night without startling every couple of minutes because the horror came back in my dreams night by night for a while.

One day, a couple of months after that incident, my mother appeared and we went to a photographer. While we had to mount a play truck made from wooden parts, several pictures were taken. And I remember that I had to dismount and mount it a couple of times, because I was always too fast for the photographer. Before he could take the picture, I was done with the job. I have still one of those pictures. I was able to convince my mother to take us out of that orphanage into another one where our sister Connie was. I do not know if she was all the time there or not. I'm not sure how long we were in that second orphanage, but it was by far the better one. At least we did not get bashed for trivia. Try to imagine that you kick a piece of wood around which is always laying in the way, that's how I feel when I remember on those years.

I have some pictures from that time and whenever I look at them I try to understand what really happened to me and why. I see pictures with my sister Cornelia and me at the second orphanage but my brother Michael is not in those pictures. I can't remember if he wasn't at that orphanage or if he was sick at the time when those pictures were made. And I remember that my mother visited us a couple of times. The last reminder from that time of life was a photo taken on a cold and rainy morning in a cemetery at a funeral.

Many years later I should learn that at this funeral was buried a little boy who was the result of a relationship of my mother with another man whom we never met because he did not wanted us to be there with her. That was probably the reason why we had to endure the odyssey through the orphanages. I don't know what the name of that little boy was nor the cause of his death. It was in that village where we would finally settle down for some years and become a family again, or at least something comparable to that.

It Was Not What It First Appeared to Be and Why Home Doesn't Always Means Home

We settled down in a small village in central East Germany named Reupzig. It took a while till we had everything to call it a decent home, but finally we were all together after years of uncertainty, horror and pain. I remember on ice-cold nights when Michael and I lay together under one cover because we had only one bed for us and there was no money for coal to heat the furnace. And I remember that at the very beginning of our life in *Reupzig* we had a funeral. Connie told me later that another child of our mother is buried there. She also told me that this was the result of a connection, maybe marriage who knows, with a man in Cottbus. And that he was the reason why we had to live in the orphanages for about three years.

For some reason, at first unknown to me, our family was not really well appreciated in that small village and even we children didn't need long to get approval for those sentiments. During the day we were in state-controlled child care, because our mother had to work to make ends meet. If I remember right, at this time she worked at the school to supervise the students in the afterschool club. Students had to stay at school to finish the homework and to be indoctrinated in an effortless way in socialism and the necessity of the dictatorship of the party of the working class. I remember one day we played outside in the sandbox when my sister suddenly cried out loud and when I turned towards her, her face was already covered with blood. One of the other girls hit her with the edge of her shovel over her head. The wound needed to be stitched several times and the girl who did it got some harsh words.

Another occurrence I remember was with the carousel. For some reason, I could not stand—and still can't today—a spin around in the carousel without vomiting. Once a week we had a special hour when the nursery teacher told us nice little stories about the heroes of the battle of the SED and the heroes of the great brother, the Soviet Union. Whenever the weather allowed doing so, we were outside, sitting all around at the carousel, and she telling her stories. One day when we were all sitting in that carousel, she got a call on the telephone and left us all alone. Two of the boys, knowing about my difficulties with the carousel, immediately started to turn it around. The boy on my left side, two years older and much stronger, kept me down on the seat and it didn't take long till I vomited. When the nursery teacher came back it was already over. I was in the grass trying to come around, the carousel at a standstill, and I got punished for leaving my place without allowance.

These are just two of those recurring events and it took me years to overcome my fear, fight back and more important to understand why we were a permanent target for the other children. First of all there was the general rejection of all of those people with German heritage who happened to live at that territory which now had become Poland and partly Russia. Since there wasn't enough usable living space, partly because many of the buildings were still laying in ruins, and because of the extreme increase of the density of the population, people perceived the incoming refugees as intruders. This was usually the main problem in urban environments. It was somewhat different in rural environments, where the whole atmosphere was more or less based on the fact that most of the families have lived there for centuries and knew each other. Now there were suddenly strangers around and whatever happened badly was surely caused by them.

In addition to that, most of the people in Reupzig did not have a bad time before the communists took power. They were farmers and blacksmiths and shoemakers and bakers. They were not rich, but also not poor, and they were free to do what they thought necessary. And they had not forgotten the horrible aftermath of the German capitulation and what happened then for three days when the American troops retreated and this part of Germany came under Russian control. The horror of rape, robbery, and murder was still burned in their minds. With that, the new political system wasn't really welcome since everybody knew it was based on the power of the Russian tanks.

And then there was that incredible gift my mother had to use the smallest amount of textiles to tailor dresses. Considering the still-existing bottleneck for nearly everything, what made life a little bit more shine than it was, women loved to have a new dress tailored after the latest models found in West Germany's fashion magazines. Even though textiles were also on the list of shortage in East Germany, especially modern textiles, many of the people had relatives in West Germany, and whenever possible they would send a package with things unavailable in East Germany or as it was mainly called for a long time the Zone or East Zone.

Since my mother loved to sing also and was pretty good at that, she founded a choir and invited other women to join her. They would use one of the large rooms at the second floor in that huge, manor house where the sire lived before the Russians came. Because of her talent with tailoring dresses, she asked every woman to bring a certain type of textile, and she would tailor all the dresses for them, charging just a small amount of money for it. And she was really efficient using the smallest possible amount of textile for a dress, and don't get me wrong, that was really something nobody else could compete with her. With that talent she was able to get her own dress made from the remnants of more than twenty other dresses she had made. This might have been some kind of theft, but nobody noticed it since she asked for much less textile anybody thought she would need.

Although there was another woman in Reupzig who was a professional dress tailor by trade, after the choir was completely dressed in perfectly tailored dresses, she was almost flooded with requests for tailoring a special dress for the women of the village. And my mother is also very talented in knitting. I have pictures where my siblings and I are completely dressed in knitwear made by my mother. Now as great as it appears at the first moment that she had all those great orders, there was another problem. My mother couldn't keep a promise. Never! And I believe she can't keep it today either. She was always late with finishing those dresses and there were incidents when people came one or two days before a celebration, even weddings, and retrieved their textiles and accessories to take them to that professional dressmaker in Reupzig whom would finish it in time, working day and night and charge an *arm* and a *leg* for it. This certainly did not increase the likeness for my mother, and we as the children would be confronted on the street or at school by the children of those who had believed her, because of the turmoil in their family.

Now since my mother had that unique talent she would get orders anyway, especially when the textiles were rare and expensive and when she did what was expected from her and she was able to do, it was always a great success. But as said before, once in a while she would just screw it and it would be the topic of the village conversation for some days. Since the children of those families knew about that, we were often the target of their mockery. Often we had to wear clothing which was given to my mother from other families in the village when their children were grown out of the size and it was still in good condition. Kids can be really brutal in their mockery and we had to endure this kind of treatment for all of the reasons above.

This was actually amplified by the fact that our gang of four, about which I will go to in much more detail later, was considered the enemy of a group of children from autochthonic families of the village. Several boys of that group were two to three years older than us and they outnumbered us by at least four to one when they were all together. It wasn't rare that Michael and I were victims of their attacks and got beaten up several times, especially when we were caught by ourselves. If we could not hide the bruises and scratches when we came home, my mother would drag us through the whole village to the homes of those who just had beaten us and we had to say that we were sorry for what happened. She never understood that we were the victims and the others were those who started the fighting. The next morning we would be again the aim of the mockery for that. With a few exceptions, there weren't many people in Reupzig who had a really positive appreciation for the nonnative and our family and we children would every now and then have to pay for it.

Supply with the food and other stuff even in the late 1950s was still difficult. I recall that I walked to the only small shop we had in Reupzig with the food ration card in my hand and we got only a certain amount of butter, eggs, and other stuff. Meat was nearly unavailable. The milk was carried in small cans with a handle made from aluminum and we got 1 liter per day, because of us children. One day when I had to get the milk from that store a multitude of people were standing outside the store and I recognized that they all waited to get in the store. So I lined up with all the others, mainly women doing their daily grocery shopping and listened to their conversation.

"Did you hear about the butter that arrived this morning," an elder woman who was the wife of one of the leaders at the agricultural collective type 3, asked one in front or her. When she turned around to answer, I recognized her as the mother of one of the kids I went to kindergarten with, Roland.

"What butter?" Roland's mother asked.

And another woman right in front of me, whom I did not know, said, "We can get butter without ration cards today. A so-called gift from the Soviets, the so-called class brothers to those of us under his thumb..."

I could clearly see how the anger about the politically incorrect statement of that woman in front of me was changing the color of the collective leader's wife's face to red. But before she could begin to give her a dressing down, the shop door was opened and the attention turned to the daily concerns.

I eventually got into the store room and could see it. A huge cube of butter approximately of an original size of 20 x 20 x 20 inches, now half of it almost gone, sat on top of the counter. I had never seen such a luxury, and at this time it was luxury for us. Even though we did not need to use the food ration cards we could not by any because it was just too expensive. But step by step life became easier and I remember that we, Michael and I, did find after a couple of months a first friend.

He lived in the same house on the first floor and his name was Wilfried. But nobody called him by his real name, not even not his parents, and when they did, we all knew immediately that there was danger in delay. He was known to everybody in the village as Stepper. I don't know how he got this name and actually I can't even remember having asked him. He was of sturdily build and much stronger but at the same age as I was. He liked to prowl around as we did and since neither his parents nor my mother really appreciate that, we sometimes got in trouble for it. But he was a friend whom we soon started to trust and who knew nearly every corner around the village because he was born there, yet his parents were from Pomerania. He was a real friend; we went through thick and thin, yet he never really laughed. I don't remember once hearing him laughing out loud. His highest expression of fun was a bright grin. That grin that we used to call from ear to ear. But laughing out loud? No, not Stepper. I can't say why, because I never asked him that either.

On weekdays the nursery school was over at 5:00 p.m., but my mother was often at school till 6:00 p.m., and we had some time to spend during the week. The best though was Saturday and Sunday afternoon. We just could do what boys liked to do at this time. We had no computer games, electronic gimmicks, and all that stuff that keeps kids out away from nature and inside the house. Stepper got a pocket knife on his sixth birthday and for several days he was the most appreciated boy in our village. Even our *enemies* came to have a look at the knife, to check its sharpness and to feel how it lay in one's hand. It did not last very long, just a few days, but it brought us another friend. And with that we created later the "Gang of Four."

Jürgen came from a family that lived in a settlement at the outskirts of the village which was where the former mower and day labor of the laird lived. He was the third or fourth eldest son, and I'm not sure on that because there were eleven children in his family. He was fast, with the same stature as me, and he laughed a lot. He was always good for plotting a joke and seldom thought about the consequences, which could be painful considering the strictness of his mother. His dad was a skinny, small man and worked at the only underground coal mine in East Germany. His mother, the total opposite of his father, large and heavy, had the total control over the family. When she raised her voice, Jürgen, even miles away from home would turn his head and say: "I have to go home now." And gone he was. We learned rather early in our friendship with Jürgen to accept her, because she did not make a difference between hers and others' children. If you misbehaved, you were in trouble.

Reupzig is a small village, actually a double settlement separated by a strip of woodland with approximately eight hundred people living there. It is first documented in 1160, and I have really great remembrance on the eight hundred-year jubilee. The village is clearly dominated by a large and whilom very impressive manor house, three-stories high with only two stories and a habitable attic. But because of the tremendous height of the ceilings it appeared as high as four stories. It had a large farmyard with an incredible number of stables which actually were horse stables original and were used by the Agricultural Production Cooperative as necessary. That estate included a large garden encircled by a twelve-feet-high brick wall. This garden was the place where the state-controlled childcare was placed.

Later that year we got a new dweller. His name was Helmut, and a couple of months later he and my mother got married. I can remember the ceremony at the church and that there was a party with a lot of people but that's it. Later I discovered that he had lived for many years with a woman at the settlement on the outskirts of Reupzig where one of our friends came from. Initially everything was fine. He was very talented, he worked hard, and we had a big surprise at Christmas that year. Since he was a man with many talents and very skilled in any kind of handyman work, people came to him to get things repaired and he was well-known for that, especially with everything that had a combustion engine.

At the time my mother and he got married, he was working for a company in the next largest town, Koethen. This company was specialized in digging wells and he made a good amount of money every month. He was a hard worker and worked as the foreman of his group. Usually they were on the road all week long and he came home only on a weekends. The company he worked for organized a company Christmas party for the children and the parents could deposit gifts which were handed over during that party. Every kid had to recite a poem. When I think back on this time, I think it was the only time in my whole childhood that I was happy and felt that I was a lucky child. But it didn't take long to change.

Later that year my stepbrother Andreas was born. It was the same year I started school. That was great, because I loved to learn reading, writing, and mathematics. Since the school was in our village, I marched every morning along a small path between the backyard gardens of the village to the school. The school was an old-brick building in that style from the early 20th century, a typical neo-gothic building of its time. We had one classroom with the first and the second grade and one teacher for both classes. I still earn disbelieving looks when I mention that today, because nobody considers it true that at the end of the 1950s in Germany such kind of schools still existed. But it's true. I went through both classes in that building and when I reached the third grade we had to go to the neighboring village which was larger and had several buildings used as provisory school buildings. It wasn't until I was in fifth grade that the new school building was finished and all classes spread out over the whole village moved into one building. But at the time I started school, two classrooms was still the way in our village.

I think it was the time when I was in second grade when my mother had one of her outbreaks—as I'll call it for this book. She got a prescription to have a treatment at a health resort. Since Helmut was working out of town all week, he couldn't take care of us kids and so we were split to others. I can't remember where my sister and my brother were at this time, but I remember very well where I was. Our pastor and his wife took care of me for those four weeks my mother was at the resort because they didn't have their own children. Actually it was a good thing. I had my own bed, in my own bedroom. I eat meals regularly, three times a day, and they were very thoughtful, actually too thoughtful. I had not one minute without being under control. I tried whatever I could to escape, at least for some hours, the overprotective care of the pastor's wife. And then there was this breakfast. Not that I did not like it, but I had to eat an oatmeal- gruel soup every morning before I could leave the house.

Terrible! Although it's very healthy, I hated it. And later in my life I thought more often than not back at the time when I had enough food to eat every single day.

However, the treatment of my mother at the health resort ended in a family drama. At that time, I did not understand what was going on. All I registered was that the situation in our family changed within few days after my mother was back. Helmut began to drink. And I mean drink, and when he was drunk, he terrorized the family. This went on for the next ten years with some breaks. Let's say periods of war and terror alternated with periods of peace and kind of a family life. With the beginning of the third grade I had to travel to the neighboring village which was a little more than three kilometers, roughly two miles. We had to use the public traffic and the bus left at 7:30 a.m. We had to walk about ten minutes from the bus stop at the school village to the school building, and most of the time we had to hurry to be in class and ready at 8:00 a.m.

The teacher, his name was Herr Krug, was very strict but fair. And we had a nickname for him. Whenever we know he wasn't close enough to hear us, we called him Spassi. I don't know where that name came from and I think he already had that nickname when we became his class. He was not from our villages. He actually came from the district city and he came on his bicycle. He had to ride almost 12 kilometers, approximately 7.5 miles, on his bicycle every day. Later I learned that he was punished for being a teacher during the National-Socialistic dictatorship and was not willing to join the communist party. He never laughed, and when I think back I believe he was filled with bitterness. But he had an authority and nobody really tried to play a joke on him.

When he wrote on the blackboard and somebody dared to chat, he would suddenly turn around and throw the piece of chalk in his hand at that student. Now, that is normally not so bad, except when Spassi threw it. He had a nearly 100 percent rate of hitting you on your head. And depending on where it hit, it hurt. One of the boys of my village, his name was Roland, and he had a slight stutter. He was smaller than me and his father was known for his strict upbringing.

One day during the break, somebody started to throw the sponge through the room after cleaning the blackboard for the next hour. Immediately the sponge flew back and forth through the room until Roland got it. He thought that this dry sponge was no fun at all and soaked it, squeezed it a bit so that the water would not drip in his hand, and threw the sponge right through the window, missing the student he had targeted. Unfortunately the window was closed, and that wet sponge was heavy enough to break the glass. At that noise of breaking glass, Spassi entered the class room and everybody was scared stiff. Now, Roland was not one of the brightest in our class, but he was always honest. When he was up to something, he would stand for it and accept the consequences. Being who he was, he immediately confessed that he threw the sponge through the window. Spassi did not say a word. He grabbed Roland by his clothes and hung him on a hook right beside the blackboard, using the suspenders which held up his pants

Then he gave us a lecture about our unacceptable behavior and the problem to get glass for a new window and how much he was disappointed about not being able to leave the room for just a few minutes. And all that while Roland was hanging on that hook beside the blackboard like a doll, being as quiet as a mouse. When Spassi was done, he took Roland from the hook and carried him to the corner in front of the classroom where Roland had to stay during the rest of the time facing the wall.

During all the time we had to wait for the bus to get back to our village, Roland was unusually silent and did not play around with the other kids. He was afraid getting home because he had a text in his notebook. And even though Spassi was strict, it was nothing to compared to Roland's father. So he knew what he had to expect.

The next year my stepsister Susanne was born. Weeks later Helmut had an accident. Somehow he was hit by a part of machinery on his head and severely injured. It took months for him to recover and when he was able to work again, he started to drive an earthmover at the second largest construction area in East Germany. This was called *Halle Neustadt*, German for Newtown. In a giant project, a new town was build designed with the modern style of buildings which would later be used as a snidely name for whole subdivisions *die Platte* German for the plate. It referred to the technology to have the complete wall of a room finished offside in a manufacturing process. A reimbursement structure of steel bars was laid out in a form, together with the windows or doors or whatever had to be in that wall and then it was filled with liquid concrete. Using several vibration tools insured that the concrete was free of air pockets and when it was hardened, the complete wall was transported to the construction site. A crane lifted the wall into place and the construction workers welded the steel bars together, inserted plastic sheets for insulation purpose into place and filled the gaps between the different plates with concrete. Within a couple of weeks they build complete houses as tall as twelve floors and in some cases twenty floors. Many years later when we had the honor to live in such a six-story building, we had a decent experience with those. Anyhow, Helmut started to work there as the driver of an earthmover and he made good money. And for a while everything appeared fine.

Then my mother got another prescription for a treatment in a health resort, I don't know what the real reason was at that time, but the cycle started again. The pastor couple wasn't there anymore—they had left the country and fled to West Germany just hours before the communists closed the last door into freedom by building the wall in Berlin—so I couldn't stay with them. This time my brother Michael and I were sent to the district town Köthen to a couple who had no children. It was a *night-mare*. The whole apartment was a mess and the woman had nightmares. Very often I would lay awake at night and listen when she made noises in her dreams because I couldn't sleep.

The school was in a very old building loaded with history in the center of the castle, and under different circumstances it would have been a dream to have school there. One of the world's most famous composers and music masters Johann Sebastian Bach lived, composed, and played music from 1717 till 1723 in the very rooms where I had school during the second half of my fourth grade. But I was permanently tired and hungry, because of those nightmares and very often there was just nothing to eat. And we seldom had all the material we needed to follow the teaching.

I do not remember what the reason was that we had to stay for nearly six months, but I believe it was to end the school year before changing school again. As all nightmares, this too ended somehow and when the summer vacation came we were back at the small village and *home*. That year we moved into the former manor house, that large three-story house where the squire lived before the communists gained power. Now it was used as the state-controlled childcare.

In the first floor was also the administration of the LPG. We moved into the rooms on the third floor where the former servants lived when the original owners were still there. In the second floor was a large ballroom, and I mean really large, and some other rooms. One of those was used as the public library, which played a huge roll in my life for many years. My mother had taken the responsibility for the library and as so many times in our life, when she took responsibility to do something, we kids ended up with doing actually the work connected to that responsibility while she would collect the revenue to extend the constant shortage on money.

So very often I found myself sitting in the library and managing the lending of books to the people of the village. And I enjoyed it. It was that place where I could escape the cheerless world we lived in. Especially in fall and winter, whenever I came home from school and was able to escape I'd sit there and read. I can confirm from personal experience that the expression "Reading is Cinema in your Head" is true. For hours I was in a different world. In my book world I rode on the back of the camels with the explorer through the Arabian desert and felt like part of their expedition. I experienced the limitless wideness of the Sahara desert and I suffered with them when something went wrong. I was scouting through the immense forests of the American East and saw myself riding on half wild horses through the Wild West prairies. I pitched my gold claim on the Yukon River and was digging for gold nuggets on the icy river banks. I shed endless tears reading about the up and downs in the life of Jack London's *White Fang*.

These hours in between handing out books and sorting the shelves, these hours without being confronted with the darkness of a family life where love was a nonexistent word, these hours composed the childhood I love to remember. I read Leo Tolstoy's *War and Peace*, *The Leather Stocking Tale* of James Fennimore, and uncountable books about expeditions and the exploration of the African and American continents. Many of those books were remnants of the belongings of the baron who once owned that property. Although the communists had cleaned out the inventory before they left it for the public library, there were several books, especially about United States of America, they would not have tolerated at the time when I read them.

Anyhow, we moved into those rooms in the third floor and it was just more space for the larger number of family members. No comfort at all. We had to carry every drop of water from the pump in front of that building upstairs to the third floor, and every drop of waste water downstairs to the slurry area of the horse barns. Even though the rooms were large, we had only three rooms and a kitchen. There was one large living room, one room for the children and one for the parents. We lived there for about three years.

In fall, we had a one-week school break, and as far as I remember it was a traditional school break and based on the time when Germany was still mainly an agricultural society, to allow children to help their parents with the harvest. And with that we did have school break, but it wasn't really free time. Living in a village actually meant from a certain age on, school break wasn't free time at all.

Our village had different types of agricultural cooperative in the early 1960s. One was type 1 and the others was type 3. Type 1 meant the farmers still owned their livestock, but operate their farmland together. Type 3 meant everything was brought into the cooperative and was managed like a manufacturing plant, but under the rules of socialism. Type 3 was usually the association of the so-called *Young Farmer*, those who had no land before the communists took over either because they came from the now Polish occupied territories, or because they were peasants. They had been given land in the course of the socialistic land reform and most of them had no clue how to manage a farm. On the other hand, since so many people needed to be satisfied with the land reform, the land they got wasn't really enough to feed a family.

With this background all of these people really enjoyed the idea of throwing everything together and having somebody with experience take over responsibility. Having the security to get paid a monthly salary, and at the end of the year a kind of a profit share if the cooperation made a profit, was the absolute solution for them. Type 1, though, was a complete different story. As already described some chapters before, traditional farmers with the declaration of enemy of the state usually couldn't withstand the enormous pressure and joint the collective but chose as long as it was an option the type 1 cooperative form. All of the children would by nature work with their parents or relatives during harvest season. That meant usually at a certain age there wasn't much having fun at fall or summer school break. It usually began with working at the fields or wherever a helping hand as small as those of us kids was needed.

Late in summer it was time to harvest the hops. Since 1956 Reupzig was an area where hops were grown and the type 3 agricultural cooperative had enough cultivable acreage to grow several hectares of hops. Hops were grown using a huge structure of beams leaning towards each other at a certain angle and mounted together at a high of approximately eighteen to twenty feet. Long steel wires connected them on the top, reaching across the field, and were secured to the ground by huge stretching screws. Thinner, so-called up-guide wires were strained from the top connection wires to the soil and anchored there. The hops rank were trained around the up-guide wires and climbed up during the year, producing wonderful smelling hop cones. Late in summer almost to the end of the summer school break we were encouraged to make ourselves useful and help with the hope cone harvest.

The harvest usually began early in the morning and it was already chilly at that time. The men would walk along the rows of hop twines and cut the guide wires with a cutter on a long rot. The women and we children would then collect the hop cones into huge baskets which were carried away by the men when they were filled. We actually liked this kind of work. It was light work, you could sit on a small stool and it smelled awesome. During the first years of the hops era in Reupzig, we had always enough work to earn some additional money for the always-dwindling family budget. Some years later the type 3 agricultural cooperative became the only cooperative in our village. One reason was that the older farmers finally retired and their children did not enjoy their parents' hard work and used the opportunity to join the type 3 cooperative. Another reason was that some of the farmers just gave up, recognizing that the big disadvantage they had compared to the type 3 system was only punishment and why should they endure punishment for honest work when there seemed to be no rescue in reach? That was the time when the success of the type 3 cooperative became better and better because of the impact of the knowledge those farmers brought into the organization. The cooperative began to grow more hops and started to grow more onions, peas and carrots contrast to the other cooperatives around us. With this success they were able to build a huge building and a machine that would harvest the hop cones from the twines direct. There were not many hands needed anymore to operate the machines and we children actually missed that.

School breaks were times to work and earn some money, but there was still enough time to play as kids like to do, although we played differently then children do today. We climbed on trees shot at each other with bows and arrows we had built from hazelnut tree branches and common reeds, built our own hideouts in the bushes on the edge of the fields. Getting the best reeds for the arrows was always a challenge. Since there were not many places to find them in our area, we had brave the ponds on whose edges the best reeds grew. They often did not freeze over completely and had only a thin layer of ice on top. And as it is often in life to get the best you have to risk something more when it is worth the risk to you. And then there was the rivalry with the "enemy gang." They too would like to get the best reed to build decent and effective arrows. Those reed spires would be hidden in dry places and sorted during winter time and they had to become real dry and with that hard enough. They had also to be turned around from time to time in their hiding place to avoid bending.

When spring finally arrived we would begin to look for the best hazelnut branches in places we thought only we knew about. Those branches needed to be at the right length and thickness because they had to fit the person who would shoot them later. They could not have any knobs or knurls and needed to be as straight as possible.

With all the requirements it wasn't always easy to find the right one. But most of the time when the battles with the enemy began, we all had our bows and a large amount of arrows. Normally we would openly march to one of our not-so-secret hideouts which were at the edge of a large Greenland where cattle would graze; just across from the edge were the backyard of the family property of one of the members of the enemy gang ended. It was approximately eighty yards across the grassland between those edges. When they saw us walking towards that hideout, they would sometimes attack us immediately and we would take stand and shoot arrows at them. The arrows were topped with a cap cut from a piece of elder branches which had a soft core and allowed to push the arrow into that branch as far as necessary.

Over a couple of years these caps would become more and more sharpened until one day one of the enemies' arrows ended up sticking at the side of Stepper's head and would not fall down. He began to scream and shooting stopped. When I looked at him I could clearly see the nail at the top of that arrow cap sticking under the skin on the side of his head. I ran over to him, broke the arrow off and calmed him down, assuring him that he would not die, at least not immediately. Since the shooting had stopped, the enemy came carefully closer to find out what happened. The guy who had shot the arrow with the nail immediately said that he did not want that to happen but all his friends were scared and were all over him, how stupid that idea was and how dangerous.

Nothing against a fight and a brawl, but this could have cost an eye and what did he think his parents would say about that? We did not dare to remove that nail and with that we walked back into the village towards the nurse station where once a week the doctor would look after the sick, but the district nurse lived there and was there always to help with the small and sometimes not-so-small injuries of the village people.

When she saw the nail in the head of Stepper she was immediately on him, cleansing the surrounding area with iodine tincture, which created another scream from Stepper at a level that my ears started to ring, and then she grabbed some kind of pliers and began to carefully pull on that nail. Stepper's screaming became even louder. She must finally have had enough of all that screaming and ripped the nail out with one hefty pull. And it was over. Stepper stopped screaming at the same second the nail was out. I don't know if it was because he was surprised that he was still alive or because of the bravery of the nurse.

The next act was to check his medical records to see when he had gotten his last immunization against all those bad bacteria and when she was satisfied with that, we got to hear a dressing-down we thought we would never hear from her. She was always so nice. But this was too much for her. We begged her not to tell our parents about the incident, and after we had promised her never again to shoot arrows at each other, she said she would think about to keep it to herself. That was all we could negotiate. And she kept her word. She did not tell any of our parents about that and we had no reason to do it ourselves. Now, this fact wasn't known to our enemies and they lived in fear for several days. Finally we had a meeting right in the middle of the battlefield and we negotiated a kind of a ceasefire.

It would not take long until one of the guys broke it by starting a brawl with one of us, usually me or Michael when we were by ourselves and had no support from Stepper or Jürgen. I was an almost permanent the target of a kind of ambidextrous antagonism by other children in our village and at school and so was Michael. This was going on for several years and we did not really have a chance to stand up against these guys. One reason was that I did not really liked to come to blows since I'd got beaten often enough for almost nothing by my parents, mostly my mother, and another reason was that I was just not strong enough. But one day would change anything dramatically.

In fall that was the potato harvest. Almost 95 percent of all of the enemies of our gang of four were working on the fields of the type 3 cooperative. We were free to choose, and with great joy we opted for the type

1 cooperative. That had several reasons but the main reason was money. Although we got only ten pfennig per basket collected of potatoes, the potatoes grown on the fields of the type 1 farmer were larger and were laying in soft, sandy, and well-cultivated soil. The machine which brought them out of the ground was a small harvester pulled by two horses. It had two blades mounted on both sides of the machine pointing slightly downwards and almost—but just not—meeting at the center of the machine. It would shovel the potatoes with the loose soil onto a belt right behind the blades which was build from a number of steel bares covered with rubber and held together with a chain. That chain was driven by a sprocket connected to the wheels of the machine, so it would move whenever the machine moved and transport the potatoes to the back end of the machine. Since the belt was also running over several oval drums and by that jumping up and down, the soil would fall through the openings between the steel bars and only the potatoes would reach the end of the machine where they would fall down in a nice wide row.

And it was a joy just to pick them and fill the basket, at least a joy for the first couple of hours. Because even though it was relatively easy to collect the potatoes, the constant necessity to stoop and go up and stoop and go up was virtually back-breaking. But we got good money and were able to fill at least ten to twelve baskets in an hour and with that we would make at least ten marks, sometimes even twelve marks in a day. You wouldn't get the money in your hand when you delivered the basket at the horse cart where the potatoes were collected and then transported to the storage. The woman who handled that business would hand you a coin, embossed with a sign and the number 10. At the end of the day you would then go and change the coins into real (I mean East German money which wasn't jokingly considered real money, it was called toy money) money which we could take home.

At home my mother was already waiting for us to deliver the wage of the day because there was always a lot of month at the end of her money. She would wait with an order to go to the bakery to buy bread or to run to the *Konsum* (German for shop) to buy something for dinner. Since nobody really knew how much money we earned a day, Michael and I would try to keep some of the money we made. Even though it wasn't often much, sometimes just thirty or forty *pfennig*, we had to be very careful when we hid it. If my mother would have found it, we would be in trouble. Most of the time we were successful, and at the end of the week school break, I did have three to four marks saved. And I kept it a secret because I had a dream one day I'd own a camera.

Now for the children with parents who were members of the type 3 agricultural cooperative that was a different story and probably part of the deep enmity between us and them. Since the type 3 had many more members the fields they had laid together were much larger, sometimes 6-8 times the size of the type 1 fields. That was the reason why they could use modern machines for the harvest and to be able to use bigger more modern machines was the reason to put their fields together in the first place. On the other hand even for those fields of the type 1 cooperative which were large enough to use those machines they seldom had the pleasure to get those machines from the general rental station. This was mainly because the type 3 cooperative had the primacy, then they left the machines often on their fields even when the harvest was done and often enough the machines were defective when the type 1 people finally asked to rent them. Over a couple of years it was just the normal way of life that type 1 cooperatives—as long as they could exist—didn't even bother to ask for those machines. And that had additional and very specific reasons.

After some years of using these huge and often very heavy machines, often called combines, the ground was heavily compressed. This wasn't really good, especially for potatoes and onions. And the compressed ground did not take the rain in as evenly and fast as the friable soil. And then there were the stones. It seemed as if there was an endless well of small to midsized stones on every single square foot of those fields and it soon became a special assignment for students and teachers throughout East Germany, especially late fall/early winter to walk the endless fields of the type 3 cooperatives and collect stones.

Now our classmates with their parents, members of type 3 cooperative, had to work on their fields during potato harvest school breaks. And although they got twenty *pfennig* and sometimes even thirty *pfennig* per basket potatoes collected, they were in a much worse position than we. Because those cooperatives were the favored customers of the MTS

FREEDOM'S NIGHTMARE

Maschinen und Tracktoren Ausleihstationen (German of machines and tractors rental station) they mad heavy use of them. And later they would have those stations just integrated into the cooperatives and with that the type 3 just owned these machines.

Such a potato-harvester combine would be pulled by a huge tractor, powerful enough to pull the machine with its large blades through the hardened, compressed ground. Those blades would cut about ten inches deep into the soil and lift the soil and the potatoes onto the steel bar belt, which would transport all of it up to another steel bar belt about five to six feet above ground. This belt was followed by two other belts vibrating with different frequencies to allow the earth to fall off the potatoes and finally a transfer belt where on both sides up to four women would stand to sort out stones and earth which had not fallen off yet. They would also take out damaged potatoes.

At the end of that belt was another belt rectangular to it, and that belt transferred the potatoes onto a trailer, pulled by another tractor along the machine. Since this tractor just pulled away when the tailor was filled, and another one would come alongside, the machine could be pulled through the field without stopping. Could! If there wouldn't be some disadvantages of the modern technology, the permanent lack of spare parts which lead to halfhearted repairs, the negligent attitude towards the *stuff nobody really owned*, and the impact the usage of those heavy machines had on the soil. Several times per hour the driver had to stop the tractor and remove heavy chunks of earth—hard as stones—from the blade at the beginning of the steel bar belt because it wouldn't break up. Despite all the well-engineered technology, many potatoes did not free themselves from the hardened earth sticking to them. That was the reason why the children were called in to walk behind the potato harvester-combine and collect the potatoes falling off the combine-harvester. This was often very cumbersome because the earth did not dry up quickly after the typical fall shower because of the compression and there would be sometimes really large puddles. The children could never collect as many baskets as we did, and even with the double or triple amount of payment they did not make nearly the money we did. And they had to carry their baskets often over a long distance with sometimes a decent weight of potatoes already in them until they could empty them to collect their coins.

One year during the potato harvest season, I think I was in sixth grade, an accident happened which would be talked about for a long time in our village. It was a very nice late fall day. After the morning fog had lifted and the sun came through it was warm and sunny and the earth was warmed up, we had fun collecting potatoes. All morning long we had the screaming noise of aircraft engines accelerating right above us into an enormous climb flight. Since the airfield used by the East German Air Force was only a few miles away, and the flight corridor and training area was right above our heads, the aircrafts would do all kind of acrobatics and were often not really high into the air when they turned into climb flight exercise, because we could still see the aircraft's contour when it turned towards the sky.

We had just begun to collect potatoes again after finishing the lunch break, when one of those aircrafts turned into a climb flight. Everybody stopped speaking expecting that typical screaming, screeching noise of the engine. The screeching, screaming noise began as always and then suddenly there was quietness. Total *silence*. The aircraft's engine failed. Everybody looked into the sky where just a second ago the aircraft had attacked earth's gravity and there it was—in a swaying fall towards earth first but immediately caught by the pilot and brought into a gliding descent. Our gang of four watched it, shielding our eyes with our hands against the bright shining afternoon sun for a few seconds, and as soon as we could determine the direction and the probable area of impact, we started to run.

Although many of the adults began to call us to stay there, there wasn't anything short of chains that could us hold to the potato field. Running cross country wasn't easy and we stumbled several time and our eyes moved constantly between the way we ran and the falling aircraft until we lost visual of it. But at this time we had a pretty good idea where it would make its impact. Since it was several kilometers from the field to that place of impact, it took us about two hours.

At approximately half of the distance we were just entering an already harvested onion field and I watched my steps. I suddenly saw something blink on the ground. I reached down and what I grabbed was a piece of plastic. It was a very strange piece of plastic. It was approximately 3 inches long and 11/2 inch wide and about an inch thick and it had a form that reminded me slightly of a fish. Since we were in a hurry I did not wander long about it and accelerated to catch up with the others, who were already a distance away.

When we finally reached the area where the aircraft came down, there was already a line of soldiers blocking the way closer to the point of impact. The point of impact was direct in a mud hole of which we had many around our village. As far as I understood, it was said those were bomb craters from the Second World War when the allies attacked the strategic railway knot point at the district city Köthen. When they got hit by the air defense guns they tried to unload the bombs to get out and back home. Those bomb craters would later fill with water and trees would grow around them and some of those places were beloved playgrounds for us.

We began to move around the cordon which hermetically secured the bomb crater to get some more information about the whole story. After putting all the parts and snippets of information together each of us had collected we understood that the aircraft in fact hit the bomb crater and was buried so deep because of the impact that the military needed heavy equipment to get it out. Till that time they had no indication whether or not the aircraft was still in one piece. We also learned that the pilot had given his life by staying in the aircraft and steering it away from the settlement right beside that bomb crater. And actually the building next to the bomb crater was the Kindergarten where about ten to twelve children were holding their lunchtime nap. He disobeyed the order of the commanding officers to eject because he knew that his aircraft would hit at least that one house next to the crater if not scratching through the whole settlement.

Within a few minutes this story about the pilot made the round among all of the spectators and everybody was moved by the heroism of the pilot. Finally it became late and we had to get home. Knowing that we would have to expect some trouble, we did not talk much besides repeating our adventure over and over again, examining it from all possible angles. Although I still had that piece of plastic in my pocket, I did not mention it and was continuously thinking about what that could be. Finally when we arrived home it wasn't too bad, because the news about the crash of the fighter aircraft was already known and the East German TV news had already briefly reported on it.

Since it was just around the corner from our village, people were standing in front of their homes talking about it. When we said that we had been at the place of the impact, we were questioned by the adults about what we had seen and what we had heard and all the obligatory punishment for running away from the potato field and coming home late, without the days payment on top of it, wasn't really an issue anymore. We were finally dismissed with the order to wash and go to bed. I put the strange piece of plastic under my pillow and thought I'd use the next time at the library to see if I could find out what such thing a was used for on an aircraft.

Next day when we came to the potato field everybody was talking about the crash and that the pilot did not used the ejection seat to get out of the aircraft but stayed in and saved the lives of those children. This would go on for days but I did not participate. Something was wrong in that whole picture. When the day was done, I finally could not hold it anymore and talked to my friends about the piece I found on that field about a mile away from the crash point. After everybody had thoroughly investigated it we were silent for a couple of minutes, and that was something. Finally Stepper came up with the question, what if there are still more of those pieces laying around, waiting to be discovered? We looked at each other and without a word all jumped up and we were on our way to that place at the edge of the onion field where I found my piece the afternoon before.

When we arrived at the scene, the field looked different, very different. And I believe that if it would have been not that way, my friends would probably have called me a liar. We were so astound that we looked at each other and began to laugh and could barely stop. The whole area with the size of approximately one hundred by one hundred yards was cleaned up. And I mean cleaned. Not even the smallest piece of vegetation was on the ground. The day before it had looked like a harvested onion field. This same area where I found that strange looking piece of plastic just a little over twenty-four hours ago now looked like anything but a harvested onion field. It was *besenrein* (standing expression in German for clean-swept). It looked like it had been brushed with a huge broom.

FREEDOM'S NIGHTMARE

The disappointment of my friends was considerable and we decided to walk to the settlement where the airplane impact happened to see if we could find out more. When we arrived, the area was still under control of the military but at a smaller size. Just the bomb crater was guarded by a cordon of soldiers. Several adults were walking around and tried to get a glimpse at what was going on at this mud hole, but it wasn't much to see. We heard that they had already discovered huge parts of the crashed aircraft, but were still looking for other parts missing.

And we heard something that planted a thought in my mind which would not get quiet and would bother me to find an answer. Some of the bystanders swore that they had seen the lift of the cockpit part of the aircraft out of the mud hole. The cockpit with a part of the fuselage was dangling on the straps when the crane lifted it up into the air to turn around and place it on a large flat-bed trailer. At that specific moment they were able to see right into the cockpit which was filled with mud and no pilot was in there. That would destroy the whole propaganda of the heroic pilot who sacrificed his life to save the children of that small settlement. But all that was spoken off the record and as soon as someone from the large number of officials came closer (or even someone nobody had seen before), everybody fell silent or began to talk about the weather. On Saturday afternoon the potato harvest for us children was over and we had off.

Usually we would try to play somewhere but I had to go and serve at the library. It was welcome to me, because now I had the opportunity to research about that plastic. I had to exchange some books for readers first, but when that was done I began to go through books on aircrafts. Most of them were not very detailed but the popular scientific books on that theme had enough information about what I was looking for. That piece of plastic I found out was with a high probability a part of the cockpit turret. It was made from a specific kind of plastic which could be formed under heat into any shape and was then specifically treaded to reach the specific characteristics needed for this application. When a pilot needed to leave the aircraft in midair he could not just jump out because those aircrafts were much to fast. Pilots of this kind of aircrafts are actually sitting on a rocket system built right under their seat. In case of a failure on the aircraft which doesn't allow the pilot to land safely he was to pull the ejection handle and eject himself out of the aircraft.

Since the cockpit turret was hermetically sealed and could not just be opened by hand by the pilot, it needed to be removed first. A small ring of explosives would blow the cockpit turret away and then the rockets under the pilot seat would start and blow the pilot together with the seat out of the aircraft. There were still many questions unanswered, but I was sure now that the pilot had ejected himself out of the cockpit before the aircraft hit the ground, and I was holding a piece of evidence for that fact in my hand. Combining that with the rumors about an empty cockpit and the clean-swept area where I found that piece created doubt in the story about the heroic pilot which was in the mean time the front page story all over East Germany.

And yet there were still many questions. Why did we not see the pilot coming down with the parachute? Why did we not see the pilot's ejection from the aircraft when we looked up to the sudden silence at the sky? Was it possible that this small boom I believed I had heard minutes after the engine of the aircraft fell silent wasn't a part of the engine failure but the ejection seat rocket's ignition? But what could I do? Nothing! The general opinion of the people around me was exactly what the newspaper wrote, and even though I had a kind of evidence in my hand, nobody would believe. Yet I tried.

There was this one man who was the driver of one of the horse carts we were using getting to the fields. He owned a small house with just a few cattle and swine and had brought a small farm into the agricultural cooperation type 1. A few days after the incident when I was walking home from a soccer game we had played on the other side of the village, he caught up with me with his horse cart and asked if I'd like to hop on. I joint him because he did allow me once in a while to take the reins and I really liked to have control over the horses, although he did not allow making them trot.

After a few minutes I directly asked him, "What do you think about the aircraft crash."

He did not answer immediately and after a short deep breath he said, "Well, they say it was an accident and that the pilot is a hero because he could have ejected himself out of the aircraft before it crashed. But then, so they say, many children would be dead now instead of one pilot." And after a while he said, "That's what they say...if it's the truth."

I couldn't hold myself and answered, "I doubt it."

He looked at me frowning and then asked, "Why is that?"

I grabbed in my pocket and showed him that piece of the cockpit turret plastic which I carried with me ever since I found it. I told him how and when I found it and what I had figured out reading the books at the library.

He looked back at me and his gaze was now filled with concern and I believe I saw some kind of fear.

He said, "Boy you better get rid of that piece of plastic and forget about all of it. And you better forget what we talked about and don't tell anybody a word, because we may both disappear when the wrong people get wind of this!"

I did not understand why it should be dangerous to try to find out the truth about that aircraft crash. If I was wrong and all I thought was just childish fantasy, fine, but then I'd know for sure and the boring questions would be answered. But what if I was right? All those articles, statements in newspapers and news were just lies, fake? Slowly it dawned in my mind that he might be right and this was just too much for me. I did not understand really what he tried to tell me because I was just ten or eleven years old when that happened. I kept the cockpit turret piece of plastic for several years as a kind of a treasure, but lost it later when we moved to the island.

During some research for this book I thought suddenly I should try to find some confirmation for that aircraft crash at that time. What I found was actually really surprising to me. The aircraft was a MiG-21 PF serial number 76-0511 and the pilot was First Lieutenant Wolfgang Bohla. He was training for a parade when the engine failed with a known failure but unknown reason. And yes, he did catapult himself out of the plane. The reason I did not and probably nobody else saw it was because he used the ejection system at the last possible second. The aircraft was exactly five hundred meters over ground when he ignited the ejection system. And I believe he was a hero for waiting to the last second and getting the plane clear of that settlement.

Considering everything else around the permanent unreliable aircrafts, I learned that between 1956 and 1986 a total of three thousand Russian aircrafts of the MIG Type crashed. And a few months later this same pilot at the approach of the runway had the same failure with the same type of aircraft. But instead doing what he did when his other airplane crashed, handling the sudden blockade of a bearing at the turbine the instruction said to reduce the push, he kept the engine in full speed and landed the aircraft at an extremely high speed but safely. That allowed the engineers of the design team *Mikrojan* to find the reason for the failure and solve the problem. I have no idea why the propaganda system of East Germany did not come out with the truth at the time, but since everything with the military and especially with the aircrafts was secret, it probably did not fit their efforts. On the other hand, after trumpeting the heroism of the pilot in a hasty news blast, they could just not have the truth come out. And actually I did forget completely about this incident until years now, writing this book.

Many of the farm tracks in our area were lined with fruit trees. Although there was this one main road with the cherry trees, the farm tracks were mainly lined with plum trees. During the time when every farmer had his own fields, those trees were a welcome add-on to his reservoir of conserves for the winter. The plums would be pitted and filled into glass jars; water would be filled in and then cooked for a while with the lid and a rubber ring held down by a steel clamp. When they were cooled down, the surrounding atmospheric pressure would keep the lid closed and the fruit would stay good for a long time. We did that with several different fruits so that we had stuff in winter, because you couldn't buy it at the store. By the way, you couldn't buy any fruits even in their time either at the store.

Now, with the creation of the agricultural cooperatives, those trees suddenly had no direct owners anymore. And even though everybody knew each other, at harvest time there seemed to fall a cloud of *envy-and-me-first virus* over the village. People suddenly became greedy to get the best tree at the farm tracks which belonged to their cooperative. After a couple of years with a lot of arguments and often ending with families who were friends within living memory becoming enemies, one year the village council decided to number the trees and sell the right to harvest to the folks. The price was low; I think I remember it was just two to three marks per tree and when you paid the fee you could grab the number out of a basket in form of a paper roll secured with a small ring. With that everybody had the right to buy the right to harvest as many trees as he was willing to pay for, and with a little luck you could catch a real plentiful fructiferous tree.

My mother was going to get her trees on the first day possible, because she thought with that she would have the largest number of lots and with that best chances to get the best trees. Now, sometimes it was, sometimes it wasn't true. But, anyway, we got three trees the first year, and as always, when my mother took on a job or work, in addition to her normal job—I believe at this time she worked as a nursery nurse—we children ended up doing the work. So it was with the plum harvest.

This was usually later in fall and we had to do it after school since the fall school break was already over and used up by the potato harvest. After school we would get our homework done, take some baskets, and go out of the village to the farm track where our tees would stand. We did not have a ladder so we had to climb into the tree and balance on the thicker branches to get to the plums. As it is with nature, the most beautiful and ripe plums were on the far end of the thinnest branches the tree had. Balancing on those branches which were able to hold my weight, I tried to get those, and sometimes it worked out and sometimes not. And sometimes those small branches just broke. That was a problem, but there wasn't much you could do when a branch was broken off the tree.

Another problem was that those plums from the outside of the tree tasted just too good to be thrown into the basket. And when you had eaten one, there wasn't much strength left to resist the temptation to eat the next beautiful and sweet-looking plum and then the next and the next.... At the end of the day, the basket wasn't full and the plums in it weren't really the ripest and best. So Michael and I decided to enter the third tree to make up for our mishap. Since we had already eaten more plums then we could really bear, we didn't eat much. But it became really late that day and the sundown was almost over when Connie came to the plum trees on her bicycle to look after us. She tried to help us to get at least one of the baskets filled, but it was already really dark and we couldn't see the plums clear enough anymore. Then my mother arrived at the farm track with her bicycle. She wasn't really happy and told us to come home now. Because of the late hour she did not wanted me and Michael to walk all the way home, so she took me on the carrier on her bicycle and Connie took Michael on hers.

It was fall, but many days we still had great weather and the sun was shining warm and bright during the day. Shoes were a rare thing when I was a child because they were expensive. Whenever possible we wouldn't wear shoes, especially not to climb into a plum tree with the harsh bark and resin bleeding out of the tree where the branches had been trimmed in spring. So we were barefooted. That late in the evening, after climbing through the tree all those hours, I couldn't feel my feet anymore. They were so cold that I had lost all the feeling.

And then it happened. My right foot got caught between the spokes of the wheel and with a scream I jumped of the bicycle. Since it was too dark to see anything, I climbed back onto the carrier, bit my tongue and with tears in my eyes I arrived home in terrible pain. When my mother investigated my foot by light of the kitchen, it looked awful. The big toe was already swollen and the toe nail stood up in the air. She tried to rip the nail off, but it was still too firm in its nail bed and all it did was increasing the pain. I could not go to school the next days and had to wait until the next week Wednesday when the doctor would come to our village. At that time the nail was already fallen off and he discovered that the toe wasn't broken. With that I got a suspensor bandage and could go to school again. Plum harvest however was over for that year.

Another regular work we had to do was weeding. For some years we had a small garden at the other side of the village. I think my mother leased it from an older lady in that part of the village and we would grow all kind of vegetables, herbs, and we had indeed some fruit trees in there too: two or three cherry trees (sour cherry of course), two or three apple trees and some red currant and black currant brushes. That weeding was like hard labor for us boys. When our friends walked by the garden on their way to play at one of our secret places at the bomb craters, we almost joint them. But the fear of the punishment was much greater than the temptation to run off and play.

But here were other temptations right before our eyes. Especially in summer when the berries began to ripen on those currant brushes we often couldn't withstand the seduction to eat them. As long as we didn't eat too much everything was fine and nobody would notice. Then there was that little apple tree which had its apples ripe to eat late in August, just before school would begin again. Oh yeah, we caught some heavy drubbing because of our inability to withstand the temptation, since hunger was often a standard companion in our youth.

Late September and into early October was the time for another temptation. Every boy in our village loved nuts, to be more accurate walnuts. There were several very great trees in our village with the ability to carry a lot of walnuts every year; actually some year more and some year less but always more than we thought the owner of that tree really needed. And therein lay the greatest dilemma. Those tantalizing walnut trees grew in family gardens we had no business to be in. To get at least some of the walnuts before the owners harvested them we had to get into those gardens and get the walnuts from the trees and get out again before the owner would notice that we were there. And that was the problem. They knew about that. It wasn't an invention of ours. This game was going on for centuries. Now it was our turn and we surely did not want to fail.

One garden had three of those fantastic walnut trees and the fruits were always second to none, even in bad years. This garden was only accessible from one side, and that side was covered by a brick wall a little over two meters high. One day our gang of four decided on the way back from school that it would be a good day to check if the walnuts ready to harvest. We couldn't wait too long because then the owner would just have taken them all away. So we met later this afternoon to plan our attack at the walnut garden.

"I'll go in together with Jürgen. What do you think, Jürgen, are you up for the task?" I said, opening the strategic planning session.

"Why not? I'm all for it, and I'm almost as fast as you, Harald, in case we have to outrun the dog," he answered with a smile.

"Wouldn't be a big loss if the dog rips your pants apart," said Stepper. "I'd suggest Michael position himself on top of the wall, so he can see both the walkways, inside the garden from the house and outside, since you never know which way old Meyer is coming."

"Come on, Stepper," now Michael was actively stepping into the planning, "after you've now setup all the difficult places with a lot of danger in case we get busted, what is it you think you will do during the time we risk our skin?"

"I'd go and watch the street side. You all know that Meyer did use the surprising way from around the house along the street last year when he caught the Schlosser boys. They ran directly into him, because, you know, when you see him, there is almost no time to escape."

Jürgen threw in the question, "What about the signals—we have to have different signals for each side where he could come from."

Everybody had a whistle since those were cheap plastic, and they used them to give signals when they were playing at the bomb craters.

"No," said Michael, "it's enough if we have one for outside and one for inside. Because when he comes on the inside of the garden, you leave through Winter's garden on the backside, where the loose pickets are. When he comes on the outside, you have enough time to get through the door in the wall."

"Okay," I said, "that's it, and here is how we do it. As I said before, Jürgen and I go in and grab as many nuts as we can get. Stepper watches the street side because he's right, that's a dangerous route not to be watched. Michael lies on top of the wall where he can see both ways."

"But what about the signals? We have not set the signals yet," Michael said.

"Wait a minute," I said, "how about we use one blow on the whistle for outside and two blows for inside."

Stepper and Michael immediately asked, "Is that outside for both, the garden way and the street side?"

"Sure," I answered, "any additional signal would only be more confusing, and the escape way is the same."

With that, everything was talked through. I stepped onto Stepper's shoulders and entered the brick wall. I lay on top of the brick wall for a while and when I felt everything was okay, I jump into the garden. Jürgen followed immediately and a few second later Michael positioned himself on top of the brick wall.

FREEDOM'S NIGHTMARE

Jürgen and I were hasty collecting the wall nuts under the trees and filling our sweaters which we had carefully inserted and secured with their bottom end within our pant belts when we suddenly heard the whistle blow once. That must have been Stepper standing outside the garden seeing the owner walking towards the small garden door which he could open with a key but from the inside you didn't need a key.

Now it was all about speed. Within seconds I was on my way towards that small door in the brick wall, and at full speed I recognized the mistake too late. The owner, Mr. Meyer, wasn't on the outside of the wall where he would have a larger distance to bridge than I, because he had to run all around the house corner to get to that door. He was on the inside. I accelerated once more and was at the highest speed I could run through the grass of that garden yet was still at least a few steps ahead of him towards the door. Jürgen had already recognized what was going on and was almost completely out of the garden through the back side fence. I could not turn around to follow him because my advantage would shrink immediately over a longer distance and I knew I had no chance at all to escape. With approximately two or three steps ahead of the owner I reached the small door in the brick wall, pulled it open and jumped through it, knowing that on the other side of the adjacent small walkway a ditch ran with a lot of high grass which would dampen my landing.

Yet at the same time I set on to jump, the owner was near enough to swing the garden hose at my back. And he hit his target. Although it was the only hit I had to endure, it hurt tremendously. But no time to be sorry because he was still on my heels and the only way to escape a next hit was to get up and run as fast as possible through the adjacent brushwood. I did lose some of the nuts I had collected, but most of them were secure under my sweater. When I finally heard him fall behind, I slowed down to catch my breath only to hear him yelling behind me,

"I know who you are, and I'll tell your mother about it." And with that he turned around and walked home.

Finally, we all assembled at our play area at the bomb crater, and I was really angry and curious to find out why the wrong signal was given. I did not need to investigate much.

"I blew the whistle twice, but it failed after the first blow. And as much I tried, I could not get a second blow out of it," Michael immediately admitted.

Still angry, I demanded, "Give me your whistle!"

He handed it to me, and when we investigated his whistle, we found a piece of fiber probably from his pants pockets sticking right in the airway.

"Now, does anybody believe that Meyer really recognized me?" I asked my friends. Looking around at each of them, I saw them all shaking their heads, but Michael, still somewhat skeptic, said, "What can you do? If he recognized you, we'll have a nice evening and maybe a couple of weeks without fresh air in the afternoon. For now let us enjoy our prey," he said and began to examine the nuts.

With that, we broke up the green outer skin which still covered the walnuts with much care, because when the liquid from those shells touched your skin, your skin would get brown. To have those brown stains on your hands was proof among your peers that you had been brave enough to sneak into another garden to get walnuts. On the other hand, it was the ultimate evidence that you had been the one who barely escaped the owner and that would mean another painful number of hits onto the backside. Since the latter was more serious then the first, we decided to be very careful peeling the skin of the walnuts and had a great feast.

We came home just in time and it appeared that the farmer who's garden we had infested did not report to my mother yet, or wasn't really able to recognize me when he was running behind me through the brushwood.

Three years later we moved again, this time into the second floor of a farmer's house. The owner lived on the first floor and we had the whole second floor. There was still not much comfort and we still had to use the outhouse but we had now a number of bedrooms so that I had a room with Michael and the girls were separate. It was at this time or shortly after that Helmut got sued and ended up in jail. I was too young to understand what happened and years later my sister Connie told me that he had tried to sexually abuse my sister's friend. She was one or two years older than Connie and at this time in 8th grade. I think he got two years, and as a result my mother and Helmut got divorced.

FREEDOM'S NIGHTMARE

My mother started to work at the childcare and she took the job to clean the childcare room in addition. As again, whenever she took responsibility for something, we kids ended up doing the job. Oh I hated to wipe, wax and to polish thousands of square feet of floor in that childcare area. During the week it was only to dry mob and to put away the toys. But the weekends were gone. Mainly on Saturday we had to do it and we tried to shortcut wherever possible to rescue at least some time of this day. That had consequences. Often very painful consequences. For the smaller misdeeds she just used the wooden spoon, but for the larger ones, such as not being home in time, she took her shoe. It hurt. But it never changed anything because we always felt the treatment was unjustified because we got beaten for things kids normally did at our age—being on the street in the woods and playing around. And that only after having already finished homework for school and most of the hundreds of duties we had to do in addition at home. And come on, what boy in the world really loves to wash dishes and wipe, wax and polish floors? And instead going out playing with the few friends we had, we had to go to do gardening, weeding and all that stuff.

One year, the East German government paid a tremendous amount of money for wild harvested chamomile. I don't know how much it really was, but we, Michael, Connie and I, ended up harvesting chamomile for weeks and had the little stepsiblings to watch too. There was a permanent temptation to do everything else than that. Especially when other boys from the village showed up and started to mock us doing girls jobs. The result was always the same, we just let the chamomile be chamomile for a couple of hours and when we came back, we were in trouble, because my mother has been there to check what we did and we were gone.

But we also had those days when we went to the woods with our friends and build a little hut. There we played what boys played in those days with no electronic games and TV shows and we were happy and time flew by. Most of the time we just forgot what waited for us when we would get home and those thoughts only came back when the day finally came to an end and we walked home. Although our minds were still mainly occupied with excitement from the games we played, the fear of what the punishment would this time slowly took over. And with every step closer to home, it became the main thoughts in our infantile minds.

Usually it was a spanking by our mother either with the wooden spoon she used for cooking or, worse, her slipper, which had a wooden inlay under the sole of the shoe. Michael usually screamed at the top of his lungs while I bit my tongue and tried to not even weep, because I didn't want to give my mother any idea I felt it was justified to punish us for being children. That was how I saw it and therefore I'd not scream and often enough she became angrier and hit even harder. Later I realized that on many of those occasions when we had disobeyed her orders to do certain things and went out into the fields or woods, her punishing us with spanking was only partially for the disobedience. Sometimes she just let out all her frustration about things weren't as they should be.

Now, I have to confess that sometimes to discipline us was justified, as it is with all children and mainly boys more often than girls. We surely did monkeyshines and were punished for that too. That was when we get caught shooting with our bows at animals. Or as I remember later when we started to build rubber band guns shooting dry peas—you know those which are really hard when they are dry and yellow. We did hide behind some bushes and would try to shoot at the girls' naked calves right above the knee socks. It would not harm but felt like a delicate pinch. We were amused by their looking around and wondering what had happened, until somebody grabbed our neck and pulled us out of the bushes. That was when we knew the punishment was justified. The lacing was usually the least problematic part of it but it helped to remember next time when we thought to plot a monkeyshine to be cautious to either not get caught or to not overdo it.

I can't really remember that we were intensively participating in church but I know that we were at church on Sundays every now and then. One day I was approached by one of the elder boys, his name was Siegfried,

"Harald, would you like to help me on Sundays at church?" he asked me as we were waiting for the bus getting home from school.

"I don't know." My answer came with some hesitation, since I did not know what I had to do. So I asked back, "What do I have to do?"

Because of my hesitation, he became friendlier and began to explain, "You'll get fifty Pfennig, as much as I get for pumping the air for the organ." And going on he said, "It's not really hard work—we have to pump only when the organ is played, and the rest of the time we can watch church from above."

I thought for a moment, having a picture in my mind of me standing beside the organ player and watching all the people down there in the pews. Getting money for that was even more exiting. So I answered, "Do we get paid right after church or some day later?"

Siegfried, immediately realizing that he had me nailed for the job, was pleased and answered, "We get paid right after church is over. And the pastor is always friendly and says that he's pleased with the work we do."

There was no reason to hesitate any longer, and I answered, "Yeah, sounds great to me. What time do I have to be there?"

"Be there about half an hour before service, so I can show you everything you need to know."

With that I was hired, and my Sunday church work began.

Next Sunday a half an hour before church began we met at the church. We went upstairs and behind the organ and there it was: a large balk from wood approximately fifty centimeters above the floor which was connected to a large compressible piece of leather formed like a harmonica. It served as a large air pump to pump air into the organ flutes when the organist played the instrument. Since there wasn't storage of buffer for the air, we had constantly press the balk down to pump air into the organ when the organist played. The balk would compress the harmonica style leather bag and then decompress by the counterweight on the other side. Hey, I was really busy. There was not time to rest when the organ was playing and we both enjoyed the time when the Pastor preached his sermon even though we did not understand much.

Now, you have to understand that the people in that village were farmers and really proud that they had a still operable organ. Therefore the elders made it clear to any Pastor that they would like to have the organ played during Sunday church as much as possible. With that those fifty pfennig were hard-earned money. I did this I believe for at least one year, maybe two years. But I remember that sometime later they built a motor in to pump the air and it was over with earning money by being at church on Sunday without being a pastor.

Taken at Job that paid for the camera

A Divorce Does Not Necessarily Mean Separation and How a Visit at the Jail Revokes It

One day my mother told me that I would not go to school but we would travel to Dessau. That was the town where Helmut was in jail and she would visit him. We used the bus and both of my stepsiblings were with us. The reason why I had to go was to watch them while my mother was in the jail for the visit. It took relatively long but when she came back she was somehow happy and we traveled home right after. If I remember right, it was because Helmut did not have to serve the full sentence. But there were still several months for him to stay.

Finally, Helmut got released from jail and to our surprise he moved into our apartment. He started his job with the construction company in the town Halle Neustadt—yeah, they still worked on it, a large project—and to so he didn't liquefy (which means changed into alcohol, the complete paycheck) at the end of the month, his check had to be picked up at the company office at the construction area. Most of the time I was sent to collect the paycheck and bring it home. Since this was a day-long trip and payday was a working day, I missed school on these days. My mother fudged an excuse why I missed.

FREEDOM'S NIGHTMARE

First I entered the bus to go to the district town. There I had to catch a train to go to Halle and the railway station was in the center of the old town. Now I needed to enter another bus to go to the Newtown, and there I had to find out where on those many square miles of construction area the office of the company was at this time. Because of the ongoing construction it was always somewhere else. Usually it was in a portable shed and most of the time I found it in time to catch the company shuttle to drive back to the district town. Sometimes, I couldn't get there in time and then I had to go back the same way I came. And sometimes it happened that I missed a connection and I ended up at the district town to late and the last bus to our village was gone. Then I'd walk and the distance was roughly ten miles. That seems not an awful lot to walk, but remember I was around ten years old and when I had to walk that distance it was always late and other than in summer it was dark. However, Helmut had accepted this procedure and with that the family had money for food and all the other stuff we needed at least for a part of the month. But he did not have money for himself. And that was the time when I became an apprentice of several special trades.

As mentioned before Helmut had *golden hands*. There was nearly nothing what he not could do, repair, build, and, his very specific skill, to organize. During those years in that small village Reupzig he rebuild four different motorcycles from scrap, drove them for a while and finally found somebody who paid enough for it that it was worth to sell it. He could virtually make gold out of scrap.

I remember one day he took me with him to visit a friend of him and they drank a lot before, late at night, we started to drive back home. Suddenly in the middle of nowhere the motorcycle started to stutter and went silent. We hustled the motorcycle back to his friend's house, approximately six miles, because we needed light; and he started to dismantle the engine. He replaced the sealing between the cylinder head and the cylinder. Now that wasn't like it sounds. There were no spare parts in a store or with the motorcycle in a spare part box.

He had to produce such a seal ring by taking an exercise book cover, laying it on the cylinder and with a very small hammer and just so very careful little tick-tick hitting. He hammered a perfect seal. Now even very strong covers of exercise books are not long-lasting seals on a combusting engine, and we wouldn't drive far with this repair. But he really knew his job. He used special grease normally used for the water pumps on water-cooled combustion engines such as the engines of tractors and therefore available. He carefully worked it into the cover paper, now the cylinder head seal of the motorcycle's engine. He added a good solid layer of grease to both sides of the cylinder and the cylinder head where the seal would lay and then he mounted everything together. Now I was all on edge to know if it worked and thought he would be too and would start the engine immediately. But instead, he went into the house of his friend, by now it was long after midnight, and had another couple of drinks and cigarettes with him as they reminisced about the past, mostly the war. Finally we got out, he hit the kick starter, the engine began to run and we drove home.

I experienced this absolute confidence in his own work a couple of times, and I need to include another story here to make that as clear as possible. Since he was always short on money—mainly because his salary was confiscated by my mother and she could never have it spent fast enough—he got the fuel for his motorcycle from all kind of dubious sources.

A very good source was the Russian army. Russian soldiers would sell you everything in exchange for a bottle of vodka. Especially the enlisted men, who lived a life worse than slaves and sold whatever they had whenever they could. There was an absolute weapon ban for private people in East Germany, and even if you had a hunting license, which required at least a decent reference and membership in the SED, your hunting weapons were securely stored at the hunting club's safe. Yet, the murder rate with weapons in East Germany wasn't much lower than in West Germany, at least if you were able to see the real numbers, and those included murder with illegal possessed weapons. One source for illegal weapons was the Russian Army. The best and easiest thing to sell was fuel. When it happened that they were on the road with just a sergeant and not an officer, they would stop at your wink, put a hose into the tank and suck till the fuel came out to fill what container you ever had. Unfortunately, sometimes that stuff wasn't really clean. What happened then was that the carburetor got blocked with dirt.

One night Helmut had taken me onto an organization trip as he called it. This time it was onions. The LPG in our village had some pretty smart farmers among them and they did very well because they were real farmers before they were pressed into the LPG. One of their real successful crops was onions. They had large fields of onions, and at harvest time we could earn some money by cleaning onions and filling bags. That night we were on the road to "organize" a 100-pound bag filled with onions to sell it to another friend of Helmut who lived in the district town.

We drove out of the village to the onion fields and passed them to get as far as possible away from the street. I had to hold the bag and look around so that we did not get seen, while he filled it with the onions. The filled bag was then put onto the luggage rack and fixed with a rope. After driving out of the field and on the street for a couple of miles, the engine of the motorcycle started to stutter and stopped working. Now, this time it was a different situation. It was nearly midnight, and we were really in the middle of nowhere. Helmut took out his cigarette lighter, put it into my hand and said, "Hold it so that I can see." In the glare of the fuel-operated cigarette lighter he dismantled the carburetor totally, placing all single parts dispersed on his coat he had placed on the ground beside the motor-cycle. I nearly burned my fingers, because at any time I changed from one hand to the other, he reminded me to keep the light where he needed it, which caused me to change less often. After approximately forty minutes he had finally dismantled the carburetor, cleaned each and every part by swashing it with gasoline and blowing into every hole, and mounted all together back onto the motorcycle where it belonged. Now again I could experience his incredible self-confidence in his own work. He took out his tobacco, the cigarette paper and rolled a cigarette. Then he took the lighter out of my hand and lit the cigarette, smocked it totally and then he hit the kick starter to start the engine. And the engine ran.

We did not drive to his friend this night because it was to late, but these are the events, when I became so fascinated about his skills that I nearly forgot all the terror and horror we experiencee when he was drunk and angry about something, mostly my mother. This was going on for some time in a constant change between peaceful weeks of working together on several projects and days and nights full of horror when he was drunk.

One night I woke up to a very strange noise. When I set up in my bed I was covered with broken pieces of a preserving jar and the cherries from it. I saw the mark on the wall just a hand over my head and I was scared to death. I remember another occasion when my mother ran out the door and he threw a knife after her. The door closed and the knife stick in the door exactly on the place where her head would have been if she had needed a second more to get through the door.

I remember days when he came home drunk and waked us kids in the middle of the night because he was hungry and he would like to get something to eat and we had to cook for him. One time there was nothing but potatoes and he told me to dress myself. When I came back with my clothes on, we went down out on the street, walked two houses to our neighbor's, and he opened the farmstead door with a lock pick. As already explained he was excellent in his skills, but this was new to me. We walked into the farmstead and there into the chicken barn. All the chickens were roosted and asleep. He grabbed a shovel and hit one of the bigger chickens with the shovel handle directly on the head. I hold my breath because I saw us already in jail. The chicken just turned over and hung upside-down. I'd thought the whole chicken barn would turn into turmoil. But no, noise nothing happened. He took the chicken on its legs and off the roost, put the shovel back on the place and said to me without any excitement in his voice, "You always leave a place as you found it. I learned it the hard way during the war." I was speechless, scared, and fascinated at the same time. As we walked back home, he said, "You can't steal geese or swine this way, but with chicken it's easy." The chicken was still unconscious when we came home and he took a knife and cut its head off. It was two in the morning when I finally could go back to bed. I had to get up for school at six in the morning.

Again, my mother had a special talent to take on jobs which we had to finish. One of those was the child care cleaning, and we hated it. We hated it especially in summer when we had school vacation. And there were several reasons for the hatred, one being cherry season. The street between our village and the next was edged with sweet cherry trees and they got ripe mid July. It was a special challenge to get onto one of those trees and get cherries eaten and collected before the keeper arrived on his loud and smoky auto cycle. Since he used it to shoo the starling away, he had dismounted the silencers from the exhaust and so we could hear him coming. There was a competition who could guess the best how far he was away and when was the latest, yet securest time to jump off the tree and escape.

This went on for a couple of years, and sometimes we get caught, and that had consequences. He had a handy piece of a garden hose, and when we did not get fast enough ahead of him he would just hit us on the back riding on his auto cycle beside us. Than everything changed one year: there was a new guy and he was different. Very different! He used us boys to help him keeping the birds out of the trees, and as compensation we were allowed to eat cherries as much as we wanted. He carefully choose those he would use for the job and watched that every day somebody else get lucky. He taught us how to eat the ripe cherries without breaking braches and had a lot of stories to tell. Time flew so fast that we often were late getting home. Not for dinner or so as you would think. No, but for doing the job we were supposed to do, cleaning the child care. Each of us had a specific section to clean, and when we were late, my mother had to move in and clean it herself. That was not how it was planned, and when we were late it had always painful consequences. One Sunday while we were at the cherry tree alley and the harvest was in full swing, we totally missed our obligations.

When we finally came home late in the evening, we were beaten and punished with room arrest for two weeks. During that time we got water and bread and couldn't leave our room. It was summer and summer school break. I was ten or eleven years old and my brother one year younger. It was the sheer horror. We had to write proverbs five hundred times, *you shall not lie; the sun brings it to the light.* And if we made a mistake in between and had to correct a word, we had to start all over again. Sometimes we had really nice summer vacations.

When I turned ten, I got my first job during the summer break at the LPG. Together with my friend Stepper we worked at the chaff basement of the large barn where the straw was stored. The chaff was used as an admixture for the hog feeding. We earned five marks per hour and we worked approximately ten hours a day. The combine harvesters at this time had a closed trailer where the chaff was blown in from the combine harvester. We had to empty those trailers and to move it from the basement opening in to the basement. It was a horrible work and the dust from the husk burned in the lung. But we needed the money because at the end of the money my parents earned there was a lot of month left. And often we had no money to buy the food we needed, and then I was sent with a piece of paper into the store. On that piece of paper was written something like, "Please give Harald this stuff; I'll pay for it next week." So the additional money I earned was highly welcome.

After two weeks the barley harvest was over and with that the job. I had been able to put aside some money, and with that I had enough to by some parts I needed to realize another dream I had: a bicycle. And that was a little different than it is today or it possibly was at this time in the free world or even in East Germany in other families. I couldn't just walk into the next store and buy a bicycle. A bicycle was too expensive and probably not even available. But I could have an expedition to the garbage dump and search for bicycle parts, usable to rebuild a bicycle. And after our gang of four had made several trips to the garbage dump, I had all the parts together I needed. The frame, two nearly perfect rims and a not too much damaged saddle. I brought the rims to the bicycle repair shop. It was actually an elder man, a widower, who lost his wife and one leg in the war and started a small repair shop for bicycles and sewing machines in our village. He promised me to put complete new spokes in and align both wheels correctly for the money I was able to pay. And I'm pretty sure it was not the price he normally charged for it. Over a couple of days I worked on the frame to remove the rust and paint it with the black color I had bought. I dismantled the bearings on the headset and foot pedals, cleaned all parts and remounted them. I had bought a cover for the slightly dam-aged saddle, and with that it looked like new. Three days later I could pick up my rims, now wheels, and it was just great to see how the new chrome spokes sparkled in the sun. Both axles were also fit for being mounted after I had replaced the bearings and cleaned the back wheel axle mechanic, including the back pedaling break.

Since my money wasn't much, I had to cut corners, and one was not to buy the rubber bands, which would go on the inside of the wheels to cover the screws of the spokes from the tire-tube. Either because of the quick and cheaper work of the bicycle man or because it was normal, there were several sharp edges at the inner side of the wheels on the spoke ends and I did not recognize those as a problem. Full of pep I was going to work. I mounted the tire tubes and the outer tubes and pumped the air in. I mounted the axis and then the wheels on the frame. I put the chain on and discovered that it was too long. I had to cut the chain and to replace one of the chain links with the chain lock, to be able to close the chain on the bicycle.

Now, as all was done, I put the bicycle on the wheels and had a couple of minutes break. Just looking at it was great, and I thought it was the best looking bicycle in the entire village. After I had enjoyed the accomplishment of several days of hard work for a couple of minutes, I jumped on the bicycle and made my first round, for sure to my friend Stepper first. He was as happy as I was, and after he drove some rounds we sat down and talked about what we could do now since we were all much more mobile. And while we were sitting there and dreaming about a trip to the neighbors' village swamp to collect common reed as basis for the arrows we needed for our bows, I suddenly realized that both my tires were flat. Just that, flat!

Almost immediately I realized that my attempt to save money had just been blown away. I had to push my bicycle back home, and all the way I was concerned not to increase the damage on the tire-tubes because to buy new tire tubes was out of question. I had to walk over to the other end of the village where the bicycle repair shop was and buy two of those rubber bands. When I came home, it was too late to repair the tires. Next morning I repaired the tire tubes by glueing patches of rubber from an old tire tube over the holes. It needed two additional repairs till I finally could buy a vulcanizing set, which allowed me to repair the tire tubes correctly. The problem was the glue. It was a very bad quality, and as soon as your bicycle was exposed to the sun long, the glue softened, and the patches would move away from the hole and everything began again. The vulcanizing sets were expensive, and all I could do was get smaller sized sets for Helmut's vulcanizing tool he had for his motorcycles.

The next year Helmut had started a new income system. During summertime, especially when I had school break, he would call in sick with his company. Since you could have six weeks paid sick days in East Germany and the company headquarters were far away, it was only in the hand of the doctor to decide if he was sick or not. The doctor usually showed up every other week in our village, and in summer when he had his own vacation probably only once a month. Helmut used this to practice his new additional source of income. Thanks to his incredible ability to fix nearly everything broken or worn out, he was sought after in the surrounding area of our village. And he could use a helper, and with that I was back in business. I had the dream to buy a camera and with working for him it was possible to put some of the earned money aside.

Pouva Start - the camera I dreamed about

Every morning around six we would leave home and ride on our bicycles to the place to work. We worked exclusively for farmers who still had their livestock and only the fields were part of the collective work. As I described before, those were named type 1. We did practically any kind of work. We painted rooms, repaired roofs, built hog houses, and repaired barn doors as well as harvesters and other machines. There was actually nothing that Helmut could not repair or build or somehow put together. He was extremely proud of a large number of paint rollers he had collected over time and had a special talent to combine background color and pattern color so that the farmers' women were always very excited about his work. There were several occasions that are burned in my mind that happened during those weeks.

One was when we had to repair a barn roof covered with the typical European roof tiles. It was a huge barn, approximately 55 yards long and 33 yards wide and 30 yards high at its top. The roof had a bevel of 45 angular degrees. None of the available ladders were long enough and we used some ropes to bind three ladders together so that it could be laid on that roof. Helmut grabbed a number of roof tiles and walked up the ladders. When he reached the top, he swung his leg over and glided to the place where the tiles were missing. Within a few minutes he had replaced the broken tiles and filled the gaps where tiles were missing. He called me to bring some pan tiles and mortar because he had discovered that there were some of those missing too.

Now those pan tiles weren't light, and the bucket with mortar wasn't either. I took three pan tiles under my left arm and the bucket in my right hand and began to walk up the ladders. Very carefully, moving the bucket with the mortar one step at a time, I tried to get up on the roof. But Helmut wasn't that patient and asked, "Shall I stay overnight on the roof top? You can stand up and walk the ladder upwards, just balance with the weight in your both hands," he commanded me. It took all my courage as an eleven-year-old walking up that ladder. But it worked, at least for the largest part of the way. Just short of the top I lost balance and could barely keep myself from falling backwards by using the weight of the mortar bucket and swinging it forward. That had consequences. The bucket landed outside of the ladder area and crashed several additional roof tiles. I lost my payment for that day, and had to learn to walk ladders up and down the whole evening while Helmut had some beer with the farmer.

Another unforgettable situation happened when we had to repair the roof of another barn which was covered with mineral surface roofing paper. The roof was approximately 15 yards above ground and very light beveled, approximately 10 to 12 degrees. Helmut had agreed with the Farmer to put a complete new layer of that mineral-surfaced roofing paper on. For that we had to heat up the tar, which we would use as the adhesive. It came in solid rolls with approximately 15" by 45" and 100 lbs weight. I had to break it apart with the ax and put the pieces in the tar cooker to liquefy it. Then I would fill it in two buckets and we carried them up the ladder on the roof. Helmut had in the mean time rolls of the mineral surface roofing paper carried up on the roof and also two brooms. He had just thrown them onto the roof and had not entered the roof before completely. Now with the liquid tar in the bucket we both stepped on the roof.

The work itself was relatively easy. We brushed a section of the roof with the tar, rolled the roofing paper over it and then brushed the next

127

section. This was going on till the first tar bucket was empty and he said: "Go down and get a bucket of tar while I finish up this one." I grabbed the bucket, marched to the ladder, and stopped. The ladder end was just a few inches above the rim of the roof and there was no way to step onto the ladder. I tried several different body positions to lower myself onto the ladder steps, but vainly. Helmut was in the mean time done with the other bucket and, without turning around, he yelled at me, "Where are you with the tar?"

So I walked back to him and said, "Sorry but there is no way to get onto that ladder—it's too short."

He looked at me like a bad joke. He walked over to the ladder and tried it himself. Forward, backward, on his belly sliding towards the ladder and I don't know what else. I had tried all that before. No chance. He finally gave up and said: "We have to wait till somebody shows up and can help." At lunch time, the farmer's wife came to call us for lunch. We explained her that she needed to send the farmer and two or three others. When they came and saw us sitting on that roof they couldn't stop laughing. By moving a huge hay cart onside the barn and lifting the ladder onto that card, the problem was solved. We stepped down from the roof and had a great lunch without having accomplished too much that morning.

And I remember on another very painful lesson I learned during that summer. This hot liquid tar had the tendency to spray all over the place when you were not extremely carefully by brushing it on the surface with the broom. And it was not always possible to avoid hitting the steps of the ladder or some other corner with the buckets filled with that hot liquid stuff. After all I was just eleven years old and those buckets were heavy. With that I had usually several spots of tar on my skin, mainly my face. Not really thinking about it, I started to wipe it off by using cigarette lighter fuel. It worked well and I could get rid of the spots. What I did not think about was that I had another couple of hours to work in the burning sun and that the cigarette lighter fuel needed to be washed off with water. It took just a few hours if at all, till I felt the result of my cleaning action. It was so painful that for a couple of days I had trouble sitting inside the room for lunch or dinner longer than necessary and had to cool my face frequently till the burns were healed.

Very often, especially on Fridays when we got paid for the week work, we ended up in a saloon on our way home. I had to sit for hours drinking lemonades and eating frankfurter and listen to the conversation Helmut had with other likeminded people. Mostly they would talk about motorcycles, cars, and engines. And he was well-known as an expert on those things near and far. He also got leads about jobs at farms around our area, and that would pay off because when he contacted those farmers and could name his references, he always got the job. I had to stay with him, because he did not want my mother to know that he was at the saloon.

And we got more siblings. Another stepbrother was born 1966 and a stepsister in 1967. Connie was actually taken out of school in summer 1967 and sent to be trained as an assistant nurse at a hospital, owned by the East German Lutheran Church. The health problems of my mother became current again in fall 1967, and right after Christmas she was hospitalized at that same hospital. And the terror at home went on. We didn't even have many opportunities to escape the terror since our friend Stepper wasn't in the village anymore. His father had quit working for the company he had worked for for almost thirty years and had taken the job as sexton of St. Martin in Koethen. When Helmut had finally consumed enough alcohol and came home late at night, most of the time we were already sleeping, but he demanded us to come out and do stuff we hadn't done correctly in his opinion. So it could happen that we started to clean the floor of the kitchen in the middle of the night, or we had to cook a meal because he was hungry, and more often than not it just happened that there wasn't anything to cook, so he would demand me to go with him and organize something, which usually meant steal a chicken, or a duck, or something else edible.

Finally one day the constant fear about the coming terror at night was too much to bear. Michael and I decided to leave. Just run away. We did not have a specific destination to go at first, but just being away from terror and beating seemed like a dream in a very far future. So we went out and turned towards the district town. It was already late in the evening when we decided to walk out because we had heart that Helmut was sitting at the restaurant and was already at a certain level of drunkenness. We just couldn't bear the thought to live through another night of terror. So we walked along the main road, and whenever a car or truck would appear we jumped behind a tree or into the ditch which was dry.

It was early in spring as I remember and soon after sunset it became very chilly. Since it was only a little over eight miles we arrived at the outskirts of Koethen a little after midnight. We had talked through all the possibilities we had and finally decided to ask Steppers parents for help, mainly because we did not know where else to go and secondly we knew Stepper's father was a serious man.

When we finally reached the door at the annex of the somewhat strange church building, we had to knock really hard to wake them up. After we told the reason why we were on the street at this time, Stepper's mother heated up some leftover from supper, which we virtually gulped down in a few minutes.

Next morning, Stepper's parents had some talks with us, and we insisted to go to the place where our sister Connie and my mother were. So they bought us the train tickets, and with that we were on our way to the city of Dessau. After about an hour and a half we arrived at the train station in Dessau, and since we had visited our mother two or three times since she was in hospital we knew the way. We created a huge swivet when we arrived at the hospital, especially when we explained why we had run away from home. The hospital was, as I mentioned before, operated and owned by the Lutheran Church of East Germany by their organization called the *Inner Mission*. They had enclosed a kindergarten and a dormitory for the nursing students.

The management of the hospital decided to take us in their custodial care in agreement with my mother until she was relieved from the hospital. The administration organized our school transfer, and the next Monday we walked the first time to the new school. Since we were new in that town and the way to the school was about thirty to thirty-five minutes to walk, one of the sisters came with us, first of all to show us the way we would have to walk every day from now on, and secondly to present us, and I really mean present, like a trophy to the school principal and the class teacher. She really meant well to do that right, but I wished the earth would open up and swallow me when she introduced me to the class teacher in front of all the other students.

FREEDOM'S NIGHTMARE

The 7th grade in the German school system added topics such as Chemistry, Introduction to the Socialistic Production, and Metal Working to the schedule. Every other week we had to go to a specific workshop at the other side of the town for one day. There, at the manufacturing facilities of the former *Junkers Werke*, where once the famous airplanes of the German Lufthansa and later the aircrafts of the German Luftwaffe were produced, was now the production of gas heaters and burners for gas stoves and ovens. We would learn how to use different tools to form a piece of metal into a useful something. I really liked it and had much fun and very good grades. Wednesdays we would go to a church near the hospital and have *Christenlehre* (German for Sunday school). Since that church was on the way to our school, we would just stop on the way back from school, wait for the time that the Pastor, or sometimes when he was occupied with more important stuff, his wife came and began to teach about Jesus and the stories of the Bible. Honestly, I can't remember anything I should have learned there. The same way I did very badly at school too. I dropped dramatically in arithmetic and science average. Mathematic, Physics and Biology, as well as Geography, and History were topics I loved and learned normally with ease to get a B plus with doing much, not even homework, and A grades when I actually prepared for tests and did my homework. Now I was collecting E on mass and barely could improve to finish with four D grades on my year-end report.

But I do remember an incredible story related to that little church, and the picture confirming the truth to it is burned into my mind for as long I live. The pastor reminded us that during WWII, Dessau was the target of several severe bombing raids by the allied air forces. Usually they tried to hit the Junkers aircraft manufacturing, which had several manufacturing facilities spread out all over the city. During one of those bombings a firebomb hit the little church we were sitting in. The bomb went through the roof and exploded on the church floor. The fire spread out rapidly and all of the pews were in flames within seconds. But when the fire reached the wall where the cross with the life-sized Jesus figure hung, it stopped and extinguished by itself.

We were sitting there in awe, silent and astounded, and listened to the story of that miracle. And we could see that this wasn't a lie, because we had the evidence right before our eyes. The Cross with Jesus' figure was still hanging on that wall and was burned up to that part right beneath Jesus' feet. During the following years I totally forgot about this wonderful story and became such a denier of the Christian faith and everything what had to do with God, that I wonder today how God was able to pull me back under His jurisdiction, trying to make me a tool for his kingdom. But that wondering usually takes only a few seconds, knowing that we have an almighty, loving, and all-merciful God.

End of March, my mother was released from the hospital, but we had to stay in Dessau to finish school there and not change again in the middle of the second semester. Yet on weekends we were allowed to go home. Not every weekend though, and with that it became very boring. With whether improving and the days getting longer we began to fall back into old habits and build pea guns, bows, and slingshots, of course secretly. If one of the nurses would have discovered that we had such things, we would have had a hard time with the director of the complex.

At the end of spring, it became warm, and many weekends were really nice and sunny, and we were granted to ride our bicycles from Dessau to Reupzig. Now that was something. Actually it wasn't really that we got allowance to do it. One weekend when we were home, we asked to get our bicycles with us back to Dessau so that we would have a better way to get to school. At this time it wasn't a big deal to have your bicycle in a train in East Germany. You just needed to buy a ticket for the bicycle and bring it to the baggage wagon. You handed the conductor the ticket, he gave you a number which was matched with a number glued to the bicycle and that was it. In Dessau we would walk to the baggage wagon, would hand over the number and reclaim our bicycles. That was the weekend we got our bicycles to Dessau. The nurses were in a swivet.

Since we had to cross an extremely busy street in the morning to get into the street where the school was, they would not allow us to use the bicycles to school. But in the afternoon after homework, we could now roam the neighborhood. Since this area was mainly built with smaller homes with gardens around, it was really nice to cruise around there. In the meantime we also connected with two or three kids from the homes next to the hospital complex, but it wasn't really a substitute for our friend in Reupzig. Although it was just Jürgen since Stepper was moved to the district city with his parents, we would be able to do much more stuff then with the *city guys* in Dessau.

The next weekend wasn't actually determined to be a home weekend, so we decided to dare the ride. We went to the library and studied the maps and we saw that it wasn't really that far. Roughly nineteen kilometers (approximately twelve miles) to ride, and that wasn't really a distance for us. So early on Saturday morning we created some sandwiches and jumped on our bicycles and on the road we were. I had copied the main route we had to travel from the maps in the library using a pencil and a piece of parchment paper and had noted the street names and numbers to know when we had to change direction. On our way was a small town with a jewel of German Rococo architecture of the late 1700. The castle of Mosigkau is one of the few still existing Rococo ensembles in Germany and includes a Orangery and several paintings of the Dutch masters such as *Zephyr and Flora* of Peter Paul Rubens as well as *The Prince of Oranien* of Anton van Dyck. It was built between 1752 and 1757, and it is said that the conceptual design was made by no one less than the famous Sanssouci Architect Georg W. von Knobelsdorff.

Now, it wasn't really on our radar to use our first—and at that unauthorized—trip home by bicycle to make a sight-seeing tour through that castle. We did not even think about that castle even though we had learned about it in history at school. But when we closed in on that town that gorgeous Saturday morning we couldn't avoid seeing it through the brush first and then down the street on our right hand side, passing by. And we stopped. After looking down the road leading to the castle we turned and pedaled towards it without saying a word.

Of course we did not enter. I don't even know if it was open at that time and if it ever has been able to be visited by the public. But what we did was to enter the unusual labyrinth of hedges as tall as a man. We had a lot of fun trying to go to the center without running every lane several times. You can actually see the labyrinth from a bird's view on Google Earth. Suddenly I heard a church clock ringing and stopped to count and it was already noon. Immediately we jumped on our bicycles and resumed our tour towards Reupzig. When we arrived shortly after two I believe it was, we expected at least some kind of trouble since nobody knew that we were on the road. But since we were traveling off main roads, and actually there wasn't much motorized traffic at this time, especially on weekends, in East Germany, it wasn't a big deal. Another reason for the non-excitement was the fact that this demonstrated that we could travel back and forth without spending money, and that was always good news.

For the remaining time in Dessau we would travel on weekends by bicycle. Saturday morning home and Sunday afternoon back to Dessau. After we got used to the roads we had to travel we got braver to spend time at several places on our way, especially at the Mosigkau Castle and the park surrounding it. It wasn't much of a Tourist attraction as it is today—as it was with many historical or famous places in East Germany. This was mostly caused by a total lack of private initiatives. Since all of those places and buildings were *Volkseigentum* (public property, or better yet state-owned property) there wasn't any possibility for private investments. And those who were employed by the state-owned management of historical or famous places had no interest to do more than necessary or required because it did not change a bit for them. And there are hundreds of places like Mosigkau Castle throughout the East German territory which were neglected for years and had finally been salvaged because they were destroyed beyond repair or restoration.

Only after East Germany became a member of the UN and their several organizations, they were forced to declare their historical buildings and places which were considered world heritage. They did that mainly with the flow of international money in mind and where their own communistic main interests lay. The places which were restored with that money were such as the town of Güstrow, because it was where the communistic Ernst Barlach had created some of his sculptures. Although he died in 1938, he was joyfully pocketed by the East German communists as proof of the geniality of their philosophy. I had huge trouble seeing anything in those sculptures when we had to write essays but ugly pieces of senseless wasted material. But granted I am not really gifted in recognizing brilliance in artwork besides organ music from Bach.

Finally we did have our last day at school—even though the results of that year were devastating at least for me—and we left Dessau for the last ride home with some kind of gloom. When she was released from hospital, my mother had started to work at a chemical plant in a town named Wolfen. There was the 1909 established AGFA Wolfen where in 1936 the worldwide first multi-level-color film *Agfacolor Neu* was developed. After being partly demounted for reparation by the Russians and operated until 1953 as a Russian SAG plant, it was given back and transformed into a *Volkseigener Betrieb* (VEB) German for people-owned plant. For several years they fought the GDR administration to keep the international well-known brand named AGFA but lost the final law suit in 1964 and created a new name ORWO Color. My mother was operating an overhead crane to fill the coal bunkers at the power station which supplied the steam and energy for the chemical plant.

The summer of 1968 was another remarkable summer. Our village in the center of the central German lowlands, flat as a plate as far as the eye can reach, was encompassed by fields, and those fields were accessible by farm tracks. Suddenly that summer of 1968, many of those farm tracks were flooded with Russian troops. They had all sort of equipment, and today I know from my time at the armed forces and from history that this was a fully equipped armored division. They were officially part of a maneuver called *Danube,* but they were in reality preparing for the occupation of Czechoslovakia. At this time that was unknown to me and I guess to 90 percent of the soldiers in that division also.

We were teens, we had summer school break and due to our very intensive and well-performed communistic indoctrination, they were our friends. Don't get me wrong, those soldiers were extremely friendly towards us kids and even to the adults because what we found out within a few hours was that they would exchange nearly everything for a bottle of schnapps, vodka at the best, but korn (made from wheat) was also good enough for barter a lot of things. Most of the people from the villages around that area just got as much fuel as possible. The most mysterious thing though to me was the price. Let say a farmer came with his car—most likely a *Trabant* sometimes a *Wartburg*, which were the only cars officially private owned at this time—and he happens to have a 3/4 liter of vodka. They filled his fuel tank and that was it. Some came with their tractors they had rebuild from scratch or those they had kept hidden during the period of condemnation, and the Russian soldiers filled these tanks from the diesel-fired tanks. And it was always just 3/4 liter bottle of schnapps. We kids used the opportunity to try our language skills and to see if what we had learned at school was useful. The result was devastating. The talking speed of the Russian soldiers was too fast and so we did not understand much but with gestures and some of the words many times repeated we made our way. It did not take long to find out that we could use fruits as barter objects to get things in exchange from the soldiers. Now the question was what? We did not have cars or motorcycles to barter for fuel. And finally we found out that they were willing to trade in cigarettes for fruits. With that we descended on the early ripe apple trees in and around the village like a swarm of locusts.

The Russian cigarettes were not really high quality, but I knew that Helmut would highly appreciate them. And from him I could get money for it. At the end of that day, I had eighteen packs of those Russian *Papyrossi,* which I sold for 5 East mark to Helmut. After dark we went back to that farm track where the Russians camped we had traded all day long with and they had camp fires burning and were sitting around, drinking secretly the schnapps they had traded during the day, singing melancholic Russian folksongs. Several played guitars, and some accordion, or harmonica. We came home late, and as always when we had forgotten to finish the jobs we got ordered to do, we were in trouble. But a very special day and a somewhat unforgettable night was worth that trouble.

Next day, the soldiers were gone, and I think it was just a couple of days later that we heard about the invasion of Czechoslovakia by the troops of the Warsaw Pact. We realized immediately that the troops with whom we traded were part of that. Although we did not understand the consequences of that invasion it was somehow a strange feeling to know some of the soldiers who were part of it. The invasion itself was used as a huge propaganda event in the East German mass media, and most of the time it was about the bad West Germans and their accomplices at the belligerent NATO who happens to ignite the counter-revolution in Czechoslovakia to destroy the achievements of the communist party for the Czech people.

This summer was also the time when I turned 14, and that was the age in East Germany when you had to apply for your ID card. Now, that wasn't just a card, as many of the readers would automatically reflect to their driver license or state ID card. It was a small booklet, probably 2 by 3 inches, and contained several pages with all kind of data about your person. At a certain age you had to carry it with you all the time and had to show it to an authorized person on their request. I was very excited when I heard that some of my friends had already applied for and went to the municipal administration to apply for mine too. The secretary handed me a form, which she said I needed to fill out and have it signed by my mother. At night when my mother came home from work, I presented her the filled-out form and asked her about the physical address of my real father. She said that she did not know and I should just write Austria, because that's what she thought he would live since he was an Austrian citizen. I did not pay much attention to that, filled out the form and she signed.

When I brought it to the community administration next day, the secretary looked at it and said something like oh, oh. Then she said I should come back in two weeks for the ID. Just a few days later, my mother was working nightshift, which enabled her to do more things during the day, and the community policeman came to our home and wanted to talk to my mother. They talked for about half an hour and he left. My mother did not tell me what it was about but I had the feeling that it had something to do with that ID card. It took another four weeks until I finally had my ID card in hand. Years later I would remember that and I would understand why it took them so long to come up with that ID card. But then, I did not care. I had it as all the others in my age, and with that there was one reason less to be teased and mocked.

The peaceful time didn't last much longer. Again, my mother was sent for treatment to a health resort. Actually I never understood how she was able to get these prescriptions so regularly, but somehow she was there every three to four years or so. But that wasn't really the point. The point was that at any time she went there a new episode of terror began when she was back. The reason was that she just couldn't withstand the temptation of having an affair, a serious affair. Helmut reacted to that the only way he knew, and that was getting drunk. And as it was at any time when he got drunk and was angry, we had terror. The power of the alcohol was to strong. Helmut couldn't just resist, and the nightly terror of an extremely aggressive drunken man came back. But this time it took only a few weeks, and because my mother and he were already divorced he was ordered to move out and moved into an apartment in the neighboring village.

Even that summer school break ended and we had to go back to school. A lot had changed since we had left the village almost eight months ago. Using the bus in the morning wasn't free anymore. Every student sixth grade and up had to pay for the ride or see to it they got to school and back home in time. Only those with disabilities were allowed to use the bus above that grade. Now that wasn't a big problem for me and Michael. We were used riding longer distances with our bicycle. But autumn was fast arriving and the weather could be very ugly in our area. We did not have really useful weather clothes, and often enough we came to school completely soaked. It took sometimes hours to get dry, and then we were on our way home and had to endure the rain again. With the lack of nutritious food, such as fresh fruits and vegetables, because that was always rare in East Germany, we were often sick. This did not bother Michael much, but I loved to learn and went to school often already carrying a cold or flu.

I had a new class teacher and I was definitely not his favorite student. One day when he returned a test we had in mathematics, which I actually liked, although physics was my absolute favorite, he couldn't avoid to announcing that my mother could not come and accuse him of being extremely negative towards me, because mathematics uses numbers and numbers don't lie. It was obvious that he had an argument with my mother at the last parent-teacher conference of which I did not know anything about. Him blaming me in front of the whole class as being sissy and complaining about being treated unjustly made my angry. The antipathy was surely mutual and not just shortly discovered. His son was now in my class and he was a disgrace not only in his behavior, but also in his grades in any of the disciplines. The only surprising exception was mathematics, which happened to be taught by his father. This was so obvious that even we children recognized it, but the parents did not say anything out of fear for the grades of their own kids. Since he was also the boss of the party cell at the school—remember the socialist party had the leading role everywhere in East Germany—none of the teachers dared to criticize him even slightly. To the contrary, in my opinion, his son shouldn't even have the grades he had in most of the other disciplines. Anyway, it appeared that my mother couldn't keep her mouth shut, and I earned the results.

In that one test I had earned a C grade and I was really sure that I had enough points for at least a B grade. That was my opinion when we had compared our results after finishing the test during the break two days earlier. Since we had to go to the gym, which was a walk of about ten minutes, there was no time to recheck the results of my equations with one of my friends Roland—his nickname was Mausi—and with that, I totally forgot about it until I came home.

It was mandatory to have tests signed by one of your parents, do the corrections and then you had to give the notebook back to the teacher. I presented my test to my mother so she would sign it and she wasn't really happy. She told me that she had an argument with my class teacher because he was unjust in his assessment of our performance, which meant Michael and me, and now I did just confirm that he was right in that. She signed the test with anger and ordered me stay in house for the next two weeks to improve my mathematics and other skills. Now, that was something I did not take easy, and walking back to our room, I went over my test and began the correction home work, which was also mandatory. Within a few minutes I find out that many of the results the teacher had marked as wrong were actually correct. How was that possible? I have to confess that my handwriting is horrible. Many times I had to think for several minutes looking at my own notes to find out what I had written during school hours. And it looked like that was the main problem here too. I did find at least enough points to move the result above 80 percent, and with that into the range of a B grade.

That same night our landlord's wife came up and brought a pair of jeans because it was too small for her son, and she thought my mother could use it for one of us. And it fit almost perfectly for me, just a little too long, which my mother could correct in minutes. Now, that was something. Suddenly I had a pair of jeans, and not just some jeans, those were original Levi's jeans. I could barely sleep that night and next morning full of pride I walked to school. And that was really something. Almost all boys had to touch them and to feel the strong textile.

In East Germany, it was not only not available, but also an almost forbidden textile. The socialists hated it and called it a sign of society decay to run around in cowpuncher's cloth and make a style out of it. But whoever had relatives in West Germany and were able to provide things not available in East Germany would ask for things like jeans for the boys and panties for the girls. Years later East Germany was able to provide somewhat comparable jeans and panties from home production, but the quality never came even close to those from West Germany, not to think about the fame. The excitement though lasted only a few hours, because for one, the next lesson began and other boys had Levi's jeans too. It was just unthinkable that I had access to jeans like that and I was brave enough to wear them to school. I did not think about that fact for a minute. As I said, it was absolutely surprising to many of my classmates to see somebody with the Levi's jeans—that symbol of rotten Western decadence—at school. The reason became painfully conscious to me next day.

As always at the last day of the month, the whole school would line up to muster. That was usually the event when the director—who by the way was my teacher in German language and literature—would credit publicly the three best students of the month and also the three worst students of the month and he would read out loud the reprimands issued during the month. For that those who received a reprimand had to stay in front of the square of all classes while he read out their misdemeanors. Since this was a normal thing going on every month, I did not pay much attention, was chatting with Mausi, and when my name was called out I almost missed it.

Somebody behind me gave me a push and all eyes were on me. I was sure that I wasn't among the three best students and was also pretty sure that I had not receive a reprimand, and with that I walked really slow and hesitantly through the rows forward. Then I heard the principal calling my name again and asking me if I thought that he had the whole day to wait for me. So I accelerated to the front where the panelized others still stood and made front towards the classes. My class teacher, who not only happened to be the socialist party cell leader, but also the vice principal, stepped forward, opened a notebook and read out loud about the great comforts of the socialist society, all the positive things we children had since we lived in a country where the workers class had the leading roll, where the rotten capitalistic system was defeated once and for all and how the great leader took care that each and every student reached his highest possible potential.

Yet, he carried on; there are those amidst us whom are unable to appreciate that. Those who would love to dishonor the accomplishments of the socialism and would run around like a capitalistic propaganda pillar. He walked over to where I stood, grabbed my shoulder, and turned me around. And with one pull full of hate and anger he ripped the Levi's label off my jeans. Holding it up in the air with a triumphant voice he shouted, "We will not tolerate defamation of the socialistic culture of the German Democratic Republic!"

I have to confess, I had tears in my eyes and I was so furious that I was close to running away from that place. But I immediately realized that it would only make it worse and just stood there and endured his hate for the capitalist world for about ten minutes. He finished with the threat that everybody who would dare to come with a symbol glamorizing the western life style would have to consider harsher consequences than this. With this I was allowed to enter the rows of our class and the event was over.

Nobody, and I mean nobody, dared to even look at me. Not even the few friends I had, including Mausi. Silent and lost, I walked back to the classroom where the next two-hour lesson would start in a few minutes. Contraire to the usual cacophony it was silent in the classroom. So silent that even the principal was astounded when he entered the room. I believe to remember that this was the most silent two hours I have ever experienced in my whole school time, probably with the exception of the day when the other Roland hung on the black board.

I had a lot of trouble when I came home and I lost the jeans. I could not wear them anymore. That was really ridiculous because later when we were at the island, nearly every boy and even girls wore jeans, with and without the imperialistic symbols of the manufacturers, because their fathers worked in the fishing industry and with that had the ability to buy stuff at so-called Duty-Free shops. But that was later.

A few weeks after that incident with the jeans symbol, I virtually exploded in anger. I was surely not the smallest in our class, but by far not the strongest. We had a guy in our class, his name was Hartmut, and he was almost a head taller than the average, was heavily built, and had a broad back. We were at the first few months of the eighth grade and he looked like he was in the tenth grade or so. Our classrooms were equipped with three rows of double-seated tables which were arranged in three

141

columns, called window column, middle column, and wall column. I was seated in the middle column and there in the middle row. Hartmut was sitting right behind me and he was the uncrowned king of the class and probably the whole age group at our school. That because of his strength, and what he had there too much, he definitely lacked in knowledge. He always tried to copy my writings, and for that, he would push me sideward from behind to get a look at my notes. If he would have been friendly and would have shown at least some kind of gratitude for doing so, I would probably be more willing to let him catch a look or two. But he was a bad boy. He was really bad, he teased me all the time, called me names and often would blow a punch at me, just because he had fun to hurt me. This day that changed.

This day would change actually everything in Michael's and my relationship to all the other boys at school and in our village. But at this time during the fourth lesson at school and the first lesson in German language, I did not know about it. We had to do a silent tutorial flexion of verbs, and I did not want Hartmut to use my work to improve his grades. Because he knew that this time it was his turn to be called to the front and to present his results, he became more and more insistent to copy my writings. His whisper became louder so that the principal already looked up from his own readings and looked around. And then it happened. Angry that I did not let him copy what he needed to get the tutorial done and knowing that he wasn't able to finish it himself, he beat me with the edge of his ruler, a thirty-centimeter-long piece of steel, right over my head.

The pain was incredible. I had immediately tears in my eye and I forgot everything around me for this moment. It was as if the time slowed down. I stood up, turned towards Hartmut, who was just about to stand up too, but not fast enough to stand completely. With that he was at the right position and the uppercut I threw at him hit him directly on the right spot, the tip of his chin. Since I had all the momentum of my body still in a turning movement and he wasn't standing completely, the different height did not matter. He uttered a strange tone and went down to the floor.

A second later the principal was over me, grabbed my arm and pulled me away from Hartmut into the corner of the classroom and shouted at me, "Stay there!" It took him and some girls who came with some napkins soaked with water to get Hartmut responding to them, and then they lead him out of the classroom to the teacher's room where they had a place to lay him down. Slowly I came to myself and began to realize what just happened. Looking around I saw a lot of unbelieving amazement. Just then I began to feel the pain in my hand and recognized that the knuckle which had hit Hartmut's chin began to swell. And then the horrible pain on my head came back to my conscience again, and when I touched the hair at that spot, my fingers were wet. Blood! I almost broke down. I can see blood without having a problem, but as soon as I see my own blood, my nerves collapse.

All that happened so fast I think there were barely more than five minutes gone from the time I hit with the ruler until the principal came back into the classroom. He came back to that corner where I still stood since he had pushed me there. He shouted at me if I had lost my mind, if I had not have enough with the problems I had already been running around as a marketing pole for the imperialists, and now this. Finally he had to take a breath and I, almost whispering, answered, "He hit me with his ruler over the head."

At first his face came down to my face so close that I thought he would bite my nose. He said, "You dare to—" and stopped in the middle of the sentence. At that moment he saw the blood already beginning to run down on the side of my head.

He asked, "Why didn't you say anything?" He grabbed my arm and pulled me out of the classroom to the teachers' room where they had a first aid room. In the meantime the community nurse had arrived to deal with Hartmut and to check if he had a concussion, which made me somewhat proud for a second or two. She removed the hair around the bleeding area, put some iodine tincture at the wound and stapled it with three staples together. With that I was send back to the classroom and the period went on.

Since we older students could not use the school bus anymore without to paying, and money was always an issue in our family, we would just walk home. Since Michael had one period more that day, I waited for him. While I was sitting at the corner of the schoolyard, touching the band aid on my head every now and then, since it still hurt, two boys of our village from the enemy group came over. Both were one grade higher than I was and had several times over the last many years knocked me around.

They had heard about the incident at school, which wasn't really a wonder because it was a sensation not only for the students, but also for the teachers. After all this years we, Michael and I, had been knocked around over and over again, and the teachers knew that I did not backfire normally. I guess they were still puzzling over what had me exploding.

Now these two guys came and wanted to know how true the story that I knocked out Hartmut really was. So they started to tease me, kicked at me, and were laughing all the time while calling me names. Anger began to cook inside of me and this time. It was not the anger of despair, but furiousness about these guys who found fun in beating boys like me. They would never feel the same pain and helplessness unless somebody gave them a lesson. And something else was included into that furiousness—the confidence to be able to beat them in the same way I had Harmut just a few hours ago.

I jumped up out of my sitting position and lifted my right knee at the same time. Since one of the guys was standing almost over me and was approximately 5 inches taller than me, my knee, supported with the whole momentum of my upwards moving 140 to 150 pounds, hit him right on the spot where men have the weakest point. With a loud grunt, unable to say one word or to scream in pain, he went down, rolled into a fetal position and grasped for breath. I looked at the other guy and said, "What about you, you want to join him?"

He looked at me speechless, and with his face white as a whitewashed wall said in a stutter. "N...n...no, I...I...I don't want anything from you. Please don't do that to me!" The other guy came slowly to himself, and with the help of his friend they hobbled away. I sat back onto the wall at that corner of the school yard and needed some time to calm down. I had learned that day to be not a victim any longer; and I learned something else, something what I have memorized for the rest of my life. As long as the malicious guys on the block do not have to fear the same harm they do to others—most of the time weaker than they are—as long as nobody stands up to them, they always win. But as soon as you answer them with their own recklessness they quit and run. I learned that the only language evil understands is the same language they like to use. I know that is somewhat not according to the teaching Jesus did, but I strongly believe that life, liberty, and the pursuit of happiness are God-given rights, and that every single human being has the right to defend himself, even by the use of force.

Never again did anybody try to harm me or Michael. We were not mocked, or teased, or name called, nothing. The next day when I came into the classroom Hartmut was sitting in his place, his chin was still swollen and begun to color. When I reached my place right in front of him, everybody held his breath, because they believed that he would beat me up like never before. But to the contrary, he stretched out his hand, and I took it more automatically than thinking about it. He said he was sorry and I said it too. And that was it. Although the theme of every single break for several days was how I did knockout two of the most feared guys at the school, I did not take much pride in it, because after it became known at home, I was locked in my room after school for weeks.

And another difference to all those health resort trips became obvious. My mother declared that she had found her sister, which she was missing since 1935 when her family was separated due to the death of her mother. As far as I understood it was her youngest sister. She had been adopted by a family living on the largest island of Germany, Rügen, in a small village near the town Saßnitz. On Christmas of 1968 Uncle Egon and Aunt Ruth came visiting us at Reupzig, and during that visit my mother and they negotiated our move to their village. Many months later I discovered the conditions for that move. Because we did not have any money to finance a move of a complete household with six children, Connie was in apprenticeship at that time, our family had to contribute to the costs. My uncle and aunt were both working at the agricultural cooperative at their village and the house we would move into was owned by them and would be renovated by their workers and on their costs. My mother had to sign an agreement to work at the agricultural cooperative and so would my sister Connie.

Connie was actually taken out of school in summer 1967 and sent to be trained as an assistant nurse at a hospital, owned by the East German Lutheran Church. To be able to close the deal she had to leave that apprenticeship and went to work for the agricultural production cooperative at that village where we would move, because the house we would live in needed major repairs. But the deal was made and right after New Year, Connie was sent up to the north to become a nobody in that village, working for the LPG. Then early in spring, I think it was the beginning of March, because there was still snow in some corners of the farmstead, we began to pack our stuff for the move to the island. It was the main topic of any conversation day and night, because we children were very curious about what we had to expect. I think it's always a special feeling when you suddenly discover that there are people in this world who happen to be your cousins and you had no idea about their existence. And it's still the same today. I had that feeling when I first time talked to my cousins in Cincinnati in 2003, children of my Uncle Harry the baby brother of my mother. And I had the same feeling when I talked for the first time in my life with my cousin Ingrid in September 2010, the daughter of my father's sister Irene, whom I found in Rio Rancho, NM.

Island Ruegen

MOVING TO THE ISLAND

Sunday School Was Not on Sundays and the Main Theme Wasn't the Bible

T HAT DAY WHEN the moving trucks arrived, we did not go to school. Although we had been preparing for the move for quite some time, there was still a lot to do. At that time in early 1968 the overall situation had improved, but there were still shortages on many things you'd need. Moving material, such as boxes or stuff to wrap fragile things like dishes or glass in weren't available at all. Over several weeks we had started to pack and wrap all kind of stuff. Everything that could break during transport needed to be wrapped into old newspapers. This wasn't really something that Michael and I liked to do, but there was no escape and we had to help get things prepared.

Since Connie wasn't there and I was the oldest of the children I had most of the load on my shoulders to get it done. And I could really count only on Michael since the other siblings were Andreas 7, Susanne 6, Matthias 2 and our youngest sister Gundula less than a year of age. It was a terrible time, and it became even more loaded when my mother came from work and saw the small progress we had on some of the days. And then the day was there.

The trucks arrived late in the evening; I believe it was a Friday. Early in the morning we began to load everything on the trucks. Now, don't consider those trucks normal moving trucks. No way! Those were normal transportation trucks with a three-seat cabin a tarp over the load compartment, and each truck was towing a trailer which was also covered with a tarp. We had to move the coal out of the basement and load it onto one of the trailers, and that was the job for me and Michael and it took us nearly the whole day. But it was necessary because coal for private purposes were highly subsidized according to the family size and the reduction of the purchase price of nearly 90 percent was only once per year available. We would not be able to afford to buy unsubsidized coal.

Since we never had enough money when needed it, we had bought only common brown coal instead of the coal briquettes. It was a dirty work since it was already falling apart and a great deal was just dust. When we were done and all the stuff was somewhat spread over the two trucks and the trailers we went to *bed*, sleeping on our mattresses with some blankets and because of the cold weather kept our clothes on. Early in the morning our mattresses were placed on one of the trucks cargo area where the adults had formed a specific place to keep Michael and I secure from the head wind. Everybody entered the trucks, and our ten-hour trip to the north began.

The first hours we were still tired enough just to sleep with some interruptions when the trucks slowed down or had to stop completely. After a little more than two hours we entered the Autobahn and the travel speed became more consistent. When we left the Autobahn after noon we had a lunch break, and without any additional breaks we drove straight to our new living place. It was already dark when we arrived and unloaded only the real necessary things for the night. Next morning at daylight Michael and I began to check the near surroundings of the house and found out that there was a barn with several additional spaces as well as a large garden and a small forest through which the walkway went towards the street. We had not much time and were soon called back to help unload the stuff and bring everything to its place.

This wasn't as easy as it first looked like because half of the house was still under renovation. The rooms for the children, beside that for Michael and me, weren't ready to move in, and while we were carrying stuff in masons and painters were still at work. They weren't really happy because we were continuously interfering with their work. It took several more days till we came to a regular life. In the mean time Michael and I had the opportunity to arrange our stuff in our own room, which was an attic conversion, and we were almost separate from all the others. Now we still had to go through the main entrance to get upstairs to our room, but soon we realized that it was very easy to jump out the window.

We met our cousins, Norbert and Jürgen. Norbert was almost a year younger than me and Jürgen about two years younger than Michael. After a few days of gauging each other, we somewhat connected. Although we did a lot of activities together over the next several years, we never really became close friends as we had been with our gang of four in Reupzig. Norbert and I developed a kind of a friend-enemy relationship affected by a permanent rivalry at school. It just happened to be that we were at the same class. Michael and I begun discovering the environment of our new home together. That wasn't really easy because there were certain circumstances we had to get used to. First of all there was the way to school. Not only was it approximately a mile longer, roughly 3.5 miles, it was hills up and hills down. And there wasn't any kind of public traffic at all.

The village we lived in now wasn't really a village. It was a small settlement with double houses. And about three quarters of a mile further up the road was the former manor house where the squire lived before the Russian Army came. The communists took over the land and the house, and for the first couple of years refugee families lived there until they could move on. They did not take much care about, and as everywhere material and qualified workers were rare, and with that the huge manor house, once a symbol of the Rügen manor-house architecture, was about to fall apart. The roof leaked on all ends and only a few rooms were still usable.

An old man lived there. He was very embittered and never spoke to us more than bad words to scare us away. The part of the building we lived in was the former house of the gardener. And since it was actually an extension of the whole manor house, just somewhat smaller, it took us not long to find a way through the attic and some holes in the walls to get onto the attic of the manor house. That was like a treasury place for us and we found newspapers from 1934 to 1936. Unfortunately the leaks in the roof had done a lot of damage to those newspapers and all we could read were fragments. But it was very interesting to read that stuff and to find out how the newspapers were at that time. Here it was when I found out that in 1936 the so-called *Rügendammbrücke* (bridge that connects the island Rügen with the mainland) was the first bridge of that size completely welded, made only from steel and not riveted. It was an amazing story how the engineers fought to get the technology right and convince the administration that it would hold. This actually created that thought in my mind to become an engineer and build bridges. However, I could never realize that dream because you couldn't just become what you want in a central-controlled dictatorship. At this time I did not know about that.

To the house we lived now belonged also a large garden and a barn which could accommodate livestock and had an attic for straw and hey. Since the drainage system out of the house wasn't done when we moved in, we still had to use the outhouse, but that wasn't really a problem, we were used to it. The drainage system was never finished and the situation became more difficult some years later when suddenly the water well did run dry. The whole area we lived in was enclosed with a large forest called the Stubnitz. There were huge, very old beech trees as far as the eye could see, and the distance between our house and the forest was occupied by huge open mining chalkstone diggings. Several were already abandoned and full of water, but the current digging was large, and the operation was going on 24/7. A narrow gauge train system was used to transport the chalkstone to the plant where it was processed and almost 80 percent of it was exported.

Over a couple of weeks we had settled in and life began to normalize. We would all wake up as early as 5:30 a.m. to get ready for school, and since my mother had to be at the agricultural cooperation at 7:00 a.m., where she had to work according to the agreement, it was always somewhat hectic to get my seven-year-old stepbrother Andreas and my six-year-old stepsister Susanne ready to leave with us. My mother would take care of the babies and take them to the *Kintergarten* (German for childcare). We needed to take care of Andreas and Susanne because they could not walk that distance to school all by themselves even though their school started sometime an hour or even two later than ours. We had to take extra care in winter time, when icy winds were blowing over the top of the hills we were walking along until we could reach the cover of the forest, where the road lead down the hill into the city Saßnitz.

A few weeks after we started there at school the great event took place. My cousin Norbert and I as well as all classmates had *Jugendweihe* (roughly translated as youth dedication). This was, and to a certain degree still is, an East German phenomenon. It was adopted in 1954 in the GDR as an obligatory pledge to socialism, displacing the Christian rite of confirmation. We had all to wear suits, and the ceremony was at the grand hall of the cinema since none of the schools in town had a hall big enough to hold all the students and their relatives.

All students of the 8th grade of all schools were seated in the front rows, and every principal of the schools would give a speech about the new status we were about to enter and that we were now considered adults and that we had to prove ourselves worthy to be a part of the collective of the socialistic fatherland and so on. That took about two hours until we were called to come up to the stage. Seven at a time we would stand on stage while a student from the senior class of the respective school would read the oath and we would confirm the oath by saying *Ja das geloben wir* (German for "Yes, we pledge that").

Students from I believe 5th grade would than present a book with the title *Weltall Erde Mensch* (German for "Universe Earth Men") to each of us and that was it, at least for the official part. After the ceremony all the families would have a festive dinner, and you would get some presents from your relatives and by tradition it was money. Since this was a rare thing in my family at all time, it wasn't much I expected to get and so it was.

Then there was another tradition. This was the time when the newly defined adults were introduced officially to hard liquor because you were now an adult. This was horrible for me because I did not like it at all. Too many bad experiences were connected to alcohol and burned into my mind. But I could not refuse the glass with korn presented to me by my uncle because he was a very dominant man and lost easily his temper. I drank one glass and was able to empty two or three more into the flower pot beside the chair. I actually did not check if the flowers survived, but that was my lowest concern. When I finally got out there into fresh air, I already had difficulty. I went home and that was it.

As soon as the Youth Dedication was done, my cousins' grandma insisted in having the real thing also, not only that bogus socialistic copy. What she meant was confirmation. Since we all were Lutheran and baptized, she insisted on having Lutheran confirmation too. My mother actually had no opinion at all because over all the years her focus was switching continuously between being totally compelled by the communists—she actually applied for membership in the party and was refused—and wanting to go to church, which only happened sporadically. And my uncle and aunt fiercely denied.

My cousins' grandma, living in the house with them together, actually had some wealth. We wouldn't consider it much today, but under the GDR situation, it was something since it was jewelry and some high valued stones, as I learned later. She had secured all of that during the escape before the approaching Russian troops from East Prussia to the island Rügen. The debates over the issue of whether there should be confirmation for the boys or not became intensive over the next couple of weeks. One of these debates was going on when I was at their house to finish some mathematic homework with Norbert.

The argument became loud, and I could hear my uncle say, "I don't believe in those fairy tales, and that book is just a bunch of phony stories written by greedy priests to make people pay for their expensive lifestyle! And I don't want my boys to be confused with that stuff!"

Grandma was a small person and already in her eighties, but she was resolute, and when she had a specific opinion, she wouldn't move for anything. This day I thought for a moment that there was a different person in that argument. With a loud and certain voice, she answered, "It's up to you. I'll sell my stuff and give the money to the church! Then you don't need to wonder any longer how much it might be worth!" That was probably the signal for my uncle and aunt to cave in and agree, but not without negotiating some conditions. He said, "Okay, I'll let them go to that stupid thing and make myself a laughing stock, but one condition, that education hours are held here at the settlement not to lose more time than necessary." And with that it was sealed.

Each family with at least one member working at the agricultural cooperative had at least two to three pigs, several chickens, geese and sometimesrabbits. That meant that every child had to help with the work those animals caused, and it wasn't little. Usually two to three hours after school were necessary to get done what was on our list. Since the LPG members got allowance in all kind of forage crops such as low-quality potatoes, wheat, barley, fodder beet and so on, we were able to raise some swine, and at least one got butchered for the family. And in some years additionally we had two meat cattle, which were sold in fall to the one or two privately owned butcheries still existing on the island. And last, but not least because we liked the meat very much, at least a dozen geese and ducks, as well for a couple of years several dozen rabbits. That required a lot of work after school. It began by firing up the huge cooking pot, which was built in a separate room beside the stables. It was a huge feed boiler formed as half spherical and set in stone. We would fill the boiler with potatoes and water and cook them. Then we would smash them and mix them with oatmeal and feed it to the swine. For the rabbits we would have to go out to the grassland and cut fresh grass, and that was not easy since I was still too small to handle a scythe correctly.

Since Uncle Egon was with the agricultural cooperative for many years and had a very high rank there as one of the most respected foreman, he had many more animals then we and with that our cousins Norbert and Jürgen had much more work to do. But they had also more technical equipment, such as an electrical heated potato cooker, and with that it took them not much longer to get it done than Michael and me. And then there was another advantage they had. My uncle had years ago discovered a source for fish offal. Saßnitz had one of the largest production facilities for fish conserves. By the way they still produce fish conserves and you can buy them in the US. He had done somebody some favors, and for that this someone owed him. Since this someone worked at that facility and was responsible for the treatment of the fish offal—practically everything you'd remove from a fish before you'd put it into a conserve—he became the source of extremely cheap swine food. Normally this someone had to operate all that fish offal through a special heat treatment process which dried out the offal and then it was ground and sold.

Since nobody was able to control the amount of fish offal converted into fish meal, my uncle got twice a week enough fish offal to feed his 6-8 swine with that stuff. With that the feeding of the swine was as easy as it gets for my cousins. The only problem was the extremely rotten stink they gave off when we met after the work was done. As long as we were able to play outside it wasn't a problem and the smell gradually disappeared after a while. As everybody did, we also butchered one pig for us, and all other animals were sold, including the cattle. And next spring, everything began again. One day I asked my uncle if the meat of his pigs would not taste like fish. And he said no, because that's the reason why we stop feeding fish offal 4-6 weeks before we sell them. Actually early in summer he would decide which one of the pigs would be the house butcher pig and that one would never get fish offal. The same was with the chicken, ducks, and geese. Those for the families were separated and fed with wheat. All the others got fish meal, and believe me, the eggs from those chicken had a defined taste.

FREEDOM'S NIGHTMARE

Now, all this work was in jeopardy because grandma insisted that the boys have confirmation, and for that they needed to be educated. But with that compromise my uncle and grandma had achieved, the loss of working hours of my cousins was reduced to an acceptable minimum. Once a week a young pastor from the church in town would come up to our settlement and try to teach us for two hours about the Bible, Jesus and why it mattered to know about all of that. That meant that my uncle could not stop at the tavern and down some beer with korn—a hard liquor made from wheat. He had to go straight home to feed the animals. And he did not really like it, but the alternative wasn't wise. If he would have ever been able to sneak into the room where we had the lessons in biblical education, he would have probably dropped dead.

The main objective of that youth pastor wasn't really to get us much educated, but to get spare parts for his bicycle or stuff he needed to repair something else. He offered trading cards of West German soccer players, which were an absolute novelty for us. Since we wanted them seriously, we would try everything to get the stuff he would change for them. I remember that one day he needed a new dynamo because his was burned out. He had probably forgotten to take it off the wheel when he rode his bicycle downhill the last steep part of the road into town. I knew that happened because I had that experience with my mother's bicycle one day and the dynamo virtually disintegrated, and I could just avoid plunging and killing myself. It was somewhat dangerous to ride downhill that steep road, covered with cobblestones and very badly maintained without light, but with good brakes and a little luck it worked out.

The education time was finally coming to an end, and with four weeks to go it was decided that we had to be trained about the whole procedure in church so that we would know what to do when and where. The senior pastor did almost lose his temper when he discovered the depth of our knowledge, or better the non existence of knowledge at all about the things we should know after almost four months of teaching. With that we had four weeks of intense teaching two times two hours, plus, per week right after school. We finally had our confirmation Sunday, and together with several other children from town we had our question and answer session, which went pretty well to the relief of the pastor. The few people who still attended church, mostly at the same age as my cousins' grandma, were happy, smiled at us, as the pastor handed everybody a New Testament with the Psalms and Proverbs included and then it was over.

I can't remember why Michael and I walked home by ourselves and not with our relatives and whether or not my mother was even there. On the way home, right after we had walked up that steep part of the road, where the cobblestone part ended and gave way to a dusty, or muddy, depending on the weather, farm road, there was a rather large brush. We had talked all the way since church about what an insane stuff that all was and why we even bothered to talk about all that and now since we had it behind us, we could go on with life, real life. Right at that place in front of that brush I committed one of the ugliest sin I did in my whole life. Not knowing that it was a sin or what sin really meant or why it should even count at all, I threw the New Testament as far as I could into the brush. Then I turned around and asked Michael, "You want to keep it and read it and become a pussy like that priest?" He took his New Testament and threw it into the brush too. I have to confess that at that moment, I really meant it.

Indoctrination qua Education

Education or Better Indoctrination or Are Teachers Actually Party Propagandists?

I was already on my way to becoming one of the best students in my class, and the socialistic/communistic doctrine taught was easy for me to pick up and repeat at any given time without problems. Within a few months, I had erased all the bad grades I had gotten in Reupzig and was second in mathematics, physics, biology, history, and geography. My year-end report card had already four A grades where at the last year were only D grades. None of the teachers had a specific antipathy against us, and with the ability to pick up most of the topics easily, I had real fun again going to school. My favorite school subjects were German literature and physics. German literature was about reading books and memorizing poems and ballads. And again I could indulge in my love of reading books. I became the horror of the women at the city's library. Every Tuesday after school I would walk into the library and seldom would I leave with less than five books.

Although the East German centralized school system favored Johann Wolfgang Goethe (the peerage had been preventively eliminated) our teacher loved the works of Friedrich Schiller and so did I. I almost enjoyed memorizing Schiller's ballads such as the "The Diver," "The Song of the Bell," and "The Hostage." What a joy was it to debate the intentions of

Schiller with his plays, such as *The Robbers*, or *Intrigue and Love*, *Mary Stuart*, *The Maid of Orleans*, or with intense persuasion the proposition of Schiller with his play *Wilhelm Tell*. That play gave me a specific opportunity to argue with my teacher about ways to change oppressive or unjust situations.

During several lesson hours we reasoned back and forth whether you have to be part of a system to change it, "*Change from Within*," or to be outside and act as a Rebel, "*Fight from Outside*," with the attempt to avoid contamination by the wrong system and the protagonist itself. We had hours of reasoning—even after the lesson hour was over for that day—whether or not the submissive rejection of the music instructor Miller for the attempt of the nobleman Ferdinand von Walter to marry his daughter or, as I preferred, the firing squad massacre on those Hessian-Germans who refused to serve the British against the Revolution in America, was the real focus of the play.

My German teacher was as most of the teachers were, a member of the SED, yet she was very interested in encouraging her students to debate issues controversial to the socialistic doctrine of a just society. She was a good-looking woman in her mid-forties, and contrary to her husband, our music teacher, she enjoyed a huge sympathy of the students. She never needed to be loud or correct even the worst characters we had in our class. During the often heated discussion I never realized that most of the other students either didn't follow our dispute at all or participated more or less halfheartedly. I tended to prefer the system change from within, while she vehemently defended the position the "*changer from outside*" represented.

Slowly but steadily I grew into an advocate of the idea that you have to be on the inside to be able to change the bad things in an otherwise great philosophy as I saw it then. She always reasoned with the concern of being contaminated by the system before you're able to change it when you're a part of it. It was always friendly and never aggressive, and that's why I many years later when I met her in a then free East Germany I was actually surprised that she was totally embittered about the collapse of the communist system in East Germany. I came to the conclusion that her real attempt was to build a better Germany after the catastrophic results of the Second World War and she was disappointed with the first attempt, equal

FREEDOM'S NIGHTMARE

to East Germany, and probably much more about the loss of the second chance. When the East German communistic system collapsed many of the citizens, mainly the members of the SED, believed they would have a new chance to build a better Germany and were totally disappointed that the mass of the people had enough of social engineering experiments.

The school subject *Philosophy of Socialism* started and was something special. This was not only because it was the subject where I did not need to pay much attention at all but because of the teacher. She was a tall person, often with not matching clothing, which I did not discover but was the permanent issue discussed among the girls during breaks. She had a rather masculine facial expression which mirrored perfectly her deep voice. And she spattered when she spoke, and that resulted in empty two front rows in her lessons. Although Immanuel Kant was the clear favored philosopher together with George W. F. Hegel and Ludwig Feuerbach, we were led to the final development of Marxism and Leninism, Karl Marx, Friedrich Engels, and the leader of the Russian revolution W. I. Lenin, whose real name actually was Uljanow.

Reading the required literature and understanding the take of it for the justification of a revolutionary uproar either bloody as in Russia or as tried in Germany after the failure of Germany in World War One, or just by gaining majority through the democratic system was relatively easy for me. I struggled for a while with the general line of the teaching that after the conquest of the political power through the use of the democratic system or through a bloody revolution, the opposition needed to be eliminated. Since there was enough evidence that this wasn't done according to their own teaching, I considered the revolutionaries not much better than their adversaries. To my surprise the teacher accepted that point of view arguing that they had no choice. To prove her point she developed the situations with the failure of revolutionary attempts throughout history, beginning with the rebellion of the Gladiators against the Roman Empire, the failed peasant uprising in Germany, the failure of the German Revolutions of 1848 and 1918. History teaches that if you come to power and you fail to secure it by eliminating your enemies, you will fail to keep power sooner or later. Very quickly I realized that she wasn't really interested in a controversial dispute, and since most of my classmates weren't interested in that at all, I just said what she wanted to hear and wrote in tests what was required and that was it.

Since the communist party who ran the show everywhere no matter what corner of our lives were not really interested in an opposition either, I decided to go along. That gave me the opportunity to read books during those lesson hours which stretched out to two times two hours a week. I moved to the last row and there to the wall lane. Since I was a good student with very good grades, the bad guys who were usually sitting in that area welcomed me. My neighbor's grades increased dramatically and our teacher appreciated that since she thought he was inspired by me to learn better about the subject. Actually, all he did was copyi my notes and my writings during the test. Those were actually the years when my opinion about the philosophy of *Changing from Within* strengthened my determination to become a member of the party myself and then work together with likeminded members—which I definitely believed were in there—to change the party to accept more individual freedom. Because that was what I really took from those disputes with my German Literature teacher, that by all necessary need for order and justice, the freedom of the single individual to determine his own future was the basis for the unfolding of the human possibility to reach his highest potential. I could not understand at this time why a party which was so determined to free the workers class from the yoke of oppression would do so and at the same time put oppression onto the same people by denying them their individualism. Although most of my classmates did not have the same philosophical understanding, and actually they rolled their eyes when I tried to reason with them. These were friends.

Nearly all of them had their fathers working at the fishing cooperative, and with that they had access to goods from West Germany, which were sold at so-called Duty-Free shops. You needed a special printed paper, which was called *Devisen* and represented the allowance fishermen got for days at sea. Depending on your rank on a fishing vessel you would get a certain amount per day as soon as the vessel left the three-mile zone. Based on this many of my classmates and friends had access to literature, clothing and other stuff I had never seen before we moved to the island. Especially the literature, which included everything from Mickey Mouse through mail order catalogues to cowboy stories called *Westerns, which were* highly sought after and would be exchanged secretly against newer ones or whatever was worth to be given for it. When you were able to get into one of those exchange circles, you could have a new trashy book every week. As long as adults did that and kept their mouth shut everything was okay. But some of my classmates had the ability to capture trashy books from their parents when they were through with them and they came back from the exchange round.

Those books became a part of the exchange at school, and that was dangerous. The socialistic propaganda considered those books *Schund- und Smutzliteratur* (German for pulp fiction or trashy literature), and having that at school get you at least a rebuke. Since those had to be signed by the parents, it was not an easy task. That was because the parents would not only get to see that rebuke and had to sign it, but the school would also inform the supervisor of the collective at the workplace. And because of that your parents would be an item on the agenda for the next collective meeting. Since the upbringing and teaching of your children in the spirit of Marx, Engels and Lenin towards an adequate member of the future socialistic society was part of the collective's assessment for the year-end ranking among all the collectives throughout the company, your parents were in big trouble. It could mean not to get the expected pay raise, or not to get the holiday place at the highly subsidized vacation home owned and administrated by the Free German Union (FDGB). And then you were really in trouble.

Knowing about the far-reaching consequences, everybody handled this issue with highest care. At minimum once a month without any notice, the principal or the vice principal would appear in the middle of a lesson hour and everyone had to empty his book bag onto the desk and they, the principal and teacher, would go through the rows on their hunt for that moral- and ethics-decaying trash. In case somebody had a book with him, we would all work together to move it around behind the back's of the teachers, and I can actually remember on two occasions that somebody was caught at another class, never in our class though.

Generally, the struggle against the infiltration of the minds of the socialistic future workers class with western, equals to capitalistic ideas and lifestyle, was a permanent, never-ending activity of a certain agency within the central controlled education system. I remember a specific lesson for which we had visitors from the district city. They brought special equipment which our school did not have and demonstrated how brain damaging it was when we would listen to the music of bands from the western world. Another interesting lesson with specialists from the State Security Police—they were officially from the education department under agency at the district city—was about to be alert for imperialistic provocateurs and terrorists. Especially on the eve of a possible invasion, the imperialistic aggressor would try to destroy precious infrastructure and facilities. One of the men tried to ease the situation a little since nobody dared to say even one word, because we knew whom we had as guests. So this guy asked a question, saying: "What facilities in your environment here in Saßnitz do you believe would the aggressor love to conquer and need our special defense?" After a few minutes of hesitation and some glares from our teacher, classmates begun to list facilities such as the Saßnitz harbor and the Fish processing plant. Suddenly my desk neighbor, whom I never saw to lift even a finger, certainly not in *Philosophy of the Socialism*, was waving his arm straight in the air. In absolute disbelief I looked at him and then at the teacher and saw her face switching between joy over his sudden awakening and fear of what might come out of this, and before she could do anything to stop what was coming, the guy from the *Indoctrination Group* called him.

"Now, what do you think the imperialistic aggressor is keen on?" he asked.

And my neighbor with the innocent air of a little child said, "The pigpen in Lancken." The whole class exploded in laughter and jubilation for several minutes, and it took all the might of the teacher's angry voice to get the class calm down.

The guy from the Stasi crew did not really know what hit him and tried to put a good face on the matter. "Thank you, but I meant more valuable installations or equipment," he said.

Whereon my classmate answered, "I don't know anything about a more valuable installation, because my father always says that if somebody gets his hands on that pigpen, we're toast. I think that does mean it's pretty valuable, doesn't it?" Again enormous laughter brought the class-room into turmoil.

To the great relief of the two guys and our teacher the break bell rang at that same second and I never saw people, including our teacher, leaving the classroom at that speed. To understand what was so extremely funny you needed to know that on one hand it was ridiculed at all that the imperialistic aggressors would want to have any of the plants or facilities in our area. On the other hand it was for sure based on the general condition of that pigpen. It was the most derelict, dirtiest, and closest to the structural collapse than any other building in the whole community. He actually meant that they're toast if anybody saw that hulk, because it would surely be demolished. And that was all his family was able to do.

Another indication of how deeply involved in the indoctrination of the centralized education system teachers really were, was the way I was able to get the necessary permission by the Stasi for higher education and to get the degree I wanted to have. Although my dream was to build bridges ever since I had read the article at that old news paper from 1934 about the *Ruegendamm* bridge, I knew that was an unrealizable dream. During the last years of high school I developed the idea to become a professional for cooling systems and use the centralized education system to get my degree through the local fishing company. That would ensure that I could go to sea. But when it finally was time to apply for the study, the local fishing company did not send students to specific education anymore. They proposed to become a professional electrician, and I thought that was a good alternative. Every time you applied for something, your supervisor had to write an appraisal. Usually it started with a hymn of the great leader of the communistic party, and at the time it was written for me they were still feeding upon the eighth party conference and the great speech the leader had given there. Then they listed all your positives and whatever you had on negatives. And that was for your whole lifestyle, your personal abilities, and operational skills as well as your environment such as what your family looked like and what people you chose to spend your spare time. And then the most important part and most likely extended over a couple of pages was your stance towards the communistic party, the communistic society and so on. All that had to be backed up with examples. And it was required that the supervisor did that every year.

All of those appraisals defined me as a first class communist, well educated with an incredible knowledge of the literature of the Marxism-Leninism and an outstanding ability to lead in terms of the communistic party. I wrote my application, and because of a very favorable opinion I got from my teachers, and, as I would discover many years later, very positive backgrounds check by the STASI, I was invited to an interview. And I think it was never the intention of the communist party in power to hide the propaganda part of the job of a teacher. It was actually an intense part of their education and study to be efficient in that part besides teaching the subject. You'd never graduate from a teacher seminar if you did not have excellent grades in all the political subjects, required as a must at those universities. And based on that, the students were used in any political aspect the communist party saw necessary. I remember that one year we started to write picture postcards to the American President. Now that was something. And we did not do this because we loved the American President. And those postcards did not show a nice view of our little town and we did not invite the President to honor us with his visit.

The postcard showed a picture of the so-called innocent fighter for freedom and antiracism Angela Davis, as we were told. She was imprisoned on a false accusation of murder. Because she was a member of the Communist Party of the United States and was fighting against the racist government, the FBI director J. E. Hoover—which is by the way one of the most hated men of the East German communists—had fabricated false evidence in a murder case and she was threatened to be murdered by the injustice system of the US. This action was nationwide organized and highly supported by the political organizations. I think we wrote three or four of those cards over a period of several months. And the efforts were successful. Sometimes in 1972 she appeared on East German TV together with the General Secretary Erich Honnecker and received great honor throughout the communist bloc. And in 1973 she appeared at the *World Festival of the Youth and Students* stage together with several revolutionary elements from around the world. Years later, I had completely forgotten about that, and when I started to write this book I discovered that we actually helped to free a woman who was actively involved in supplying the arms which were used to kill a judge and several other people. And more surprised was I that she had become a distinguished Professor Emeritus at the college of Santa Cruz, CA.

HARALD ZIEGER

A Mailman, a Long Morning Break and Why They Hate Dogs or the Other Way Around

Although I loved school and enjoyed physics and mathematics, as well as geography, biology, and history, chemistry was a riddle wrapped in an enigma. I can't really say why it was but I never could get my mind around the mol and all those chemical formulas. (The mole is widely used in chemistry instead of units of mass or volume as a convenient way to express amounts of reactants or of products of chemical reactions. For example, the chemical equation $2 H2 + O2 \rightarrow 2 H2O$ implies that 2 mol of dihydrogen (H2) and 1 mol of dioxygen (O2) react to form 2 mol of water (H2O). It was easy to learn the periodic tables of the elements, but that was it. Maybe it was because for about half a year we did not have a teacher, and when the lessons finally started again, the teacher was returned from retirement, could badly hear what you said and after the first experience with the ignorant and badly behaving students he just gave up. It was actually the only subject where the students did not have any kind of respect or fear.

He wrote on the blackboard while telling the secrets behind the hiero-glyphic characters but nobody really tried to understand. Even though you'd like to understand what he was trying to teach, you could barely hear him because the class was noisy and he spoke to the blackboard. There was all kind of stuff going on behind his back. Some made their homework for the next subject, some were talking about what they would do after school, some were reading books, like I did, and there were actually some who tried to follow the teacher. He did get our attention at least regularly at the end of each month when the monthly test was coming up and he started the lessons with the sentence: *Today we will recapitulate what we have learned, or better what you should have learned during the last weeks.* That was the point when everybody put aside whatever he or she was doing and listened and tried to get at least a clue what this subject was all about. So did I. But as said before, I somehow had extreme difficulties understanding all those mol and spin and I can't even remember what else. Years later at the Institute of Technology, I had to write a thesis in material science and I had to relearn the hard way what I missed in those years. Another part of the lessons to get our complete attention was when he demonstrated the aftermath of chemical reactions when you went on to combine certain substances either in the right way, or what could happen if you did it the wrong way.

With all the work around our house and the animals and the garden, we were quite busy and usually had not much time for playing in the woods, but when we were able, we had the best playground a boy could find in the world. That forest behind the chalk extraction was large and we had plenty of room to build huts. But it became more and more rare since were growing up and getting more loaded with homework. On weekends we played soccer and when temperature allowed went swimming at the water-filled unused chalk extraction lakes, although it was strictly forbidden.

One day on my way home from school I suddenly heard somebody talking aloud in front of me and the voice sounded very familiar. I accelerated, and when I came around the corner, I saw Michael standing in the middle of that dusty farm road talking to a dog which was sitting right in front of him. It was a male German shepherd, black with some brownish-yellowish stains around his nose and eyes. The dog was obviously very interested in what Michael had to tell him, because his had was moving from one side to the other, while his ears where straight up. No, that wasn't right; only one ear was straight up, the other one was bent sideward, which gave him a funny appearance.

I closed in on both and asked Michael, "What is going on with this dog?"

"This dog followed me since I left town and I can't get it to turn around and leave," he answered.

I said, "He might be hungry and need some food."

Michael replied, "If we take the dog home with us our mother will just explode."

"We don't need to tell her, we just give the dog something to eat and send him away," was my answer.

Michael asked, "How? If he won't stay back now, he won't leave from home either."

Tired of the discussion about what could or could not happen, I moved on, pulling Michael with me, and we started to walk towards our settlement because I thought the dog would just stop following us. That didn't work well; he just kept following at a certain distance. We finally decided to take the dog with us and reasoned that when it had eaten it would probably run away anyway. What a huge mistake that was.

While walking home, we puzzled about his name and tried to call him by several of the typical names Germans in our area would give to dogs, but nothing changed. Anytime we said a name we looked over our shoulders to see how he reacted, but he was just trailing behind at a constant distance. I can't recall who it was, but when we called out the name *Harras* to our surprise he accelerated and within a second was on our side and kept there like a very well trained dog. We looked at each other and that was the moment we decided that, if there was nobody reclaiming Harras as his own, we would keep him no matter what our mother would say. At home we found some leftovers from the day before and fed Harras, and he gulped it as if he hasn't had anything for days, which was probably very close to the truth. Later we learned that one of the breeders on the island, about thirty-five kilometers from our place, who was famous for breeding dogs for Police and Army, had excluded Harras because of the difficulties he had to uplift his right ear. The dog escaped on the transport to a medical testing lab and was straying around for several weeks when we finally took him in. That was actually the point when my mother stopped insisting that we gave the dog away.

Soon we discovered that Harras was a very well trained dog and mastered the subordination commands with excellence. I began to go to the dog training, which was organized by the police of Saßnitz, and since one of my classmates was the daughter of the chief of police in our town, I got allowance to go with Harras through the full training the K9 unit would do with their dogs. And he did great. The only flaw he really showed was patience. He just had none. When we went through the exercise where one of the policemen would wear all those security clothes to illustrate the bad guy, it was enough for Harras to see the guy taking the stuff from the ground to get dressed and he would just storm to attack if I would not keep him down. It took several exercises to get him to a point to wait for the command to attack the *gangster* instead of attacking the guy in the same second he began running away. Another exercise was called *Stellen und*

Verbellen, which meant to pin the subject into a corner and bark, but don't attack. The last part of that command did never enter Harras's mind. The trainer put a plastic foil onto the ground and a piece of chicken fence over it. They connected a hand generator with one wire to a piece of chicken wire and the other to ground and wet the ground and the wire. I had Harras sitting on my left side as a required position, and when I gave the command and one of the trainers would crank the generator. That did not impressed Harras at all. He jumped on that wire and onto the arm of the imitator gangster and would shake him as much as he could, ignoring the current through his body between his forelegs on the chicken wire and his hind legs on the ground completely. Only after the generator was screwed onto a table and two men were cranking the generator together with all the speed they could would Harras finally realize that there was something that hurt him and he would begin to obey the command and stay off the guy and bark. I think it took three or four rounds for that.

He was an awesome dog and we had a lot of fun. Sometimes when somebody forget to close the yard gate, it happened that Harras would sit at the top end of that steep part of the cobblestone road and wait for me or Michael coming from school and he would joyfully jump onto us and runback and forth. But he would never hurt any other child even though we discovered that younger children going home from school would throw stones at him, which he dodged cleverly. When we played soccer I could lay down my belongings on the ground and say "Watch it, it's mine." He would lay down with his head towards the stuff and would not move a millimeter until he got a different command from me. At that point in time, not even Michael could take stuff that lay before him.

And he was very watchful when he was alone at home. That was actually administrated in a rather strange way. He wouldn't have any problem to let anybody into the yard, but never out without someone from the family accompanying this person. It happened that even my uncle had to call after one of us to get out although he was not fearful with dogs at all and most of the dogs would just show the white tail when he kicked them. He tried that once with Harras and Harras had his toe and did not want to let it go easy. He usually asked me or Michael to get him leashed. But sometimes he just forgot about it, especially when the dog wasn't visible when he arrived and when he was at the yard gate he would call for somebody to take the cur away. All that was really harmless, but one story which really brought us into trouble was when we almost lost Harras.

One day the original mail carrier was on vacation and a new, completely unknown to Harras or us, mail carrier was carrying the mail. He entered the yard, dropped the mail into the basket at the door, and turned around to leave. But there was a problem. Harras was standing right in front of him and gently snarling. He showed his perfect set of teeth. Beside the specialty of Harras to let everybody onto the yard but not away, I don't really know what it is that dogs and mail carriers have against each other. So this guy tried to use all kind of tricks to get out of the yard, but nothing worked. Harras did not really bite the mail carrier but he grabbed a couple of times his pants and pulled him back away from the gate so that the pants were finally shredded on both legs.

Sometime between 9:45 in the morning and 2:50 in the afternoon when I arrived at the scene, he gave up and set down on the stairs and waited for help. He was almost unable to talk to me because his voice was so croaky that I could barely understand his hastily announced threats. I guessed that he had screamed for help for a while before he realized that there was nobody near enough to hear him. Loaded with anger he walked away, turning around the outside corner of the open yard and almost ran into Michael who arrived from school. Looking over his shoulder Michael asked me why the mail carrier was so angry and all I could do was point to his pant legs. And without any word necessary to say he understood and we both broke out in laughter so long and heavy that it began to hurt. Harras was sitting at my feed and looked at us with that one ear up and the other one bent sideward, and he looked like he wanted to say it's not my fault, I gave him several warnings.

The summer school break wasn't far, and with that the report cards looked around the corner. Every teacher gave those who were in bad situations a chance to better their grades by either working a specific assignment or preparing for an oral exam in front of the class. Those oral exams were frequently chosen because you did not have to write too much and could use your talent to talk yourself around when you did not know the answer to a question. The assignments required the students to study intensely a specific assigned theme, to elaborate an article about it, present the findings in front of the class and answer questions from the teacher as well as the students. Since I was able to balance my weakest subject grades chemistry at a C, I wasn't quested to do any additional test or assignment. One of my classmates asked me for help with mathematics and physics, and twice a week for about two months I went with him to his home after school. Volker was a very silent, introverted boy and his passion was playing Handball. He was almost a head taller than I and was really good at it, actually so good that he played at the district team in our age bracket. He was an only child, and when he was a little boy his father had been lost at sea. His father was only one of many fishermen to whom this had happened, and though modern technology had reduced the life-threatening hazards of the work dramatically, it was still a risky job. I met his mother only two or three times because she worked as a tour guide at the local travel agency and often went on multiple day trips.

Also at that time there was a work to be done which I hated from the bottom of my heart. Every member of the agricultural cooperative had to thin out, later to weed out and then a second time to weed out one "morgen," which is approximately 1.5 acre. Since we were two, Michael and I and my sister Connie and my mother could actually come in the evening and help, and we would be done in a few days with the first step thinning.

But Connie appeared seldom since she was busy with meeting boyfriends and my mother never came to help us. And as so many times in the past she joyfully volunteered to work the mandatory acres of the cooperative leader and the party secretary and some other lazy people with enough money too. Because those people would pay a lot of money to get that hated work done by someone else and my mother always was short on money, it was the perfect fit. Not for Michael and me.

One year the field we had to work a total of 4 morgen, which totaled to 6 acres, and we had to walk about 3 miles to the field. When we came home from school, we would try to find something to eat, which often enough ended up in hopelessness, would grab the tool and march to the field. Since we did not like the work at all and had to pass the soccer field and walked by the swimming place at the chalk lake, it took us a while to get to the field. We were also not really fast in doing the work itself, and with that we were not having real progress.

The first work, thinning the plants, was necessary because the seeds were put into the earth with a machine, and many seeds were direct together the whole row. We had to decide which of the multiple plants per approximately half a food was the best and pull out all the others. And that yard for yard and hour for hour. The sun was burning down on us and we had at least three to four hours to work each day before we could consider calling it a day. The next step was weeding. A few weeks after we had finished the thinning, usually already mid of July and within the school holidays which we loved to use otherwise we would use a different tool and remove the weed between the now separated and larger beets. Since we were usually late, some of the weeds were taller then we and that wasn't really funny at all.

There was a guy on those fields all the years and he was an original character in town. Everybody knew him by the nickname Hektar, but his real name was Hering which wasn't much better because we lived in a fishing town and that was what the fishermen mostly caught at the Baltic Sea, herring in German with just one r = Hering. But nobody, and for sure not we kids or teens, would dare to tease him for his name. He was in extremely good shape and was a hard-working individual. The only "negative" was that he did not "Live to Work" as the general German attitude was. His attitude was "Work to Live." He would work on the beet fields for about three to four weeks and would clean twenty times the area we did in eight weeks if we would have to do that much. When he felt he had worked enough he would dress himself up and would be the amazement of the dance halls in our district until the money was gone. Then he would go out and look for another job nobody else would like and would finish it with persistency and endurance second to none. And the cycle would begin again.

He was always traveling around with his bicycle and that was something different. Since he was usually working from dawn to dark and sometimes even in darkness without a break longer than it takes to eat a sandwich or to have a gulp from the water buddle, he had all the stuff he needed on his carrier. Now this carrier was special. It was welded together from very thick steel bars especially for him, and the mechanic who mounted it to his bicycle had to reinforce the frame of the bicycle so that it could hold the load possible to put onto that carrier. Wherever that bicycle was parked, you knew immediately whom it belonged to.

There was a story floating around town which I never could get proof for. The story was that he once was stopping at an intersection with his bicycle standing with one foot on the back pedaling brake when a car could not stop correctly and hit the carrier of his bicycle. Standing on the back pedaling brake the bicycle was pushed somewhat forward and that was it. Because the car was just a little too fast to stop correctly, nothing really happened to Hectar or his bicycle and for sure not to his carrier. But there was a problem with the car. Since it was one of those famous East German cars, the Trabant, made from Duroplast, a composite of resin with cotton fibers or sometimes because of supply difficulties even with paper inlays, it was damaged badly. Since spare parts were rare, actually almost unavailable, that was the real calamity.

One day when I came home from school, my stepsister Susanne, she had just started first grade was sitting outside on the stairs, said, "You better don't go in there." I stopped, look down at her and was about to ask her why when the door opened and two men were carrying our TV out of the house. My mother was behind them talking about the payments she had already made and that she would pay all the rest at once. But the men were like deaf and dumb. Turned out, the TV we had gotten a few weeks before we moved away from Reupzig was bought on a payment plan.

I actually did not know that this even existed in East Germany and for sure it was in place only for a short time, because I never heard of a possibility to buy something on credit again. As far as I remember there was a short period when so-called "*kinderreiche Familien* (German for families with many children) were able to buy high-value technical goods on a payment plan. I remember that day in Reupzig very well when we got our first TV. We didn't have an antenna and we had a very bad reception with the inside antenna. But since almost everybody in Reupzig had a huge antenna on his roof, mostly built by some amateur with access to aluminum rods and steel pipes, my mother found somebody who would build one for us too. With that a few weeks later we were able to mount a huge double YAGI antenna, and with that we were able to watch West German TV also. Not in very good quality, but good enough to watch.

But this was in Reupzig. Now we were at the North-East corner of East Germany and the possibility to receive a decent West German TV signal was zero. However, at very specific weather conditions we were able to receive a strong enough TV signal from Sweden. Since nobody understood the language in our family it wasn't much influencing at all. And I think I remember correctly that most of the time it was about Swedish folk music. It was at one of those TV evenings watching Swedish TV when I saw the group ABBA the first time. They sang the song which later became one of the hits, something about the ring of a telephone. Now the TV was gone and my mother was in a very bad mood for several days. It wouldn't take her long to get a replacement though, a used TV. She loved to sit in front of the TV and watch figure skating and the TV variety shows and at the same time knitting or sewing.

A Soccer Ball and a Log Can Create a Major Change in One's Appearance

At the beginning of the new school year we began to play against a soccer team formed by the boys living at the outskirts of the city of Saßnitz. My favored position was defender, but most of the time we played 3-3-3 system with a free man behind the three defenders called sweeper, and that was what I really liked. I was well known for standing strong and not being easy to go by. Soon I got the nickname Iron Block and many strikers would just give up when I was in front of them because—although always, at least most of the time, fair—I used all kinds of tricks to separate them from the ball. One weekend we were playing and I was in my favored position playing the sweeper. The goal keeper of the other team had captured the ball and was about to kick it towards our goal. He waved with his free arm to the players of his team to move closer to our goal. Knowing that he had a real good goal-kick I walked backwards towards our goal keeping my eyes on the ball to be at the right position when it came down. At the same time I noticed the opposing striker running towards me and the possible point where the ball would hit the ground, looking every now and then over his shoulder.

He finally positioned himself in front of me just a few feet sideward on my right hand side. The ball reached its zenith and began to come down and it looked like I was standing at the right place to get it. Suddenly I saw the opposing striker moving closer to me and I knew he had a very good feeling for the ball too. And it came as it often was the case, He was just a step closer to the point than I was, which wasn't normally a problem for me to stop him. But this time it was different. When I realized that he would get his foot onto the ball before me, I did what I always did in this situation: I jumped upwards to get my head on the ball and redirect its trajectory. At the same second I realized my mistake, it was too late. The ball, made from leather and still a little heavier than normal from the play on the wet grass the day before, hit me direct center face. It was a perfect shot, and if it hadn't been for me standing, or better jumping, into its trajectory, it would have been an unstoppable shot and goal. The opposing striker was ideally positioned to hit this ball a few inches above the ground with all

175

his might by getting the ball center on his boot. I did not hit the ground with my feet. The momentum behind the hit in the center of my face was so strong that it turned me backwards and knocked me out.

I can't remember hitting the ground, but my friends told me later that I came down almost horizontal. When I regained consciousness I lay on the side of the field and all the head of the players were looking down on me. My whole face burned as I remembered from the day when I was burned from the fuel in my face, and something warm and wet ran down my cheek and into the collar of my shirt. Trying to find out what it was, still being not fully conscious I touched my nose and almost lost my consciousness again by the additional pain that touch created.

Somebody came and gave me a huge piece of fabric which I used to wipe off the blood from my cheek and neck. After a while I could sit, and several minutes later stand up and thought I could go ahead and finish the game. But only a few dribbling steps were necessary to make clear that there was no way to play another second that evening. I was sitting down and watched our team lose the game. All the time tears of pain were floating down my cheeks, and although the bleeding had stopped, I felt that my nose was swollen and was growing more and more. I knew something wasn't right with my nose because breathing became more and more difficult.

When the game was over, I said to my brother, "Michael, I need to go to the emergency room at the hospital to have somebody look at my nose."

Michael answered immediately, "I really thought you'd never say that, let's go." So we both began to walk across the city, because the hospital was on the other end of town. Harras well behaved, trotting alongside me.

When we arrived at the hospital, there was no nurse or doctor at the ambulance/emergency area. No wonder, it was Saturday evening and we were served by a Universal Healthcare System. We walked towards the desk officer's desk, where a woman was sitting and reading a newspaper. When she looked up from her reading and saw my face, we did not have to say a word.

She grabbed the phone and talked to somebody: "You need to come down to the emergency room now, because there has been an accident."

She led us into the waiting room and said, "Sit down here and wait, the doctor on call will be here in a minute."

After a few minutes a woman entered the room whom I remembered to have seen a couple of times but did not know that she was a doctor at our hospital. She looked at me and began to ask some questions, very professional and with a friendly warm voice, "How did that happen? What did you do? How long ago did it happen?"

Probably with the main reason to distract my focus from what she was about to do. She used some of those wadding rods and shoved them up into my nose, while talking to me, "It might hurt but I need stabilize the broken bone" I believe to remember she said.

That was the first time that I realized that my nasal bone was broken. I'm not sure whether it was that message or more likely the pain, but I just passed out. When I came to myself, I lay on a treatment table and all she could do was done. She was sitting on a desk and was writing the facts of that accident into my medical record.

By the way this was another specialty of the perfect organized (one of the explicit characteristics of Germans) central controlled system. The administration had every part of your life a record. Whether it was your education from kindergarten through school and university, military time over your work until your death or your health record from birth to grave, or your behavioral record from your first steps as an adult (when you received your identification card) to your death. Every single step, accident, event and incident was recorded and available to those who needed them to build their opinion about you; not everybody in the system, but you. You'd never see what was recorded about your life. Writing these lines, I tried to imagine how much longer the East-German communists would have been able to stay in power than they actually did if they had the electronic and computer systems available today.

When she was done with filling the record, she looked over to me, and recognizing that I was back into the world of hers, she said, "Sorry, I could not do much; you should have had somebody putting on a nose bandage and ice on the nose. Come back next week and I will look at it."

That was it and we could leave. Harras was patiently waiting all the time and Michael had looked after him when my treatment was done, so he was already outside of the hospital. We went back home and did not talk much. First of all I wasn't really in the mood to talk much and secondly it was already late. My mother was in a swivet when she saw my face and was actually not concerned at all that we came late and she had to do the work feeding the animals. I believe she was actually concerned, at least until another problem caught her attention. For some days I had to fight the pain in my nose every step I took besides the teasing of my classmates about all kind of reasons why my nasal bone was broken. But slowly it did get better, and at the end of that week I could breathe almost normally and could walk, even run around without pain driving tears in my eyes. Then the next weekend came.

Actually a weekend we liked every fall, because we would go into the young forest plantations with Uncle Egon and several others and would cut out the slimmer trees to lighten up the area for the better ones so that they'd have more room to grow. These were young forest plantations approximately 15 to 20 years old, and since we were in an area called the Stubnitz, all those trees were beech trees or oak trees. My uncle usually contacted the forest office late in summer and would ask for permission. He would then fill a form with the names, addresses and number persons of the families included in that permission. He would pay a relatively low fee, and we had the allowance to cut all the wood we would need to heat the homes during wintertime. While the men went in and started to cut the trees with their axes, we would just follow them and take the trees, remove the branches with a smaller hand ax and throw them onto a pile. When that pile was at a certain height and the men were moved to a certain distance we would begin to carry the trees out of the woods onto the forest road. Uncle Egon would then during the week drive there with the tractor and us boys again and bring out all the trees we had harvested and spread them evenly among the families.

Later that day, I think we were already at the third pile of trees, carrying the last pieces of them to that pile, when the final surgery on my nasal bone took place. I was on my way back into the woods and my cousin Norbert was coming in my direction with one of those trees on his shoulder passing me on my left side. That was when his dad called to him, asking something he obviously did not understand. Since Uncle Egon was working about twenty yards into the forest slightly to the back of my cousin, he made a right turn to ask his dad what he just said and that turn turned out horrible for me.

FREEDOM'S NIGHTMARE

Not paying much attention to his move, I realized that oncoming tree, with the thickness of a grown man's upper arm, too late. The tree hit me dead center on my nose and the last thing I felt before I went unconscious was a strange creaky noise inside my head. This time I woke up with blood all over my clothes, lying on the ground aside of that forest road beside the pile of trees we had carried out. My uncle, my cousins, my brother and all the men with us in the forest were standing around me and looking down on me. And with that, seeing all those faces, I was sure I was at least still alive. My uncle said something like, "See he's back; let's get to work and Harald when you have rested enough, see that you get back too. We don't have much time because winter is coming and it will be a hard one."

Everybody turned around and walked back to work, but Michael and my cousin Norbert. Norbert actually said that he was sorry and I think it was the only time I heard something like that from him. Michael tried to clean up the blood that was all over me, but I did not like it at all and began to scream in pain. I wasn't really able to see clear yet mainly because of the tears and the incredible headache I had. I might have had a light or even medium concussion, but there wasn't much room for being sorry for yourself in our family and at that time.

After a while I could sit and about half an hour later I was on my way into the woods to carry out the cleaned trees. I could not go back to join the others removing the branches because every single hit with the hand ax was as if I got hit on my nose again. And the blood began to flow from my nose again when I had to bend over to cut some branches. So I decided to just carry out the trees, and even that wasn't easy because I had to go down onto my knees without bending over, lift the tree onto my shoulder and then go up with that tree and walk it out to the forest road. When we finally got home, my mother was almost angry at my uncle for not having me brought back home so that I could see a doctor. Now it was Saturday night and there was no way to see a doctor before Monday morning. So all that could be done was cooling the nose with some cloth soaked in cold water.

Monday morning I went to the hospital and the doctor—who wasn't an otolaryngologist, but at least not gynecologist. This time he looked at my now not only swollen, but also already colored in green blue and partly yellowish nose, and said: "How long is it since this happened.

I answered, "It was on Saturday."

Whereupon he immediately said, "No, I mean the first hit." Then he looked into my health record and read for a while.

Looking at me again he said, "Lay down on that treatment table." He looked into my nose with that instrument that has a lamp build into it. I grit my teeth not to scream because the pain was horrible.

After he was done with the investigation he gave me some pain killer and said, "I can't do anything because the original crack in the nasal bone was too old and had already begun to heal, although in the wrong position and angle. I did just move it a little more sideward to make it easier for you to breathe."

He went on to say, "It is necessary that you get surgery, but your surgery will not be covered by the universal health care system. You will need to find an otolaryngologist who will do this and pay for it out of your own pocket. I can refer you to one at the city of Greifswald."

This was the nearest city with a medical university and the most recognized professors usually were allowed to have their own private practice. Although that sounded great for a second, it was impossible and I knew it immediately. We did not have the money for that and I did not bother even to tell my mother about it. My nose healed over several weeks and all I kept was a strange-looking nasal bone and difficulty to breathe while sleeping. This kind of surgery wasn't covered by the Universal Health Care system, because it was considered an aesthetic surgery. There was not coverage at all, as long as the outcome of an accident or illness did not affect functionality, meaning your ability to proceed with your job.

The next weeks during fall went on with a lot work, as hay and straw needed to be stored at the barn attic, and fodder beet and potatoes needed to be put into large heaps, covered with a thick layer of straw and on top with a thick layer of earth. That would keep it fresh for several months and we could take out of it the necessary amount at any time needed, carefully closing the whole back again when done. Also all the arm thick trees we had cut at the forest and finally got them home needed to be cut into pieces and split so that it could be used. To keep it in order, it was traditionally stored in huge rounded heaps by creating a circle with about a ten-foot diameter by putting two rows of split wood as a kind of a wall and then throwing all the other wood into the center. At the height of a normal man it would be closed by laying the split wood in the form of a circular roof.

And then the winter came. That winter 1969/1970 was the most extreme winter I could remember till that time. The road we had to walk to school was defiled in parts and filled with the blown snow so that we had to walk on the fields to get to school. And on several days the wind was blowing over those fields all day long and we had trouble to walk either to school or back home. School shut down? Are you kidding? I can't remember one single day that school was closed because of winter storm, at least not during my school time.

Years later, 1978/1979, it was a different story. But at that time people died and trains were frozen onto the rails in certain areas, and even the Baltic Sea was completely frozen over and they had trouble keeping the ferry line open to Trelleborg/Sweden.

It was said that the Baltic Sea was frozen over in during the winter 1969/1970 too, but I can't remember if that is true or not, since at this time we had not ever walked that far and had not conquered the distance to the cliff line yet. That would happen next spring for sure since we had heard that there was some awesome fishing possible at certain places at the coastline. In the mean time we enjoyed winter as kids as good as possible with having a huge hill to sled down and often spend all day long finding out who was the fastest or could ride the sled the farthest down the hill. Harras was always with us and running aside the sleds and trying to stop them, biting into the wooden side of the sled, and several times he was almost rolled over by them. But he was in his element hunting the bad guy, and at this time it was the sled.

Towards the end of winter, still a lot of snow on the sides of the road and night temperatures below freezing, I developed a closer friendship with one of my classmates, Dirk. His mother was married a second time. He did not know his biological father because he was still a baby when his parents got divorced and when his mother married again and had another baby, a girl, he felt rejected. Maybe these similarities began braiding a bond which should have held for many years. It was only cut by his decision to drink himself happy. Dirk was somewhat different from all the other classmates I had. He did not go along very well with any of them and was quickly losing his temper if anybody said something he did not like. Although he would often get the short end of the stick, he would never back down. That made him a lot of enemies, and many others wondered why I could go along with him. I guess it was, besides the similarity in our family history, the fact that I just told him to stop it when he tried to do something stupid and told him that he was an idiot to lose his only friend. He had some difficulties understanding mathematics and physics, but was in general at average in all other subjects. With that we used a lot of time to do homework in math and physics before I walked home.

It was early spring when he suddenly appeared at about 10PM at our home, throwing stones at my window. When I looked out and saw him, my first thought was he was about to make his threat to run away reality. I jumped out of the window and asked him if he had completely gone crazy.

Calming me down, he said, "I had to come out because I need to tell you the news immediately."

I asked him, "Do you have any idea how late it is? I have to get up at 5:30 tomorrow morning."

"I know, but I need to tell you, I could not wait, I'm coming direct from Sargard. I ran the whole way up here, and I'll run the whole way back home. I'll become a boxer!"

I thought now he was completely insane. He was about fifteen years old. "If you want to start a boxing career, you needed to start at the age of four or five, not at fifteen," I answered really tired. Then I turned around and walked to the door to get up and into my bed.

He yelled, "Wait, Harald, you will see that I'm serious because I met a real legend."

That caught my attention. "Tell me about it."

He began to explain how he was caught at the train without a ticket and thrown out in Sargard, two stations before Saßnitz.

Angry about being caught, he started walking home and, as we did all the time, used a shortcut, walking along the old road from Sargard to Saßnitz, which wasn't used anymore and ended after about half a mile in a small walkway. Right at the end of that road, there was a house nobody really paid attention to.

Dirk said, "This time a man was standing there and asked me what I was doing. I told him about my misfortune, being caught without a ticket when I was almost home and how I had to walk all the way home. I was already turning around when this guy suddenly was all over me. What was I thinking, cheating on those who work hard to keep that train running?"

I could still hear some anger in Dirk's voice that this guy gave him a good telling-off.

"Then he asked me if I knew who he was."

I asked, "Did you know him?"

Dirk laughed and said, "I had no clue who this man was. So I answered, 'No, should I know you?' The man told me that he was a boxing legend. He boxed 129 boxing challenges and won 111, and he was one of the most successful box trainers in East Germany. I tell you, Harald, for some seconds I really feared he would knock me to the ground for my misbehavior. He invited me into his house where his wife offered me lemonade, and then he showed me his collection. His name was Leo Weichbrodt."

I had to confess I had never heard that name before and neither had Dirk. Then he said good-bye and began to run home.

Next day at school he said to me, "I have not slept at all and have created a training schedule."

"For what do you need a training schedule?" I answered without really paying much attention to him.

But he brushed my question aside and said, "You have to help me to get in shape because I'm about to participate at the district championship in May."

I was blown away. "Do you know how stupid this idea is, that is so stupid I can't even find words for it. You will have to fight against people who have trained for many years probably five days a week and won't stand a chance."

But he assured me that Leo Weichbrodt would train him and he would work hard to be fit for those fights.

My part was to push him through with his physical training. The next weeks were almost a nightmare to me. Although he was carrying my school bag uphill and downhill running to our home, I had to run with him, and I hated running long distances. I could never understand how somebody can enjoy running for hours and hours. I love short distances and I was pretty good at it. Actually I was so good that my teacher wanted me to start at the district school championship. It always took all my fantasy in excuses to avoid it. It wasn't because I did not like it, but because I knew I would have trouble keeping promises. I knew I could not guarantee I would be at the trainings necessary to get faster, and I knew I could not guarantee to be able to travel to the qualifications for those championships. Not because I was such an incredible unreliable scalawag, but because the omnipresent shortage of money at the absolute untimely moment made it difficult for me to commit to anything where even the lowest possible amount of money may be needed.

I will never forget the bitter feeling I always had when I had to go to the grocery shop with a piece of paper in my hand. On that piece of paper was written a phrase like "please give to my son the follow stuff, I'll pay it next week when I get my payment." Then a long list of groceries followed, desperately needed to feed my little siblings and of course us.

It took me sometimes hours to get the guts together walking into the shop and presenting the paper, because I knew that the sales clerk would loud read the paper so that everybody in the shop could hear it and would than usually say, "Aha, has your mother squandered all her money again!"

And all the women in the shop would look pitifully at me and I wished the earth would open and swallow me at the spot. Knowing all to well that there wasn't any guarantee that I'd be able to have even those 5 mark or 10 mark or 15 mark at the time when I'd need it to fulfill a commitment, I just avoided any.

Anyway, I had become the physical trainer for Dirk and he was demanding. As often as possible I used my mother's bicycle. I would take Harras on the leash, wrap it around the handle bar, and would kill two birds with one stone. So I had Harras pulling the bicycle and Dirk running behind it, round after round through the hills up and down around our settlement. Since one round was about 1.5 miles, he had to run at least 5 rounds. Harras loved to help by pulling the bicycle when we got uphill and he rested when we were downhill or on flat terrain. Mondays, Wednesdays and Fridays Dirk was in Sargard to train with Leo Weichbrodt and on Tuesdays, Thursdays and Saturdays we pulled him through his miles. On

Saturdays we kept it easy just to get him running but without much stress. And it worked. I had never thought that he would have a chance to even get qualified for the district championship and I believe neither did his trainer. But when he started the qualification fights everybody was surprised. A newcomer, no name, was knocking out one well-known fighter after the other.

Years later he told me that he thought the reason was that he'd trained with a flyweight boxer. Based on that, he never inherited the tactics of the heavier weight boxers as he was at the half-medium weight class. He was trained to focus on speed and precision of a few combinations of straights and uppercuts. I saw him hour after hour repeating the same combinations hitting a 200 lb. sandbag hanging from a beam in our barn. That sandbag was adjusted so that the upper edge was just a little higher than his head because he knew that many of his opponents were a little taller than he. On that sandbag he had marked the spots for the lever, the solar plexus and the chin area with red color four times around the sand bag. With incredible speed he would dribble around the sand bag and repeat the straights and uppercut combination onto the marked areas until he could hit all of them at least five times in a row. Then he would have a five-minute break and after that he would go again. He did this for more than three month every other day two to three hours. With that he was absolutely in top shape when the qualification for the district championship begun.

I was never a great fan of the boxing sport. Not even at the time when my friend Dirk started his career as a boxer. But after all that excoriation I needed to see him boxing at least once. When he finally brought me a ticket to his fight at the semifinal I could not avoid being very proud of what he had accomplished yet still wondering how he really found the encouragement to go through all the torture as I called his training regimen. He won that semifinal, and the final both fights were over within the first round with a knockout of his opponent. After high school he went into an apprenticeship as a mechanic at the Fish Processing Plant and became state champion several times in his weight class. Because of that, the East Germany Navy was very interested to get him when he had to serve his time. He voluntarily contracted for three years—mandatory was 1.5 years—and for that he got the allocation of an apartment which was extremely rare for his age.

A Certain Decision of My Mother Touched a Sore Spot or Marital Arguments

I think it was almost the end of May when my mother decided she needed to travel back to Reupzig. The reason was that she had not gotten any alimony payment from Helmut for my four stepsiblings. Although you would think that was the reason why the money was always shorter than the months, that was only half of the truth. But, yes it was a problem, and I understood that she had to do something to get the money. Connie had to take care of the little ones, and I took care of Andreas and Susanne who were at school age and went with me and Michael to school every day. After a few days, I believe it was less than a week, my mother was back but unfortunately not by herself. To my surprise and I have to admit, anger, Helmut was with her. I thought the world around me would collapse.

For over a year now we had peace in our home. Sure, we had a difficult life and it was hard with school and all the work we had to do, but we had peace. No flying saucers, knives, or other objects to endanger our lives, no screaming and beating in the middle of the night; all of that was coming back into my mind within a split second. I could not grasp what happened and in my head, and there was this one question screaming at an almost unbearable sound level, *Why again, Why to me?*

My mother explained that Helmut was at the edge to rot away. She could not get an address at the administration for child support because they said he hadn't been reporting to the police since he was released from the labor camp. I asked, "What labor camp? What are you talking about?"

My mother answered that when the alimony payments stopped last fall, she called the child support at the district town Koethen and complained about it. The administrators found him not working at a regular job, just working for what he needed to eat and buy hard liquor. They filed a claim with the court and the judge decided he needed to learn to work and sentenced him to a labor camp because of his antisocial behavior. Because of a decision of the communist leadership those camps were closed in spring 1970, and he suddenly was free, but in such bad shape and health that he could not find any work. And he did not report, as he was obligated by law to the police station in the area to give an address, mainly because he did not have one. He lived in barns and huts and wherever he could find a place.

I finally agreed that she probably couldn't let him die like a straying dog and accepted that he would now live again with us. His biological children weren't really much happier than I, because at least the older ones could pretty well remember the terror we had in Reupzig. But at first all looked fine. For several months everything went well. Helmut recovered fast and got his old strength back. He got a job at the machine repair shop of the agricultural cooperative. Since he was an excellent marksman in almost all trades connected to machines with extraordinary skills, he soon became the man to go to if you wanted to have things done right the first time. My mother had made an arrangement—to which he did not even need to agree, because all his income was under jurisdiction of the child service court anyhow—that all his payment would be paid out to her directly.

Sometimes Helmut offered me the possibility to work with him at certain repairs on the weekend. He negotiated a five mark per hour payment for me, and I was happy to earn some money. Although it wasn't much, especially on a weekend, it was more than I could get working during school break at the cooperative fields. I thought that if I could convince the foreman of the machine repair shop that I was a useful helper, he may hire me then too. With that I put all my attention into the job and learned a lot of things. The most difficult task though was welding. We had two different kind of welding systems at that time. One was the Oxygen/Acetylene welding and the other one was electrode welding. The first one was somewhat dangerous if you didn't know what to do; you could actually flatten the building. Some of the older readers may remember those carbide lamps used at the dawn of the 20th century. You put some rocks of carbide into a reservoir, filled water on top of them and then closed the reservoir tight. The chemical reaction between the water and the carbide produced the gas which you could light and had a pretty good light.

The same system worked with the welding, just a lot larger. Together with the oxygen it produced enough heat to cut steel or to melt it so that you could weld steel parts together. I had a lot of trouble to adjust the gas streams from the oxygen and the acetylene to create the right size and color of the flame to work. But the electrode welding worked great and I became pretty good at it over time. Again I was in a situation to learn a lot of tricks about mechanical work and how to do things a little differently, and with that easier and at a better quality. I learned to dismount and mount bearings, to use the right lubricant and most important to keep the lubricant clean, because contaminated lubricant was the main reason for premature bearing failure. And I learned that it often was more important to know how not to do things. Anyhow, summer came and school break and I did not get the job I wanted at the machine repair shop. I don't know the real reason, but I guess the cooperative needed us more on the fields than at those special jobs, although the machines were extremely stressed during harvesting season, and based on a low level of quality, breaks were omnipresent.

I could do nothing about it and went to work as the year before. In the morning at 7:00 a.m., we would all be at the cooperatives main yard and the operation manager would group the different helpers to the several working brigades composed of the members of the cooperative. For the next eight weeks, and often including the weekend, we would help at the field to get the hay onto the trailers pulled by tractors, load straw onto trailers or unload the straw at the barn or would even build straw-stacks, with the straw coming from the field when there was no barn for the straw. I took every single opportunity to work, even on weekends, and I volunteered when only a few were needed, because I had a dream.

About two weeks before the school break, we were walking back to school from the sports field, and on that way we had to pass the sports shop. That was when I saw that great bicycle there. I went into the shop and had to get my hands on it. It was the absolute top brand in East Germany a Supersport Diamant. There were two brands available at that time, this one and Mifa. As it was with all the other stuff, you had the luxury to choose.

"C'mon, what's bad about having the possibility to choose?" you may say.

We could choose between average and top quality. Not bad hey, what else do you need to choose between? You see what comes from too many choices. Your closet is filled with stuff you never use. We did not have that problem. Actually more often than we liked we had no choice at all, because there was only one brand available and usually the average quality brand. The great leadership of the party tried desperately to comfort its people by reducing the headache of choices. And most of the time for many products, they did not just reduce the stress of having to decided between different brands; they eliminated that stress totally and replaced it by a funny game. I'll explain that in more detail later.

But here was the unique, once in a lifetime chance to choose the highest available quality brand of a bicycle. And not just that, it came as the luxurious design, the Sport Edition. I was thrilled.

I walked over to the clerk. "How much is it?"

"It's 230 Mark," she said with a distressing smile, and I almost died on the spot.

I nearly missed the beginning of the next lesson at school because I couldn't just leave. I walked around that bicycle again and again. From that day on all my thoughts were focused on that bicycle.

Since my mother had her and Helmut's income, I wrenched the promise from her that we, Michael and I, could keep our money from the school break work that year. That was the reason why I took every single job at the cooperative I could get, even on the weekend. One weekend they needed a helper at the mill. Saturday morning I reported at the mill.

"I can't believe that you're the guy the operations manager has sent to help me," said the miller, looking at me, shaking his head.

I was approximately 5 feet tall and weighted roughly 120 pounds. Many of the bags he needed me to move around were the same as I in weight as well as in size.

"Please don't send me away. I need the money because I'm saving it for my dream bicycle," I begged him.

Finally he gave me some other work to do. Until the last couple of weeks in August I had more than 200 mark earned, and since I had the agreement with my mother that I could keep my money that year, I did not give it to her. I had to remind her sometimes when she asked where my money was, since we got paid weekly. Knowing that it was not appropriate to have the money just somewhere in a desk drawer, I hid it at a special cache, a very special one. We had this small wood- and coal-burning furnace in our room upstairs at the attic. It was an old fashioned furnace with a steel frame, furnace tiles on the outside and a hot air labyrinth created by fire bricks on the inside. Since the furnace wasn't heated during summer time, I used that labyrinth to hide my money. Not even Michael knew exactly where to find it.

Two weeks before the end of the summer school break it happened. We were working on a straw pile at a field outside of a village about six miles west of Saßnitz. We were almost done because that pile was already twelve feet high, and we never got more than fifteen feet high with the straw pile. It was already late in the afternoon, the day has been hot and everybody was aware the weather could change and in a day or two we would get a lot of rain. Based on that, we had already been notified that we would build another straw pile right next to this one and would work until nightfall.

We were done with the arrangement of wisps from the last delivery. As always we would at first build a balustrade with a ring of wisps on the edge of the straw pile and work from there inwards to build a complete layer of wisps. So we had done the balustrade and I was turning around looking out for the next tractor trailer, which was just turning around the corner of the street about a half a mile away. Knowing I had a few minutes until the trailer would be at the unloading position, I lowered myself backwards to sit on the wisps I just had placed at the edge of the straw pile. In a split of a second I realized that I was going much too deep to sit down but it was too late. I could not stop myself and was in a free fall backwards down approximately twelve feet to the ground.

I woke up several minutes later by the rattling of the tractor trailer where I was placed on some wisps only to lose conscience immediately again. I remember waking up again in the shaking cabin of a truck and passed out again immediately. I have no remembrance of the arrival at the hospital and the first two days. I was wondering where I was when I finally woke up and trying to look around caused so much headache that I almost passed out again. I heard a lot of voices sounding, like several people were in the same room, but could not see clearly because one of my eyes was covered. I tried to fall asleep but the headache was just too much. After a while a nurse appeared, smiled at me and said, "Fine that you finally woke up."

"Where am I?"

Whereupon she answered, "At the hospital."

"How long?"

"Two days. You have a very heavy head concussion. You need to lie flat down for at least two weeks before you can even think about getting up."

"What about my eye—why is it bandaged?"

"You had almost cut your right eye when you hit the ground, because there was a piece of the bottom of a glass bottle right where you landed."

But I was lucky because that glass cut only into the upper end of my eyelid. And since the bottle might have been dirty they had sanitized the complete eye and covered it to avoid any risk for infection. In a few days the eye specialist would be in town and would look at it, but it seemed to be okay. She told the others in the room to be as quiet as possible because I needed rest and left. Later she brought me some painkillers and I was able to fall asleep.

This was going on for several days, waking up to have something to eat and getting painkillers and sleeping alternated, and only sometimes was I awake long enough to get a glimpse of the others in the room, mostly children younger than me. That was probably the reason why there was almost constantly a noise level I could barely endure.

One day the ophthalmologist accompanied the ward round. The bandage on my eye was removed—not without pain, since the skin—dry blood from the cut did not get off easy. He looked at the eye, did some checks with a special lamp and said everything looks fine with my eye. But the concussion was still severe and I was not allowed to get up longer than I needed to use the restroom and for eating.

I believe I was in the hospital for almost three days when the first visitor appeared. My sister Connie came and brought a bottle of apple cider. She talked for a couple of minutes about the shock everybody had when they heard about my fall. I asked her about Michael and she explained that he was not allowed to come in because he was considered a child and therefore could only visit me under supervision of an adult. And my mother was too busy and would probably come on Sunday at official visiting time. She left after about half an hour.

You can imagine my surprise when my mother appeared Friday night at about seven in the evening. She also brought a bottle of apple cider. You may wonder what it was with the apple cider. Actually that was the typical gift you brought somebody to the hospital in East Germany, because first of all there wasn't much more else you could bring such as orange juice, or maybe bottled mineral water. And secondly, all you got to drink was peppermint tea or coffee substitute made from barley malt.

My mother said, "I was so shocked when I heard that you fell off of that straw pile. I'm so sorry that I couldn't come earlier, but you know how it is with all the work until late night...And then all that work at home."

Yeah, I knew, and actually I asked myself how big her concerns really could have been as a mother when it took her almost a week to find time to look after me.

Then the hit came. "Harald," she said, "I need you to tell me where you have hidden your money. I need it because I have no money and nothing to eat for your siblings. I will have nothing to eat for them until end of next week when I get my payment."

Because she was employed at the cooperative, she got paid once a month. Still having a headache during the time I was awake, it now increased to a hammering pain in my temples. Not because she wanted to have the money I worked so hard for almost two months, not because she, once again, had burned all of her and Helmut's money through before the end of the month, but because she was virtually about to shake me down with the inability to feed the children.

"You need to remove the furnace pipe at the back of the furnace. Then, grab around the left side of the fire brick air labyrinth. There you'll find the 205 Mark I earned so far," I said, with tears in my eyes. "I saved for my dream bicycle, every single Pfennig. And I want it back!"

A very strange feeling started to grow inside of me. A feeling I could never really explain and I still can't say what it was. It was some kind of a mixture between a hate of myself and a hate for my mother. A hate which wasn't creating violent thoughts towards her, more a creation of hateful disgust.

"You'll get your money back with the payment next month, I promise."

I answered in a very clear, ice cold voice I did not know I was able to use against my mother until that minute, "*Darauf kannst Du Gift nehmen!*" (German for "You can bet your life on it!")

I'm not sure whether or not she really heard it, or even understood what I said, because she had what she needed and was already at the shop with her mind, buying the stuff she needed. A few minutes later she left, and it was then that I realized that something was different with me. Something inside of me had changed. It was as if a very important part of my inner human being had been emptied by this, and that what was there before had been replaced with a huge icy something. I won't say hatred, but—as I said above—disgust was all I could feel. Maybe psychologists have a name for it, but I don't care. And at that time, I did not know such kind of people, nor had I heard that they exist.

This feeling is gone. I have long forgiven her and all I feel is compassion, because she doesn't listen to me when I tell her about the forgiveness through Jesus Christ and the peace she would have accepting Him. Finally I was discharged from the hospital. I don't know if my family was informed about it, or my mother had to work and couldn't come, but since school had already begun again, none of my siblings could be there. And honestly, why would they, besides Michael?

At night Michael asked me, "Why did you tell her about the money?"

"Michael, what should I do, she had no money to buy food for all of you and pay the bills for energy"?

"What's new with that?" was his answer.

Then he turned around and fell asleep. I wanted to tell him that she had promised to give me my money back so that I could buy my bicycle, but I knew his answer would have been similar. I thought for a while what I could do if she did not gave me the money, but there wasn't much I could. With that I turned to my book to read.

I was reading a lot.

The local library in Saßnitz was the place where I went at least once a week. The maximum number of books I could borrow per week was five, and depending on the size of the books I went through one of them sometimes in a night. When my mother realized that the light was still on in our room, she would call us out and threaten with consequences if we did not shut the light off immediately. We did not have small reading lights, and with that I was forced to use a flashlight to read. Now that needed a lot of batteries, and sometimes I did not have battery replacements. That was the time when I was using every free minute during the day to read. And one of the opportunities was the school lessons in Philosophy or Political Economy of Socialism.

There were still some weekends when our cousins, Norbert and Jürgen, with me and Michael would do some really interesting things. One weekend we decided that we would walk through the forest to the cliffs and would try to fish there where I was told to get real good fish. Fishing rods weren't really expensive, although not with the quality you know these days, but good enough to have fun. And then, as it was with all the stuff, you needed to be lucky to get the right one. I was checking in with my dream bicycle almost every other day. Yeah, it was still there and not sold after about three months; it was just too expensive for the average people to pay that amount of money for a bicycle. And no, I did not get my money that following month.

During one of the visits to the sport shop, I saw a fishing rod singled out and with a price reduction mark on it. When I asked the clerk, she said that this was a mistake by the wholesale delivery because it had a very heavy casting weight of about 200 gram maximum. Normally in our area they were using fishing rods with maximum casting weight of 70 to 90 grams. The fishing rod was 2.10 meters, and I got it for just 15 Mark, which was a joke. Since I had an old fishing reel all I needed was new fishing line since the standard we had was smaller, and for that what I had in mind I needed at least 0.5 mm fishing line. With bending a piece of wire into the shape of a fish and casting molten lead around it I created the bait for the fish I was about to catch.

On the weekend we made our way to the cliff in about three hours, starting early in the morning. It took us a while to find the best way to get down to the water line, but finally we were ready to start fishing. With the long fishing rod and the heavy casting weight, it took me a while to get used to, but then I could throw the weight really far out into the somewhat bumpy sea. After the third or fourth throw, suddenly there was a hitch on the fishing line, and when I did the yank to hook securely whatever was caught out there, the fishing line began to move sideward.

FREEDOM'S NIGHTMARE

I was excited because I was sure I had a fish on the hook. And it began a fight to get it to the sands, which made me think about a huge fish. But when I had it finally there so that I could get it lifted out of the water and throw it onto the stony beach, since I did not have a scoop net, it wasn't such a huge fish. It was a mackerel approximately a little bit longer than a foot. I did catch two more, yet smaller ones, and we decided to make a fire and broil them over the open fire on sticks. There was enough driftwood lying around to burn hundreds of fires all night long, so it was easy to get the fire burning and keep it that way. We had to search for a while though to find the right sticks to put the fish on so that we could keep them at the right distance to the fire. That didn't work out all the time, and several areas of the fish skin were burned and black like coal, but since we did not remove the scales we did not intend to do anything with the skin. We had a lot of fun and telling stories back and forth and holding the sticks with the fish sometimes too far and sometimes too close to the fire. Time went by and nightfall began.

We were almost done with the broiling when the place where we were sitting suddenly was bathed in bright light. Jumping off of the tree stumps we were sitting on around our fire, we were scared to death. We looked around, but could not see anything because we were almost blinded by the bright light. It appeared that the light came right from the corner of the cliffs, approximately 120 feet above our heads. A moment later a voice was shouting at us.

"Put your hands in the air and don't make the slightest move," commanded that voice.

Then we were surrounded by a group of uniformed soldiers from the East German Navy, pointing their AK 47s at us. When their NCO realized that we were just some kids, he commanded them to lower the weapons and closed in on us. I for sure was scared.

"What are you doing here at this time?" he yelled at us. "You should be home with your mom and not at the beach, breaking the law."

"We have the approval from our parents to fish here," Norbert answered with a still shaky voice.

"So," the NCO yelled back at him, "did they gave you approval to make a fire at the beach and irritate the navy? See that you get the fire out and yourself out of here at lightning speed or we will arrest you."

We didn't need more than that to have us move as fast as we could.

We walked away with the light beam always on our heads. And whenever we turned our head back to the place, we could see the group sitting on our reignited fire and eating our fish. I was so angry about that, that I was tempted to follow the proposal of Jürgen, because he felt betrayed the same way I did.

"Let's walk back on the cliff line to the point right above these guys and throw stones down onto them."

But knowing that not a single centimeter of coast line was unreachable by the huge floodlights mounted on 130 meter high towers along the coast, I said, "Keep marching—let's get us home."

Since these guys did not have our personal data, we were sure that we would not have any additional consequences to fear, but the shock of their sudden appearance and staring into the barrels of their AK 47s was enough.

Then at the end of October, it happened. That was the month the cooperative paid the members a year-end bonus together with the monthly payment. That meant more than twice the normal payment. My sister Connie was there to pick up her payment and that of my mother because my mother was out of town for reasons I can't remember. When Connie came to the house—she had not lived with us for several months because she had a boyfriend and had moved in with him—I was there.

"I'm just dropping the money," she said. She did not want to wait for my mother coming home.

"Where is the money?"

When she handed it to me, I counted exactly 205 Mark from it and put it in my pocket.

"You can't just take that money from her. If she counts the money, then I get in trouble because it's missing. Mother knows exactly what she has to get," she protested in total disagreement.

"Connie," I answered, barely holding my temper, "you know that it's mine. And you know that Mother promised me that I'd get it back this time."

I went to my room, grabbed the rest of my saved money from the new hiding place, and yelling over my shoulder, running out the house, said, "Tell her I'm going to get my bicycle!"

FREEDOM'S NIGHTMARE

It was almost five in the afternoon and the shop closed at six in the afternoon, which left me little time to reason with her much longer, so I walked out and was on my way partly running and partly just walking as fast as possible. I made it to the sport shop just a few minutes before they closed and proudly counted the money onto the cashier's desk. Since I had been there so many times, promising her that I'd get the bicycle soon, she had a huge smile on her face, "That is great you finally realized your dream," she said. "I wish you luck with your new bicycle. "

When I came home that night, my mother came down on me like a storm. And I let it all go down on me without saying a word until she finally slowed down in her tirade. But when she said that I was an egoistic, selfish and unthankful boy, taking the money needed for food for the whole family to satisfy my greed, it was too much.

"Do you remember that day when I, selfish as I was, lay in that bed at the hospital? Probably not," I said, barely being able to speak.

"Do you remember that I was there for about three days until you showed up? Probably not!" Now fighting the tears, which started to fill my eyes, I went on, "Do you remember that I could barely speak because of the pain in my head. And at that time I didn't know for sure what happened to my eye. But that didn't concern you either. The real reason why you even bothered to show up was the money, which was what you needed."

Realizing how I spoke to my mother made me hesitate for a moment, but then, it broke out again, "It really doesn't matter whether you have those 200 Marks or not—at the end of the month, we will have no money to buy stuff we really need!" I said.

"If you really believe I had no right to take my money back, why did you even bother to promise I'd get it back?"

It was a very bad conversation and I did not feel right about what I said, but I just could not take it anymore. I wanted to let everything out, about the nights when we went hungry to bed because there was nothing to eat, about the days and nights when the rooms were cold because we had nothing to heat the furnace, and so many more things which came to my mind at that moment. But I did not say it. I just walked away, and an indescribably sadness overpowered me. And again, I swore to myself that I'd never have a life that way when I grew up.

197

As if it was an unknown natural law, Helmut begun to drink again. At first it wasn't much to talk about. He'd go to the bar after work and have a couple of beers and snaps, and when he came home my mother would scold and nag him and we would hear that for some time even though we were separated through the ceiling and in our room. But it became worse and worse, and it was finally at a point again we had known so well for so many years. He would come home late at night, usually long after midnight, begin to throw dishes and all kind of stuff demanding food and threatening my mother. One night it was so bad that Michael and I feared for the life of the younger siblings. We went down to their rooms and found their door already barricaded. They let us in and we looked the door again. But we soon recognized that this little room door, made from press-board on a frame from wood molding, could not withstand the onslaught of that angry out of control man.

Before long Helmut began to hammer on the door requesting us to come out. In the mean time we all got dressed and went out of the window. Michael in front and me at the back, we walked as fast as the youngest sister could—she was just two and a half year old—through the snow towards the main settlement. It was after midnight and we had to knock the door of my uncle's home intensely to get them out of bed. My uncle dressed himself and walked back with us to our home. He went in to the house, grabbed Helmut by the arm, and threw him onto the chair. He told him that he would break his bones if he would not stop it immediately. Then he placed him onto the couch at the family room and threw a blanket over him. Since Helmut was really drunk, and it was long after midnight and he was probably exhausted by all the bluster, he fell asleep almost immediately. My uncle made sure that we could all go to bed and then walked away. Next morning Helmut acted as if nothing had happened. Although he tried to be friendly to his own children they were scared and forwent him where ever possible. Over the next several weeks, things calmed down and everything seemed back at the normal pace.

But it did not take long for Helmut to have another outbreak. When I heard from the then 10-year-old Andreas that his father was at the bar and had already enough but wasn't coming home soon, I decided that we would not let him into the house. My mother did not agree, but as usual when it came to the point, she went to her bedroom and would just lock herself in. I locked the house's main door when it was time, and when Helmut arrived, he could not get in. He began to scream and threaten one after the other of us to be killed when he would come in and was kicking against the door as hard as he could. But the main door was an old door and made from oak wood and very solidly built. After a while it was silent and we took a deep breath of relief. We almost fell for it, but I instinctively knew that he would not give up that fast. He would need to be exhausted to capitulate.

And there it came. Like a thunder crashed the ten-pound sledge hammer into the window frame of the kitchen window. The whole window moved about ten inches inwards and the breaking glass was flying all over us. I jumped to the light switch to shut off the light to, at least somewhat, reduce his orientation. It was just in time because the next hit was against the brick wall which did not do much damage. He finally gave up and disappeared. After an hour or so, Michael and I went out to the barn and we found him sleeping in a corner at the straw wisps. Relieved that the threat was over for the night, we could go to bed also. And again, next day it was as if nothing had happened that night. And if there wouldn't have been the damaged window, I would probably believe that I had dreamed all of that. In the afternoon after school, my frind Dirk came with me and together we repaired provisional the damaged window, putting plastic over the broken glass, and fixed the frame as good as possible. Again several weeks passed and everything went back to normal.

In early spring my mother quit her job with the agricultural cooperative and started to work for the chalk mine. There was a switch point where the trains coming from the different extractions needed to be directed and managed. Since the mine was working around the clock, she was working morning, afternoon, or night shifts. She made much more money and had a regulated working time and a much healthier working environment. Another change happened in spring. Suddenly one day we could not get water from the well. First I thought the pump or the motor had a defect. But as soon as I had removed the cover from the well, I realized that there was no water in the well anymore. Our well was a hole, probably hand dug, with approximately a 2.5-meter diameter and a bricked wall.

The water level was normally at about 5 meters. But now I could see down there several more meters the dry sandy ground. I could not believe it and called Michael.

"Hey, Michael, come out," I called after him.

"What's the matter? You're yelling as if the moon fell down to earth," he called back. That was a standard expression of his.

He arrived at the well, and I said to him, "Can you see any water down there?"

He looked down, and with an unexcited voice, he said, "No, no water there. Somebody stole our water over night."

What happened was easy to explain, as soon as we knew. The chalk extraction closest to our house contained the cleanest and highest quality of chalk. To continue to harvest chalk from that specific mine, they had to lower the water level so that the huge bucket excavators could get the chalk out without drowning. The chalk processing plant had started in fall to dig a lowering well, and when it was deep enough, to pump the water out. With that it finally happened that in spring the water level was so far lowered that they could begin to harvest the chalk, but our well was dry.

For several weeks Michael and I were forced to carry water from the settlement, where a public water pipe was accessible, to our house. Every single drop of water we had to carry with two five-gallon buckets filled with water from the settlement to our house. We had to walk that distance several times until we had filled a huge butt and several other containers. Later we would use a beam across our shoulders to reduce the stress on our hands. After many letters written to the administration, and several groups of people coming and looking into our well, I don't know till today what that was good for, they finally had the cooperative to bring a water butt with about five hundred liters and replace it every week. Sometimes those responsible for the exchange of the water butt would forget about it, especially in summer when they had so much work with harvest. Then the water would start fouling and we would carry water again for several days until the cooperative remembered the promise. Based on this the local administration decided to move my mother and the children into an apartment in Saßnitz. But that was much later when I was already off to get my electrical degree.

Spring was almost over when Helmut had another outbreak. This time the situation was different. Because of the last rage attack, he was ordered—I can't tell by whom—to sleep upstairs in that room at the attic Michael and I called our home for several years. Although we absolutely disliked it, we had no chance, we had to move. Since we had two smaller living rooms, one of which was barely used at all, it was converted into the bedroom for Michael and me.

That day when Helmut came home drunk and ready to terrorize the family again, my mother was working nightshift. I was at the hallway waiting for him. I told him that I'd no longer tolerate his terror, and only if he would go peacefully upstairs and sleep off his drunk I'd let him enter the house. He begun to yell at me, threatened me and was actually at the edge to attack me physical.

That was enough for me. I remembered how Dirk was hammering the sand bag and how he explained why he did specific steps, aligning his body so that all of the body's strength would be behind the punch. All that raced through my mind in a split of a second, and my fist hit his chin at the exact point. He stopped in the middle of the sentence, his body went limp and he slowly sank to the floor. I called Michael to help me, and together we carried him upstairs and threw him onto his bed. I was still shaking when we were back downstairs and it took me a while to calm down and realize what I just did.

Yes, he was drunk, violent and had terrorized the whole family so often that I couldn't even count it anymore. But on the other hand I could almost feel the shame rise inside of me that I had beaten an adult, who also was my stepfather. The feeling was strange. On one side I felt that excitement that I was able to stop that evil from doing us additional harm; on the other side, I was feeling somewhat guilty. Next day when I came home from school, I tiptoed to the room at the attic, and after listening for any kind of noises for a few seconds, I carefully opened the door. Helmut wasn't there. He was gone, and he never came back to our home again. Years later I saw him in Saßnitz on the street with a handful other drunks, but that was it.

Time was flying by, and the final year of high school came. Although the condition at home did not improve very much, the terror of a drunk we had endured for so many years wasn't there anymore. I was able to keep my success level in many of the subjects with the exception of Music, Drawing and Sports. Now Music and Drawing was somewhat understandable to me, and even my mother and my class teacher found some kind of reasons for it. Since the breaking of my voice I just couldn't hold a tone. And then all of those strange rings with flags on them put on different lines on the paper, and if there weren't enough, they just draw more of them somewhere; I'd never get a hold on the secret of why and where.

At the drawing lessons, everything that did not require a ruler or triangle wasn't working out for me. If I was asked to draw a dog, it would always create a strange look on the face of my teacher. When I was done drawing an animal, it could be everything but what it should be. With iron will I memorized the lyrics of the songs we needed to learn and always came away with a C grade in Music, but in Drawing, it was just the mercy of the teacher that she gave me a C grade for my artistic accomplishments.

Now with sports, that was different. I loved sports, and as said before especially sprint and apparatus gymnastics more often than not I missed the lessons or just could not participate because I did not have appropriate clothing. I didn't want to say that we had no money to by sport shoes or gym shorts, so I said I forgot it. And the rule was if you forget your sportswear you got a second chance, and when you did not have it next time it was counted as not passing, which meant E-Grade. Sometimes I was able to borrow sportswear, but that was so embarrassing that I did it not often.

Anyway, the final month came as fast as always when you think something will never end, and with it a number of final exams. Mandatory were a written final exam in Mathematics, Literature, Physics or Biology and Chemistry. Whether you had to make it in Physics or Biology was decided by the teachers, and since my A-Grade in Physics was solid, I was nominated for Biology, where I'd have the chance to improve from a B+ to an A- grade. Since the education was centralized, the tests for the final exam were unknown till the night before even to our school, when the principal would receive them. After the written exams were done and evaluated, the teachers decided who would go through oral exams either to improve the grade or to avoid the embarrassment of failure. Those who failed had an additional chance in fall right before the next school year began, and if you did fail that then you would have to repeat the last year completely.

I was honored to improve my grades in four subjects, including Mathematics, because with my written exam I had inspired the idea in my teacher's mind to get me to an A-Grade. Instead of having some free time and fun, I suddenly was back into learning mode. But even that went by and finally there was the great celebration of graduation. Since I graduated third out of sixty-eight students, I was honored to sign into the Book of Honor of our school.

That last summer school break was different. Because of my mother working at the chalk mine, I was able to get a job at the processing plant. That was huge, because of the money I could earn. And since I was now old enough, I could also run nightshift, which paid extra. However, I totally underestimated the hard work I had to do. The chalk was heavy and stuck to the shovel, and especially when it rained, I was barely able to lift the shovel. But after several days and some tricks I learned from the workers there, I gained some more strength and it became more and more routine, and all that hard work paid off because when I began my three and a half year undergraduate school in electrical engineering, I had some money to buy necessary books and clothing.

Now, our undergraduate program was a little different from what I learned it is here in the states. We could not just go ahead and chose a school which we liked or find more chances to survive the rigorous elimination process. At the beginning of the 10th grade year you'd try to determine what kind of profession you would most likely have a chance to get accepted by the corporation which offered the occupation for the profession you'd like to study. Than you'd apply and if you were lucky your favored corporation would invite you for an interview. If that went well, all was set and it only depended on your success at school for the remaining years. That was the process I had gone through as described in another chapter before. If you would not keep your grades, you would just go through a trade education. That wasn't bad in general but it would take you another three to four years after you'd finished that apprenticeship to be able to get a degree, if you wanted to get one.

The education was organized in a way that you were an employed student at that corporation and they would handle the whole education if the corporation was large enough. Otherwise they would send you off to school either of their choice or the one that was suitable. School time was usually 4 weeks in a row and then two weeks practice at the corporation the first two years and vice versa the third yea. The last half year was filled with realizing the project the corporation together with your leading professor at school had decided. You'd have to build something in practice and you'd have to write a comprehend thesis about it. It could vary between the different professions and industries, but in general, as stated so often before, everything was centralized, regulated and controlled. There wasn't much room for variation allowed. In my case, the Fishing Corporation had their own educational system for the theoretical and practical education of their students, but that was limited to mechanical and nautical degrees. Because the need for electrical graduates was much smaller, we would be sent to a central school for theoretical education. Yet we, the electrical students, had to move into the dormitory and abide by the rules. Now, that was something different than the dormitories here in the US. It was one large four story building with about two hundred rooms. Each room was equipped with two bunk beds, four lockers and four small desks, as well as a larger table in the middle to seat all four students. Each floor had two large bathrooms with showers and vanity only and two large additional bathrooms with water closets. Since all students were male, that was enough for all. I was the last one reporting to the dormitory administration and was send to my room where I'd live for about half of the time alone until a new student came to move in. Since our education was external, we had to get up long before official rouse, so we were accommodated in separate rooms yet on the main floor.

During the weeks of study at the external school we had to travel by train to the district city. The train was leaving the station at 6:00 a.m., and we had a way of approximately twenty-five minutes fast walking. School lessons started at 7:00 a.m. and with breaks lasted usually till four in the afternoon, sometimes till five on days we had laboratory. The number of hours per subject was clearly defined by the central commission of National Education and included regular tests and exams at the end of every semester. We would be back at the dormitory at around 6:30 p.m., and often had a lot of homework to do.

After the four week turn at school we would have our two weeks practice at the Fishing Corporation. During the first year it was straight organized with one teacher in a workshop who would train us in basic skills a professional electrical engineer needed, such as to file a piece of a round bar perfectly square, file another piece of square bar perfectly round and put a thread on it, and cut a disc of a round bar, file it flat on the upper and bottom side and change the round into a perfect hexagon. Finally drill a hole in the center and add thread to it so that the now created nut would perfectly be screwed onto the created bolt.

I still believe that the main issue with the first year of practice was to get us some basic skills, mainly work ethics and work discipline, those proverbial German characteristics. But the whole thing turned out to become a nightmare, especially for some of us who never had any kind of experience with housekeeping and punctuality. Our teacher's name was Mecky, and he wanted to be addressed as Mr. Mecky. I'll remember for all of my life the minute I arrived at the workshop. He was standing at the open door and was holding something in his hand. When I past him, he yelled at me the number two. Just that, two! Not knowing what that was about, I went into the workshop and found that I was the first and chose a workbench right at the large window where the light was falling onto my left side. Since I'm a right hander, I'd always have some light at my work. All the others appeared within a few minutes and Mecky came in, closed the door and walked over to the first guy at one of the workbenches who was the last one coming in. Poking his fore finger at the sternum of that guy he yelled, "You"! We looked at each other not knowing what he meant as he again yelled, "You!" and then adding onto that, "When you arrived I told you a number!"

The guy answered six and Mecky yelled, "Six hours" then he walked over to the next poking his forefinger onto his sternum he yelled, "You!" Knowing what was required he answered his number and then the next and finally it was on me.

When I answered two, he turned around, walked to the center of the workshop, and yelled at us,

"Men, you are wastrels. Everybody was late, but since this was the first day, I'll grand you mercy before justice, and your number is only single hours to work longer! Next time it will double and then triple and so on!" That poor guy at the first workbench was just sentenced to six hours to touch up because he was six minutes late. I was so lucky that I had been out of bed much earlier and had my bicycle and with that I had only two hours. The problem was that the main factory gate was just on the opposite end of the city. That was a distance of about five kilometers, and many people not familiar with the city just underestimated the time needed. Although there was public traffic, busses just to go mostly when you couldn't use them. Never again was I late during all the three and a half years.

Another foible in our opinion was his extremely developed sense for order. Every single tool had to be placed back at its place at any given time, even when we were using them continuously, and every single tool had its specifically marked place. This was something he was extremely watchful of, and we learned that the hard way too. Our workshop was relatively close to the main gate, and the shape of the company ground was determined by a small, flat area between the quay and the steep hill going up about 100 meters right behind the row of buildings and the train rails. The whole harbor was about 2.5 kilometer long, and right at the center was the central dining hall where all the workers would get lunch. Since we had only a thirty-minute lunch break, we had no time to lose to get there, get our meal, eat and walk back to be in time and not getting punished with additional hours.

One day, we had to stand in line for some minutes to get our lunch and were just seated when Mecky appeared at the door of the large dining hall. He walked over to our table and to our complete surprise did not yell, but almost whispered, "Back to the workshop and order your tools now." We jumped up all at once, put our lunch into the trash belt and ran back to the workshop where he was already waiting for us since he had the allowance to use his bicycle on corporation property. When we had every tool where it belonged, the lunch break was over. These two incidents are burned into my mind for all time. I'll never forget them. Did I like it to be treated this way? No, surely not, and who would as a young and rebellious, "I know it better" nineteen-year-old?

But why is it burned into my mind ever since? Because I learned that a certain value of housekeeping was the basis for good quality of work. Considering the age of Mecky, he could have easily learned his lessons on a workbench at Krupp's machinery factory before WWII. He had some very memorable proverbs which he used to repeat during the day several times and which were usually mucked proverbs our grandparents used to know. Something like: "From a dirty workbench can't come quality products" or "Nothing is in hand with a dancer." The latter he would use when he checked the file work, which was never accurate enough but at often he would just resign and let it pass. Although I brought some preexisting skills to the job and probably overestimated that and underestimated Mecky's determination to make useful members of the socialistic society of us "useless elements of a lost generation" as he preferred to call us, I had some difficulties achieving the quality he required. The only comfort was in the knowledge that every one of us had the same problem.

School was much easier for me, and I loved especially the hours in the laboratories.

When the second school week period ended, we were not allowed to go home. All of the junior classes were fitted up with uniforms, boots and other stuff of the GST and we were transported by train to the station in Sargard, close to the barracks where we would be for the next week. After a train ride of about forty minutes we had to line up in marching order and marched about 5 kilometers to the village where the barracks were. There were trainers from the NVA who handed the male students a KK47 a 22LR version of the AK47 as earlier explained, while the female students were equipped with all the stuff a medic would need.

This week pre-military training was called Vormilitaerische Ausbildung in German, and considered part of the education. Some of the students tried to take it easy but soon realized that this wasn't the way to go. I remember that four or five guys were jumping over the fence at night and went to a restaurant to have some fun. They were captured by the patrol recruited by the guard commander, and since he could chose his patrol out of about 450 male students, they were all tall and tough.

Next morning it rained cats and dogs, and those poor guys had to rake the roll call square for hours, only interrupted by running several rounds because they complained it was cold and they were soaked. The drill sergeant, one of those guys from the NVA, was very caring and said they would dry up if they would just run some rounds and heat up themselves. It wasn't really funny for all the others from their platoon, because they had to go the obstacle course several times during that morning. At about noon the rain ceased and the sun broke through the clouds here and there, and with that the punishment ended because now the trainers had no fun anymore. No other absence without leave happened again during this week.

And as described in earlier, we would storm hills, fight an invisible enemy to clear trenches and sneak through bushes and up and down sand dunes. This wasn't as funny as it sounds at first. Teens love to play soldier—at least German teens at this time—but those bushes were sallow thorn bushes and you needed a great deal of care not to get larded like a piece of pork to be cooked. Finally even that week was over, and when I came home I was so exhausted that I slept almost the whole weekend.

The first year went by and the practical teaching changed. We began to rotate through the different departments of the company, and that was very interesting since there were times when we would go on board with the foreman we were assigned to. The third year became again somewhat difficult because now each of us was assigned to a master electrician as an assistant to work with him together on repair orders for the fishing vessels. It was challenging because now we had to prove that we were able to apply the theory and the little practice we had learned to the practice in life, which wasn't really easy either.

Those weathered professionals, even though they did not have a degree, had a huge amount of knowledge about how things work in practice, and that was sometimes different than the theory in my mind. Before I could run all kind of calculations through my head and figure out what value needed to be applied in that certain situation, my foreman had already come up with the solution just based on his experience. When I later in the evening at the dormitory went through the application and put all the numbers together I'd often be surprised how exact his estimations were.

On weekends—not every weekend, but sometimes—I walked home since it was only a little more than five miles. But more often than going home, I would meet with three friends from the dormitory, Michael would come down to us and we would all together travel to a small harbor next to a small village direct at the shores of the large brackwater lake Großer Jasmunder Bodden. There was the sailing station of the Fishing corporations' nautical classes. We would rig one of the cutters and sail all weekend long. And that was what I loved the most during all those years. When I entered the cutter and we had hoisted the sails and the water began to create this typical gargling noise, then I felt free. All what happened was in my hand, controlling the tiller and the sails I directed where and how fast the cutter would sail, and for that time I forgot everything on land.

It was at this second year at undergraduate school that I became more and more involved in the youth organization, first at the Fishing Cooperation and then at the city youth organization. Soon I was chosen to represent the youth group of the corporation at the area assembly of the FDJ and almost at the same time was chosen to become a member of a special group of students. All of the different Fishing corporations were combined under a central administration called Combined Fishing corporations. This group of students was invited to present specific problems of the educational process to the General Director. That happened once a quarter and was both instructional and funny.

Later I became what was called the Secretary of Agitation and Propaganda of the city youth organization and was delegated to the Festival of the Youth and Students of the World in Berlin. And there she was. Angela Davis was standing on the honorable stage when we marched down the Karl-Marx-Allee, the boulevard where the socialist dictators would have their parades.

Back at home I was leading a group of youth leaders to organize propaganda events on special days which were important for the communist movement. I trained them to organize special FDJ meetings at school classes and so-called Youth Brigades by inviting elder, mostly retired "fighters against the Fascism." Youth brigades were formed after Erich Honnecker took the position of the Secretary General of the SED, which made him the most powerful person in East Germany. The idea was to form workers collectives with members not older than 30 years to have at least some kind of guarantee that all of them were totally indoctrinated by the communistic philosophy and in complete agreement with the socialistic doctrine of total control of the individual through the collective.

It was during the second year at undergraduate school that I applied to become a member of the Party of the Workers class, the SED. I was becoming deeper and deeper involved in that kind of work, because as described before, I believed in change from within. I was actually obsessed with the idea of the change from within so much that I did not realized that my active argumentation against the total control of the individual was already creating some frictions and disapproval at the leadership of the district organization.

This total control of the life of individuals at those youth collectives was up to the point where the collective would decide whether or not a member of the collective could date a certain person, depending on the political history of that person. It went so far that the leader of the Youth Collective would have access to police records and could request a briefing from the regional STASI office. Unconsciously I began to sabotage those efforts by delaying or forgetting to transfer the request for those requests. I did not participate in our weekly leadership meeting, when I knew that a punishment of an individual for so-called destructive behavior to the collective was on the agenda. And I actually began to do things I'd have discredited others for just a few months earlier. Slowly, yet steadily, I began to realize that the "Change from Within" did not work; it just didn't work.

One of my classmates, Hartmut, was an incredible fan of the US music band CCR. For those who are younger than thirty-five, the Credence Clearwater Revival was a real famous US band and loved by my generation in East Germany. It was somewhat tolerated to listen to decadent music of capitalistic bands at home, but there where unwritten rules for university students. Being a student at the university you risked to be expelled if someone would publicly discredit you for that. My classmate had almost all of their songs on tape, and was very eager to get the rest of them too. One day he said that there would be played two songs in the radio at 10:00 p.m. Since I had the best transistor radio one could buy in East Germany at that time with the short wave band spread into two different tunable scales, he asked me if I'd be willing to help him to record these two songs.

FREEDOM'S NIGHTMARE

When I arrived a few minutes before 10:00 p.m., he was already on the edge because he thought I wouldn't come. He guided me into the backyard of the three-story apartment house where he lived with his parents and where he had built a very strange construction right at one of the telephone poles at the fence of the backyard. A number of fish boxes, usually poorly nailed together from waste wood, were stacked on top of each other, and on top was the tape recorder.

Now remember, this was East Germany and it was at the beginning of the 1970s. That was a band machine where two open reels of tape would be wound from one end to the other pulled through a carefully adjusted magnet head to magnetize the coated plastic band. And those machines didn't run off of batteries. They needed real power. For that he had lined up a large number of power cords knotted together right out of the window of his parents' bedroom. Happy to have me there, he grabbed my battery-powered radio, placed it on top of the alarmingly unstable pile of fish boxes right next to the band machine, squeezed the telescopic antenna between the ground wire and the wooden pole and began to tune the radio in to the frequency he knew the songs would be played.

For a few seconds there was only a static crackling noise, and then at exactly 10:00 p.m. our time, the transmission began. Since he had to use a microphone to record the songs, that band machine did not have a direct wire connection, the microphone was placed directly in front of the radio speaker and he had the volume on maximum. Now, imagine a clear early summer night, full moon lighted the backyard so that we could clearly see and could be seen, and most of the people already in bed or even asleep to get up to work in the morning.

And suddenly with a loud voice probably to be heard throughout the whole city the speaker said, "This is the Voice of America. Washington, DC, is tuning in!" And then Yankee Doodle began to play. My blood curdled and I wished the earth would open up and swallow me. It was so loud that I thought the whole neighborhood might stand upright in their beds. But Hartmut was already at the volume control and reduced it at least somewhat. The problem with that was if anyone called the police or even recognized Hartmut and reported the incidence to the STASI, we would be thrown out of the university and could even end up in jail for that, because broadcasting music or statements of the class enemy in public was punished by law. And Voice of America was definitely the voice of the class enemy. He got his two songs and finally that was over. Although the quality wasn't anything you would talk about, that wasn't really the point for him.

On a weekend, several weeks later, we had a delegation from a West German youth group of the Communist Party of West Germany as guests in our city. The whole SED and FDJ leadership from the region was there, and the conference with speeches back and forth went on all day long. The main theme was to show these young West German communists the Real Existing Socialism. In my position as the responsible person for Agitation and Propaganda, I had masterminded the cultural part of their stay. And I wanted them to see the real world we lived in, not that Smoke and Mirrors they usually got shown. I had to bypass several security barriers and we all had a great night together at the only discotheque in town.

Because the music played there wasn't approved by the Agency for upholding the Cultural Integrity of the Youth of the GDR, it was half illegal. Yeah, we had such stupid things, and believe it or not, they were extremely powerful, because it was a STASI controlled organization. Based on some brutal beating some of their agents allegedly had to endure, they were armed and had the right to use their arms.

The disc jockey had no license and he played mainly illegally imported and black market vinyls. That was the reason why you couldn't get a place there if you weren't there hours before opening. Since everybody in town knew what position I had at the city's youth organization and they knew that I was a great fan of that discotheque and would never reveal that to anybody in power, even to the contrary had warned the lessee of the restaurant a couple of times that a control was scheduled by the Agency, I always had access and could use the back entrance.

It did not go unnoticed by the regional boss of the FDJ that the West German Youth Group disappeared after dinner and nobody knew where they were. He was beside himself and called the FDJ leader of the Fishing Corporation, who was my direct boss for the FDJ work. He told him that the western youth group had been reported missing and that I was probably responsible for that. My FDJ boss answered succinct something like, if they are with Harald, I wouldn't worry, and they will be alright. And believe me those West German youth communists had fun all evening long. To the excitement of our youth and them, there wasn't much different between them and us; they enjoyed being young as much as we did, at least at nights like this at the *Schacht* as that restaurant was nicknamed.

The next day was a horrible day for me, and it wasn't just that the FDJ boss of the Fishing Corporation came down on me in the morning. There was a special meeting arranged of the combined leadership team of the corporation, and the city FDJ group as well as the FDJ Secretary of the regional office was there. The only item on the agenda was me.

I can't and actually won't remember and write down all the pathetic socialistic-communistic philosophical phrases were brought against me. Because of the cruelty of my misconduct, which included the long-term attempts to alter the political basis of the doctrine of the Party of the Workers class, I was stripped of all of my positions and reduced to a member of the Party as well as the FDJ. There was though a slight resistance by several of the members when they voted to remove me from the board and to recall my delegation to the Advisory board of the General Director of the Combined Fishing Corporation. But it was only a short moment, and those who wanted to give me a chance were in minority.

When I was asked to present my last statement, I told them that they had long lost the trust of the working class. That they were living in an ivory tower of a socialistic-communistic dream world, blinded by their own inability to see that all their phrases did not produce anything people could buy or strive for. I was angry and totally stirred up about my failure to actually reach that what I called the Change from Within. Discouraged, I had to recognize that a "Change from Within" wasn't going to happen. Although I recognized at that very moment that I failed, it took me several more years to understand and completely internalize that it never would be possible. The real devastating thought years later was the awareness that I should have known it since my high school years when the discussions with the German Literature teacher ended in her saying something like, "You will see, later, when you're a little bit more experienced, what life is all about." It was the awareness that a totalitarian regime cannot, never ever, be reformed. It needs to be washed away by the uprising of the suppressed people. But at that moment, I was not that far in my own realization and was just disappointed.

The exclusion from the leadership board had a major impact on my school and work life for the rest of the undergraduate education. Although I finished with good results, I never again achieved a level of interest in learning and doing the best I could. I did what was necessary and that was it.

My theoretical thesis was about a complex control system of an ice-block manipulator at the processing room of the fishing trawlers. I did very well since the theme was interesting, had direct practical implications and allowed me to be at the trawlers when the next vessel got that system installed. Since I knew most of the electricians from the time I worked there, it was always a great moment when they realized that the system was my development. My practical exam wasn't all that exiting, not because of the system I had to build, but where I had to do it. I had to calculate, design and install a cooling system at a basement of a warehouse with five compressors and five different temperature-requiring cool rooms; one of them was a walk-in freezer. The problem was the building was built during WWII, and for what reason ever, the people at this time loved steel bar reinforced concrete for their life. To get a hole into the wall to mount something was a nightmare. Amplified by the absolute uselessness of the drill bits and the permanent overheating of the power drill, the frustration seemed endless. That was the time I begun to understand the meaning of the phrase: "It must hold until the painter comes." But I knew from years of experience that even the toughest job gets done with endurance.

I graduated with a degree in electrical engineering and had somehow managed to make it with a total C grade. But I couldn't share my joy with anybody from my family. I can't remember why Michael wasn't at the commencement, and for my mother it was probably not possible to travel to the district city where the ceremony took place, or was it because I had definitely not matched the expectation after I was reduced to a simple party soldier. I don't know, and if it wasn't for this book, I wouldn't even bother to think about.

One consequence I never really spent much thought on was that Michael, who was always following in my footsteps, was right behind me.

He chose the career of a machinery technician at the technical school of the Fishing Corporation. I mean he had during his time made his way through several leadership positions within the company's youth organization and was on the way to become a leader like me. I never thought that our opinion about the state of the socialist party would differ that much.

As I should learn just a few months later, he was in absolute agreement that anyone, who did not subordinate himself under the absolute truth of the party doctrine, had no place in a leadership position. The idea of a free exchange of ideas to form a better society under the free will to decide who would and who would not willingly be a part of it was absolute foreign to him. He understood from the first minute that the Dictatorship of the leading Party of the Workers Class required the absolute dominance of the party. To him, that included even the most private areas of an individual, because he saw it as the incubator for trouble. This discrepancy would grow to an extreme position. But that was much later, and since we were on total different work assignments, I can't remember seeing him more than just occasionally.

Anyway, that was the greatest moment in my life so far. And a week later I was on my way to enroll as the assistant electrical engineer on one of two Fabric Trawlers the Fishing Corporation owned. I was so excited that I almost missed the train. The Fabric Trawler was too large and had too much draft to enter the harbor in Saßnitz, and it was therefore stationed in the harbor at the state capitol. The senior electrical engineer was a *foreigner* as we called those who were not from the coastal area. But he was good and had a lot of experience since he had worked with the corporation for over twelve years.

Managing the electrical systems of the Fabric Trawler as a senior engineer, you had a lot of responsibility. The crew was about 48 people; the vessel was 120 yards long and 26 yards wide. Although the senior electrical engineer and I shared one cabin, he was considered an officer and therefore he would eat at the officer's mess. To my greatest surprise, this Fabric Trawler was completely running on DC power. All the main installation was DC powered, and for the nautical equipment as well as for the Radio transceivers and all the emergency systems we had two huge AC Generators. The first trip was not that far; we left the harbor, turned east-north-east and rounded the island Rügen just to get around the north cap, which is named Kap Arkona.

Although the Fabric Trawler—surprisingly named *Stubnitz,* the region where I played for several years—was equipped with everything necessary to catch fish itself, that trip was setup to take over the catch from the cutters. These were specially designed type of fishing boots built between 1958 an 1963 at the Shipyard in Stralsund which would play a specific role later in my life. With a total length of 26.5 meter they were excellent situated to handle the conditions of the Baltic and the North Sea under almost all weather situations. On this trip our Fabric Trawler took over their catch of sprats a kind of a Herring with a maximum length of about two inches. We would usually just freeze them and store them into the hold, which was cooled down to minus thirty degree Celsius roughly minus twenty-two Fahrenheit, which made it really funny to work there on electrical installation. Everything became like glass at that temperature, and since silicon isolated wires were almost unknown, I mean like gold dust as we loved to say, you'd be really careful what you did. Within the first few days I learned my daily routine of specific tasks I had to accomplish, and after that everything that was necessary to be done. And for only three electrical personnel aboard of such a vessel, there was always enough work. The third electrician was an electrical journeyman with a special education in ships electric.

The biggest difficulties we had to deal with were short circuits, caused by the corrosive saltwater. There was virtually nothing secure from corrosion besides stainless steel, but you can't make everything from stainless steel. Junction boxes and limit switches got filled with sea water especially at the fish processing area almost every single shift. Since the processing area worked around the clock, three shifts at eight hours each, we had constantly to be at alert. Soon I learned to read electrical schematics spread out over several pages and still remember where what contact was connected to. Especially the so-called landing switches, actually used in elevators to indicate the landing to the controller, were used here in a complete different application. With its multiple contacts at different stroke length of the movement were multiple functions realized. This was an add-on study at high speed because only processed fish meant money earned, and you could be in big trouble when those guys at the processing area weren't able to process fish for a longer time.

I was both exited and completely overwhelmed at the same time. But it was very encouraging when I figured out what went wrong, found the defect and could repair it without asking the senior engineer. And week by week I became better at it. During my off time I would read as much as I did earlier when I was a child or watching the movies played with a cinema apparatus at the crew mess on Tuesdays and Thursdays. But those were usually old movies which had been played at the city's cinema during my time as a student, and with that I was seldom at the showing.

One night I woke up because something was different with the movement of the trawler through the water. The senior engineer woke up right after me asking what was going, and when I said I didn't know he asked me to check it out. As electrical engineers we had access to the bridge and any normally locked control room at any given time. I dressed and walked up to the bridge where the third nautical officer had his shift. Always at night was the third NO in charge. I had to get up at night to repair some stuff because I was on call for electrical issues at nights. The senior would not do that as long as he wasn't really required to help, and that was always a bad thing to call him out. Because of those events, the third NO and I had become relatively close and knew each other since we had lose contact at the dormitory during study time.

The third NO was outside at the bridge wing with his powerful binoculars looking seawards at the dark water, which was at this time flooded with the light from the two large floodlights we had on top of the compass deck. I walked over to him and asked him what was going on, and he said that they had received a *man over board* message twenty minutes ago and had started to lead the whole flotilla of about twenty cutters in a search routine. From that point of the person missed last seen, we would go back for twenty minutes, which was about two miles, then turn ninety degrees and go another twenty minutes and then again turn ninety degrees. With twenty cutters, ten on starboard and ten on port of the fabric trawler in the center, we would cover a one mile of width with each turn. So I went back to our cabin and told my boss, who in the mean time had already gotten up and brewed a coffee for both of us. Since this was a specific situation there were rules on board of a vessel, and one of the rules was that the electrical engineer on duty had to be at the machine control center. We wondered why the third machine officer did not call one of us, and then we realized that the assistant electrician was on duty. The senior asked me if I'd be willing to take the first part and he would release me later. I agreed and walked down to the machine control center while he went back to get some more hours of sleep. Since the assistant electrician was not qualified according to the maritime law and the specific rules of our corporation to be on watch in these kinds of events, we had to replace him.

At the machine control center was at this time the so-called 3rd MO (machine officer), and since he was at the same age as I was—we had actually lived at the same floor for two years at the dormitory, we were good friends. I checked the control instruments for the generators and the auxiliary aggregates and joint the engineer and his assistant with my cup of coffee. The electrical assistant was more than happy to be released and get some more sleep.

Keeping an eye on the instruments, I asked Wolfgang, "Do you know details about the man overboard alarm? Since you've been on watch when it happened, and Rolf is on the bridge, you need to know more."

He grinned at me. "You've been on the bridge. Why didn't you ask Rolf? He could have told you."

"Wolfgang, you know how it is, he was too busy looking through his glasses and barely said anything. And I didn't want to stay too long at the bridge because the Old could come back any minute." The Old was the usual nickname for the captain, although you'd not dare to use that in his presence.

"Okay, okay," he said, "about thirty minutes ago the third NO received the Mayday call on channel 16 from one of the cutters after one member of the crew did not appear at the night watch meal." And he went on, "They searched the vessel and then called the trawler with the official man over board message."

That started immediately the search procedure which was part of the education of all the nautical officers. The crew of the cutter searched the complete vessel three times without finding him. At about eight in the morning, official watch change took place and I got replaced by the senior as well as the 3rd MO by the chief engineer. Tired as I was, I went direct in to my berth and slept several hours. Waking up later in the afternoon, I felt that we were still steaming in search mode, and that meant nothing good. Not for that poor guy whom we were searching for and not for the whole fleet because we did not earn money if we did not catch fish. At the same second I condemned myself for having such thoughts. After a short meal I walked up to the bridge and there were all NO's including the captain looking ahead and sideward through their binoculars.

The 3rd NO, Rolf, came over to me and said, "One of the cutters has fished up the slicker of the missed fisherman."

They knew it was his because every one of us wrote his name into the special working clothing you got from the corporation to make sure nobody else would confiscate it. After forty-eight hours the search was discontinued. The captain of the Fabric Trawler, who was at the same time in charge of the whole fleet, gave a short statement over the command system which was also transmitted to the cutters by radio. With that the routine work, fishing sprats, with even greater intensity to regain the losses, resumed.

We were only 28 days at sea and had a total of 1200 metric tons of sprats frozen in our hold. That meant, for me, that I got a salary of about 1,280 Mark which added to 18 mark base pay per day. When we were back at the harbor, there was something that really made me smile when I was called in to the cabin of the chief engineer. He was paying out the so-called *Devisen-Scheine* which allowed me to buy stuff at the Duty Free Shop at any harbor in East Germany. Since I was a junior engineer, I was entitled to 2.50 devisen per day totaled in 70 mark *devisen*. That wasn't much you'd think, but for me, who never ever had the ability to think about buying stuff in those shops because of no access at all, it was like Christmas. And since it was a duty-free shop, it meant no tax on anything there, and you could get a pair of Lewis Jeans for 28 Mark devisen. Cigarettes, for example Marlboros, not available at all in East Germany, were 1.25 per pack and so on. Luxurious consumer goods, unthinkable for the average East German people, were available at almost no cost. There was a lot of joy about the ability to buy those things Surely after the first trip it wasn't much, and I saved most of it since we were only 5 days ashore, But there was some kind of doubt growing about a government system, which denied the majority of their people the same joy.

As said, just a few days later I was back on board and we were out for another run on sprats. Everybody was excited because this was a good season, and if we could repeat that luck we had on the first trip, we would make good money again. And since we had lost some days during the last trip because of that tragic accident, we thought we might even be back earlier this time. And everything went fine until the second week or so. Work was tough and almost uninterrupted were some defects to repair. Fish was coming in around the clock and the processing center was at 100 percent capacity. That stressed the material and led to more defects than ever experienced during the first trip. There were days when I had not more than two or three hours sleep in 24 hours. But I learned a lot and all of this was a great advantage since I was working on a reputation to get my own ship when it was time to take responsibility. Then it happened.

Fishing, especially with the modern fishing methods and tools, is a dangerous business. You have to be alert at any second when you're on deck and the gear is moved. I believe it was the second week when we suddenly stopped and lay still in the water. Now, the sea wasn't really calm, rather rough, and the Fabric Trawler, even at its large size, began to bob up and down as well as moving from port to starboard back and forth. Even when you were at the deepest storage room you felt immediately that something was going on. The work I did wasn't really critical at that moment. I dropped my tools and moved upstairs, using the smokestack stairways to get up to the compass deck where I had the best view. Not to be astounded to much, our assistant electrician was already there. And he knew exactly what was going on.

I asked him, "Assi, what's going on, why are we dead in the water?"

Proud to be able to tell me, he answered, "On one of the cutters a decks man was standing in a kink of the towing line for the net and when the net hit the water while the cutter was at a speed of about 6 to 8 knots, the net pulled the towing line out and took the decks man with it."

I thought for myself, "He had God's saving hands on him and probably 100 guarding angels, because the kink opened up under water and he could get free."

He continued, "The crew could fish him and get him back aboard, but his leg was several times broken. Later we learned 7 times, 3 times the lower leg shinbone fibula and 4 times the thighbone."

The Assi, as he was called by everybody on board, went on to say, "The captain had setup a Mayday call, and since we were close to Swedish coast line, the Swedish coast guard had confirmed to send a helicopter."

Within a few minutes I was at my cabin and back on the deck with my camera. That must be a great opportunity to get some pictures. After about twenty minutes the helicopter appeared over the horizon, then the noise was to hear and became louder and louder. In the mean time the weather had gotten bad and wind had increased. The only somewhat safe place to get our man from board was at the bow. A call came through the intercom for the electricians to take down the bow antenna of the radio transceiver system. When this was cleared, the helicopter flew round and the pilot mastered to hold the helicopter stable over that small size of deck at the bow. They lowered a man with a special stretcher, and our doctor and the man from the helicopter placed the crew man in to the stretcher, and both the stretcher and the man from the helicopter got lifted up. Then the heli-copter disappeared into the rain-shower and continuously vanishing light.

Since the Assi was member of the board hobby photographer team I did not hesitate to accept his offer to develop the negative and get a con-tact copy in positives. Knowing his reliability considering his normal work I should have known better. He totally botched the film and I never saw any pictures I took from that helicopter event on our foredeck.

We came home two weeks later after 26 days full ship, and again it was a nice feeling to get another 1,780 Mark pay to my bank account. But there was a huge setback waiting for me also. The call to serve my manda-tory term in the East German *Nationale Volksarmee* (German for National People's Army [NVA]) had arrived. With that in front of me, I had a nice good-by party with some of the crew members who had become friends over the time, and some of them I saw several times during my active duty and they had always a bottle of whiskey (not available in East German shops) and some cigarettes for me.

In the Army now

GOD REALLY NEVER FORGETS YOU

I Became a Brake on the Golden Carriage to Communism Because God Sent Me an Angel

DESPITE MY NASCENT doubts about the absolute power of the government of the SED, I was a perfect product of the communistic education, manipulation and brain trimming centralized education system when I entered the National People's Army. But there was that strange feeling of the already beginning rebellion inside of me. Very silent very little, but I felt something was wrong here. I had begun to see and to understand the discrepancy between the words and the actions. I began to see a different picture of this communistic society. It was very blurry yet and everything else but clear what it really meant. The dictatorial organized system of the military, the often extreme brutality with which the general soldier was treated, and the perseverance of the indoctrination of the communistic defense doctrine, everything was just the opposite of what we got told.

Every month we had a two-day political education and we got explained why communism is better than the rotten, parasitoid capitalism and that the great communistic victorious Soviet army would win the defense battle against the blood-thirsty capitalist aggressor. But I could compare the heroic words right after with the reality, and what I found was different, very different. Roughly 30 percent of all our vehicles were out of order because of missing spare parts. We had to cannibalize two or three of them to get the rest running. Officers were drunk during their time on duty and often not able to drive home by themselves, so solders had to drive them home and then had to walk 6, 8 or sometimes more miles back to the barracks. When they came later than 12 AM, they were arrested for absence without allowance.

But we lived a life of luxury compared to the Russian soldiers stationed in East Germany. Their conscription time was 2 years and it was hell on earth. Russian officers had the right to order corporal punishment. Their food was often what was left over by the officers. We have a saying in German: *Das fressen nicht einmal die Schweine*, which means "Not even swine would eat that." When we found something really disgusting we would say not even a Russian soldier would eat that. I served at a special

223

army caserne where non-commissioning officers were educated in technical specializations. It was named *Technische Unteroffiziersschule* (German for Technical NCO School you'd probably call it NCO boot camp). It was not really a caserne; actually it was a large complex of ten buildings. Each building had five stories and was one hundred meters long. Between each of the buildings was a free area of approximately twenty meters. The whole complex was the former National Socialistic propaganda construction of the Third Reich and stretched out over more than three kilometers along the finest beach on the whole Baltic Sea coast line of East Germany in Prora.

I got drafted as truck driver for the education unit responsible to train the NCOs for the corps of engineers. Since the military basics had been trained during the college or high school time most of the soldiers did not need a long training in the basics such as March lock-step, or to exercise. But anyhow we had a sixteen-week boot camp, and since all of the future NCOs had been volunteers for longer terms than obligatory, mostly ten years, it was pure horror for me to be at boot camp with them. They were so besotted to become the perfect NCO that they exercised their routines even when we were off duty. This was especially terrifying for the 5 enlisted men among 110 NCO students in our unit.

One of the guys in my platoon, we called him *Kirsche* (cherry), was stupid! I mean really stupid! It was just scary to experience his trials to achieve the limits to get out of the attention of the First Sergeant. He wasn't even able to dress himself correctly under normal circumstances, and when we had alarm in the middle of the night, he brought punishment on the whole platoon because he wasn't able to dress correctly. So the other guys in the room started to train with him every single evening and weekend to get dressed within the requested time in case of an alarm. I recall the first of those special trainings when they tried to simulate that he's asleep at night and then blow the whistle to give the signal. He slowly sat up in his bed and said, "But I'm not fallen asleep yet." First I thought he was mucking his comrades but he was serious.

Another frightening episode was one day at the shooting range. During boot camp we would be twice each week at the shooting range. The main reason was to get those extracted who were really good shooters.

Kirsche was placed on my right hand side in the shooting line and we had to shoot several different targets. Now, everything in Germany is usually well organized, let alone in the Army. At the daylight exercise we had usually three different things to accomplish. First, three single shots at a target at one hundred meters, then changing the magazine and shooting at a special target what we called *father and son*, which simulated a belt-fed heavy machine gun with automatic fire, and then five single shots at a target at three hundred meters. After each exercise we had to secure the weapon, replace the magazine with an empty one and demonstrate the secured weapon to the line NCO by saying a specific sentence and pulling the trigger to approve that the weapon was secured.

I soon recognized that Kirsche was an excellent shooter. And since he was a future NCO which meant he was voluntarily serving longer than necessary, he did not care about being sent to the border security troops. That was a permanent threat to all of the enlisted men, and I'll explain that later.

He scored twenty-nine with three shots at one hundred meters and twenty-four at three hundred meters. But let's stay in sequence. When he finished his exercise with the requested short automatic bursts at the *father and son* target, he went through the security procedure and when the NCO came to him he said his sentence pulled the receiver back and let it go to press the trigger. Now try to get the picture. He lies on the ground on my right hand side. His AK47 with an apparently unloaded magazine is laying on his left forearm pointing diagonal in front of my head. The firing adjustment level still on auto he pulls the trigger and before he even realized a burst of approximately 5 or 6 rounds gets fired off of his AK 47. The bullets begin to hit the ground right in front of my head approximately four to five meter away, but with the recoil of the burst, one bullet after the other comes closer.

That was all I needed. I jumped off of my position in the firing line and ran away. The commanding officer finally stopped me at the end of the firing line. "Soldier, stop now!" he yelled at me. What are you doing? This is not a play ground to run around!"

"I have absolutely no desire to be killed by friendly fire from an idiot," I answered still scared to death by the level of idiocy on my right hand side.

Now let me explain why normally none of the enlisted soldiers was eager to score high on target shooting, even though you could get a lot of benefits when you were good at it. And I was good but did not let anybody know. The reason was very simple. All the excellent shooters were automatically registered for service at the border between East Germany and West Germany. And since they had proven to be excellent shooters they had to hit the fleeing people, to kill those who tried to escape the paradise of the working class, to kill those who knowingly risked their lives crossing the death-stripe under the fire of the AK 47 in the hands of excellent shooters, mostly not older than 18 or 19 years, seldom 20 years old. I did not want to be one of the soldiers at the border line. Because I did not want to kill people who risked their lives for freedom, I missed sometimes the target. Although I was still a communist at this time, I could not understand why we had to kill people who did not want to live in East Germany and would rather get killed. Something in me said it was wrong.

Later after the boot camp training was finished we five enlisted were move to separate quarters and the future NCOs began their specializing training while we enlisted men became truck drivers to ensure their training sessions. During that time they were also regularly called to duty to perform the watch on the objects of the casern. Kirsche was applied to a section where people of our battalion would try to sneak in over the fence when they were back late from furlough, which was usually limited till 12:00 a.m. The average soldier in the East German army had no right to furlough. It was granted on the mercy of the Sergeant Major of the company and only possible Wednesdays and Saturdays after duty.

Since there was a permanent fear in the screwed minds of the leadership in East Germany that the evil capitalists would attack the socialist workers paradise, a minimum of 65 percent permanent combat readiness was mandatory. With that the number of soldiers who could go on furlough was small, and when you got caught coming back late you ended up in jail for at least three days and furlough was history for the next two or three months. Knowing that, whoever was late and knew that his own company was on duty that night would jump over the fence and his comrades would not report that. Normally! Not though when Kirsche was on duty. But that was unknown to everybody till it happened first time.

One of the enlisted guys who was with me in the same room during the boot camp time with Kirsche was late, and since he knew Kirsche was on duty at a specific section he decided to jump over that fence. Now those fences surrounding an East German military complex weren't low. They was approximately twelve to fifteen feet high. And because he had some drinks before he caught the strength to start the action he was exhausted after he had climbed the top of the fence direct on one of the poles. Now he was sitting on top of the pole and rested and trying to figure out how to jump down without to ripping his uniform on the barbed wires which were mounted inwards on the top of the fence.

Suddenly a loud command reached his ears. "Stop or I'll shoot!"

He recognized the voice and yelled back, "Hey, Kirsche, it's me." And happy to see a comrade, he added, "Don't give me that shit. Help me to get down here."

But not with Kirsche! Kirsche was important. He had his order and he insisted, "Come down or I'll shoot!" So the guy just jumped down from the fence ripping off his uniform. And Kirsche, obviously totally stressed out with the responsibility he was confronted with for first time in his life, considered that jump as an attack onto him. So, he broke a warning shot.

As I said before, he was an excellent shooter and we had learned how to shoot warning shots and we had trained that over and over again. As our trainer always said just don't shoot the earlap, but it must move by the airstream of the bullet then its right. At the short distance the bullet was fired and the marksmanship Kirsche had, I believe every single word the guy said when he complained that he felt the bullet passing his head. Now he lay down on the ground and did not move an inch. Even though Kirsche requested that he would stand up, yelling at him, "Get up on you knees, fold your hands behind your had and cross your legs!" exactly as he had learned it during boot camp. It took the section commander only a few minutes to arrive on the scene and get the intruder arrested and, according to the procedure, Kirsche relieved from duty. The intruder got ten days arrest, and Kirsche had a day off for excellent service on patrol. Unfortunately to him, he needed the whole day to clean his underwear.

One year our unit was redeployed for a special maneuver for four weeks at the eastern border river Oder. It was early in spring and we were transported by train. All that was done as it would probably happen in case of a war. We were thrown out of bed sometimes after midnight by the alarm sirens, got our stuff and marched to the car pool. Our NCO was already there and we started the trucks and drove back to the barracks were the NCO students already were standing to be picked up. Loading all their stuff and a ton of other material was a strange thing. Nobody spoke and it was just so unusually quiet, because nobody knew what was going on. We had no clue whether this was for real or not, till we arrived at the railway station and the NCO informed us that we were on the way to a mutual maneuver with the Polish Army.

The transport took about ten hours, and when we finally unloaded train, we were in a small town near the Oder River. The camp was built directly at the river side of the dike. It was a nightmare. We had to use our personal rain canvas, which was just large enough to cover an average person's body. With some pieces of wood we build a tent and filled a large potato bag with straw to lay on it. The difficulty was in the details as always. The meadow was until a few days ago flooded and the ground was still soaked with water from the river. Now that alone wasn't really a problem, since we had enough straw to refill the bags every day. But in March in that area you still could have temperatures below freezing point, and we had exactly that.

However, with the thick woolen uniforms and woolen blankets we had, we did not really get too cold during night. But it happened though that some guys were frozen with their backs onto the straw bag, and in the morning had severe trouble getting up. The only solution was to have enough blankets, but the demand was far above the resources. And with that it happened that the one or other soldier needed to be lifted off his straw bag in the morning. The situation was worsened by the constant layer of fog we had for the first couple of days. And we found it very wrongful that the NCOs and the Officers all slept at the commanders' office about two miles away. Only those who were in charge stayed at the camp. And since they were officers and not just plain soldiers, they slept in large 10x10 tents with cots for them and wood-burning ovens. Another cut into the propaganda picture of the equality of all who served the workers class. Although I was not yet in real opposition to the system, it began to make me angry.

FREEDOM'S NIGHTMARE

It was the same year that Andreas was arrested by the city police after he and two of his friends had broken into several cars and stolen radios. He was fifteen years old, and it was a horrible experience for my mother. The judicial proceeding was at his school because of his age and to demonstrate to the other students what happened when you broke the law. I was prompted to appear as a character witness and for that I got 3 days leave. In the evening when I was sitting in the family room reading in a book, suddenly my mother yelled after me and said, "Harald, come because Christiane is here." I did not know what she was talking about, but I walked into the kitchen and there she was. All what I recalled was that incredible long blond braided hair as I had seen it months ago laying on the cover of her bed in the hospital.

Months ago, my mother was in the hospital because of a surgery she had on her foot and I had visited her. Now, with the National Healthcare it wasn't much different than with anything else in a communist country. At least six, sometimes eight people were placed in one room. Usually there was one washbasin in the room for all and the bathroom was on the corridor. By the way that wasn't much different when we came to Austria and later to Germany, because all have nationalized healthcare. The only difference was that those who had enough money to pay extra in an additional private health insurance had the right to get into a two-bed room with enclosed bathroom. So I went to the hospital to visit my mother, and in the bed next to hers lay somebody I could not identify. All that was visible was a very blond, very long braid. Everything else was covered by the blanket.

Now she was standing in my mother's kitchen and smiled. Many months later I'd understand that the Lord has sent an angel to rescue me. I can't explain it but it was something I'd never experienced before. We felt immediately connected and began to talk. We talked the whole night about nearly everything young people in our situation, in that country, would talk and so much more. In the morning she drove me to the caserne and we promised to see each other again. We began to date, and a couple of months later I was discharged from the army.

Christiane worked as a radio operator at the radio station in Glowe and had a very strange shift system to follow. This radio station she worked

229

at was a very important part of the East German information system. Through it the country kept contact with all vessels swimming around the world. It was a hard job, but the income was well above the average income of a woman outside the armed forces, the party bureaucracy or government institutions. To become a radio operator at that station was a long way for her, and she had to sacrifice a lot of spare time to get through the specializing school. And she had to hide her believe in Jesus Christ. If she would have confessed publicly that she was a Christian; she would never have seen that school from inside, let alone get the job. How did she get there?

Christiane has been raised as one of three children, all girls, at her grandparents' home. Her mother moved back to her parents' after she was divorced. Christiane's grandfather was a very faithful man and so was the whole family. Every night he used read a part of the Bible after dinner. She grew in such a divided environment that she became silent. One must try to imagine how a little girl feels when she learns at night how merciful the almighty God is and the very next morning at school gets punished for belonging to a Christian home.

There was a time when she had to stand up in the classroom and the teacher pointed at her and said, "This is the enemy of our glorious future. She, her grandparents and her mother are those who want the famous communistic society to fail. Because of those kind parasitic elements still living among us, the comrades have to struggle with the setup of the communism." She was at the third or fourth grade at that time. She would not pass the several socialistic extracurricular tests because she just could not say those things needed to get certified. For that she was permanently blamed for being "not one of us."

As explained before, it was mandatory in East Germany to have an education in a certain profession after high school. The possibilities near to the village where she lived were limited. She began a vocational training and became a professional electrician. This was anything but what she liked. The people on the shipyard, a hundred percent navy vessel builder, were reckless, ragtag, and their colloquial language was more than dirty. So she left after her graduation. That was not what the communistic society liked really much and all the time she needed to find another job she was permanently under social attacks. It needs to be understood that in a society where everything is central controlled and regulated, the power of the SED is absolute; there is no room for any kind of individualism. The main part in everybody's life is the collective. The individual does not count, has no voice, nothing to say at all. You couldn't just decide to change something in your life that influenced the collective and get away with it.

But it appears that it was a little different with her. Maybe it was her perseverance, maybe it was that the communistic supervisors had given up on her, or maybe it was just because the Lord was with her, but she found a job which really met her interests. She went to school in a small town south of East Berlin to become a radio operator. She not only learned to operate high-power transceivers but also to transmit and receive Morse-coded messages that she had to type direct into a text on a typewriter. The time there at this specific school was a good time on one hand because she could meet with her aunt from West Berlin a couple of times. Although it wasn't possible for people from West Berlin until the mid seventies to cross the Berlin border, because her aunt had a West German passport she could enter East Berlin and meet with Christiane. But on the other hand all that stuff with the communistic indoctrination began all over again. After graduation she moved to that small village on the north eastern coast line of the largest German island where the radio station was and started that job. That was 1970, and she was still there when we met.

She picked me up at the base when I was discharged from the army and we spent the weekend together. During the first several times we were together I felt insecure, because even though I had developed severe doubts inside of me about the society we lived in and the communistic system in general, I was not ready to abandon all that that I had been indoctrinated with over so many years. We did not really debate the differences in our political views but slowly I changed. Though I didn't notice it for myself at first, and it took almost two years to be ready to confirm, I had become a Christian.

I had to go back to my company next Monday and I was back on sea before a week was over. At first I was assigned to a small vessel, one of those cutters which served the fabric trawler I worked on before I was drafted. It was 26.6 meters (approximately 73 feet) long and had 7 crew members including the captain. The big advantage with this small vessel, which was mainly operated in the Baltic Sea or North Sea, was that the trips were relatively short up, to twelve days. That was of a special interest for both Christiane and me. I made two short trips as a machine assistant to the master machinist, because there was no position for an electrical engineer. Since it wasn't my real profession I did everything to get back onto a trawler. But we used this short time to know each other better and to understand one another more. And I still wonder how it worked out so well with us because at this time, beside all the changes I went through in my political opinion and started to discover again the Bible, I still was strongly bonded in the communistic party and their system of teaching and control.

We had not really much time together during the first months, but she was special and had planted a seed in me. I began to remember my time when I went to church, and we used every minute together to talk about her Bible-based home. It changed me completely, but not over night. It was a long process and sometimes very painful. Step by step I became a Christian. But that is not comparable with a Christian in America.

You need to know that Christian life in East Germany, based on the Lutheran Church which was infiltrated by the STASI, is not a Christian life as you know in a free world. We learned after the collapse of the communist world that the STASI had the secretary general of the Lutheran Church of East Germany in its pocket. He received the highest possible civilian decoration off the hands of his STASI case officer. And the bishop of the area we lived in was over more than 20 years a reliable unofficial Employee of the Ministry for State Security. Pastors were paid with West German money to stay in East Germany because the East German Socialist United Party was more than willing to let them go, contrary to any other person. What do you expect from leaders of a church like that? Where do you get your strength and courage from for the daily fight in such an environment? To believe in an almighty and loving God, try to know more about Jesus, being together with a small group of believers, mostly elder women praising the LORD and praying was part of it.

From the first moment of recognition that something inside me had changed, and brought back the time when God meant something to me, I always felt a little bit inspired by the great apostle Paul. Did we not have a little bit in common relating to our opinion about the Christians? Was he not a prosecutor of the Christians? Even though I did not prosecute them, but I laughed about believers, made jokes about God and named those who believed in him "the breaks on the golden carriage towards communism." I know this statement created some kind of an outcry; Apostle Paul was a Jew, and he believed in God before he became a Christian, but I did not even believe in any kind of almighty power above men, besides the dictatorship of the SED. How could I dare to find some kind of equality between me and him? And yet, there was, and still to a certain part is, something what made me to feel some kind of congeniality with him. I can't really say when I became a Christian and I wondered ever since, for a long time caught in my own uncertainty about my faith. Mainly because of the fact that so many Christians have some very incredible stories to tell about their experience discovering Jesus. And maybe because of my special situation, I'd explained, there was no such thing as a flash light or an internal shock.

After those short trips aboard the cutters I was sent out with a trawler where the electrical engineer was having some health issues and would be omitted for a while. It was late in fall when we left harbor and the trip was scheduled to last forty-eight days. And the trips in winter time could become really tough. Everybody wanted to be home on Christmas. And even though the vast majority of the East Germans had no real relationship to religion anymore, it was that time in the year when even the toughest sea men got wet eyes thinking on home. The weather was continuously bad, rain and wind and only moderate fishing results were replaced by light to medium storms which did not allow to fish at all.

The area we where fishing was normally lucrative at that time of the year, but that year was just a nightmare. Finally beginning December it became clear that we would not be home at Christmas, and the mood aboard reached its deepest point. The captain realized that he needed to do something and called a crew meeting, all men in the mess. He explained that he wasn't happy about the situation, but he couldn't change it. And he said that the easiest to not be angry about the situation was to forget about situations you can't change. That easy! Focus on things you can change

233

and try to do the best possible there. This short sentence actually started something in me which I never forgot in my life.

I began to focus on my own education about the books of the Bible. I had already begun to read, but now I intensified reading and focused on the book of Acts. For some reason Apostle Paul and his change from a persecutor of the Christians into the most fascinating fighter for Jesus Christ, and especially his role as the Apostle to the non-Jews, appeared very congenial to me. I thought that this was a thing I could control myself and only I could do it for me. The captain finished the meeting with the announcement that we would go up to the Gulf of Bothnia to go after the winter herring which was known to be there during that time.

We passed through the strait between Sweden's Aland and the Aland island of Finland. The crew was in a much better mood because everybody had great expectations about getting decent catches. The wind was steady at a relatively high level, but with this captain fishing wasn't stopped until 6 Buford. There were huge steel plates with a size of 100 x 150 inches used to hold the net in mid-water as well as the bottom weights composed of multiple steel blocks, fed onto a steel bar dispensed on the deep. Those weights easily had 300 pounds to hold the net bottom side open against the upper net side being kept leveled by the steel plates, pulled through the water. All that stuff was hanging on hooks and tangled and moved around with the movement of the vessel with the rolling sea. It was dangerous and the decks crew had to be very alert all the time. A second of inattention could bring you a broken bone or worse, death. We made good progress and had almost three quarters of our capacity on frozen fish in the hold when the weather turned from bad to horrible.

First thing I noticed one morning was that strange sound along the vessel's side. Ice! We were driving through ice. Everybody on board knew that our trawler had only a low ice class. I don't remember the correct class we had, but I remember it wasn't much. When I went up to the bridge, I found both NOs and the captain there looking out at the sea, which was completely covered with ice. It wasn't thick yet, but the real problem was the wind. It had turned over night to East-North-East and became stronger and stronger every hour. Since we were already running south, I wasn't worried because I knew we were not far from the strait, about a day trip. Three hours later the situation had changed completely, and I was concerned now, as every other man on board was.

We had a horrible storm and we could not run it out, meaning our trawler could not travel fast enough through water to stay ahead of the waves. So we had to turn and go against the waves. The ice storm from the winter polar region coming direct down the Gulf of Bothnia was the most horrifying experience I had in my whole career aboard a fishing trawler. I'll never forget that noise of the ice floes scratching along the trawler's side during the time the trawler was entering the hill of the waves. Then, the trawler reached the tipping point, would slide down the wave and crash directly into the next wave. The breaking sea crushed over the bow and up to the bridge where the rotating sighting glasses had difficulties keeping the sight open for the NO. This crash into the wave almost brought the trawler to a standstill, and the movement of the trawler was more that of a wounded animal, angry and shaking off the pain, than a vessel being in its element, the sea. It seemed to take forever before the bow came out of the wave and the climbing to the top of the wave began again.

There was no point even thinking about going to sleep. For about three days we fought the storm, barely making any distance against the wind and the ice waves, but at least the ice was reduced and driven out of the Gulf by the storm. When we were finally able to turn around and begin fishing again ice wasn't a problem anymore. I remember that the radio operator told us that he had heard a message that the storm had ripped a light house from one of the thousands of small islands in that area where we had just survived one of the heaviest storms there. Yet another problem became obvious. Fighting the storm with running the engine at 90 percent power almost permanently had consumed more fuel than usual. Even though that we did catch a good amount of fish, we would have to break off and go home with approximately 80 percent loading capacity filled. Not bad considering the payments, and although Christmas was gone, we had a good chance to get home for New Years Eve.

The vessel was finally at the pier I think it was right after Christmas, and I was really happy to have some days off to spend with Christiane. But soon I learned that wasn't to happen. The workforce dispatch caught me and sent me to harbor watch at the Fabric Trawler "Granitz," just arrived from the shipyard in Poland where it has been rebuilt over several months. Since I wasn't married, I could not escape. The only way to get around it would have been to get a sick prescription, and that was not possible since the harbor doctor, the only one who you could get such a prescription, was on vacation. I was disturbed, but when I learned that Christiane had to work also, I used the time to have some quiet hours aboard.

Eventually it worked out for me that a senior electrical engineer on a trawler had left, and I got his job. That meant that I was now much longer at sea. The sea journeys as we called them became longer. One reason was that the trawler where I worked now had a much larger capacity to load frozen fish. A second reason was that the extreme overfishing by an enormous number of fishing vessels of all nations around the Baltic Sea and the North Sea led to less and less results at the traditional areas. But instead of stopping or reduce overfishing, the Russians broke all international agreements before even the ink was dry on the paper. The increasing development and the implementation of modern nets and echolocation technologies allowed them to fish at regions never thought before. From beginning May till late October most of the trawlers of our company were now far in the north, at the Barents Sea around Spitsbergen. The island was at this time commonly used by the Russian and Norwegian industry. They exploited the inventory of seldom ores such as manganese ore, magnetic ore and copper or molybdenite.

The fishing activities were mainly done 200 to 250 nautical miles south of that island, too far away from home to go back and forth when the loading capacity was filled. Therefore we discharged our fish to supply vessels. They brought mail—highly appreciated—and took mail back home; also, we got fresh food. Sometimes crew members needed to be replaced and they came with the supply vessel too. If you had not a very good reason to be replaced, you usually were on board all the time, sometimes three months before you saw land again. With one exception I had the luck to be on board without seeing land over that time.

Try to imagine, you leave your home port at the end of April or beginning of May. The nature is still in its winter sleep. Everything is grey in grey, no green on the trees, no flowers in gardens and often enough icy snow-rain showers. When you come back and you see land for the first time after three months nature is in its full gorgeousness. Everything is different. Then after a few days, usually 5 to 7 days for necessary repairs and revictualing, the next trip starts. And then you come back and it is almost winter.

When I experienced this the first time after I met Christiane and started to discover God as the creator, the impression of that change in the appearance of nature was so overwhelming that I instantly confessed to myself that there had to be a creator because this miracle couldn't just happen by chance. This picture of creation, transforming from nothing into an incredible gorgeousness of colors and flowers and different shades of green on the multitude of trees, was fascinating any time I came back from a deep sea fishing journey where I had no other color than blue. Yeah, there were different shades of blue, but all was blue, sometimes with a slight tinge of green, but that was it.

On the Hook to Barendsburg

What Deep Sea Fishing, Russian Nautical Navigation, an Almost Lost eye, And a Rope in the Propeller Had in Common

The East German commercial fishing industry had two severe problems. Alcohol was the biggest problem. One reason was that you usually had, beside the professionals, a lot of low-level qualification people on board, and they used any kind of reason to drink and get drunk. The second big problem was the so-called illegal leaving of the republic, or as the people called it, skips off. Since the border between East Germany and West Germany was so secured that even a mouse would die by crossing the dead strip, the opportunity to work on a vessel which enters foreign, meaning western, ports was a great temptation. And the secret police knew it. Although the fishing vessels rarely entered foreign harbors where people had a chance to ask for political asylum, most of the people on board who had the intention to skip off had absolutely no chance to get hired onto a vessel of the mercantile marine.

But as the vernacular says, you can't look into men's heads. It happened time and again that people could outsmart the secret police and walk away. Therefore the secret police had special educated members of the *HauptVerwaltung Aufklaerung* (German for Head Office Intelligence HVA) which were absolutely unknown to anybody working in normal jobs in any kind of companies. And for sure they were on each vessel. Not even the captain knew which member of his crew was one of those special officers. And abiding the rules of the great leader Lenin, there was a second guy of this breed on board and they didn't know each other as well. Because as Lenin said, "Trust is good, control is better." You remember the movie *Hunt for the* Remember *Red October* with Sean Connery starring as the captain asking his chief officer, "Do you know who is the KGB officer on my ship?" And the answer was twofold, "Your ship? Nobody knows."

And yet the temptation was so big that some people often took all those sacrifices, no family life, having no real home, living a vagabond life just for that very moment to get the chance to run away. Confronted with that reality, I was again pushed a step further away from the socialistic doctrine, which forced people to renounce themselves just to get out of the Worker Paradise.

These STASI officers for special operations were everywhere. It appears that roughly 9500 officers for special operations had been trained and sent out during the existence of the STASI. Unfortunately all files and documents about this top secret and very special unit are vanished and could not be discovered since the STASI finally was dispersed in 1990. There are rumors that the STASI internal security guard had taken advantage of the usefully "initiated" storm of the furious people during a protest rally in front of the STASI Headquarter in Berlin on January 15th 1990. While the mob of the people rampaged through the STASI offices, these guys used the situation and destroyed most of the highest top secret files and took some with them to make a business with it. You may remember on the so-called Rosenholz files. It's still unknown how the microfilms with detailed information about the spy active for the HV-A ended up in the hands of the CIA, but most of the files were copied onto CD-Rom and handed over to the German Government. It is still not accessible for the German people. Another dark chapter of the East German terror regime remains in the dark for political reason.

At the end of the spare time between one of the spring and the summer trips, Christiane and I were on the way to the harbor because I had to leave that day, and I ask her to marry me. She did not answer. I was a little shocked, and all I could do during those few minutes we had before

I had to go through the gate into the harbor was ask her to think about it, because we had at least three months till I would be back.

When the vessel finally left the harbor that day, I was uncertain about our relationship as never before. Why did she not answer? What is the reason for the reluctance? I had to witness more than once the break-up of relationships that friends and colleagues went through, and most of the time was it because of the extreme long separation between partners. Several weeks later came the first supply vessel, which usually brought some goods, food, spare parts and mail and with it a couple of letters. In one of the letters she asked about my ring size. So I realized that was a yes.

We didn't have so fancy stuff as they have today, these ring gauges. And I needed to be careful not to get the news out to all on-board because that would have been a reason for a big party. And as said before, alcohol was a problem on fishing vessels. And yet, there was the doubt in me every single day on that vessel, reams of miles away, why should she bind herself to me? However, somehow I got it done and could measure the ring size and wrote it into my next letter. But there is no mailbox in the middle of the northern part of the Barents Sea. It took a couple of weeks till the next supply vessel arrived and mail could be exchanged.

For a reason I never could discover, the captain and the chief engineer had a kind of love-hate relationship. Our trawler was permanently out of trim, and they accused each other of being responsible for that. The chief engineer told me that the captain had a propensity to hoard all kind of running rigging and cable ropes. One has to understand the situation in East German economy. You took whatever material, spare parts or any kind of goods you could lay your hands on when you were responsible for running a department. And there was no difference in the fishing industry, although the supply was much better than for any other industry. You just never knew when you were able to get certain things, and so you just loaded everything you thought you might need once.

Since the trawlers were handled as a kind of an independent business unit within the company, we had to "buy" all this stuff, and then when we came back from the journey we "sold" our fish to the company. All that was imaginary, but it was a little bit of a first contact with business economics. So when the captain got the rumor that there was something in the warehouse that he believed was valuable for future trips or for exchange with other trawlers he just *bought* it.

This was one of the first secrets of socialistic economy rules you usually learned at a very early age: buy whatever might be valuable, even if you don't need it yourself and now. You never know who may need it later and for what other goods you can exchange it the other guy has. This was the basic rule of life in socialism. No matter what it was, deep sea fishing, repair of machines or building material or anything else you may have had a need for, you needed something to barter for, and even if it was the favor of a friend you'd need. That was what all things had in common. Money wasn't worth much, because the basic law of human coexistence, although denied by the socialistic philosophy—Supply and Demand determine the Price—was working on a daily basis. That was the common ground to survive in a centralistic controlled economy, and it is common ground to be successful in a capitalistic environment.

At my first minutes on board of that specific trawler it just happened that I ran into the captain when he was on his way to the warehouse because of a tip he had gotten from somebody and he needed a hand. Since I had just signed in the ship's articles with the chief mate, the captain did not know that I was chartered as the electrical engineer. So he just ordered me to go with him, and I had too much respect to disagree. Actually you did not argue with the captain of a vessel, not at the time in East Germany, and I'm pretty sure it is still the same today. We had a very good time together at that warehouse, and when I started to look for some electrical supplies I thought I might need, he finally realized that I was his new electrical engineer. He apologized for being rude and not having asked what my function was on board. I accepted it and he was very helpful to get me connected to the treasury guardian of the electrical department of the warehouse.

That was very a important person to me. And that was because of another very important rule of the East Germany, and probably all other communistic economies throughout the Eastern Bloc—the appreciation of a warehouse department lead, and with that the gifts he could receive, were directly proportional to the ability to have so-called gold dust available. Not everybody came to know the true promise to walk through the special areas where the gold dust was stored. The magic word was, as so often anywhere else in East Germany, "Do you have something FDGB?" Wherein FDGB meant *Fuer Den Guten Bekannten*, which actually was a malapropism of the appropriation FDGB (*Freier Deutscher GewerkschaftsBund*). The meaning in this case was getting something only friends would get so it was for the well known friend.

The captain's introduction gave me that connection, and I became included in the FDGB club of the electrical warehouse department. With that I was able to get in example the extremely rare self-adhesive Teflon tape needed to repair the plastic welding stations in the freezing department. When we got back to the trawler he invited me for a coffee, and that was the start of a very good relationship. Every morning after I had breakfast I made my check round through the different departments and ended for a first Q&A at the control room to have a coffee with the engineer-in-chief. Not only because of he was my direct boss but we had to talk things through, like what was on the map for the day on preventive stuff, what I had scheduled and I had to check the log-file of the three other machinists to see if anything had happened overnight that had to be taken care of. And every morning he complained that the captain had loaded the trawler with another bunch of unnecessary cable ropes and steel waste and he could pump the fuel from one bunker to the next and couldn't trim the trawler because the captain was a hamster. And indeed we had a very strange situation on this trawler; it was always out of trim. The nautical personnel blamed the machinist for being incapable of trimming the fuel tanks, and the machinists blamed the nautical personnel for worsening it by hoarding steel waste.

And because of being out of trim, everybody had a special piece of wood called the "coffee wood." Over all the time that this situation existed there had been a kind of cult evolved to put as much creativity into the design of the coffee wood as possible. The coffee wood was approximately two inches long and one inch wide, and the height was from approximately 1/8 of an inch to a one half inch over the total length. Hence it was possible to have the coffee cup filled independent to the current grade of tilt the trawler had at this day. Usually it was when I just had finished my coffee and the chat with the engineer-in-chief, and I always wondered how he could know that, the captain called through the P.A. system, "E-Mix to the bridge." E-Mix was the standard nomination of the electrical engineer on a trawler. Even during my time on a fabric trawler with nearly fifty people and two electrical engineers and one electrician, *E-Mix* was the standard call for the electrical engineers, and the electrician was called the *E-Assi*, even though you had to have an engineering degree to get the job.

When I arrived at the bridge, he had already two cups of coffee ready and started at first with a kind of questions about the chief, which he really never expected to get answered, "Did the chief complain again about the cables and ropes? We have already removed some and he is still not able to trim the boat. It's impossible to do him justice. He is an old nagger. If I'd not know him for so many years I'd long have thrown him over board," he finished now with a smile on his face.

When he was done we usually went through the electrical stuff mainly as far as it affected the winch and fish echelon system or the frosting system in the converting area and cooling system in the cargo hold. And then he told me one or another story. I do not remember all of those, but soon I realized that he was not that kind of captain that you would expect on a trawler under the flag of the socialistic East German dictatorship. Later I learned that he was the only captain who was not a member of the SED in the whole company.

Once he told me a story about an incident which has never appeared in newspapers or was publicly talked about. There was that small village in the northern part of the island where Christiane worked at the radio station. Also in that village was a foster child home which I knew about because it was well known to anybody who lived on the Island. It was a foster home for children who were taken away from parents either were unable to fulfill the requirements of the socialistic educational system or much worse their parents had tried to leave East Germany without allowance, were caught by the STASI and put in jail. Until the responsible bureaucrats had decided which one of the childless comrades and reliable communist couple would be entrusted to raise those children, they were *parked* at that foster home. That word *parked* was really used by these people.

A couple of years ago, long before we had moved to the Island, late in winter the kids from that foster child home made a hike along the shore, and some of the kids run onto the ice. Although it still covered a wide area from the shore into sea it was fragile since the salty water of the Baltic

Sea needed really cold temperature to be strong enough to hold people and that did not happen too often. Especially along the cliff line are many large boulders laying in the water not too far from the shore line, which attracted some of the kids. With the ice field wide enough into the sea, the kids could easily reach one of these large boulders, and four of them climbed onto it.

All that happened within a few minutes of negligence of the nursery teacher because she was dealing with some of the kids who were behind the group. Now, the ice was fragile, and just at this time the wind blowing on the shore increased. Within a few minutes the ice field which had bridged the water between the shore and the large boulder with the kids was a field of ice debris. There was no way that the kids could go off that rock.

The nursery teacher reacted immediately, left the elder kids on the shore and ran with two of the younger kids back to the village to the next fisherman. Within minutes they were in the water with their rudder boats trying to get to the rock. But the wind was already too strong at that time. The boat crashed on another rock and the both fisherman could barely rescue themselves. In the mean time several other fisherman, the other nursery teachers alarmed by the elder kids, and the village policeman arrived at the scene. The fisherman tried again to get a boat to the rock, but failed as the first time.

The policeman walked back to the village and called the nearby Navy base and asked for help. They declined to send a vessel arguing that the water wasn't deep enough and with this extreme onshore wind there was the danger that the Rocket-Speedboat could run aground. Meanwhile the wind was so strong that the water sprayed all over the kids on the rock who had stopped weeping and the people on shore could only hear them whine. Somebody remembered that the Commander of the Russian Army unit, stationed in Saßnitz, had a helicopter and they tried to call the Russian basis in Saßnitz. Time was running out, and the technical infrastructure of East Germany in general and for sure on that Island wasn't prepared for such kind of emergency situations. After endless minutes of back and forward negotiation finally they got the commander on the phone. The answer was short and staggering.

"Net! We can't risk our level of operational readiness to fight the class enemy! And the storm may even damage the helicopter and he can't risk that either." The policeman now tried to call the helicopter squadron of the GDR Navy in Stralsund, the nearest helicopter squadron, and ask for help. It took him approximately thirty minutes to get a connection. Just to get somebody with the military authority on the phone to decide to fly this mission took another half hour. They immediately started two helicopters but it was already too late. The permanent freshening wind was meanwhile a storm, nightfall had begun and the helicopters were ordered to abandon the operation for safety reasons.

The temperature was low enough to turn the icy water spray into ice, and slowly but steadily the four kids on the rock turned into an ice pillar. The people stood on the shore the whole night, and at dawn the whine voices of the kids on the rock were long silenced. The storm calmed down. The fishermen got into the boat, rowed to the rock and broke the ice which kept the group of kids on the rock. They lay the human ice blocks into their boat and brought them back to shore. This story was never made public. For more than two weeks was the STASI in the village and made sure that nobody would dare to say anything in public about what happened that night on the shores of the village. Only off-the-record and only few people told the story years later. One of them was the captain of that trawler, who happened to be the husband of one of the women on the beach that night.

We used to sit in the map room where we were most of the time uninterrupted, and the door had a window so that we could see when somebody came to the room and we changed the theme we talked about. It became a kind of a ritual to have those coffee-morning hours and I really enjoyed it. Although we never talked about God or faith, somehow I had the feel that we had a kind of affinity, and I really don't know whether he was a Christian or not. But sure for nothing existing on earth he would have openly declared that he was a Christian. Because nobody in that environment could be hundred percent sure that his vis-à-vis was not the officer for special operations, you never opened yourself that far. I was actually surprised that he was talking so open about things which were wrong with the political system, since I was sure he did not know who those officers were. For the captain it would have been the end of his career and for sure his family would have had the whole arsenal of repression on it. Although it was an incredible story and sounded so strange, I did not question his story because he was the most trustworthy, honest and inwardly man I met during my time aboard the fishing trawlers.

And I got some kind of confirmation that this incredible story wasn't an accident when a nearly unbelievable other incident was told to me by the mother of one my schoolmates several months later. During the time the trawler was in the harbor and got equipped for the next journey, which usually took between seven and ten days depending on how much repair needed to be done, I had more time available than Christiane had. She had to work her shifts, and so I used the time and applied at the local travel agency for a job as tourist guide.

The idea was that I knew our island very well and could just use the time to earn some additional money. But it wasn't that easy. Everything in Germany is regulated, requires a certificate, and to get that you need to pass at least one test. Especially in a dictatorship where everything is controlled closely, regulation is just the beginning. So I went out and bought several books about the island, and the historic cities in North-East Germany. It was very interesting to widen the horizon about the history of these cities and especially about some places on the island where we had spent many hours as kids, not knowing that we were on historical impressive ground. I passed the test, finished the record cards, which I used for the test preparation, and got to work. Most of the time it was a tour around our island called *Ruegenrundfahrt* (island roundtrip). But there were others too i.e. a tour to the south east area of East Germany which lasted several days. Our two-day tours were to other interesting places in the northern part of East Germany, such as Rostock, Stralsund, Wismar and so on, mainly well looked for, because of the hanseatic period. I drove with the public transportation to the starting point of the tour.

One day I got a special tour, which wasn't really a tour, and travel guides were only there to help the tourists in case they had some problem. It was what was called boots trip along the coastline. One trip lasted for four hours and we did it twice per day. There was a break in between the trips. During that break the second tour guide, a woman who appeared to me as I should know her, asked me if I would like to go with her for lunch. We bought some sandwiches and sat down on one of the benches at the esplanade. She looked at me and asked me if I didn't remember her. I said, "I think I know you, but I really can't put you anywhere."

She said, "I'm the mother of Volker. He was your classmate in high school."

Now I have to confess that for some reason I'm not really good in remembering faces and have even more trouble to bring names and faces together if I haven't seen them very often. But for sure I remembered Volker. He was kind of an outsider in school like me but for a different reason. He lost his father as a little kid to the sea, he was a fisherman, and he was most of the time introverted. And I recall that we spent many hours during the senior year together, because he had some deficiencies in math and physics, doing homework. But since his mother was working, I saw her very seldomly, and so I did not recognize her face immediately. So I apologized for that and asked her, "How is Volker doing?" And with my thoughts back at that time, said, "Haven't seen him since several years now, actually since he started his apprentice as a painter, I believe it was?"

She said, "That's okay." But suddenly she started crying, and I was completely swept of my feet. After some minutes she regained her countenance and asked me if I really did not know. Now it was on me to be surprised, I asked her, "What is it about Volker I should know?"

Still sobering and wiping her tears, she began to tell me a nearly unbelievable story.

Many years later we would learn that those stories weren't really unbelievable, just concealed.

Volker went to an apprenticeship after high school to become a painter. This was a two-and-a-half year education where professional specific theoretical education with practical training alternates. And it was mandatory in East Germany as the lowest level education when you finished school. So he went through that painter apprenticeship, and on the day he passed his last practical test and got his certificate as a master painter, he went to a restaurant with his colleagues to celebrate that. After a while, they had already some beer, they began to tell jokes, and several beers later the jokes became political. Everybody raised in East Germany knew that you never told political jokes outside your closest, most trustworthy circle of friends. For sure not in a restaurant! But alcohol is the enemy of every secret!

His mother said that his colleagues told her that they were still laughing when two men perhaps from the table right behind them suddenly stood on both sides of Volker. They produced their credentials which identified them as officers of the STASI. They declared Volker arrested. That was the last time anybody saw him alive. When he did not contact his mother for a couple of days, and she couldn't find him in his apartment, she went to one of his colleagues to ask him. He hesitated even to open the door to talk to her, and all she could get from him was that her son has been arrested by the STASI. She was horrified. Everybody in East Germany knew what that meant. It usually ended with a couple of years behind bars. Just look up the term *STASI Zuchthaus* on the internet if you want to know why that thought was so horrifying. She began immediately to try to find out where he was, but she ran into extreme resistance.

It took her several months to get an answer to her letters she sent wherever she believed she could get some information. That letter she got was short and lapidary information that her son was indicted with subversive agitation and vilification of a leading person. His whereabouts could not be revealed because of the ongoing investigation. Another couple of months later she got a hint that he was in a certain prison in the southern area of East Germany, and against all reasoning of her friends she traveled to that town, only to be rejected and she had to go home without even knowing if he was there or not.

More than a year and a half later she received another letter. This one was the formal information that her son died because of cardiac insufficiency. The letter told her that he was cremated, and because of the seriousness of the felony towards the Socialistic achievements of the German Democratic Republic the place of his burial was not disclosed. He was 20 years old, 6'3", and 210 lbs and very athletic and in the best health condition, because he played team handball twice per week, and that as long as I knew him. At the time she told me about it, she did not know where her son was buried. She was sworn to secrecy about the circumstances of the disappearance of her son, and neither she nor the former colleagues dared to talk about that in public. She only told me what happened because she remembered that I had spent many hours with her son to get him prepared to pass the final tests at high school. It did not happen again that we had to work together or even in the same area, and our trawler started its second yearly journey in June towards the Barents Sea. With that I never met her again because when I came back from that journey, I went to university and lost track of nearly everything that was going on in my hometown.

The fishing activities in that area of the Barents Sea were actually real deep sea fishing. And I mean *deep*. When we put down the net for a fishing session we had much more of the steel rope in the water than usual, up to 1500 meter roughly 1640 yards. With that we had the net down on the ground at approximately 550 to 600 yards. The net had several pads of cow skins at the first part of the bottom side to cover it from the rough ground. Also the bottom side of the net and several yards of the steel rope were loaded with huge weights to hold it down while the upper side of the net was equipped with huge rubber balls with adjustable amounts of air to hold the upper side of the net high. With that the net would stay open, and pulling it over the ground, all the ground fishes would be scratched off the ground and hopefully swim into the net.

The fish we were after in that region was Golden Red Fish. During the session of towage roughly four to six hours, we could get eight to ten metric tons of fish in the net. The net was covered by a net probe, which was mounted right on the upper side of the net opening. Using the ultrasound technology, this probe sent sound waves and received the reflections. Through a cable it was connected to the trawler and the signals are sent to a display on the bridge. There a pen, deflected by the electronic signal equivalent to the amount of fish swimming through the opening of the net, was constantly writing on a continuously moving paper. When the captain thought it was enough, the real work for the deck crew begun. To haul the net inboard took up to an hour because of the length of the steel rope in the water and the huge load. Usually the net itself was approximately 120 yards long, and when the opening appeared on deck, it needed to be pulled section by section with additional steel ropes on board. That took its time, and when the end of the net where the fish was, called the stert, was on deck, we knew how successful the session was.

And now everybody who was not on watch became suddenly a butcher. This kind of fish needed to be cut off immediately. We cut off the head, slit open the belly and took out the intestines. I can't really describe it, but it is a bloody and strange matter when suddenly fifteen men are standing around a platform and butchering fish from the size of approximately 10 inches up to 3.5 feet. I still have a picture holding one of these giants in front of me. Then the fish would be slit down a skit into the freezer area, cramped into the freezer cassettes and the cassettes would be filled with fresh water. The freezing process on that trawler was using Freon 11. Since it was already banned by the EWG (predecessor of the EU) because of its assumed tremendous effect on the ozone layer in the atmosphere, it was cheap and available, because nobody else would buy it.

Since it took almost five full days to get to the fishing area, the fleet stayed there the whole season, and when we had filled the loading capacity we called one of the supply vessels which were constantly shuttled between the home port and the fishing area. We would unload our frozen fish into their cargo bay and they would leave for the home port when they got filled to their capacity.

One day I woke up early and immediately realized that something was wrong on board. When I arrived at the bridge, the captain was on the Ultra-Short-Wave radio talking in Russian and was very agitated. Then he hung up, and he turned around to me.

"Give the E-Mix a coffee," he said toward the helmsman and asked me to follow him into the map room, where we usually sat and talked. The helmsman brought my coffee, refilled his cup, and went back to his job, closing the map room door behind him.

"Gunter has had an accident. He got a piece of a steel rope in his left eye. We can't get to a port in time. You know we are to far away from any harbor. I did send a Mayday call and got a response from a Russian Super-Trawler, you know those larger trawlers we build for them, equipped with a board hospital, and their surgeon happens to be specialized in ophthalmology. We're on our way to meet them and should be there in approximately three hours," he said, sipping on his coffee. The captain was obviously moved by the situation. I could tell by the sound of his voice.

"That's the reason why we're steaming full speed."

"I thought for a moment you had some inspiration that a huge swarm of fish is waiting somewhere else," I answered.

"I'm sorry, I do not want to be rude, but how could that happen?"

"The deck hands had to replace some of the steel ropes around the net, and for that, they had to cut it to the right length. Using the tools available, a sledgehammer and a cleaver, they cut the ropes. You know how brittle those steel ropes are, and unfortunately one wire piece of that steel rope broke away and flew directly into Gunter's left eye."

Safety glasses were not unknown in East Germany, but rarely available, so they did not use them.

Then suddenly he jumped out of his seat.

"Come, let's see if we can see the Russian already." He walked out of the map room. I followed him, and we each grabbed a binocular and both looked in the direction where the Russian Trawler should be clearly visible at the horizon. Still hours away, but visible. There was nothing. The captain asked the helmsman if he had seen anything, which he denied. The captain took the binoculars again on his eyes, but I knew there was nothing and so did he.

"They should be visible for several minutes when they are where he, meaning the Russian captain, said they are," the captain said more to himself than to us others on the bridge.

Walking over to the radar he adjusted the range to the maximum, which was 60 nautical miles on our device, and buried his face into the rubber cover of the screen which allowed you to see the screen clear at daylight. He turned the bearing ring back and forth a couple of times then stepped back from the radar.

"They aren't there!"

They expression on his face was a combination of disbelief and consternation. With three steps he jumped to the VHF radio and called the Russian Super-Trawler. It took a while till they answered his call.

"Give me the coordinates of your current position please," he asked them in Russian.

The answer was clear to hear from the speaker, "Njet," which means *no* in Russian.

"We can't give you our position, but since we have your position from your Mayday call, we're on our way, just forty miles away and will arrive shortly," the Russian captain answered. You have to know that Russian vessels never gave you their position, never ever!

I thought our captain was going to explode. "You can't be forty miles away, because than I'd see you in my radar! How do you navigate your position? Your position must be wrong!" he said, having difficulties holding back his temper.

"I'm navigating with our great Russian navigation system and my position is correct! Your position must be wrong! You gave me a wrong position when you can't see us." The Russian captain's voice came loud and clear over the speaker

We were speechless. Nobody had ever heard something like that said to our captain. He was one of the most successful captains in the whole fleet because he was able to find as we said "the place where he dropped a match in the sea" the next season. The argument went back and forth for several minutes till finally the Russian captain gave his position.

We jumped to the map room where the captain immediately discovered that the Russian Super-Trawler was about 90 miles away and about 35 degrees in another direction according to our navigation system, which was C-LORAN imported from GB. This was not imported directly though, because East Germany was under the ban of this kind of technology. It had been installed on our trawlers especially for the fishing in that area of the Northern Atlantic at the harbor of the Swedish town of Helsingborg.

After six more nerve-racking hours of waiting and getting updates on the condition of Gunter from time to time by the chief mate, we finally got alongside ship with the Russian Super-Trawler. It was almost too late but yet at least the Russian doctor was real and very good in his abilities to save Gunter's eye. Since the weather was really good we lay alongside for some hours till it was certain that Gunter was okay and the captains had a long debate about navigation systems, mistakes and technical defects while slowly emptying some bottles of Vodka.

When we finally went back to fishing, the reason why we were there, everybody on board was relieved knowing Gunter would be home much sooner than we would see land. If we only knew how wrong we were.

Before the service in the NVA, when I was on the Fabric Trawler fishing with the cutters at the Baltic Sea, we had an accident on one cutter. One of the deck hands was standing in a kink of the towing rope when they lowered the net and he got drawn into the sea and under water. He actually never came back to East Germany because he asked for political asylum in the same second he arrived at the hospital in Sweden.

Why were we wrong with not seeing land for many more weeks? I think it was just two or three days after the accident with Gunter. We were heaving the net and all of us who were on watch, prepared to be ready for the next butcher session. The winches were yowling under the load and everybody was exited and looking forward to a great catch. Suddenly an unbelievable jerk went through the vessel as if we had hit a wall. The engine squeaked in a bloodcurdling tone and fell silent. Since the generators were driven by two auxiliary engines we still had electrical power and the winches worked to heave the net. But the vessel was unpowered and slowed down. The engineer and his crew tried to start the engine but it died within seconds and the indication was overload. Something was blocking the screw. Since the drive system on our vessel was a direct coupled engine-shaft-screw system, there was nothing we could do. Although it is a difficult task to get a full net on board without speed ahead, because the net isn't floating, we were able to get it on board and save the catch. At least most of it.

This situation is called an average, and at sea there are certain procedures in place when such things happen. For me as the electrical engineer it meant that I had to be at the bridge and engine room alternately to ensure that the electrical power system worked well and all nautical instruments were working. Now, remember, we were in the middle of nowhere in the Barents Sea. After a couple of radio conversations with the headquarters at home, it was decided to be towed to the Russian Base on Svalbard by one of the supply vessels that had just arrived at the fishing area and finished the round through the fleet delivering mail and spare parts. This was a mining settlement with the name Barensburg. The tramper took our trawler on the hook with a long towing line, and we were on our way. It was a 3-day trip, and with that almost double the time we would need to get into the next Norwegian port. But it did not cost convertible currency. Something the East German government was always short of.

It seemed to take forever to get to that island, and since there wasn't much to do, I began to systematically replace parts of the equipment I knew were at the edge of failing. That wasn't really easy, because often there weren't just parts to repair or replace defective stuff. Something you will never read about in books was the ingenuity required from the East German people and probably all the others behind the iron curtain. In a permanent fight to get things done without having all the tools and materials a peer would have in the Western World, you needed to have a seventh sense for how to handle situations with what you had and not with what you thought you'd need.

The inserts of the limit switches, which broke often, were rare, and certain types were not available at all. If I needed those, I would have to totally dismantle other ones and build a new one out of the parts. You really had to be inventive to get things going. The next day we could see the mountains of the island with our naked eyes, although it was still so far away that our radar did not catch it. Finally the seemingly endless trip over absolute a sea as smooth as glass drew to an end when one morning I arrived at the bridge, and I could see that we now had the mountains of the island on both sides of the vessel. That meant we were already inside the sound and within a few hours we were on the pier at a very small harbor.

The negotiations went quick and without any complication, and after a little while, several Russians begun to move machines and equipment close to the stern area on the pier followed by a man clothed with a heavy diving suit, the bronze helmet under one arm carrying the connectors for the air hose with the other hand. They connected the air hose and some-thing additional, which I later learned was the voice connection. Then two guys lifted the helmet over his head and set it down on the suite where the screwed it tight with several nuts. They started the motor of the air pump system, and when they had checked that the air was flowing into the suite and the voice connection worked, they closed the helmet opening by screwing a large round glass hold by a bronze ring in front of the diver's face. The diver marched to the pier and stepping down a ladder mounted at the pier wall, disappeared in the water.

Now I was disappointed, because standing at the nock of the bridge, I had no view onto the stern and what was going on there. Suddenly the motor of the air pump begun to stutter and the guys at the machine started to twitter. After they checked something I couldn't see and one of them run away into the barn and come back with a canister of fuel. They filled the fuel in and the machine noise went back to the former tone. Then the diver appeared on the surface holding an arm-thick, eight-feet-long piece of hemp rope in his hand. One guy at the pier stepped down the ladder and took it from him. When he was back at the pier, the other guys joint him in investigating the hemp rope.

Then elated, he yelled towards the captain at the nock of the bridge, "Nascha, it's ours, it's Russian!" and smiled from one ear to the other. At first I thought the captain would jump into his face, after all we had just had a very stressful situation with Russian "ingenuity" behind us. But he immediately recognized the situation these men where in. They were there for several years, on a godforsaken island, working in underground mines under inhumane conditions not only because of the weather, but they also seldom saw a new face. They had usually been contracted for two years, some even more, and they made an enormous amount of money compared to anybody else in Russia.

After another fifteen minutes or so the diver appeared again and had the rest of that hemp rope cut out of our propeller. The chief engineer ran a test run with the main engine and everything was just as it should be. The Russians brought all their stuff back into the barn and the captain invited all of them on board to celebrate the victory over the Russian hemp rope.

What followed were sheepish faces. The captain did not understand immediately what was going on, and the men explained that they were strictly forbidden to enter a vessel in harbor until their time was up. They feared heavy reprisal if they would come aboard. So the captain walked with one of the guys to the administration building to talk to the commander—the whole island operation on the Russian side was under military command—and when he came back, he had the allowance to throw a party for those men who had removed the hemp rope from our propeller.

Based on the instructions of the captain, the chef and his assistant had in the meantime everything prepared for a huge party. When the party was finally over, each of the Russians, including the base commander, needed to be carried to their apartments, because none of them was able to walk. Next morning we were clearing everything to leave the harbor, when a Russian fishing vessel, a small one, came in to moor right behind us on the pier. Soon it began an active barter trade because one of our crew discovered that this was a krill fisher. We changed krill for Vodka and got a lot of krill for it. The Russian chef came over to us and instructed our chef how to cook it. With all that going on, it took almost till noon to get the trawler out of the harbor and back to sea. Finally everybody was happy that normal day routine would soon begin again.

After about two days we arrived at a position which the captain believed was good to try a catch and we moved out the net. The ground sonar showed a lot of echo, but the captain wasn't really sure that it was a good place and permanently doubted back and forth. When we finally had the net back on deck after four hours, it was full. Really full! Almost eight tons of Golden Red Fish were on deck. And every single face on deck had a huge smile. And for the next couple of hours we were slaughtering Golden Red Fish. We had several good catches, and it didn't take long for others in the area to understand that the daily reported catches weren't a joke. Our captain did not like it much when all trawlers tried to catch the same fish, and he decided to call in one of the tramps to unload the hold and move on to another place.

The tramper were vessels which were constantly traveling back and forth between the home port and the fishing area and would bring all kind of provisions and the most anticipated mail, longingly expected letters from loved ones. Because of this service we were out there in the middle of nowhere, virtually where the sun did not set during all the time we were there, for as much as three to four months at a time.

Because of the radio operator and the electrician were usually very close, I had also a very good relationship developed with the radio operator on our vessel. He knew about the new tramps at the same moment when they left the home port, because they had to send a radio message to Rügen Radio where Christiane worked and she usually called our vessel immediately with this news. My friendship with the radio operator had several advantages for me beside this. It allowed me to have at least once a week a what he called "*loudness test*" to call Christiane when she was at the land-based radio station to work. It was great to hear her voice even through the atmospheric spatters of the short-wave radio connection.

FREEDOM'S NIGHTMARE

But you had to be very careful what you said because it wasn't allowed to have personal discussions through the system if you did not make it official. Official meant you had to fill a form at the radio operator's office. He would then call Rügen Radio and apply for the registration of a *Sea-Call*. After a while he would get the confirmation or denial, and when confirmed a specific time would be set up when that *sea call* would take place.

Now, one reason why this procedure was in place was the extremely "well developed phone system" of East Germany at the conditions of approximately before WWII. The second reason, and I believe the most important reason, was to have all parties in place when the *sea call* took place. That meant the STASI officer at the end of the radio wave at Rügen Radio, to be sure that the radio operator there wasn't doing or saying anything that could harm or denigrate the great socialist German Democratic Republic. And then there needed to be the STASI officer in place who took care of the phone connection station where the phone call would be received by the relatives of the fisherman, to ensure the same as the officer at Rügen radio. All just to make sure that the constitutional right to freedom of speech did not ended in a trial on *denegation of the great socialist German Democratic Republic*!

To avoid this procedure and to save the great socialist government some money, my friend and I developed this idea with the "loudness test." It worked pretty well except on time when both Christiane and he did not realize that one of these STASI officers, better known as rubber ears, was at the Rügen Radio station in the neighbor room of Christiane's office and listened to our conversation. It ended in a reprimand for both.

One of those tramps had just arrived at the flotilla and had a lot of stuff for us, among that the mail. Now that was something that brought a lot of joy. I sorted the several letters I had from Christiane according to the date and finally came to the point where she wrote that the date for our marriage was on August 5th. What a surprise, she had already arranged a date for the marriage ceremony. But that date was unsustainable. I wasn't able to be in the home port within the next four weeks. And I couldn't just leave the trawler and the team because they relied on me. I was the only electrical engineer on the vessel and there was no way to go home, especially not when you consider that we were more than two thousand nautical miles far from home. I had to find a way to let her know that this date wasn't possible without alarming the whole crew.

But first things first, I had to talk to the captain to request a replacement for me. And he had to do that ASAP. Knowing that he was off duty at this time, I waited till next morning, because I knew he wouldn't like it. Not that I thought that he was so excited about having me as his electrical engineer, but because he did not know what replacement he would get. And yet there was this kind of a very special relationship developed over time during so many hours of drinking coffee together, I mean serious philosophical discussions we had camouflaged by coffee drinking. Next morning I went up the stairs to the bridge with a heavy heart.

When we had sat down in the map room with our coffee in front of us, I hesitatingly began to speak, "Captain, I have to tell you that I need to be replaced."

"That was my impression since the first minute I met you," he said with a bright smile on his face. "I'm just kidding, I don't think you're that bad of an engineer that we need another one. Or did you make the vessel inoperable and I don't know of it yet?"

Now, it was on me to smile. "No, captain, at least not that I recognized yet. I have to go home to get married." At the same second I realized that my wording could be base for another teasing by the captain.

And here it came. "So, you don't marry, you get married? You have no saying in that?" He looked at me, and we both began to laugh loudly.

He was not arguing, but was silent for a long time.

"I'll agree to send that request to the company to get a replacement engineer for you, and I'll let you go home under one condition—you can promise me face to face that the new guy is able to do the job," the captain finally stated.

I was sure the guy who would be sent out to replace me would be at least as good in his profession as I was.

That special relationship with the radio operator allowed me to get the news about tramps, and my heart began actually to palpitate any time we got message that a new tramp was on its way. Now, Christiane did not know whether or not my replacement electrician was on board, but just the hope it could be was great. At least to that day when the radio operator got the content of the tramp determined for our vessel and no replacement electrician was mentioned.

Then the day came when the replacement electrical engineer entered the dinghy to be transferred from the tramp to our trawler. I was standing at the bridge nock watching with great expectation the dinghy closing in, to see who the guy was. His real name I got from the captain. It did not sound familiar with me, but most of the professionals weren't known by their real names. We all had our nicknames, so did I. Unfortunately this guy wasn't known at all, and when I used the evening round call through the fleet nobody knew him.

By the way, those evening round calls where initiated by one of the chief engineers after his trawler had a severe defect and no spare parts, and he called the fleet to see if someone else could spare that specific part. The answer was yes and it saved the trawler to wait until the next tramp arrived. Out of that incident we created a regular round call through all the vessels at the area, and most of the time it was just a call of the name of the trawler and *your turn*. And the answer was I'm okay.

That day I went up to the radio room and when the call, "Kattegatt, Your turn" came, I asked, "Is there anybody who can refer my new electrical engineer?" I got so many responses at once that I had to ask them, "He guys, talk one after the other, the radio operator named it radio discipline." I was so focused on getting a rough understanding with whom I had to deal to leave *my* trawler to, that I did not noticed that the captain had opened the small opening that connected the chart room with the radio room and was listening to the reports from several engineers who had the opportunity to have my replacement as an assistant engineer aboard. When the *E-Mix* round call was finally over, he cleared his throat and asked me to come to the bridge. And I knew what was coming; there was no way that he would let me go with that same tramp back home next day.

He made it clear to me, "Harald, as much as I'd like let you go tomorrow, you know that you have no right to request your relief from duty of the electrical engineer of his trawler. And if you can't convince me that your replacement is up to the job, securing the functionality of the electrical systems on board of my trawler, you won't leave this vessel before we're moored at the Kay at the hailing harbor."

"Captain, you have my word. I'll not trick you to get home. If this guy is not up to the job in time, I'll stay," I promised him.

I went to work on my earliest possible relief. The next few days we, the new electrical engineer and I went through tons of drawings of the electrical systems. My main concern was the generators, the power supply of the trawler with all the controllers and the fishing winch controller because the first was essential for survival and the second for the money. And even though many crew members saw it differently because money (meaning fish in the hold) had the highest priority to them, it was the functionality of the power supply system that made their life possible in the middle of nowhere.

What I found, though, was that even with the negative references the new man had gotten, he wasn't stupid or lazy. He was just inexperienced and insecure, and when somebody begua to hurry him, he immediately capitulated. As soon as I realized that this was the problem, I did what every good leader does. I gave him an objective, described exactly what I wanted him to accomplish, told him where he could find the tools he would need and when I expected him to be done. I also told him that I would check in from time to time to see if he may have any question and encouraged him to come at any time he needed my assistance.

And it worked. Without telling the new electrical engineer I informed the captain and the chief engineer about that kind of training program and that I'd given him three weeks, to see for myself how it went. They both agreed to go from time to time and see how he was doing and after two or three days he told me that he believed the captain has changed his mind about him to the positive. That was good news.

I slowly began to prepare to sign off. Since I had to change vessels probably several times, I had to choose very carefully what luggage I could take with me. Nearly 80 percent of all my work clothing and special tools and so on needed to stay on board. That was terrible; especially with stuff which wasn't available at the depot at home and that was with most, if not all of it the case. For instance I had produced my own survival knife. For that I had taken a machine saw blade which had the right hardness, but wasn't that brittle that it would break immediately when you hit something. I had spent many hours on the bench grinder to get the right shape and even more to hone it. It also took me many hours to create the knife's handle, since I couldn't drill a hole into the steel. Now I had to leave it there on board with other things because I'd have some trouble to explain to the border STASI who would search my belongings when I arrived at the harbor what the knife was for. Knives with a fixed blade longer than 7 cm, which is somewhat around three inches, were considered weapons and forbidden.

Finally the day came when I was allowed to have a ride on our dinghy over to the tramp, which would transfer me to another trawler that was on its way home because of some defect on the shaft bearing. I had all my belongings pushed into two large duffel bags. One was with all the stuff I could take with me, and the second one was stored away in one of the electrical storage rooms where only the electrical engineer and the chief engineer had a key. The trip to the tramp was short but rough, and when I arrived and signed on at the bridge, the 1st NO said that I'd be with them for about three days. I got my own cabin at the forecastle, and since it was only for three to four days, I did unpack only the necessary stuff. The tramp moved through the fleet and finally we met the trawler I should go home with.

To my surprise, it was the trawler Jan Mayen, named after a small island north-east of Island. There the electrical engineer was one of my classmates. Although we had lost contact between the undergraduate school and now, we had talked over the radio several times. The travel home was almost uneventful until we reached the Kattegat. That's the southern part of the waterway which connects the North Sea with the Baltic Sea. While the northern part, called Skagerrak, is north-east oriented, the Kattegat is south oriented, and that became a problem for us. It was late summer and not unusual for the time the wind came from south. But when we were almost three quarters though traveling towards the Oresund, which is the eastern part of the waterways around the Danish main island Zealand with the capital Copenhagen right on the water, it increased steadily up to a decent storm. When we finally got through the strait between Helsingoer (Denmark) and Helsingborg (Sweden) to enter the Oresund, we found a fully grown hurricane direct onto our nose.

The way to handle these kinds of situations was to stay into the wind with the bow and get the vessel just enough speed to stay above the water. On the second day I was with my friend on the bridge, having a coffee with the 2nd NO on watch, when one extremely huge wave crashed against the front of the steering house so that the whole steering house seemed to bend over backwards. When the water was gone and we could see the bow again, I thought something was missing. I asked the 2nd NO why I had the feeling that the bow looked somehow empty, when he was already on the command system to sound alarm for the leak defense team. Over his shoulder looking at me he said, "You're right; it's the foredeck cargo hold hatch." I wouldn't believe my eyes If I'd not have seen it myself, and if I'd not have experienced over the several years on board of fishing trawlers and cutters how powerful water can be, I'd have thought somebody is telling fairytales. A roughly two-feet-high square of a quarter-inch-thick steel that had formed the coaming of the hatch was gone. With the waves continuously crashing over the bow, the fire pumps placed in the foredeck cargo hold were not able to empty the hold and we had to take speed out of the trawler to get the leak defense crew able to work there to close the hole. This took a while, and during this time the trawler was thrown around by the storm and the waves like a huge toy. Another two days later we were home and the next phase of my life could begin. I got married.

Marriage, Vacation and a Firsthand Experience with East German Border STASI Officers

We married at the St. Johannes Church in my home town Saßnitz. My home town has a wonderful, relatively young church built in 1880 to 1883 in neo-gothic style, and we were glad to be married at the same church where I had gotten my confirmation several years ago. What an incredible development I personally had gone through in those years. At this time it was usual that couples lived together without being married, and a church wedding was not usual at all. My brother Michael, still a strong communist, condemned my move away from the only true way to social justice—the dictatorship of the party of the working class—and refused to set his foot into the church. After the Church ceremony we had to go to the city hall because the marriage was only legal with the additional government ceremony. There we received the so-called *Book of the Family*, which contained the official marriage certificate and where later the births of our children would be officially registered. There was a standard statement in that book that obligated parents to educate their children about socialism and the everlasting ruling role of the leading communist party.

The wedding party wasn't really something you'd remember for long, and the best actually was when we walked through the city center, a little more than ¾ of a mile, to get to the photographer's studio for the pictures. Yeah, you couldn't really request the photographer to come to your wedding ceremony or party and take pictures. In socialism, with no competition at all, all jobs secure, unemployment unknown, and payment guaranteed, why would you bother to go out to those who wanted your service? Since they had no alternative, you dictated the condition when, how and where you worked. The only alternative was to pay with *Westgeld* (West) German currency, which was illegal, but a highly sought after alternative to the worthless East German money-colloquial named play money. If you could wave with "*real money*" at somebody, suddenly everything changed. Since I did not wanted to waste my few and hard-earned devisen for a photography, we chose to walk to the studio, and many people on our way smiled at us and said friendly words.

263

The next morning we started our honeymoon trip. Since we did not have many alternatives and I could not take off more than a week, we accepted the invitation of Christiane's sister to stay for a week with her and her husband. Because they lived in Eisenach, a city very well known because of the Wartburg castle, we thought to use the opportunity to visit the place where Martin Luther was in protective custody and translated many of the books of the Bible from the old Hebrew and Greek manuscripts into German. We were not really impressed. Although the East German government tried to do its best to keep the castle in good shape, especially for the many foreign tourists, the shortage of the necessary recourses was obvious. And even with a lot of tourists visiting this historical place every year, the enclosed restaurant was a complete disappointment. The attitude of the waiters, the quality of the furniture and the food was very typical for East Germany—nothing you'd refer to. Since the city of Eisenach was in Thuringia, and no to far from the Czechoslovakian border, we decided to make a trip there before we went back home to the north.

We started early in the morning, because although it was roughly 45 to 50 miles, we needed almost three hours to reach the border. Christiane had some German Mark (the West German currency), a gift from her aunt in West Berlin, because she thought she could buy something useful there, something like bohemian crystal, which was very famous. Standing in line for the East German Border control, we suddenly detected a sign notifying East German citizens that it was illegal to own foreign currency. What could we do? The only way was turn around and cancel the trip. But we were already in an area where we couldn't turn around without creating suspicion, and so we decided to declare the West German currency as mine, because of the seaman's muster book I had, which allowed me to cross the see borders of East Germany in official occupation. With that I could reason the ownership of that foreign currency. It wasn't really much, but it was dangerous not to declare it.

When I handed the officer my document, which was obviously not the standard documents she saw all day long, all hell broke loose. We were ordered out of line, separated and questioned for several hours. Our car was searched, and I mean searched, they dismounted the cabin in a way and speed I'd never thought possible. To their credit, I need to add that they put it back together flawlessly. The problem was that my Seaman's Muster Book was only valid to cross the sea borders of East Germany and they couldn't understand that I did not realize that when we decided to travel to Czechoslovakia. On the other hand, with issuing the Seaman's Muster Book to me, the administrator at the harbor police confiscated my ID card. So I did not have one when we tried to cross the border to Czechoslovakia. I should have gone to the harbor police, told them that I plan to cross the border to Czechoslovakia, and for that I'd have gotten my ID pass back temporarily. The money wasn't even an issue.

After several hours they finally let us go, and we had at least the afternoon to spend there, in that nice little town with the still visible charm of the glorious 1920s. Yet we did not dare to spend a single Mark from that West German currency, because we feared that the border control would take us in custody for that. But when we crossed the border back from one Paradise of the Socialist Workers Class to the other, all the excitement was gone and we were just briefly checked and let go. The travel home from Thuringia back to our beautiful Island was uneventful, and the everyday life had us back soon, but with one exemption. Yes, we were married now, but I had to leave my newly married wife because I had to start a new chapter of education.

Several months before our marriage, I applied at the HR department of our company for delegation to a graduate study in Electronic Engineering. The company applied at the Institute of Technology of Goerlitz for a graduate degree in Industrial Electronic for me, and I finally received the admission with some additional requirements. Since the grades from my undergraduate weren't really good. I have to admit I was some kind of negligent after I was been expelled from the FDJ leadership functions. The condition was that I had to go to a preparation course before I could start the graduation study.

For half a year I went to a special preparation school for graduate student applicants specialized in electronic studies. Alongside refreshing courses in basics such as Mathematics, Physics and Chemistry, we had courses specially designed for electronic engineering students. On weekends when I went home, it was sometimes strange, because Christiane had her shift system—although she tried to change with others to have at least one day off—and I had to do a lot of home work and studies.

Finally at the end of May I finished the course, passed all tests with flying colors, and was ready to go to university. Since the semester started mid September, and I was still employed by the fishing company, I reported back there at the dispatcher and lucky enough he did not have a vessel for me. I was sent on leave on call, and Christiane and I used the opportunity to visit her mother. She still lived on that farm Christiane's grandfather once bought for a lot of money only to lose everything twice in his life. We had several wonderful spring days since that small village was surrounded by huge forest, and we had a lot of fun riding on bicycles through the woods.

Then one day, we were just done with lunch when the mail man arrived at the farm tizzy, waving with a piece of paper in his hands. It was a telegram for me, requiring me to report at the state capitol harbor to the Fabric Trawler *Stubnitz,* the same vessel I was working before I was drafted into the NVA. We decided that we would drive together by car to the harbor and Christiane would drive home with the car. That allowed us on one hand to have some more hours together and on the other hand I did not have to leave the car unwatched for an unknown time at the harbor. I was surprised to learn that I was assigned as the senior electrical engineer. And there were several crew members still there I knew from my time aboard who greeted me and welcomed me back, including the former 3rd NO now chief mate.

Since I had arrived relatively late, I had not much time to move into my cabin, say hello and introduce myself to the deputy electrical engineer and to learn that the electrical assistant wasn't the screwed guy we had years before when I did my deputy trips on that same trawler. There was no official announcement where we would go with this trip yet, but since the hold was full with about 800 metric tons of sprats, rumor was that it was sold to a western country. Now as the senior electrical engineer, I earned a whooping 28 mark base pay per day, and although we had nothing to do with direct fishing, we got paid the normal fishing bonus and the devisen payment. With the promotion to senior electrical engineer that was now 3.50 Mark per metric tons bonus and 3.20 per day devisen. During the area trip from the harbor to the open sea, I had to be at the machine control center where I found another friendly face grinning at me from ear to ear. The former 3rd MO was now the chief engineer. I was wondering and asked and he confirmed that he already served before me at the NVA and with that he had two more consecutive years on the same vessel.

With the end of the area trip we moved up to the crew mess because the captain had announced to have a meeting with instructions for the trip. Turned out we were on a trip to Bergen in Norway, where the whole load of sprats was sold to a fish meal processing plant. As usual, the East German government needed hard currency and was short on it, so they sold everything they had to meet their obligations. That trip was almost five days in duration, and since we had no fishing activities I used the time to get used to the changes aboard. During my time at the NVA, the Fabric Trawler had been at the shipyard in Poland and was completely rebuilt in many major functions and equipment.

So was a part of the hold area cut off and converted to a workshop-storage area for the electrical department. Before that, there wasn't a defined area for the electricians. We had to share a workshop with the mechanics, and that was in the middle of the machine room. Even though we had both AC converter sets inside the workshop, it was a huge improvement. All spare parts were right there, and we did not have to walk through the vessel and collect parts from three different places. The evening before the arrival at the harbor of Bergen, we had another meeting at the crew mess. The captain instructed all of us to behave because we were considered representatives of the German Democratic Republic. Then the 2nd NO began to instruct us about the punishments in case we would try to commit *Republiksflucht*, a special term which was used to describe the illegal leaving of the GDR. He also read the instruction not to leave the vessel without having signed out at the bridge and giving the watchman on duty a proximate idea where we considered going and when we thought we would be back.

The non-officer crew was allowed to leave the vessel only in groups of three or more people. The reason given for that was security. Then the production officer announced the working groups and shifts for the unloading of the eight hundred metric tons of fish. Since East Germany wanted to get money, they had negotiated an agreement with the Harbor unions in Bergen to allow us to unload ourselves under usage of the harbor crane.

The processing plant would place the trucks as needed. Officers were not forced to work but were offered an additional 5 *devisen* per hour working with the unloading crews. Since my greatest objective was to get a science-technical calculator bought for my upcoming graduate school, I immediately volunteered and was assigned to the first shift from 6:00 a.m.-2:00 p.m. every weekday.

Back in my cabin I thought about the opportunity to leave the country but abolished that thought immediately. Although I knew I would have no problem to get political refugee status by the Norwegians and would be in West Germany within two or three days, I could not bear the thought to leave Christiane there under the scrutiny of the STASI for several months or more and no chance to know if and when she would be able to follow officially. I knew of too many families who had been destroyed because the man used the first opportunity to leave and never saw his family again, because the STASI forced the wives to divorce the husbands, and if they refused to do so, they took the children and gave them to parents in line with the system. With thoughts like that moving through my mind, with no possibility to talk to her at all, drove me almost insane.

During the first week I worked and stayed aboard, not going into town, and was fascinated with the discipline the crane operator held his break time. That harbor was under total control of the union, and he would have a ten minute break every fifty minutes. Then a forty-five minute break at noon and another fifteen minutes at 2:00 p.m. He worked from 7:00 a.m. to 4:00 p.m. Another fascinating skill he had was rolling his cigarettes with one hand at an incredible speed. We actually challenged him that one of us could open a new pack of cigarettes, take out a cigarette and light it faster than he could get one rolled and lighted. We gave him one advantage though, that he could have his tobacco pack and the cigarette paper in hand at start. We did it several times and he won every single time. The last thing I couldn't get my mind around was when he demonstrated rolling a cigarette with one hand in his pocket. First time we thought he tricked and had a cigarette already finished in his pocket, but he turned it outside and back in, empty and did it again. Now, those cigarettes were not as perfect as the machine produced once you get out of a package, yet it was fascinating. He explained that the finished cigarettes were so extremely expensive in Norway that only rich people could buy them. With many years of smoking and operating the crane, he said, he had enough time to train himself to get it done.

On Friday after work, I signed out at the bridge, and since I had learned from other crew members where the shopping area was, I did not waste a minute and walked straight to that area. Not long after I arrived, I found a store where they sold school stuff and then another and a third one. I walked into all three of them and checked what calculators they had and how much those were. Most of them at this time in the late seventies were just simple, basic mathematic calculators. And then there it was, almost as I had dreamed. It was a TI 30, and I paid roughly 130 Norwegian Crones for it. Since I still had enough money left, and we had gotten the opportunity to change 50 percent of our earned devisen into Norwegian Crones, I bought another basic calculator with the idea to sell it at home. I actually sold it to the processing manager during the trip home when he saw me learning to use my TI 30. I showed him that basic calculator and he was exited that it would reduce his paperwork and paid me actually more than I had paid for it. There was no incentive to go into a restaurant because meals were expensive for our circumstances and we had very excellent provision on board.

I used the opportunity to walk around the small center of the city with its typical architecture, knowing that the city was actually founded by German merchants during the height of the Hanseatic League, and suddenly I stood on a corner of a street just across the police station.

I stared at the building. The dusk had already initiated the automatic street lights, and all the windows of the police station were ablaze with light. On a mast in front of a small memorial, whose meaning I could not determine because of the increasing darkness, was the Norwegian flag waving in a slight breeze. It was such a peaceful picture that I sadly, deeply inhaled the fresh air and dreamed with open eyes for a few minutes, seeing myself crossing the street, opening the door and walking into the building to ask for my part of freedom.

Again taking a deep breath, I forced myself back into reality and turned around and slowly walked back through the now dark streets, lighted with traditional formed street lamps, towards the harbor.

Next morning, Saturday, was no loading at all, and many of the crew members went into town. I stayed aboard and made myself comfortable with the calculator I'd bought, reading the instruction and beginning to solve some of the equations I knew I'd have to use at the university. And since the start wasn't really far, three months would pass like a whirlwind, as time only seemed to stand still when I was away from home, I began to recapitulate some of the lessons in mathematics and physics from the preparation course.

I planned to go again to town on Sunday though, since it was obvious that we would leave in two or three days because we would not be longer than absolutely necessary at the harbor because it cost money, real money. I used the opportunity to take the Ulriksbahnen, which is a cable car and goes up to the Mt. Ulriks. Although it wasn't cheap, I thought that the opportunity wasn't an everyday event and spent the money. And I did not regret it. Back down to sea level, I walked along the old city harbor, where a lot of restaurants and coffee shops were filled with early tourists, mainly Scandinavians, but I think I did hear some German words too. Late in the evening I went back to the ship, and since there wasn't really anything on TV that would have caused me to try to follow without understanding the language, I went to berth early.

Next morning, although I did not work with the unloading crew anymore, there was a lot of work to do anyway to prepare the trawler for the trip back home. The call at the harbor was a long journey through pictorially and majestic Fjords, it was all-area trip, requiring an electrical engineer at the machine control center. Since it took several hours, the deputy engineer and I had to substitute each other during the time inwards and we would do so outwards but with a changed time table so that he could see the part he missed inwards and vice versa. There was also a new estimation about the finishing of the unloading operation by the processing manager with a ready-to-go time at around noon next day.

Next day, many of the officers—crews were not allowed to leave board anymore—would use the last minutes to get something for their wives or children. Then suddenly the whole trawler got paralyzed. The voice of the captain through the command system sounded "Lock Down! Lock Down! Nobody leaves the ship! All hands to the crew mess!" Within minutes all men were assembled at the crew mess, waiting for the captain, who appeared only a few seconds later. With a vibration in his voice clearly indicating that he had trouble to keep his countenance, he said, "We have an indication that one of us committed *Republikflucht*! I have order from our government to leave harbor immediately! We will lie in the roads until all information is clear and different order arrives! All men at their stations; we leave now."

Within ten minutes or so we had the tug boats and were away from the pier. Sitting in my chair at the machine control center, I was so consumed with my thoughts about what could have happened to all the crew when I would have actually gone into the police station the other evening that I completely missed the conversation between my friend, the chief engineer, and the 3rd MO, talking about a lying bastard and the imprudence telling us what could happen on retaliation to our families, And now being the guy who does it to his own. By those last words I was startled from my thoughts.

"What are you talking about? Who did what to himself?" I asked.

They looked at me as if I was not from this world.

"The second NO. Are you dreaming with open eyes, Harald?" they said in unison.

Now it was me saying some bad, not printable words about him.

Just a little more than a week ago he had instructed the crew that it would have severe consequences for the whole family at home if any of us considered leaving the GDR illegally by asking for political refugee status at a Norwegian government office. And then he did it himself. The general popular outrage calmed relatively soon for several reasons. First of all he had at least the decency to do it at the end of our time there, so that everybody could have his time on land. Secondly, it wasn't really that seldom, and I believe some of the crew deep in their hearts envied the second NO for his guts to do the final step. I did. At least it was not the first time that a crew would say good bye to the workers' paradise using the unique possibility to walk right into a building of a foreign government and asking for political refugee status. I knew personally two sea men, the guy who broke his leg when he was pulled out into sea by the rope and then Gunter, one of the deck men at the trawler I was with before my school time, the guy who got the wire piece in his eye. He was dropped off at the harbor of Hammerfest in Norway by the Russians on their way home. And he never found his way back to the GDR.

The real issue here was the dishonesty of those who tried to tell everybody how to live their lives and be a devout representative of the socialistic ideals in foreign countries and then betray their ideals by showing that it was all just a façade. The real high point in that entire specific event was, he was the trawlers SED group party secretary. Writing these lines and thinking about my own journey from the largest prison on German soil into freedom, I can't avoid that he may have played a very perfect roll by pretending he was exactly what he needed to be, to get that chance. He was prepared when he had the chance, and I wasn't when I had mine. I never met him again and learned later that his wife with the two children were already at the West German embassy in Prague when the STASI knocked at his apartment door. His parents, so was told, handed them an application for family reunion. I don't know if they ever could leave East Germany before the wall came down, but for sure it wasn't easy.

Education Never Really Ends and How Life Changes as Long As You're Alive

I began my journey to become a graduate engineer at the University of Görlitz. At my time it wasn't called a university, it was called a Technische Hochschule (German for Institute of Technology). My focus was on industrial electronic because the idea was to be ready when finally electronic systems would enter the control systems of the East German fishing trawlers and replace the controllers designed in the late fifties and early sixties. But it was tough to stay focused on the study with the whole length of the country between Christiane and me, especially since she was expecting our first child.

The studies at those Institutes of Technology in East Germany were very tightly organized and left you little room for individualism. The teaching day was scheduled starting at 7:30 a.m. and lasted till 4:00 p.m., some days with laboratory exercises till 6:00 p.m. There were two hours of lecture and then 15 minutes break, then the next lectures and so on. The next day was filled with tutorials and hands-on seminars and laboratory exercises. And when you got to the dormitory you had a lot of homework to do to get yourself prepared for the next day. Especially at the Görlitz Institute of Technology, the political part of the higher educational system was extremely developed. Almost all of the professors were members of the SED, and since this area in East Germany was part of the so-called *blind spot*, an area where not even the highest sophisticated antenna system allowed people to receive West-German TV broadcasting, the availability of alternative information to the East-German politic-propaganda TV was zero. When I tried to argue certain themes at the party meetings, very carefully though, because I knew that the base information they had contradicted the facts, I was immediately accused of undermining the leading role of the workers class party and power.

Approximately in the middle of the first semester an incident finally made me shut up at all of those meetings, and I became a non-active member. One of my classmates, as I knew from personal discussions, was a devout catholic Christian and an excellent student. For the subject *Political Philosophy of Marxism-Leninism* we had to write a thesis about

273

the communistic philosophical law that "The struggle and the unity of the opposites" are responsible for the development of mankind. My catholic Christian classmate wrote an excellent thesis according to the books and teachings. But he finished it with a statement that he personally believes that God the almighty creator of the heavens and the earth was the reason for the development of mankind. That caused a furious attack of the professor against him in front of the whole assembled seminar. He required the student to revoke this laughable statement publicly. The student, standing in front of the about sixty students, refused to do so by saying: "I'm not Leo Galilei." The next day he was gone. We never saw him again at school so I guess he was expelled. I believe that this was the last straw that broke the camel's back, and the spark of hope to at a certain degree try the strategy of change from within was extinguished. Although I was at the SED member meetings once a month, I was there bodily but my mind was always somewhere else.

And together with feeling too many times alone, far from my loved ones and among people who did not care about anything but themselves, I withdrew from almost every official event at the Institute.

Although I loved the technical side of my study very much because the application of electronics in industrial applications was what I'd dreamed of, I wanted to change to another Institute. But to change university just because you decided to do so, or you did not like the distance to home, wasn't easy. I needed to put in a special application to the central academic commission CAC for changing university. The first request was declined, because at the Institute of Technology in Wismar wasn't a place available. This would have been the next possible Institute for Technology where I would get my first year counted. Since Christiane was pregnant, she quit her job at the coastal radio station to move to the village in the farmhouse with her mother. At the Institute in Wismar, I would be closer and could go home every weekend. In April, our son Lennart was born, and I could not get home before the spring break in May. Before I left for spring break though, I got the seminar group leader (the title of the professor who was responsible for our seminar group) to co-sign my second application for a transfer.

End of May I got the confirmation to change university, only not to Wismar but to the Institute of Technology for Telecommunications in

Berlin. That was a very well known institute with a huge reputation because it was founded 1924 with the support of Siemens and AEG as an external Institute of the Technical University of Berlin. Because of the separation of the Russian and the other Allied Zones in Berlin, the communists re-founded the Institute of Technology for Telecommunication new in 1948 at one of the old buildings. I could not understand why the CAC wanted me to enroll there, because there was no industrial electronic course.

But anyhow, I put all the paperwork together and sent it to the CAC as required. The time came to get all my stuff out of the dormitory, and I was sending a package virtually every single day for two weeks, until I had all my stuff sent home. And my bicycle was still a great help.

During summer break I work at the agrochemical center (ACZ). This was a kind of a centralized warehousing company for all the agricultural cooperatives in that area. Normally I was ordered by the institute to work with all the other students on one of the many Youth-Objects arranged and managed by the FDJ central student organization. There were no exemptions, and it was usually a horrible time for most of them. Now since I wasn't enrolled in Görlitz any longer, I escaped their control, yet I wasn't enrolled in Berlin yet, and with that I escaped their control and was free to find my own source of supporting income, desperately needed for my small but hungry family.

I went down to the harbor where a huge five-story granary was and asked the manager if he had a work for me for summer time. He asked me if I had a driver's license for tractors, and since the license I'd made at the army included tractors, I got the job. The problem was that the granary was infested with the grain weevil. All the grain needed to taken out of there and transported to the ACZ main depot, which was at the outskirts of the small town. Next day I got a tractor with two trailers and started the race as I called it. It was actually a really new tractor with just a few hours on it, and it was one of East German manufacturing, not one of those unreliable Russian brackets. In the evening I would just drive home with it and the next morning back the twelve kilometers to town.

Everything worked fine until the space at the modern storage building was filled and I had to unload into a storage building with one door only. Now that was a challenge. Have you ever tried to push a tractor with two trailers behind it backwards through an opening just a few feet wider than the trailers were wide? You need a lot of training, which I did not have. After approximately half an hour back and forth and back and forth again, one of the truck driver lost his patience and came over. "Have you ever done this?" he asked me.

"No, never," I answered, a little ashamed of not being able to complete that task and keeping other from doing theirs.

He jumped into the seat. "Sit down on the emergency seat and watch me," was all he said. What I then experienced was absolutely fascinating. Without moving his head even one times backwards, only permanently moving his view from the right to the left mirror and back, he turned the steering wheel with an incredible speed left and right, and within two or three minutes both trailers were perfectly lined up along the unloading chute.

"Not bad. Haven't done this for some years with a tractor, only with the truck, so I wasn't sure that I was still up to the challenge," he said, and seeing my totally perplexed expression, added, "No, I won't you to believe you can do the same now. That is impossible. But you have seen how I did it, and all you need to know is, low speed, fast steering wheel is the key. And then a lot of practice." Then he jumped out of the tractor and was gone.

I did not see him again; I think he was from another cooperative. But the next tour I disconnected one of the trailers, pushed one in backwards and when I had it empty, I did the same with the other one. Then I coupled them together and was on my way.

The summer break went by and I did not hear anything from my new school until I finally decided to call them sometime in the second week in September, since I knew the semester began September 6th or 7th. The secretary of the branch did not know about me starting there and said that she had no paperwork received from the CAC. So I called the CAC and it turned out that the responsible person was pregnant at the time when my change was worked on and may have forgotten about it. I should go to the institute immediately and they would send the paperwork in that day. Still wondering what I should do at that institute, I traveled to Berlin next morning. I arrived in the afternoon after a five-hour trip, with the train having its usual delay. At the institute I was sent to the Professor for the Telecommunication branch. He was in his office and wasn't really surprised to see me late. He looked at me and said that he had a meeting with his team in the morning and they had almost come to the decision to decline my enrollment because I lacked the undergraduate qualification for telecommunications technology.

But because of my excellent results from the prequalification course, which I did for half a year, they were willing to give me a chance. Then he explained that the Institute of Technology and Telecommunications Berlin was far ahead of the institute in Gorlitz with four disciplines taught and already had the final exams on them at the end of the second semester. The challenge for me was not only to catch up in all the other disciplines but to gain the knowledge required to pass the final exams in those disciplines they had already finished. The deadline was at the end of the winter semester.

Now, that was something. Instead of traveling home every weekend, I was most of the weekends studying, either at the library or at the dormitory. The last two weeks of January were almost unbearable. I had to pass eight exams to stay in school, or I'd be set back one year. Because that was the compromise the professor had agreed to, even after he understood that it was almost impossible to make it under the circumstance I had in front of me. But I did make it and everybody, even I, was surprised. Maybe God had his hand in here too. Even though it wasn't as glorious as I was used to, I passed, and that was important for now. Coming from the high voltage side of the electrical engineering I had to adjust to the different sinking of the telecommunication engineers, because here it wasn't about high current or power dissipation, besides in transistor power amplifiers, but about adaptation of resonant circuits, impedances and frequencies.

But I became more and more familiar with the specifics and many things became easier, except for this one mathematical procedure called Fourier analysis. I could never finish a complete equation in a single test, and that really bothered me. Another negative thing happened during the second year at graduate school. When I changed from the Institute of Technology at Görlitz to the Institute of Technology and Telecommunications, I did not declare my membership of the SED.

A few weeks into the 3rd semester the leadership of the SED had started an exchange of the membership cards, as they called it. It was specifically designed to find people like me, because of the large discrepancy between membership and collected fees. I got a reprove and had to pay a fine, which was hard since we had two children and Christiane was the only one earning an income. Although the study itself was free and every single book you needed was available at the library, you needed money for living and several books were restricted from borrowing. Mostly those from western country authors fell under that category, and even though the East German books weren't bad, some technologies were just not developed enough to have East German authors to be able write books about them. Since I was able to have at least in some of the more important subjects B+ grades, I got an academic merit scholarship that covered for most of the time my living costs and the train tickets. The final semester came, and with it a large number of exams and for four weeks we, a group of students, were sitting together on the days between the exams to help each other with things unclear. Little did I know at this time that 5 out of 17 classmates who survived the three-year elimination courses were actively spying on their classmates by reporting regularly to the STASI, but more about this later.

For the first two years at the Institute of Technology and Telecommunications Berlin my TI30 calculator helped me a lot, although it was not allowed to use calculators during exams. Yet being able to double check results much faster than without it made it possible for me to follow up with the lessons I had missed. Then, with the beginning of the last semester, a rumor began to circulate through the Institute. It said that the professor panel would allow the use of calculators for all future exams. And it was true, just a few days later, our professor made the announcement and added onto that: "But we don't want to give you a free run, and with that, the time you have will be reduced from 5 to 4 hours." That was great news because many of the students had already calculators; some of them were even programmable.

After a long weighing back and forth, talking with Christiane and checking out available types of calculators, I decided to spend our saved West Marks for a new calculator. It was a Sharp; I don't remember the type and series, but I remember that this calculator played a huge roll a few months later. It had complex number calculation, all the trigonometric functionality up to the sinus-hyperbolic, as well as the tangent-hyperbolic and to my surprise probability calculations also. It helped me a lot getting the exams in Frequency Analysis and other subjects done much faster, giving me time to re-calculate and make sure that my results were correct. Unfortunately I messed up the mathematic exam, and that was horrible. Now I had to pass all the other outstanding exams and to repeat the mathematic exam at the end of the exam cycle. I felt really overwhelmed. I used the four days between the last exam and the second mathematic exam intensively to get more familiar with the calculator at the Fourier Analysis and the probability calculation. However, I bungled them, and with that had less than 60 percent, which meant failed.

The second exam went pretty well, and I was sure I passed it by at least 75 percent. I was shocked the next day when I saw the results on the black board. That must be a mistake, I thought, because I knew that I had definitely more than necessary to pass, yet the listing said: failed. Destroyed to the ground, I was walking out of the Institute, not recognizing that the door to the secretary's office was open when I suddenly heart the voice of the professor's secretary calling my name. Startled out of my thoughts, I stepped into the room and she said that the professor wanted to talk to me next morning at 10:00 a.m. Next morning, when I was about to leave the dormitory to see the professor, I heard a voice in my head! A clear voice I had never heard before, and it was such a strange experience that I almost ran into the still closed door.

"Take the calculator with you to the meeting with the professor!" I heard a clear voice in my head saying. It was actually so clear I answered, "I don't need my calculator at school today." "Take the calculator to the meeting with the professor!" that same voice said back to me.

In my stupidity I talked back again. "I do not need the calculator," I said, and the answer was there right as before. "Take your calculator with you to the meeting with the professor!"

So I gave up and thought, *If you're now hearing a voice where nobody is beside you, you can take that stupid calculator with you.*

You need to understand that even in more evangelistic groups of the Lutheran church in Germany the ability to hear the voice of the Lord by listening to those small thoughts inside of you, or even a somewhat audible voice if it is important and you did not listen to the inside voice, was considered ceased with the end of the book of Acts. If you told somebody that you're communicating with GOD through his Holy Spirit, they would tell you that this was satanic. I had no clue that GOD was instructing me after I probably missed his words several times.

When I arrived at the Institute the professor wasn't there, yet and I had to wait for a couple of minutes. His secretary didn't say a word, and when he came I was relieved to get the telling-off behind me. In his office, the professor looked at me.

"I'm very sorry, Harald, but I can't let *that* get through. Since you failed the second time, there is only one way. You can appeal to the Rector to get a third chance and repeat the year. But I doubt it is possible after *that*."

"Professor, I don't understand what is it that you cannot let go through, and what do you mean with *that*?"

"You have written off the results for two equations from your neighbor, even though I have no idea how that was possible since I was there all four hours with several other teachers, and the tables were so far distanced. But none of my students in twenty-five years was ever able to solve those equations without the intermediate steps."

Looking me straight in the eyes, he said, "And by all due respect, Harald, you're good, but not good enough to be the first one doing so," he added.

"With that the only solution to get the correct results is to write them off from somebody else."

I could barely stop myself from bursting into laughter, because there were thousand things going through my mind in milliseconds.

"Professor, I do not need intermediate steps, because those are all done by my calculator."

"You don't need to sink that low and lie to me. I'm sure that with my reference the Rector certainly allows you a third test and to repeat this semester."

He really thought I tried to swindle myself out of a difficult situation and was visibly disturbed.

"No, Professor, my calculator really can do that, see here," I answered.

And with that I took my calculator out of my case, switched it on and handed it to him. For about two minutes he stared at that wonder of modern microelectronic, reading all the functions mentioned in four different colors on the keys with multiple functions.

Then he looked up as if he was looking straight through me. "Why is it that this, the great socialist nation, controlled by the power of the workers class, is unable to get even a basic calculator of the size of a building brick to work for one hour, and the rotten imperialists can produce these wonders as small as this?"

It was obvious that he was scared by his own words. When he looked up at me, he said, "Harald, would you mind leaving me that calculator for two or three days? I need to check it's functionality, and since the results of the exam are already official, I have to present my findings to the rector, to revoke your exam result."

For the next two day I was on needles and pins. Would he accept the use of the—to him unimaginable—possibilities of that little piece of Japanese electronic? With hesitation I walked up to his office two days later and with great joy I could leave it. He could not find any wrongdoing in me using the calculator as it was supposed to be used and the Rector accepted his judgment. But because of the huge advantage I had, they conceded only a C Grade. I did not really think much about it, because the alternatives, to either been thrown or to repeat the year on Rector's mercy, weren't even thinkable.

Who am I

WHO AM I:
WHERE ARE MY ROOTS?

I Needed to Know Who I Really Am, Where I Came From

I ASKED MYSELF WHAT kind of future our young family could really have, if I don't know where I came from. My biological father was never a subject of any kind of discussion. Actually we never talked about the family situation—current or historical—at all in our family. And if I asked I always felt that the answers changed with the time and I never got the true story of my Mother's life. It was a kind of part of her personal history—untouchable. Years later when I was able to compare her story with the narratives of my Father, I realized that I really could thrust neither his nor her description of the events. It was not really shocking anymore at this time, because I was used to being lied to from all the years from my early childhood on.

So I began to look for something what would give me a lead to find out who I really was. And this *looking for whom I really was* started years back right after I became engaged with Christiane. One day when my mother was in the hospital, we, Christiane and I, had the chance to browse through the documents my mother had collected over all the years. Since this stuff was not sorted, it just filled a large drawer in the living room cabinet. Suddenly I was holding a letter in my hand which was different from all the other papers we had seen so far in that clutter of documents, photographs notes and so on.

It was written on a paper with a quality we had never seen or touched before. It was from a lawyer and came from West Germany. And it was old. The date said it was send to my mother in 1963. The lawyer wrote that he represented my biological father. He, my father. thought that my mother had his certificate of naturalization as a German citizen. The lawyer asked my mother to send this document to him because it was worthless to her and my father needed it to be able to get a job in West Germany. I did not know what this finding would do to our life, and it was years later that I realized that it was another turning point in my life. But immediately we understood that it was a hint we could start with.

So I sat down and wrote a letter to that lawyer. I explained that I had found his letter from 1963 to my mother and that I'd like to get the current address of my father. But you could not just send a letter from East Germany to West Germany, especially not to a lawyer with a peerage as name, as was the situation with his. We needed help, and help came.

Some month later an aunt of my wife's came to visit my mother-in-law. She was a first grade cousin and lived in Marburg, West Germany. We knew that she traveled a lot and we used the opportunity to ask her if she was willing to take the risk to transport my message. She was. A couple of weeks later we got the answer. The peer lawyer wrote that he was sorry, but he couldn't remember that issue. He said he was actually retired, and even if it would be correct, that I would be in possession of such a letter from him, he didn't have any documents at all from that time. I was buckled. All that risk for this lapidary and negative answer. All my hope and months of waiting for getting the letter out, gone. I feared that somehow the STASI would find it among all the thousands of letters from West Germany to East Germany day by day because the mail was searched all the time for suspicious letters. And how desperately we waited for the letter from our aunt that *it* had been delivered for nothing?

But I was not willing to give up. Actually I never gave up and it took me years to understand why that actually was never my own decision. I put all eggs in one basket. I wrote a new letter to the lawyer and put it together with his original letter from 1963 in an envelope and sent the letter out by mail. But there was no other visit from relatives from West Germany for roughly a year, and I could not wait that long. Since I had started my second year on the Institute of Technology and Telecommunications Berlin, I could drop the letter in a mailbox in Berlin, where the risk that it would be captured was much lower than in our small town. Because of the special status of Berlin as a divided town, with relatives often living on the other side of the street but a country, actually an ideology, away from each other—separated by the WALL, mine fields and machine guns—because of this specialty the mail crossing that deadly border every day was too much to be one hundred percent checked. And the Lord was with me. The STASI did not confiscate the letter I sent, nor the letter the lawyer sent back to me. It was a great joy when I came home and the letter was there.

But the surprise was not only fun. First he apologized for the denial of knowledge with the first answer, but he was too old to walk into the traps of the STASI. With the original letter, which he actually did send back with his letter, he was able to find the file with the documentation of my father's issue about the German citizenship. Since my mother never answered that request from 1963, my father found himself eventually forced to go back to Austria. As far the lawyer knew, my father lived in Vienna and was married again. But he had no contact and he had no idea what his address might be. Shock! Again everything was for nothing. With the next visit of the aunt, we asked her if she would be able to help as to find him in Vienna. She promised try to find him or at least his address on her next trip to Vienna. And again it took a lot of time till we heard from her. She was in Vienna and met with somebody she knew who worked at the police. He promised her to look into it. What a great step forward.

Finally I graduated, and through the central student agency I was sent to an electronic company that did service on the radio transceiver equipment for the East German Navy. It appeared that the so-called perfect surveillance system did not work so well; at least I thought so. Otherwise they would have found out that I had connections through my wife into the so-called NSW (Nicht-Sozialistisches-Wirtschaftgebiet, German for non-socialistic economic area). And when they knew about these kinds of connections, you never got your hands on radio transmission systems, especially not in a Navy base.

There Is Guidance When Men Look For a Way Out or Choices Have Consequences

The job at the Navy base wasn't really my first choice, and actually I was nominated for the position on the Navy Shipyard at the next bigger town just eight miles from the village where we lived. But for some reason I was sent immediately after my arrival to the Navy Base at Peenemunde. That was another thirty-five minutes travel time, and with the public transportation system in a communist country I had to wait for the next bus, which wasn't going before 10:30 a.m. I was assigned to the radio transceiver service group of a civil corporation SER, which was contracted throughout the East German Navy to service all the electronic equipment. We would not only repair defect systems, but also do preventive services and improvement implementations.

The most fascinating thing though was the Ultra-Short-Wave transceiver unit they had on every single vessel. It was a Russian system and still based on tubes, but it was build with so-called mini-tubes. Later I learned that those transceivers were actually used throughout the whole Warsaw Pact, the counterpart of the NATO, in any kind of mobile military equipment, such as tanks, aircrafts, vessels and so forth. It was actually the backbone of short-range communication. Since it was very sturdy build and not really highly sophisticated, it was pretty reliable. The only real problem was the horrible documentation, by the way everything was in written in Russian, and the unreliable lifetime of two of the mini-tubes. In addition to that, we serviced several short-wave transceivers, developed and produced in East Germany. One of those stations was a transceiver with maximal one thousand watt output power. At least the technical documentation said so and since we did not have any kind of equipment to measure that, we took it as it was written. The standard phrase we used was something like, *Divided by two and then take half of it and you might be pretty close to the truth.* I believe it was realistic somewhere around 800 to 850 watts.

The first thing I learned was, as a Newbie I had to give *Einstand* (to make my debut). The team leader was there with his car and we drove out of the post to a store where he would choose the alcohol they would like to drink and I had to pay for it. I do not remember how much it was and how many bottles of hard liquor we bought. I had a hard time to convince my new colleagues that I didn't drink hard alcohol, and the more they got drunk, the more they insisted that I drink with them. Mainly they feared that I could betray them.

At a certain level of drunkenness they finally were too busy with themselves, and finally at 2:30 p.m. when work time ended everybody moved out to catch the bus to get home. I did learn though that the work time began at 6:00 a.m. and that the bus from the city left at 5:20 a.m. That was a major problem for me because of the connection of the public transportation system. There was no public transportation available at 5 a.m. from that village we lived in to the city. And in the afternoon when I came back from Peenemunde, I had to wait till 4:45 p.m. to have a train back home. The only way to make that work was drive individually. But how? The extremely expensive fuels, in relation to my income, forbid me to use the car, at least on a regular basis. Just being hired as a Graduate Engineer in test, since I had to write my thesis and develop some system according to the requirement of the company, I did not get paid full salary for another six months. Then I remembered that my stepbrother had a moped which he did not used much and we drove to his village to check that out. After much back and forth I finally bought that very old and not really reliable moped for about 500 Mark, which was almost ¾ of my monthly paycheck.

It had a problem with the ignition system, which was in front of the engine right behind the front wheel, and whenever I drove through water, or it rained heavily, the engine would begin to stutter and sometimes give up completely. Finally I found out that there was a little hole through which water could enter the ignition system. I filled that hole with special putty used to seal connection boxes on vessels, and that made it much more reliable and it became my standard vehicle to get to work.

To get my final dot on the graduate school and become a graduated engineer, I had to design something and write a master thesis about it. In my case it was the problematic with the modern navy vessels, which did not have those two high masts anymore where they had the antenna wire stretched in between them. Therefore it was necessary to find a way to use a seven-meter single pole antenna, which created some difficulties for the frequency range the transceiver was working at. I designed a system built from inductivities and capacities, which were adjusted by gear motors and electronically controlled by a set of control cards with frequency detection and a logic system build with NAND and NOR IC's. The longest time needed was to get the parts approved even though the military had priority before any other industry. But I got it done and was finally able to travel to Berlin to defend my thesis and get my graduate certificate.

And something else we did since Christiane was with me, we got our guts together and went into the Austrian Embassy in East Berlin. Since I had my degree, there was no fear that they could throw me from school. We entered the building, almost in the center of the street along the Berlin Wall to the north of the Brandenburg Gate, and found that there were three different embassies, among them the Austrian, at the third floor. It was an old building and had a spiral stair with a landing on each floor.

At the embassy, which we could enter without any trouble or questioning, we asked to talk to somebody who could help to find my father. After waiting about twenty minutes, a woman asked us in her office.

"What can I do for you?" she asked me, after we had introduced each other.

"From several indications, I conclude that my father lives in Austria. According to the latest information I have, somewhere in Vienna. I wonder if you can start some kind of investigation to find his address and connect me with him."

"Is your father an Austrian citizen?

"I don't know for sure, but my mother said so, and I have a letter from a West German lawyer, where he claims that my mother should have a naturalization certificate as a German citizen. But she denied ever having something like that in her possession."

The embassy clerk leant back in her seat. "You know, our embassy till today is dealing with the aftermath of WWII. An estimated twelve to fifteen thousand Austrians are living in East Germany, not knowing that they are Austrian citizens."

Now, that was new to me, and I wondered how that was possible. Her answer gave me a first hint how false our education in contemporary history really was.

"When WWII was over, the Allies decided that the occupation of Austria was an act of war. Also, the general naturalization of a whole people by force, which is probably what your lawyers' letter referred to, was declared illegal and revoked. May I ask you when you were born?"

I gave her my birth date, and she went through a number of pages in a huge binder. She finally looked up at us again after several minutes,

"Mr. Zieger, if, and I have to emphasize *if*, your father is an Austrian citizen, and if he was an Austrian citizen when you were born, and if he and your mother were married when you were born, or he declared you legally his child if they were not married—if all of this ifs are positive, then you might, and I again have to emphasize might be, an Austrian citizen too."

After that statement I needed a while to answer.

"That's a large number of ifs. I lost track of how many, but how can I find out if, here another one, I'm an Austrian citizen?"

She laughed, "That is relatively easy, we apply for a citizen approval procedure, and the ministry of foreign and internal affairs of Austria will find out whether or not those ifs are positively answered."

"That sounds fantastic, but I'm concerned what the East German government has to say to that."

"No worry about that," she said, "nobody beside you and maybe your mother, yeah, for sure she, will know about this investigation of you citizen status."

"Okay, what do I have to do to get things rolling?"

"We need a lot of paperwork to be signed."

There was nothing to think about. I signed a ton of papers and got a list of things to bring ASAP and with that the stone began to roll. The question how long that would take was answered in a typical Austrian way as I'd learn later: "That depends on." When we were back on the street, we noticed a kind of a closed cabin standing across the street. The windows were sealed with a kind of a silver-colored paper or foil and only a small strip was left free. Although we wondered what that could be and why we did not noticed it when we came, we did not spend many thoughts on that because we were busy with talking about all that, what we had to do to get the ball rolling with the Austrian government.

The following weekend we drove to my home town to visit my mother, because I needed an affidavit from her that she had never applied for a GDR citizenship for me. Now this was not easy. Not because she wouldn't do that, but because my mother could never keep any kind of secret. So when we arrived and the situation was there to talk about that affidavit she had to sign, I made it very clear to her that she could not, under no circumstances talk about what I was about to reveal to her, never ever. I repeated my urge to secrecy until I could see on her face that she realized that something really special was about to happen. Then I told her about our visit at the embassy and that I'd need her signature under that specific affidavit. She said nothing, signed the paper and asked only one question, "Does this apply to Connie and Michael too?" I almost lost some heartbeats and repeated that she can't talk to anybody, not even to Connie or Michael about that.

"If, and this is a huge *if*, the request goes through and the Austrian government confirms that I'm an Austrian citizen, then, and only then can you talk about that. I'll for sure inform Connie and Michael immediately about their opportunity to do the same," I promised her.

With that we left Saßnitz and went home. With me, being now regular employed at the Navy Base of the East German *Volksmarine* (German for Peoples Navy) and Christiane working as a secretary at the district construction business, our life became kind of normal. We began to renovate three rooms in that old farm house and "enjoyed" life as good as possible. The biggest handicap was that this old farmhouse had no bathroom. Yea, you get that right. We had the year 1980, and many families in East Germany lived as if they were living before WWII. Every night we had to heat up a huge pot, holding about seven to eight gallons of water, to bathe our children. Twice a week we did that several times, so that everybody could enjoy a full bath. And the outhouse was still the norm. That was complicated especially in winter; it could get really cold out there.

To change that situation, I decided to build a bathroom in one of the no longer used barns where once the swine were fatted. Breaking down some walls and building up a new one to get enough room for a toilet and a bathtub as well as the water boiler wasn't really a problem. We had enough old building bricks I could use, and because of my apprenticeship with my stepfather Helmut, I had enough experience to do it. But the real problem was cement. You couldn't just go to a DIY store and buy whatever you needed to get the job done and that for several reasons. But the most obvious reason was, there was none. I mean there was no cement you could buy; besides the DIY store didn't exist either. There were three ways to buy things which were officially not available in East Germany.

First, if you had West Mark, or Deutsch-Mark as you may have called it. If you had that, you would write your *insane* shopping list on a piece of paper, fold it several times and place a decent amount of West Mark in it, means equivalent to the size of your wishes, and put the paper on the desk of the clerk. The clerk would take that paper and would go to the back room. There the gift would be evaluated and when it was according to the unofficial currency, he/she would come back, open a registration book and would note your name and address at the several categories you had on your shopping list. Also we had some of those highly appreciated Deutsch-Marks because of my mother-in-law's relatives in West Germany and West Berlin. We never had enough to pay these insane fees in addition to the normal price you had to pay anyhow. So this didn't work for us.

The second possibility was you knew somebody who worked at the shop where the stuff you needed was sold and that *knew* was really intensive. I mean that was a good friend, or relative or you had something in common that really made you help each other, because you had access to something this guy needed. For this situation we had the expression "One hand washes the other." And the question would be do you have something FDGB?" I explained that expression some chapters before and it really worked, if you had those relationships or counteroffer to make a deal.

The third option wasn't really an option; the third option made you a poor pick. That was the pitiful expression when you tried to buy something that required access to one of the first two options. Your name would be written in another book with all those categories exactly the same, but when the delivery arrived, the book where you name was in would only be opened when the people listed in the other book had gotten their list filled up and supplied. With that, it could take 2 to 3 years to get a new window, a bathtub, a boiler or a toilet. And that was the short waiting time. If you were living close to an area where the great socialistic building initiative was on a roll, maybe with a TV-effective evening-news report, supported by the great leader, you were at the short end. You would wait five to eight years or, as usual, forever. And everybody knew that. And based on that knowledge the culture of "What do you have that I could need?" and "I'll see what I can do that you get what you need" was wide spread.

So what we had was Christiane working at the district construction cooperative. Now, the cooperative had the same problems as all the others to get the material to fulfill their projects and were often enough in a decent backlog with their jobs. But there was that special law, which said that any project considered important for the defense of the great socialistic achievements had absolute priority. Since the punishment to corrupt orders connected to those project was severe, most of the time people tried not to use material determined for those projects. But to order two bathtubs instead one and then buy the surplus for private use to avoid that it lies around and depraves, that was considered a good attitude. But you could do that only so often. So we got the stuff we needed, and when I was almost done with the brick wall, I realized that the cement wasn't enough to finish the floor. The only way was to call in a favor with relatives.

My stepbrother Andreas had in the mean time finished his apprenticeship as a professional concrete worker and was foreman on a concrete manufacturing plant in a city about thirty-two miles away from our village. We talked about it and he told me that the concrete they used for the precast concrete slabs wasn't really good for a bathroom floor. That was because it had a special chemical which accelerated the binding process. After some back and forth, we decided it was worth the risk, and so a couple of days later I drove with our car, pulling a small trailer with a max load capacity of about 700 pounds, to his plant. Placing the trailer under the opening for the concrete, I waited that the mixing of that batch was finished. Then he opened the outlet for about a few seconds and my trailer suddenly looked like a wounded dear. That opening was designed to fill an eight-ton truck within a few minutes and was very difficult to control for only seven hundred pounds. All the planning for getting home as fast as possible to avoid that the concrete would harden before I was able to spread it out at the bathroom floor was in jeopardy. But I made it, the trailer did not break and most of the concrete was still usable and the bathroom floor was done. The joy was great when we finally could heat the boiler and everybody could have a bath whenever they wanted. And what an improvement it was to avoid the outhouse in wintertime.

I had begun to design and build my own car radio, and since modern ICs and literature wasn't widely available, I decided to spend a week to visit the spring exhibition in Leipzig. This was a very well known internationally recognized industrial exhibition, and many of the western electronic companies were there. Following spring I traveled to my friend and classmate from the time in Berlin, because he lived near Leipzig. Every morning, we would enter the rain and travel to the exhibition. I ordered business cards at a small printing company in our district with my profession but as private person. That gave me the ability to have several very productive meetings and I got a lot of information. That actually had a severe aftereffect. A few weeks later, I had just received a huge package with catalogues from a Texas Instruments daughter company in West Germany, when two spooks or squash-hats as we called them in East Germany appeared at our front door. They showed their credentials as STASI officers and demanded the literature I'd just received. I did not give them everything, only what was still on my desk, and with the remark I should not try to contact those people again, they left. I could finish my radio and get the two short wave categories and the mid wave category to work, but for the ultra short wave I missed the equations to calculate the external components on that IC because it was in those books the spooks had taken.

And I became more and more involved in the organization of our church. Our church was a small church. It was really small. That wasn't just because the village we lived now with my in-laws was a small village with about 600 people living there. This was because the decades of atheist indoctrination by the communistic educational system, formed mostly people who were atheists and with all the problems to organize your life, cared not much about anything else than themselves. I had been a perfect atheist before God's grace opened my eyes to the reality that there was something else behind the enormous creation I could experience daily, and He sent me an angel. But it was also based on a very tradition of unbelief in that area.

My mother-in-law used to say that the only thing these people believed in was *that one pound of beef gives a good soup.* She said that this was one of the reasons that the national socialists could turn this area in a hotbed. and as soon they were gone, they turned around again when the communists gained power. Our church was held in the house of Christiane's family at least since the end of WWII. Although there was a church building, built in early 1300 at the neighbor village, approximately two miles through the forest, it was in such a condition of disrepair that it could not be used for services. And for the three old ladies and our small family it was comfortable enough. The pastor—a woman—came every other Sunday morning and we could worship. She was pastor for several villages around that area and would travel from village to village. Since every church traditional had a pastor's house enclosed, she lived there although a part of that house wasn't usable also.

Eager to put my energy into the work for an improvement of the church organization, I had several interesting discussions with her. From the time Christiane's grandfather was alive my mother-in-law still had good connections to the provost, who happen to preach at the home as a pastor before he was called to become the provost. He came from time to time visiting us and we had some interesting discussions about the decline of the Lutheran church in East Germany in general and the difficulties to connect with young families specifically in our area. He had, as so many of the church leaders of the Lutheran Church in East Germany, many excuses and was blaming the bad times we were in. But he was at least interested in giving it some thoughts. A little later we got an invitation for a family weekend at a church-owned facility at the island Rügen. There we met several couples our age with little children and the same or similar thoughts about the life as a Christian family under the circumstances of an oppressive system.

We became kind of friends with some and visited them later only to experience a harsh rejection after they learned more about my history. It was not that I could not understand their fear for being infiltrated, but I felt deep inside of me a guilt. A growing feeling of being the reason that our family was not able to have a friendship with other believers, building relationships and having the children growing together with children from other Christian families. I wasn't a communist anymore, although I still carried the membership book and had to attend the monthly meetings because the Institute of Technology and Telecommunications in Berlin had corrected my personal file when I was sent to the company servicing the electronic of the East-German Navy.

Even though I considered myself a Christian, I did not really know what that meant at that time. The rejection by other Christians because of my history was hurting. Reading the history about Apostle Paul, I saw many parallels, and I know that sounds weird. But was he not mocking, persecuting and supporting the murder of the first Christians, as I did mocking Christians and laughing at them and throwing the Word of God into the bushes? Did he not have a specific experience on the road to Damascus and was changed, as I did when I met my wife Christiane, like the angel who would lead me from dark to light? And was he not one of the most fervent in preaching about his transformation and the grace of God to be able to recognize the salvation by faith, as I did when I finally found my way to confess and change? Now, I understand there is not much to compare and it seems somewhat arrogant.

Then the day came and that horrible letter was in the mail. I was called to serve my turn as a reservist. It was not unusual that you got called, but since I had children and was working at a Navy base, I thought it would somehow not happen. First step was an invitation to the military district command.

When I entered the office, a very friendly captain asked me to sit down. "You have been invited, because the military command is very interested seeing you serving as a reserve Officer instead as a simple corporal. This has many advantages for you, such as being at home every night with you family, an Officer salary and many more." He continued for about fifteen minutes, and when he finally stopped, he looked at me in joyous expectation.

"That's it?" I asked and was about to stand up to leave the office.

His demeanor changed on the spot.

"Who do you think I am? I'm making you such a great offer, and you have the audacity to reject it!" He was now so in rage that I could see his swollen carotid artery expanding at his increased heart frequency. "You will see what the consequences will be, and I'll take care of that all of your commanding officers would know what an unthankful dog you are. After all what the great socialistic fatherland had done for you, granting you this excellent education, and now you are not willing to give something back."

I waited till he was done, though I did not really hear all what he said because it was the same crap I heard to many times, then I just stood and walked out, ignoring his yelling to my back. I did not see any good of serving in the military in a godless government.

A government that was determined to erase any root of faith in an Almighty God, tolerating the existence of a church it could not just wipe out because it wasn't strong enough. When I talked to our pastor about the call to reserve service, and the thoughts I had to deny the reserve service, she was not in favor of the idea. She said I should to the contrary freely go into the reserve service and use the opportunity to tell everybody how bad it was to be a soldier for that communistic, atheistic system and that they should commit their life to Christ. She had obviously no clue what she was talking about because if I'd do that, I'd be arrested and shot for treason. But a few days later she told me that there would be a meeting at a deaconry and the theme was serving in the East-German army as a Christian.

The meeting was a few days later, and when I arrived, several young men were already there. We greeted each other just with our first names because everybody knew that we all were in severe trouble if there was one among the six who had infiltrated the meeting in order to report to the STASI. With just a few minutes' delay the man we were waiting for arrived.

He introduced himself, "I'm lawyer Wolfgang Schnur. I've been working since 1965 as a consultant in legal issues for the Lutheran Church. I'll try to answer your questions as good as I can. I don't want you to make any notes."

The first question came from a small, skinny boy with very thick glasses on his nose, which he had to push back upwards every now and then because they wouldn't stay where them should. "I'd like to know how I can deny serving with a weapon, because I don't want touch that stuff at all."

"The only option everybody who can prove, above the shadow of doubt, that he has a strong connection to a Church and is living a believable Christian life since his childhood, is to serve as Spatensoldat (German for spade soldier). As you all know, the official name is Bausoldat (German for construction soldier). And you have to be aware that those will be used for all kind of construction requirements throughout the military of East Germany."

"Those who are not Christians, but deny service with weapons, have much more difficulties to make their case and often end up serving in regular military units."

Although it was a two-year service, instead the regular eighteen month, and it was determined by continuous bullying by the NCOs which were usually discarded convicts, several young Christians decided that their faith did not allow them to serve with a weapon in their hand. There were also those who had not the conviction of Christian faith and pacifistic beliefs but just did not want to serve in the army of a system they were totally opposed to.

A short moment of silence was broken by the question of one of us: "What when I don't want to serve as a Spade Soldier? I heard that they have been ordered to work at the border to mount spring guns and burry anti-personal mines?"

"The alternative of not serving at all is jail."

Looking at each of us, he continued, "Nobody, at least somewhat sane, would voluntarily opt for that alternative. The condition at the military prison is worse than at the civil prisons. If you refuse to serve at all, you'll get five to seven years. Most of the inmates are absolutely scrupulous evil criminals who have many years and nothing to lose." He looked again at each of us, and with a very quiet voice said, "None of you here would survive that hellhole for more than a year."

Listening to all the reasoning and questions and answers, my initial enthusiasm about denial of service melted down like snow in spring.

Already having my misgivings I asked carefully, "What if somebody who served the eighteen months with a military unit, now called to reserve training, would refuse to do so?"

Wolgang Schnur looked at me, without saying a word for a seemingly long time. "You don't want go that road."

I shrug my shoulders and said, "Why not?"

"Because you wouldn't survive the punishment."

First I thought because of the still practiced dead sentence in East Germany, especially for treason, and on political enemies carried out by a surprising shot in the back of the head with a silenced P38, he meant that I'd be executed for the refusal to comply with my oath of allegiance and he shook his head.

"No, that's not what I meant. That would be too easy, as macabre as it sounds. And I don't mean that everybody who breaks the oath of allegiance to this government would be tortured to death. No, at least not officially. You would be sentenced to fifteen to twenty years special military prison and you would die every single day a little bit, stretched out over years." Quietness followed for a while.

"Do you have family?" I confirmed, and he went on, "Even more, for that reason alone you should not do that, because your family will suffer as much as you. Although not physically, but mentally, it would be hell on earth for them too.

"I think that's it. I seriously recommend that every one of you looks deep inside of himself and considers all the possible consequences, of which I could give you today only an impression of those I know about from my practice. Think about what you and your loved ones have to bare if you deny the service as required."

And with the words, "This meeting never took place, because I'm officially at a birthday party with twenty witnesses," he left the room.

Nobody said a word for several minutes and slowly one by one went out the door and home.

I did my reserve service as a normal petty officer 3rd class at the NAVY base in Peenemunde where I usually worked as a civil contractor with my company, and after twelve weeks it was done. Those twelve weeks increased my antipathy against the whole system so much that I felt inside of me the day of decision coming faster and faster. I knew I was on a collision course with the system when questions I asked were not answered but led to a personal meeting with my commanding officer. The usual day at the Navy as a petty officer 3rd class would be occupied with a lot of stuff because you'd be considered a NCO. But as a reservist you did not take that as seriously as when you served your regular turn. So where ever possible, you'd find a way to hid and get the day done, without being caught by your commanding officer.

Since they had enough to do with the regular troops it worked out most of the time. But sometimes you just couldn't avoid being there and then you had to bite the bullet and fit in. One of those occasions was the regular monthly political education very well known from my regular service time and avoided at all costs when possible. Caught by my commanding officer and having no reasonable excuse, I had to endure at least the morning session. It was about the aggressive forward operational strategy of the imperialistic NATO and that the East-German Navy needed to be ready as the spearhead of the border protection of the sea border of East Germany.

As usual at the end of the presentation with slide shows and movie and so on, there was the point where the sailors could ask questions. Some of them asked questions as required so that the training officer could deepen our knowledge. He would finish with something like, "If there are no more questions…" and that was my time. I raised my hand and told him that I was somewhat confused about the fact that we as the defending army fighting the righteous war against the aggressive NATO had huge landing crafts to land whole brigades at foreign shores yet the aggressor did not have such things, so I did not get who the aggressor really was? His head begun to change color and for a few moments I thought it might explode at any second. When he caught his breath he yelled at me to report immediately to the commanding officer and that my treasonous and defeatist question would have repercussion.

I was sentenced to cut the grass in front of the officers' mess by using nail scissors. In my STASI reports I could read almost ten years later the informant reported what I said with a hacksaw blade. Looking at the huge front yard I thought for myself I could stay there until the end of the reserve service, still wouldn't be done, and had a great excuse doing nothing else but this. And that really made my day. It wouldn't take that long though.

On the second or third day I was there on my knees with a ruler in my left hand and the nail scissor in my right hand, I looked up to a voice in my back that sounded familiar. "What are you doing there?" It was a captain who was the liaison officer between the company I work for and the garrison commander. I got up and in to attention with the scissors in my right hand I saluted, and before I could say anything he commanded me to end the ridiculous salute before I hurt myself. I did so and explained what I was doing and why. He, being one of the more reasonable people in uniform I'd met so far, said that I had asked a justified question and that the answer was stupid. He commanded me to follow and we walked to the office of my commanding officer. I had to wait outside, and although I could hear the heated debate inside I couldn't understand the wording. After a while my commanding officer came out and told me that I was dismissed to the quarter. The rest of my reserve service was eventless and the day I was dismissed from active duty into reserve again, I had made up my mind and decided to drop the shoe.

Four weeks later was the next group meeting of the communist party and my time had come. Here I was sitting among all those brown-nooses, apple-lickers and would-be revolutionaries, and could barely hold my breath. I could not take it anymore. I just couldn't. How could it happen that I have come so far? What had made my life so complicated that I was sitting here and about to risk everything, my job, my family, my freedom even my life?

I was about to do it, and the only reason why I hesitated was the thought of my young family, my wife and two little children. What brought me to a point in life where I had to decide whether to walk farther down this road or just stand up and say: "I'm done"? And I started to let my mind wander back in time. Because it was not only me, it was the question about the country also. Actually it was a twofold question, what brought this country into a situation that the citizens tried everything, and I mean really everything, up to the point risking their very life by crossing a deathly border, to leave that country. And how came I so far, to risk that everything myself? That deathly border which had eaten away so many lives, mostly young people, died in the mine explosions or under the fire of the AK 47, the standard weapon of the border guards. And those who had the finger on the trigger were often still teens. A thought flashed through my mind and before I could really develop it, it was gone. Something like, "Why do they have to kill those who even won't to be part of the victorious workers' paradise? Let them go, because they aren't really assets to the system." To the contrary, they did everything they could not to be a positive part of the system.

FREEDOM'S NIGHTMARE

Here I was sitting in a meeting of the smallest unit of the party in power as a member, yet miles away from agreement with the ideology and doctrine, the doctrine of the absolute power of the party of the workers class, which actually had nothing to do with the workers class at all, since most of the leaders never had worked with their hands for a minute in their whole life. And these people controlled every single aspect of one's life. Every!

Freedom? What was that? There was no freedom. Okay, I wasn't in jail. Wasn't I? When the area you are allowed to move around is encircled with a fifteen-feet high fence, crowned with barbed wires, secured by anti-personal mines and spring-guns—sounds like jail, or not? When those in power dictate every phase of your life such as what you're able to buy, what you can earn, what profession you can learn, which study direction you're not allowed to choose, how you have to raise your children and what to watch on TV, sounds like prison, or not?

Although it was a large prison, a little larger than 41,700 square miles—somewhat larger than Ohio—I felt locked-up. And even if many did not dare to say or express it in any kind, thousands felt the same way. This feeling was especially intensified when we were able to receive the West German TV transmission. Seeing that there was not shortage on all the produce needed for a decent life, understanding that they could go wherever they wanted to go and knowing the only way they got killed when they left West Germany was by car accidents—it made all the phrases and ideological indoctrination a farce, downright ridiculous.

It was in the middle of the meeting, I can't remember what stupid phrase somebody had just said, and the leader of the meeting with the striking name *Manfred Dumm* (German for stupid) asked if anybody would have a comment on that, I raised my hand. And within a milli-second I had the attention of everybody in the room because it was an absolute novelty that I said anything during those meetings since almost two years. As it was common, I stood up.

"I'm done with this farce. I can't take it anymore. I'm fed up listening to the lies and phrases of the blooming socialistic world. Not one of you here in this room with a little piece of your brain alive really believes one word you have said or heard. I believe in God Almighty as the Creator of the

Universe, and His Son Jesus Christ, that he died on the cross for my sins and rose again. I believe that He, Jesus, is my Lord and Savior."

It was absolute quiet in that room. You could have heard a needle drop on the carpet. "This whole illusory socialistic world you have built in your mind is fantasy, does not exist, and if you would be honest with yourselves, you would say the truth and you'd stand up with me and do the same as I do, leave this monkey house and never come back."

With that I moved around that table I was sitting or now standing behind and walked out the door.

When I arrived at home and told my family that I had told the SED fat cats that I was through with their chimera, it took only a few seconds and we all were thankful together and praised God for the guidance to end a very bad chapter of my life. But it wasn't over. Next day, I was going to work as always, arriving at the bus station, traveling to the Peenemunde Navy garrison and starting to work. All was the same. Then at about 10:00 a.m., the phone of my group leader rang and when he hung up, he looked at me with a very questioning gaze. He said that the boss wanted to see me at his office. So I grabbed one of the bicycles we had and drove to the other side of the harbor where his office was.

He wasn't really happy but he made it short. He said that I had to report to the headquarters next day at the state capitol and that he was very disappointed that I did not inform him about my step to throw my bright career away. Little did I know that to this point in time a so-called Operative *Personencontrolle* (German for Operative Personnel Monitoring) was running for over two years and that there had been procedures in place to detain me and Christiane and that the operational command to go ahead was given twice, only to be stopped every time minutes before execution. This meant that I was under surveillance for more than two years almost around the clock. But at this time I did not know that and I'll come back to that later in another chapter. So much about the truth on a bright future I had thrown away. And this lying bastard was one of the informants of the STASI with the largest number of reports about me.

Einstein Wasn't Stupid and What I Had to Do With That

When I arrived at headquarters of the company, I was checked in with the security and brought to the office of the head of Human Resources. After a short waiting time, I was led into the conference room and he came in with two other men I did not know. He began to question me about my, as he called it, outburst of insanity, what I thought, who I was, and that I would now feel the full force of the security system to eliminate me from that sensitive defense support department of the socialist Navy.

But they were not done yet. One of the guys on his side asked me if I had conspiratorial connections with the class enemy, meaning West Germany or another western country. I denied and almost laughed loud, but had wide grin on my face.

He turned immediately furious and threw a stack of photographs over the large table in my direction and yelled at me at the same time. "Stop lying to us, we have enough evidence to get you in jail for a very long time."

Now it was onto me to be surprised. These were pictures taken at the time when Christiane and I were visiting the Austrian embassy in East Berlin, and I clearly remembered that moment when we came out of the building and recognized that strange hut across the street. But I stood ground and said I did not conspire with anybody and it was just ridiculous to believe that. They got more and more angry, explaining that I lied at any time in the past when I was questioned about connections to the class enemy. That I lied when I said I would not receive mail from West Germany, I'd lied when I said that I did not receive packages from relatives in West Germany and that I just lied again saying I'd not conspire against the socialistic workers and farmers republic yet having personal connections to an embassy of the class enemy.

Then the HR director jumped in again, asking me what that bullshit, what believing in God and Jesus Christ as Lord and Savior, was all about. I began to explain why God is the almighty creator of the universe and what is in and why He had send Jesus as His son to earth.

They angrily interrupted me, saying he did not wanted to get a lecture in religious crap but wanted to know how it came that I, an obviously intelligent man with a degree as a graduated engineer could believe that there is such a thing as a God, because he couldn't believe I was that stupid.

For several minutes I did not answer. I thought about what to tell those guys about the change I had gone through over the last six years. How to explain to totally ignorant people what joy it was to discover God's love and that believing in Him was real freedom? Finally I answered with a question, "Do you think Albert Einstein was stupid?"

And all three answered in unison, "NO."

"So why do you think I'm stupid because I believe in God since Albert Einstein did too?" I asked.

One of the guys at the side of the HR director obviously did not understand the meaning of the comparison when he asked me if I thought I was as intelligent as Einstein. And the HR director added that he believed that I was not so intelligent that I could compare myself with Albert Einstein. I do not know what devil rode me, but I answered that I'd never dare to put myself in a class with the genius of Albert Einstein, yet consider my intellect far above his grade because otherwise he wouldn't sit there. That was enough for all of them. Yelling at me that I should guard my tongue, the director of HR threw me out of the conference room to wait for the verdict.

I never saw him or one of the guys, which I definitely put to the state office of the STASI, again. About half an hour later the secretary called me in her office. She handed me an instruction which contained the order to be at my workplace next day to collect my personal belongings. She told me, without looking at me, that I would be not allowed to be at the Peenemunde Navy garrison longer than necessary and under continuous monitoring during that time. She also told me that the instruction contained that I had to report the day after the next at the shipyard Stralsund where I'd start working as a commissioning engineer with the SER department.

That was a shock, but I did not react, and long before that day I had sworn to myself that I'd never let these cowards, who were helping to run a dead system year after year, see when I was hurt. I arrived late in the evening because the train connections were miserable, as most things are in a glorious dictatorship. What else could you expect from a system where people are promoted for their ability to repeat lies better than others and were better in building smoke and mirrors?

It was a sad night, and even though we were somewhat relieved that this was behind us, a new burden was loaded onto our young family. Next morning I entered the bus and everybody was looking away. It was as if I had leprosy. But when we arrived at our office where the radio systems repair group was, that changed dramatically. For almost two years we had worked together and they knew I was a reliable and decent guy. I never gave away when they had their drinking sessions even though I did not participate; they had learned to trust me. And it was to their own advantage, because at least one person was able to answer the phone. Everybody was bombarding me with questions until our group leader silenced them and began to get order into the curiosity. Some were astounded about my bravery to stand up and saying such things, others just considered me an idiot for throwing my career over board, and then there were two or three who may have thought, *I'd like to have the guts to do this, but were only silent.* I put my personal stuff together under observation of the group leader, said goodbye to everybody and left earlier to catch the regular bus to get home.

Next day I reported to my new boss at the Construction Side of the Shipyard Stralsund as it was officially called. He already had my personal file on his desk and welcomed me with a short sentence, something like, "We don't like any trouble here." With that he introduced me to the group I'd work with in the future and I was in. The group leader put me together with a man about twenty years above my age and said we would probably fit well.

Should turn out it was that way. He was expelled from his home town workplace when he had applied to leave East Germany because he had inherited an electrical installation business from an uncle in West Germany, who died and had no children. The STASI did everything to discredit him until they finally caught him by doing what almost everybody did, taking stuff from the workplace to exchange it for something else he needed. Now, I understand you would, and usually everybody in our country also, consider that theft. But when you live in a society where the money you earn can't buy what you need besides hard liquor and basic food, and that in miserable quality, you have to do what you have to do.

The STASI caught him and offered him to choose between five to seven years forced labor or to cancel his application.

Manfred, or Manne as he was called, was a master electrician and had years of experience. Since the STASI had decided that I was a too large thread to the security of the GDR working on radio transceiver systems, I was now back at the electrical systems of vessels. I was right there where I was before I went to graduate school and spent three years to increase my knowledge and get a graduate degree in electronic engineering. But soon I discovered that it wasn't that bad. As I had in mind when I applied for the allowance to get to graduate school, that one day even fishing trawlers would be equipped with electronic control systems, here it had become reality. The shipyard Stralsund named *Volkswerft* (German for Peoples Shipyard) was specialized in building fishing vessels of all kind and had been specializing in cranking them out, not just building fishing trawlers. And as with almost all of the manufactured products of the GDR 98 percent went to the great brother as the Soviet Union was called—mostly ironically—by many of my new colleagues.

At the time I began working at the *Volkswerft*, the last serious of Super Trawler was in production. The group I was assigned to was responsible for testing and setup of the electronically monitored power generation. Since there were several vessels at different stages of production at the same time, our group had multiple teams which were usually responsible for two to three trawlers. We would check the wiring and the functionality of the control systems and would then, when the generators were ready to be fired up, run a specific setup and test procedure together with the shipyard's electrical department. When everything was as it should be we would have an official commissioning run with the Russian Senior electrical engineer who had to sign all the diverse protocols which were not only required by the contract, but by international laws. Since a vessel at sea was completely self-sustaining, a reliable source of energy was vital for the survival of the vessel, and everybody took this part seriously.

After a few months the new series of trawlers begun to roll out of the welding area, several huge halls, connected to each other by rail tracks. And since this shipyard wasn't as technologically backward as many other industries in East Germany; the shipyard had already established the technology of sectional assembling of the trawler by having the hull finished with some main structures. It would then be rolled down a slipway and into the water. At the fitting-out quay it would then get most of the lower level equipment as long as the decks were still not mounted. But step by step the sections would be transferred from welding halls to the quay and lifted aboard by huge cranes, sometimes with two cranes synchrony because it was too heavy for one.

Since I was not able to go home during the week, I could add overtime and with that increase my salary. That was very welcome for a young family and improved our quality of life at least on the monetary side dramatically. Secondly I used this opportunity to increase my knowledge of the absolute new systems aboard the coming new trawler class, which was called GTS for Gefrier-Trawler-Seiner (German for the freeze trawler with the ability to use seines).

Although I had two Super Trawlers in work to get them transferred to the Russians, I used every free minute to be at the two prototype vessels. There would be two completely new systems installed which would come under our group's responsibility, and those were just stuffed with electronics. One was a completely new designed and computer-controlled energy supply system, the other was a *thyristor* activated and controlled net winch system controlling the power and speed of a thousand Ampere constant current DC motor. Here were two completely different areas of implemented electronics I had a decent education to understand what was going on inside the control systems. Now, you have to understand we were in year 1982. That computer was not the fancy, high-power machine you have on your desk or even in your cell phone today. It was actually the reverse engineered copy of the Intel C808 and was named U808.

Years later when I was visiting one of my classmates from the graduate school time I learned how the GDR, permanent short on convertible currency, was able to design that 8-bit processor. He asked me if I remember that one guy Roland from the parallel seminar group and he told me a story which seemed almost impossible, but only to those who had no idea about how desperate the GDR was to catch up with the international development in microcomputer technology.

After several years of trial and error and the failed attempt to get their hands on the manufacturing schematics and processes of a decent western processor chip, the STASI controlled organization *Commerzielle Coordinierung* (German for Commercial Coordination) was finally assigned to solve that problem. This was an organization specialized in obtaining products banned from being sold into the communist nations, COMECON. All those products were listed in a special document which was called the COMECON list. The Commercial Coordination, or CoCo as they called themselves, had established several different companies around the western world and used those for multiple cases.

The main case was to earn convertible currency by selling East German products into the western world, even though below the cost of production, if they just could get *real money* for it. That was one of the reasons that the supply situation became worse and worse every year.

Beside these trades, they used those facilities and businesses for all kind of illegal activities. They were able to buy a large batch of Intel's C808 through a business they ran in Austria and several high precision grinding machines from Switzerland through Sweden.

The Ceramic Factory Hermsdorf began to grind down layer by layer to reverse engineer the microprocessor. And it worked, at least somewhat. Although roughly 90 percent of the U808 did not work or died an early death, the East-German industry got their hands on desperately needed microprocessors.

And later they developed better designs and came finally up with a 16-bit processor, but that was long after I was gone. Okay, back to my work with the great accomplishments of socialism in the workers republic. Based on my knowledge in assembler programming, at least for that part I still could remember from school, I was able to understand quickly how the system operated and how to set commands to change values or limit when necessary. Although the processors were made in GDR, the memory chips were imported, meaning smuggled, in from western countries. That made them really valuable. If one was considered defective, it was as if you wanted to get a new ten-carat diamond. Since the geniuses at the Central Planning Commission probably never worked at a real job, I mean in a production, they had no clue that machines or systems could go defective and therefore they always forgot about planning the production of spare parts.

The solution was to go to the storage area and cannibalize the systems for the next trawler. That assured that the current trawler could be ready with just a few days delay, but you had to be careful to take at least the stuff for the sixth or seventh next vessel, otherwise you got in trouble with the colleagues who were working on the next one. Since we were not the only department doing that, there were sometimes electrical cabinets mounted on the vessel which you just took over to get it ready for setup, which were almost complete empty. The manufacturing plant at headquarter had delivered what was scheduled on time, had already charged the shipyard for it and had no cause to supply the stuff again. There were either new cabinets delivered, fully equipped and ready to be plundered, or after several months some of the defect parts claimed under warranty had been sent back repaired.

And often enough the repair wasn't worth the name because it did not work after all. One of the most unreliable units we had was an electronically controlled time relay. The GDR version of the NE555 IC just couldn't endure the head developed inside the cabinet when the thyristor controllers were operating at high power to run the winch motors. After a few months the timers became almost unavailable, and without them we could not run the winches. One day I had enough, I wrote one of my classmates from graduate school who lived in East Berlin and send him a list of components I needed.

There were three shops where you could buy electronic components, and since two of them were run by private owners who really cared about what they had, you got often more parts there than anywhere else in East Germany. Two weeks later the package arrived and over the weekend I repaired four or five of those relays.

During that repair I found that the NE555 died because one diode and the serial resistors between a contact and the IC burned through. According to the datasheet of the diode, the resistor allowed much too high current and that killed the diode when it got hot in addition. So I repaired all of the relays and wrote information to the company where the relays were manufactured. I better had kept the relays dying and spared my money.

A week later I was called to the boss and he asked me what I had in mind to interfere with a highly secret manufacturing. Even the idea to open these relays was punishable. Turned out that that timer IC was also a reverse engineered IC but based on stolen documents which neither he nor I knew at that time, but the STASI did let him know that he had to warn me that this was the last time that they did not persecute me. He said that he had put all his weight in that I did not get more trouble than I already had because he thought I did a good job with the new technology and he believed that my intention was to help.

When I had time later to think about that I had a different opinion why the STASI did not touch me. Since I was working in Stralsund at the shipyard, I used some of the overtime as well as several vacation days to travel to Berlin and visit the Austrian embassy on a regular basis. One reason was to show as much interest as possible and give the clerk at the embassy to understand that I desperately wanted to know where the investigation stood. The other reason was to indicate to the STASI, which I suspected was still monitoring my activities, would see a guy who had a regular contact to the Austrian embassy. And as I read later, it worked.

Several weeks later, the boss was promoted and moved to the state capitol to work at headquarters. For several weeks there was no boss and our group leaders were determined to run the show at that time. Then the first rumors started to make the round, the new boss would be a guy from the shipyard where we had our SED party meetings when I was in Peenemunde because the Peenemunde SED party members belonged to the group at the shipyard in our district town.

After a few days the rumor became more real and the name came up which blew me away was Manfred Dumm. My first thought was, that can't be. Was he following me? Was the STASI actually placing this guy here at the shipyard to keep an eye on me? No, no way I wasn't that important, especially since I was not at a sensitive area anymore. For a couple of days I had to answer the questions from my colleagues about this guy, who he is, what type he is and so on, over and over again, and all I could say was that he was a stalwart party hack and his wife was even more in lockstep with the communist party, because she was youth persecutor. Her job was to plead for the highest possible sentences for adolescents who violated political laws.

Then some days later I ran directly into him on my way to our workshop. And to my surprise he was very friendly and introduced me to his companion. I did not recognize him although he was from the same shipyard. Manfred told me that he was actually thinking of me because he would like to have a meeting with me later. That was a week later, but in between happened something else that almost made that meeting unnecessary.

I was working on the setup of the generator security modules and had an apprentice with me who had his practice week. To do the setup I needed to set the upper and lower levels of voltage allowed to be supplied by the generator in to the board net. The upper voltage level was to be set at three different limits for alert, alarm and shut down and the highest level was 420 volt AC. For that we had a special transformer to create this overvoltage. When I came to the second generator, the voltage control card did not work and I send the apprentice to get a new one from the workshop. To waste no time I thought to move to the controller for generator 3 and begin the adjustment there. All the instruments and the testing equipment were piled on top of each other. Holding the instruments with my hands, I moved the testing equipment with my foot over to the next section when suddenly the vessel got bumped and the voltmeter begun to slip down from the pile of equipment. I took my hands off the other instruments and grabbed to catch the voltmeter but got only a hold of the cables still connected to that overvoltage transformer. The cables slipped out of the connector and I had both blank ends in my hands, one in my right hand and one in my left hand. The transformer was still adjusted to 420 VAC, pulsing a 50 Hertz current through my upper body with almost no resistance. I had the feel jumping backwards with the same frequency but could not leave out the cable because at that moment my mussels were already cramped.

Right at the moment before I passed out, I heard steps outside the control room. When I woke up—a miracle that I did—one of the electricians form the shipyards crew was about to begin rescue breathing. They were on their way back from break and heard me screaming, jumped over me and hit the emergency button to shut off the power on the vessel. I was transported to the emergency room got some electrolytic drinks and a total check. The dizziness I had felt during the transportation was gone and I felt extremely well, and beside the blisters on both hands index fingers and middle fingers which were somewhat painful, I had nothing. Those scars are still visible today. The doctor was completely baffled not only that I was still alive, but he thought I should have at least severe cardiac arrhythmia and took an additional cardiogram. I could have told him that I thought God wasn't through with me, that He had something else in mind with me and my time wasn't come yet. But I saved it to me and my prayers because this doctor was known for his ignorance. Finally he wrote me a sick prescription for that day and since it was Friday, I informed my group leader and drove home.

With four fingers wrapped in bandage, I couldn't conceal the accident. Christiane was beside herself about the danger of the work I was doing every day and asked me what I went to graduation school for. The following week I had an additional check and that was it. My fingers still wrapped in bandage secured with some rounds of electrician's tape, I went back to work. What I did though was to bring my human savior, the electrician, a huge present to his workshop and to say thank you. That was publicly.

Privately I was on my knees to thank my Lord and Savior that He gave some more years with my family. Everybody who has just a little understanding about the danger of AC current floating through you upper body direct through your heart from hand to hand, knows that I did survive that accident because of the grace of God.

Later that week the new boss called me in his office and over about an hour and a half he explained to me how he wanted to improve the efficiency of our work. The most important part he said would be to install the position of a Test Manager who would be responsible for the organization of the several different teams of our company and the coordination of our work with the shipyard's project manager. I said that this would be a good idea because it could reduce a lot of trouble based on miscommunication between the groups and the shipyard as well. He closed with saying that he was sure I would agree with him and he was pleased that I'd like to be one of those guys. I was totally perplexed.

I had expected all kind of stuff coming my way, something like, now I'm here and if you don't behave, I can make your day a hell and so on. But no, nothing like that. Still not trusting him, and I never really did until I find out that he always played fair game with me, I asked what he would say if I denied. He said that he did not believe that I'd refuse his proposal, because it came with a decent pay raise. I asked for a few days because I needed to talk to my wife and he said that he already thought about that. Therefore he would officially send me home immediately and wanted to get my answer the next day.

When I arrived home at around noon, I had to calm down everybody immediately because they thought I had an accident again. Christiane did not needed more to know than that the new job would totally disconnect me from dangerous work. Although work at a shipyard is never without danger, the whole life is danger as soon as you leave bed, as we say in German.

Next morning back at the workshop everybody was talking about that new guy, what he wanted to change and that he had even gotten approval for several new apartments at one of the newly built parts of Stralsund. When I was finally called to the office of Manfred Dumm, I had made up my mind. When he asked me I told him that I'd take the position under one condition. Within not more than 8 weeks I would have an apartment in Stralsund. I told him that I knew of the allocation and that I wanted one of those. If he could not guarantee that I would get an apartment, I would walk out and no deal; if I had no apartment after eight weeks, I was back at the workshop and the deal was over. And he accepted. I went back to the workshop and told my colleagues that I would now work as the Test Manager, and since I knew what they did and how they worked, they could not fool me. Everybody laughed and they were actually happy that an insider was promoted who knew what difficulties we were fighting every day. And it wasn't an easy job.

The short breath of fresh wind which was blowing through the East-German economy after Erich Honnecker took total power in the position of the General Secretary of the Communist Party the SED and the Presidency of the administrative council called the Staatsrat, had long calmed down. Bedeviled by permanent shortage of convertible currency, every single product, no matter what that was, sellable throughout the western world, got exported. The brain-dead journalists as the propaganda arm of the failing socialistic construed economy sang the praises of the increasing international success of the competitive industry and the leading workers class because of increasing exports. And many of the East-German workers knew instinctively what that meant. Another longer waiting list or an additional inability to buy the long-waited-for equipment or furniture or whatever it was they had saved their money for. And not just the consumer durable goods became more and more unavailable, it was worse with the convenience goods as well as with services. The East-German versions of supermarkets, probably a tenth of the size you know and sparely stocked at all, were a mirror of the failing policies, and people became more and more frustrated. But the fear of the STASI and their informer was omnipresent, so that nobody really dared to speak openly any critic about the government and the system. Yet the numbers of jokes told among the people when they felt secure was dramatically increasing.

One example here to give you an idea, it was told that the sod of a certain agricultural cooperative was about to deliver and when it finally happened, she had five piglets but two died immediately. The next morning the responsible guy reported to the boss of the agricultural cooperative the numbers.

The boss now had the obligation to report the number of piglets to the district central bureaucracy, and out of fear to have the lowest numbers in the whole district, he reported five piglets. Those two piglets could have died later.

The bureaucrat at the district central office was shocked about the low number. He could not possibly report this low number to the state central office and when he called the state central office, he just augmented two piglets and made the number seven piglets, those two could have died later.

The bureaucrat at the state office was calculating with a promotion that year, and for that he needed to have really perfect results, better than the others. But with seven piglets, he knew he would be just average and his promotion would not happen. He thought, so what, three piglets added to the number doesn't harm anybody but helps me a lot, they could have died later. With that he reported ten piglets to the national central commission on meat supply.

FREEDOM'S NIGHTMARE

At the meeting the next week when the minister asked how many piglets we have, the commissioner for the meat supply said that he had ten piglets. The minister said that this is great news and decided, five for the people and five for the export. Since export had absolute priority, East Germany had to keep their contracts, five piglets were exported. The rest came to the butcher shops and you can imagine how that looked.

Although this story seems a little farfetched, you could replace the piglets with virtually anything somebody would want to buy. The most sought-after product was a newly marketed shopping net. The so-called Mini-Net was produced form synthetic fiber and was able to increase multiple times its size when loaded with goods, a wonder of technology, but never really an exportable product. It was necessary for every East German because there were no plastic bags or paper bags. It was your problem how you get the stuff you bought out of the shopping cart and home. And since the whole consummation economy was more and more based on buying whatever valuable product you can get your hands on, you never knew who else is looking for it and may have what you need, you bought whatever you thought was good to barter.

I remember one day when one of the electricians came to my office and said that the car spare part shop in town should get wiper blades and window seals for the car *Trabant* that day, if I would go with him. Sure was my answer. I left my workplace and we drove to the shop to get in line with about twenty to twenty-five others already there.

About an hour later the shop opened after the clerks had sorted out the delivery according to the two books I explained some chapters before, allowing ten people entering the shop at a time. When it was our turn, there were no wiper blades available anymore, but I could get ten seals for the windows. When we were back at the workplace, I pinned a paper at the black board: Window seals for Trabant 601 for exchange. Because the funny thing was, I did not have a Trabant, I had a Skoda. It took only a few hours and I had a brand new set of wiper blades for the Skoda in exchange for the ten Trabant window seals and a 3/4 liter.

Hard liquor became more and more the currency for stuff you couldn't buy, especially for stuff available at the shipyard. And alcohol was a continuously increasing problem for many people. The only way the socialistic system could do with, *that not could be what not should be*, was to criminalize those who became alcoholics and sentence them to forced labor as a special kind of withdrawal treatment.

The result was often devastating, since the alcoholics were forced to work usually at open soft coal mines and the only treatment they got was lectures in socialistic behavior. Several committed suicide because the withdraw was too much; others tried to get their hands on anything that contained alcohol, including window cleaner or aftershave. The result of drinking these liquids was infirmity over years.

During my time in Stralsund with no way to travel home after work every day, I began to study the word of GOD more intensely, but it was difficult to get my hands on good books. Soon after I was send to the shipyard, I found contact to the superintendent of the Stralsund church and was invited almost every week to his house and have dinner with his family. During that time I was connected to the inner church's work with those poor people released from those force labor camps. Most of them had no chance to find back to a normal life. They were treated as if they did not exist and got a small apartment and a weekly payment and everybody pretended not to recognize them.

The organization Anonym Alcoholics tried to get them to attend church events, provided warm meals and gave them the feeling of being human again not only by preaching the gospel but also staying connected. Many of these poor souls were rescued and became dry, and it was a huge joy to see one you knew for a long time celebrating his or her first complete year without alcohol. And it was during that time that I had the honor to be part of the church team that organized the visit of Dr. Billy Graham at the St. Mary church at Stralsund.

Although we were informed about that on a very short notice and had almost no time to get the information out, we were able to get many Christians into the church before the STASI could fill it up to the extent that nobody could fall down even if they did pass out. That, by the grace of GOD, did not happen. It was great, although I did not understand much of what Dr. Graham said, and the translation wasn't really good, and the audio quality was bad. And then there was the special job I had taken to help the mobile camera team to get around the church through the stuffed hallways and stairs so that they could have the ability to get shots from different perspectives. It was an overwhelming and incredible experience.

Finally it was reality. My boss told me I could go to get the key for my apartment, approximately 8 weeks after I started to work in my new position as the test manager SER = **S**chiffs **E**lectronic **R**ostock (German for Ships Electronic Rostock) at the shipyard Stralsund. Many of my colleagues couldn't understand for long time why I was even considered for that position since the same guy who promoted me had thrown me out of my job at the Peenemunde subsidiary.

But none of them had any doubt on my political position and opinions about the politics of the government. That not only because I made it clear at any time political discussions came up at the workshop, but also when we had these monthly indoctrination attempts called School of the Socialistic Work. The whole crew of about 80 highly qualified workers had to sit in a room from 8 AM till noon with one break at 10 AM and got told how happy they are, or they should be, to be a part of the leading class, the workers class, and not having the trouble to live in West Germany where life was horrible.

If you'd have had the ability to note down all of the whispered comments on these idiotic indoctrination lessons, you would probably have filled a whole book. Although I wasn't a member of the Union and all the other social organizations such as the German-Soviet-Friendship anymore, I had to be at these events because it was considered work time. It would not take long though to create a situation which allowed my boss to exclude me from any further attendance on these events. And that happened this way.

The lecturer, a Union desk perpetrator, was referring to a horrible crime that happened at a small town in West Germany where a worker who lost his job as a foreman had shot his wife and his four children and committed suicide. Using that tragedy as starter he then expatiated that the worker could have made a much better decision and come to East Germany, because here he would be sure that he would not lose his job, and so on, telling everybody already sound asleep in the meeting how great life in East Germany was. When he came to the end, it was standard to ask if anyone had a question, which usually led to a total silence for about 3 to

5 minutes and that was the end. Not this time. You should have heard the murmur of unbelief that Harald had a question.

"I have a question, and if you can give me a decent and logical answer, I might even be willing to join the Union again."

Now I had his attention and the eighty-plus people in the room were silent as in a church.

"Okay, what is your question?"

"If the story about that worker is true, and for the case I'll consider it is, why did he kill his whole family and himself instead to drive to our border and ask if he could join the happy people of East Germany and become a member of the leading workers class? If our great socialistic system is so extremely fascinating as you told us here over the last several hours, why is it that all of the desperate, unemployed, hungry and hopeless people of the western world aren't storming our borders to be part of the victory of the workers class in the GDR? Should all those guns and mines not be pointing to the outside to hold off the onslaught of the exploited workers from all over the world? Instead, all of those guns are pointing inwards, killing everybody who tries to leave this workers' paradise. If you can give me a logical answer to that question, my offer is still current."

It was absolutely silent. Not a whisper was heard, and many of my colleagues waited for an answer. That answer never came. The lecturer needed several seconds to catch his breath and said something like, "I do not answer defeatist and provocative questions, the meeting is over you are dismissed."

My boss ordered me never again to attend these meetings and urged me to make myself invisible during that time, which I joyfully did.

On another occasion I was trying to save the schedule for the test trip of the vessel I was responsible for as the SER Testing Manager. And by that I got almost the whole leadership team of the branch office fired. As I wrote several times before, the devastating flaws of the centralistic controlled socialistic economy required sometimes enormous personal efforts of a single individual to get things done and done in time. I had a vessel two days before the scheduled trial trip, with the alarm system on board not completed. The alarm bells had not arrived in time, and although I had cannibalized the stored items for the next two ships which brought me a lot of critics from the two other Testing Managers which had been hired after me, I still needed six alarm bells to get the safety system ready for the trial trip.

Let me here explain a little bit how production in a central controlled socialistic system works using these desperately needed alarm bells. In the case of the alarm bells our company would send in a request for those bells on the basis of the shipyard's plan for how many ships they would build in the following year. Knowing how the system worked, a good local planner at the company would add at least 20 percent more.

The Central Planning Commission would then go ahead and add up all required alarm bells from all companies throughout East Germany, and knowing how the system worked, would subtract at least 15 percent towards the later years mostly 20 percent of the requested demand and place the order for alarm bells with the manufacturing company. That meant almost zero reserve for error or defects. And you need to know that in a centralized and strictly regulated economy with fixed prices and planned demand, competition was an unknown word. With that, you had only one alarm bell manufacturer.

When the year began for which the planned alarm bells were ordered, the company would send at the end of each month the planned number of alarm bells according to the order of the Central Planning Commission. With every defect alarm bell sent back under warranty the number of missing alarm bells increased until you finally could not mount enough bells to get the safety system certified for the trial trip. The main focus of the material clerks at our branch was to contact in endless phone calls the material dispatcher at headquarters to get the stuff repaired back or the new ones delivered. But that never helped much.

Now I was under enormous pressure, because I had made a deal with the shipyard's production director. If I got the ship ready for the trial trip on time, he would make sure that I got a truck to move my furniture from my in-laws home to the new apartment in Stralsund. He was not the number one at the shipyard, but he was the most powerful one and you did not want to disappoint that man. After a short visit at the storage, only to find out that nothing came in the morning, I went straight up to the material clerk's office and asked him for the phone number of the alarm bell manufacturer. Although I knew that it was forbidden to call them direct, I knew he had the number. Hesitatingly he gave me the number, and after about two and a half hours I got through and had their office on the phone.

The woman was very friendly and reminded me that this was illegal, but called the colleague who was responsible for the delivery of those alarm bells I needed. He told me that he had eight of the warranty repairs ready to be shipped, but according to his requirement log those were not to be shipped before the end of the month with the normal shipment to save fuel.

I told him that he would not have any fuel when those alarm bells wouldn't be at the shipyard tomorrow morning, because then the vessel would not go on trial trip, and with that the Great Brother (as the Russians were widely named) would not open the oil pipe for another gush of oil. He said he couldn't do anything even if he wanted, because he had no truck ready at all for the next several days. I asked him if he could make sure that those alarm bells be brought to the central railway station and he confirmed that would be possible. I told him to stay close to the teletype to receive my instructions which train at what time. That was the most reliable information system in East Germany until the collapse.

I went down to the workshop to find the apprentice and instructed him about the train journey he was about to make. He was actually excited about it and agreed immediately. With the secretary of the boss we found a good train connection which would bring the apprentice to the city and back over night. We immediately sent the data by teletype to the company. She was a little concerned about the action. She suspected it to be somewhat out of the regular, but when the confirmation from the alarm bell company came, she was as happy as I was.

Knowing that everything I could possible do was done, I went with a good conscience into the milestone meeting with the production director and confirmed the next afternoon ready from our side. He looked at me with a doubtful gaze, but said nothing. At six thirty in the morning I picked up the apprentice from the railway station with eight alarm bells and drove him home to get him some sleep. Then I went to the shipyard, got the team on board to install the alarm bells and was on board until the system was checked, certified and ready to go. With that it was already 10AM when I entered the office building where several of my colleagues with grins on their faces told me that the boss was in a swivet and wanted to see me as soon as I came in.

When I entered his office, he was on the phone with headquarters and I could definitely hear the yelling voice of his boss out of the phone. Concerning the permanent bad connection quality and instability of the phone system in East Germany, this was something to remember. When he hung up he could barely hold his countenance. After he heard my side of the story he did not say anything and I was dismissed. The ship went out on a trial trip at 5:00 p.m. and the next week I had my truck to move.

We were really happy to have our own home for the first time as a family, although it was somewhat strange with two little children to live at the 6th floor, in American counting 7th floor, without an elevator. The Central Planning Commission was not able to plan enough elevators to be manufactured to serve the multiple construction places throughout East Germany, and since Berlin had absolute priority in everything, they changed quickly the law, which until then required buildings with more than 4 floors to be equipped with an elevator, now it was 7 floors.

These buildings were somewhat strange and usually called the *Platte*. It came from the technology which based on prefabricated concrete slabs either with windows, doors or the installation pit completely installed already. I did explain that several chapters before and this technology was the same after more than twenty years. As I saw more often than I wished during the time I went to the construction side where our new home was built, those plastic strips did not go down into the guides as they should. The workers would then go ahead and hammer them down into place. This often enough did not work out very well, and especially in winter when the plastic shields became bridle by the low temperature, they just broke off, when the guide was filled with hardened concrete. There was also not much attention paid to the sound insulation of the installation pit, which went from the first floor up to the sixth floor at the bathroom. You could hear the bell ring from the apartment at the second floor as if it was yours at the seventh. And since all the bells were the same, remember, central managed manufacturing and planning, that bell from the second, or any other floor in that house had the same sound.

In our apartment the bedroom window faced northwest. And the fall storms with heavy rain blew the rain right into the children's bedroom at the bottom side of the window. It cost me two bottles of hard liquor to fix that problem by getting the insulation putty which was used at the vessels. That putty was the only stuff available that could withstand the weather.

Another problem was the heating system. Those buildings were equipped with night-storage-heaters. They would automatically switch on at night when the power usage was low and the price was cheap and should hold the heat and slowly discard it during the day. But soon we realized that was a huge *should*. As many things in East Germany the reality was very different from the planning. As soon as the energy production got deeper and deeper in trouble with the burning of the energy-inefficient soft coal, the electronic control system at the heaters were altered to reduce the power used to heat the storage elements inside the highly insolated heaters. With the reduced power the stored heat was much less and latest at five in the afternoon the heaters were cold.

Even during the day when the wind blew through all the leaks around the windows and the wall connections, and the apartment never got really warm. So one Saturday, I took one of the ovens apart and removed the electronic controller to take to work. At work were several colleagues who had all the same problem but nobody had ever tried to do anything with the electronics. I got a hold of a former classmate who was managing an installation department at the construction site in Berlin and he sent me the schematics of the electronic for the heater. Looking at the schematics it was immediately clear which components were needed to get the heater to heat at full power when necessary. I also found out that there was actually a connection for an external temperature sensor. I ordered the stuff I needed, and as usual several more components usable for barter deals later. I soldered everything into place at all of our heaters and whoa, what great warm apartment we suddenly had. I was warned though by my friend, that the manipulation of the heaters was considered theft. This was because we did not pay heating per kilowatt-hour rather than a flat rate.

A few days after that, the pastor came to us because we were about to organize a children Bible teaching and he was fascinated with the difference in our heating system. He promised not to talk to anybody about it, and I changed his electronics too. I had to do it twice though because one of the electronics burned totally out after a few days. After I looked a little closer I recognized that there was a leak right behind the electronic and the extreme heat with the increased power level burned the electronic. But otherwise it worked well.

As said before, I used many of my vacation days to travel to Berlin and visit the Austrian embassy, mostly by myself to reduce the risk, but often with Christiane, and on these occasions we left the children with their grandma. My suspicion that mail wasn't secure from being read by others wasn't really farfetched and one night confirmed by friends from church who visited us. She was working at the central post office of our city and she said that there was definitely a special department where all mail, listed in a specific list daily updated by the city office of internal affairs which was the head of all police forces in the city including the STASI, had to be sent. It was known to most of those who had relatives in West Germany that their incoming mail was not only opened regularly, but often confiscated, especially when money was included. But it was completely unknown to many and to me, that this would also happen with outgoing mail. This was another reason for us not to use the postal service at all for mail to the Austrian embassy. But in the following spring, we decided to take a couple of days off and take the children with us and visit the Austrian embassy and have some fun at the Berlin amusement park.

So we packed our travel baggage, loaded the car and we were on our way to have a great time for a couple of days. We had planned to be at the embassy on Tuesday and stay for two or three days in Berlin after that. We arrived late in the evening at the hotel as close as possible to the embassy and affordable. We checked in for the night and went to our room. The reason you checked in for one night only is that the hotels, especially in East Berlin, were regularly monitored by the police, and every hotel had to report the guests with a special form. If you would stay several days in a row at the same hotel, the STASI would be informed and they would first check if they had anything about you at their files. Then they would contact the district STASI office to see if there were any special events happened over the last ten days or two weeks, and finally they would think about to paying you a visit and taking you in for some questions. No East-

German person in his right mind would check in for several nights at the same hotel.

Since we were really tired and had to get up early next morning we went to bed early. With that we missed a very important message. The result of that miss was almost devastating to our small family. Next morning when we get up, we spent not much time at the hotel. Just a short breakfast and that was it. Hotels in East Germany at that time, beside so-called Inter-Hotels which were prohibited for East-German citizens, had no TV or radio at the rooms and the breakfast wasn't really anything you were interested in. After the breakfast we went to the room, packed our baggage and stored it in the car. Since we were hotel guests, we had a parking spot at least till noon. Then we were on our way to the embassy.

Don't Try to Outrun the STASI Especially with Two Little Kids Under Your Arm

It hit me like the soccer ball in the middle of my face many years ago. How could I've been so stupid? The clarity came over me like a flashlight in the middle of the night. Focused on the visit at the embassy and knowing that we had done it so many times without having any trouble, I had totally neglected the explosive political situation East Germany had been in for a couple of days.

One factor probably was that the East German media did not even mention it. Thousands of East German citizen were able to enter the West German embassies all over East Europe. Nearly every West German Embassy in countries of the communistic block, such as Poland, Czechoslovakia, Hungary and so on, were occupied by masses of East Germans who demanded to be released into West Germany. Because of the inability of East Germany to block the western media from reaching into East Germany, even if they tried really hard, many people were informed about this situation, and so were we.

In the same second when I saw two men from the state security police walking towards my family and me, I realized how empty the street was, unusually empty. And these two hadn't been there before. I was sure when we entered the street one or two minutes ago there was nobody, the street was empty, zero, nothing. Yet that should have warned me that something was wrong. And looking over my shoulder there was another team.

Now from both ends of the street where the Austrian embassy was nearly in the center, these two two-man teams of the state security police walked towards us. I looked to Christiane, who had already seen both and realized in a flash the situation.

"We have to hurry," I said.

She nodded, and we accelerated. And so did the STASI. But with two little kids, four and five years old, we stook little chance of outrunning them. And we realized that immediately. Christiane took our daughter Melanie and I our son Lennart on the arm and walked now really fast. We knew we couldn't make it, because the Austrian embassy was at the third floor of the building. We passed through the door and knew we had to make a decision none of us liked.

"Let Lennart down and run, that at least one of us is safe," said Chritiane.

I hesitated. But she was right. If they caught both of us, that would be the end. At least three to five years in jail, and the children given to strong communist foster parents. No, that should never happen. She was right; at least one needed to make it into the embassy. I set Lennart down and started to run upstairs. Christiane was a couple of stairs behind me, and when I reached the mezzanine, I could hear the voice of the state security police talking to each other:

"They are up there—we have to stop them."

I arrived at the third floor, rang the bell, and instead of the door, a small porthole was opened.

The face of a woman appeared.

"What do you want?" she asked not really as friendly, as it used to be the case.

"I'm Harald Zieger and I have an appointment with Mrs. K." I yelled at her, since I have a rather strong voice and was still breathing heavily after running up the stairs.

At the same time, it happened—and I believe by divine intervention— that Mrs. K inside the embassy was on her way back to her office heard me.

"Let him in, he is an Austrian citizen!" she said.

So the woman opened the door and I turned around where I could just see Christiane with Melanie under her arm and Lennart in front of her walking up the last steps. The woman behind me asked me:

"Would you come in. Please, I must shut the door."

"No! My children and my wife are behind me."

At that very moment the first of the two state security police man appeared maybe two or three stairs behind Christiane. Since the stairs in that building were spiral stairs, it seemed he would be able to grab her heel any given moment. And from inside the embassy the same voice said:

"The kids are citizens too, let them in!"

I grabbed Lennart's arm and pulled him through the door at the same moment Christiane was through with Melanie under her arm, and the woman slammed the door in the face of the STASI officer.

That was how we learned that I'm an Austrian citizen. The idea of becoming free from tyranny and suppression was suddenly about to assume a definite form. We needed a few minutes rest from the shock. The fear, which was immediately transferred to our children when we started to run upstairs with the mortal fright of being arrested by the STASI, needed more time and some sweets they got from the employees at the embassy to disappear from their faces. The embassy clerk was visibly annoyed about the audaciousness of the STASI to enter the building where only embassies were, to hunt down a family with two little children. Finally when we were sitting at her office, she asked if we had planned this trip some time ago, and I said that it was just a few days ago that we decided to come to Berlin to spend some days here with the kids, and we wanted to use the opportunity to visit the embassy to see if the bureaucrats, uh I'm sorry, the colleagues, in Vienna had come to a conclusion, which obviously was the case.

She pointed out that this was the case and thank God, because the embassy was ordered by the Austrian department of foreign affairs to allow access to the Austrian embassy only for Austrian citizens. That was based on the situation at several West German embassies around East Europe and since the previous day, and also at the Permanent Representation of West Germany in East Berlin. Because of the tense situation and the limited space the Austrian embassy had, as well as the fact that there were other embassies at the same building, the embassy was closed for all foreigners. And at a briefing in the morning, the Ambassador informed the staff that the East German Government had declared the area where all the embassies were as a restricted area. That could change during the day though.

Now everything became clear to us. Since we were traveling all day long the day before and went to bed early without listening to the news, we did not know about the development at the Permanent Representation and the restriction of the whole area by the STASI in the early morning. Since the hotel where we stayed overnight was inside this area, we were not halted by police until the patrol saw us walking down the road. Then the clerk pulled out my file and handed a three-page statement to me. Because of the explosiveness of the official notice, she was directed to read it to me. She asked me if I'd accept the notice and the statement therein which I affirmed—why shouldn't I—and handed the official certificate of citizenship over to me. With the issue of an Austrian passport which I had to sign in front of her, the formal act was done.

Each and every document had required a fee to be paid in Austrian currency, which I definitely could not pay. But the Austrian department of foreign affairs knew about the dilemma East Germans had with convertible currency and had allowed the embassy to handle this situation as follows. The first time such kind of documents were issued, the embassy would pay using a special fund; all further documents would be paid in East-German Mark. During that time the woman from the front desk came in the office and said that the policemen had left the floor but she wasn't sure that they had left the building. Since the whole procedure took several hours I was a little concerned about the children and asked the clerk if I could go and look after my family. She said that the other people at the embassy were taking care of them and when we walked out the office I saw them playing with all kind toys and all kind of sandwiches were ready for them to eat, and Christiane was reading the Austrian Newspapers. When all the official stuff was finally done and we left the embassy later in the afternoon there were no policemen to see, and normal traffic was back on the streets. Full of joy and still excited about how the situation had turned into a happy ending, we decided to drive home and assimilate this great news.

Two Citizenships Are Not Really Helpful or Well-Meant International Laws Bring More Harm than Benefits

With the confirmation that I was legally an Austrian citizen by birth, the situation was totally changed from one day to the other. What could I do with this? I knew from my research I'd done earlier that year, that the GDR punished the possession of a foreign passport with several years in prison. Since I did not have an official visa, issued by the East German government, in that Austrian passport, I could not use it for anything inside the GDR. On the other hand, I was officially Austrian citizen and was still trapped in a country that I did not loved that had no love for me because I did not agree anymore with the oppressive politic of the government, and where I did not see a decent future for my children. Being the children of a traitor, as the leaders on all levels of government saw me; my children would not be able to go to an undergraduate or even graduate school. They would be inferior in any situation of their lives and had no chance to achieve personal fulfillment.

When one walked into the East-German version of the supermarket, called HO, one could not find any fresh fruits or vegetables without having a specific relationship with one of the clerks. The quality of the products offered was bad to horrible, and at any of those shops at the entrance was always the huge skeleton container with the potato inventory. Nobody cared about the appearance or how things were presented; why should anybody? There was not only no reward for initiative, but it was likely to cause infuriation among the coworkers when somebody did more than necessary. Everybody was busy to get what was needed to survive in an economy that was to a large part based on barter trading than on buying and selling.

Those potatoes were never cleaned before they had been stored at the warehouses, which were for sure not conditioned to keep the potatoes fresh; they had already begun to rot when they arrived at the shop. Each of those skeleton containers was filled with approximately 50 to 60 bags holding 10 pounds each. The load of all those bags squeezed the bottom layer to the point where the potatoes crushed and begun to molder even faster. You could measure the progress of the decay on the increasing intensity of the smell that awaited you entering the shop.

The chocolate was made from low-level quality cacao, and since East Germany had to buy it on the world markets it required convertible currency, which was always limited. With that real chocolate was seldom obtained, and what you got tasted sandy and greasy. Fruits like oranges, bananas or even domestic fruits such as apples, pears, cherries, plums were rarely available, and if so, you needed to have a relationship with one of the clerks to even get to see them. Even at Christmas, when all the parents wanted to have at least for their children some oranges and bananas, it was difficult to get them. I remember one year that the shipyard actually sold a special contingent of what was called south fruits, oranges and tangerines, to the workers. I was standing in line for more than three hours and got two oranges and two tangerines, one of each for each of my children. Fortunately the packages we got from Christiane's relatives from West Germany contained real chocolate.

To buy cold cuts and meat was another odyssey. The normal butcher shops were empty almost all week except Thursday. I still don't know why it was that of all things on Thursday meat was delivered to the government run butcher shops. And in reference to the story with the piglets, there wasn't enough to satisfy the demand. Prices were fixed and centrally controlled, and the money we earned wasn't worth much.

So from time to time some butcher—yeah, there were still some private butcher shops and even bakeries existent—found a way to get whole swine-halves to buy and to produce quality cold cuts and meat. I remember the time when even we supplied swine to a private butcher. Within a few weeks that was known in a radius of usually 25 to 35 miles, and people would come from all over the area to buy their meat and cold cuts there. You would stay at least some hours in line and you had to be there at the right time.

One of my Testing Manager colleagues had discovered that one of those privately owned butcher shops across the Ruegendamm on the island Ruegen (about thirty miles from the shipyard) had find a source for swine halves. And he said there were rumors that he had from time to time even beef. That was almost unbelievable because that would be sensational. Again, for an unknown reason, Thursdays were the days. Equipped with long lists of what to buy, two or three of us jumped into a car at around noon and drove to the butcher shop. Even though we were there about 12:30, we had already a long line in front of us. We were back at the shipyard at the right time to clock out. That wasn't unusual. Almost every worker in East Germany used the official work time to satisfy private requirements, such as buying food and spare parts, to complete official tasks or to help relatives or friends to do such things.

Another important part was to get the material organized as it was called, because there was no shop where you could go to buy a piece of pipe because you wanted to replace it in your bathroom, or you wanted to build a shelf for the children's books in there room, but you could not find a carpenter to buy that shelf. And this was the situation for nearly everything in your life day by day. Every night when the children were in bed and Christiane and I were sitting together, I looked at that Austrian document, confirming my citizenship, that official note from the Austrian government and my passport—I will not conceal that I took that passport into my bed at night for several days—and I saw a future in freedom for us and a future full of opportunities for my children.

Yes, I had a secure job, yes, I had a warm apartment, yes, I could buy the basic necessities such as food and clothing. Yes, my children had the opportunity to go to school, and yes with that we were probably better off than many million people around the world. But that wasn't all. And it wasn't all I wanted for my family. Even though many people in East Germany had accepted a life like that, restrained in anything that was outside of the collective, who had caved in and lost their individuality and that little rest of self-esteem inextinguishable in any of God's creatures was drowned in alcohol on the weekend.

A few days after that event in Berlin, we decided it was enough. The strategy was to go a different way than so many others had tried and ended as a broken family, divorced, in jail or separated from their children. We decided to get my Austrian citizenship legalized and use the ability to travel to Austria and prepare everything for immigration. I bought an issue of the GDR citizenship law and begun to study. The law clearly stated three ways to become an East German citizen, but none did really fit my situation.

At that point I remembered the lawyer who several years ago advised me not to risk my life in exchange for twelve weeks service in an army I despised. I knew that he was living at the island and from the pastor I got his address. I chose a Saturday and drove to his house only to hear that he wasn't there. I said I'd wait but was told that might be in vain. I said I'd wait anyway. It was a great day. The sun was shining, and I had a book and was just sitting there outside reading.

Late in the afternoon, I think it was already after five, a man I did not recognize at that moment entered the house. Soon I heard voices which pointed to an argument between the man and his wife, and I knew it was Wolfgang Schnur. After several minutes, he appeared at the door.

"Why are you waiting for me? It's Saturday—I have a hard week behind me. Drive home and come back on Monday."

"Do you not remember me?

"No, why should I? I've never seen you, at least not to my knowledge."

"I was in that meeting, which never happened because you were at a birthday party with twenty witnesses several years ago. You need to read this letter, sir. It's an official document from the Austrian government."

Standing in the doorway of his home, he began to read and after just a few minutes, said,

"Come in, let's go to my office."

When he was done reading, he looked at me, silent for a while. "I'll not open a case file for this. I can't probably help you much with this, but I'll tell what I can do. At first I'll make five copies of this."

He really had a Canon copy machine! And a big one. That alone was a miracle to me, I'd never seen such a machine other than in TV, West TV of course.

"I'll dictate you letters to several different local and central government parts, including the department of foreign and internal affairs."

And while he dictated and I wrote, he would once in a while seem to be lost in thoughts, only to startle and say,

"I can't understand what happens to this country."

"As soon as you can, go to the Notary in Stralsund, I believe he is open every day during the week. Let these copies exemplify and then send them together with the letters to the respective addresses."

"I remember you from that meeting, you asked about refusing reserve service. I'm really glad you did not go down that road." After a short moment of silence, he said, "I really can't understand what is going on here, what country we have become. Just some weeks ago I had a man in office who was stateless from his birth on. Even during the Third Reich under Hitler, he was stateless and did not have to serve in the military. The GDR made him a citizen. And he said that for the first time in his life he felt like somebody. But that has changed. He doesn't want to be citizen of this country anymore. He wants rather to be stateless again. Now you're here and you would rather go to all kind of trouble than to be a citizen of the country."

Wolfgang Schnur was working as a lawyer at cases for the Lutheran church in a more silent way than the more prominent and famous lawyer Wolfgang Vogel. Knowing that, I understood that he had probably seen more suffering and hardship at the STASI-run prisons than anyone else outside the system. Thinking about that while driving home, I was sure that he was under surveillance by the STASI, and for that reason really eased that he did not created a file about my case.

The following Sunday we traveled to Saßnitz to see my mother and my siblings Michael and Connie to inform them about the outcome of the Austrian investigation and to give them the opportunity to go the same way. My brother Michael was at this time a full-time employee of the district management of the FDJ organization, and he had a steep career in front of him; he actually had a delegation for the following fall to the political academy of the SED in his pocket, meant to become a real big wig. Connie was divorced and lived with her two children in Saßnitz, working as a professional waitress. We were all sitting around the kitchen table at my mother's apartment when I told them the news.

"More than eight years ago, Christiane and I discovered a letter from a lawyer in West Germany who asked our mother to send him the naturalization certificate of our biological father." I began to explain the reason for this unusual family meeting.

"What? Where did you? What letter?" they all spoke at once, and I had to calm them down.

"Let me finish my explanation and then I'll answer all your questions as far as I can. I decided to write a letter to that lawyer, although his letter was over twenty years old. We sent this letter to the lawyer with an aunt of Christiane, not knowing if it would go through on normal mailing," I said with a look at Michael, who actually rolled his eyes at that statement.

"The answer a few weeks later was negative. He, the lawyer, wrote that he is retired, can't remember on such a case and even if he had such a case, after that long time it wasn't possible to find anything. After I had recovered from that devastating message, I wrote a new letter and, risking everything, added his original letter from years ago. The answer came soon and confirmed everything including an apology because he thought it could be a trap. Our father is living in Austria, actually in Vienna."

"Could you write to him?" Connie threw in.

"Hold on for a moment, Connie. It gets much better. Now, knowing he's in Austria, but having no address, I decided to go to the Austrians direct. Christiane used the time we spend in Berlin and went to the embassy. That was two years ago, and last week we received the confirmation that we, meaning you, Connie, you, Michael, and I are Austrian citizens according to Austrian and international laws. You both have the right to go to the Austrian embassy in Berlin and apply for your citizen documents."

"How long will that take and what do we do then?" Connie asked, but before I could say anything, Michael was speaking up, and his voice signaled extreme anger barely suppressed.

"What do you mean with we? I'm definitely not included in that. Even though it might be legal, something is wrong with that. That's all false."

"Do you think I'm able to inspire the Austrian government to write such a letter? If you really believe that this letter is false, you're far more deceived than I thought you are."

"You're a traitor—people like you have no right to enjoy the accomplishments of the Workers' and Peasants' State. If the situation will ever require certain actions against the class enemy, I'll personally make sure that you are among the first who get lined up and shot." He was furious now and was yelling this at me, already standing. Without an additional word and not reacting to our mother's words to calm down, he left the apartment.

It took me a while processing what my own brother just said to me. And I knew him well enough to know that he was fanatic enough to mean what he said. I explained to Connie that she could use all the information I had and start her own application. It took her only a few weeks till she got the same official statement from the Austrian government.

Next Monday when I had checked the progress at the two vessels I had responsibility for at that time, I went to the notaries' office in town to get the five copies exemplified. To my horror, there were at least twenty people in the waiting room. I couldn't even sit down because there weren't enough chairs. After about ten minutes, the door opened and a woman came out.

"Anybody come newly in here to see the notary?"

"I need to have the notary to exemplify these five copies here," I said, and handed her the five copies the lawyer had made of the original letter from the Austrian government. She looked at me with a kind of a questioning expression on her face.

"Where's the original?"

"I'll hand it direct to the notary when I'm in his office."

"But I need the original to exemplify that the copies are identical with it."

"No, you don't, the notary who signs the exemplification needs to read the original. And I'll not leave that document out of my sight."

Several people overheard our discussion and one man asked reproachfully, "Don't you even trust the office clerk of a notary?"

"How can I, if I can't even trust my own brother anymore in this system?"

My answer must have shocked him because he fell silent.

After that the woman just gave up and went back in her office, the five copies of that Austrian government notification in her hand.

About five minutes or so later she was out again and handed the five copies back to me.

"The notary can't exemplify these copies. He called the city's' department of Internal Affairs and they said you shall come over to their office immediately."

"What is a notary good for when he can't confirm that two pieces of paper contain the same text? That's all I did ask for. And what is he worth if he can't keep a secret to himself?" I said to her, not even trying to reduce the volume. And turning to that man next to me who had just a few minutes back questioned my sanity, I said, "Do you need more to know about trust in a country where the most trusted person, a notary, is selling you out to the regime?"

And with that I left the notary office. But I knew instinctively not to go to the office of internal affairs because I had the original document with me and I would not go back to work with it either and went home first.

Later at night we decided to send the letters with those copies even when they were not exemplified and just add the remark that the notary refuse to exemplify the copies. Now, knowing that the city's department of internal affairs was already alert about my person since I was considered a threat to the political security and stability of the GDR after being expelled from Peenemunde and throw in a startled by the call from the notary, I decided to travel to Berlin and drop the letters in mailboxes at several different areas.

You may think that I was now completely nuts, but with all the information and knowing that even the outgoing mail of certain people was caught in dragnet actions, I was sure that my name was on that list too. So I took a day vacation, traveled by train to Berlin, and used several different public traffic systems such as subway, tram and S-Railway to drop the letters in mail boxes spread out over East Berlin. One letter was directed to the Minister of Foreign affairs, one to the Minister of Internal affairs, the department of internal affairs at the state and the department of internal affairs of the city of Stralsund, which I actually dropped at the mailbox on the railway station in Stralsund when I came home late at night that day. My major objective explained with those letters was to clarify my citizenship as an Austrian citizen and repeal my GDR citizenship, which had been illegally forced onto me.

The Number 1 in East Germany was not German

LET'S GET OUT OF HERE

The STASI Offered Me Dog That Won't Hunt Although I Wasn't a Hunter

IT TOOK THE control entities of the political suppressing system almost four weeks to react. Then I found a postcard in my mailbox requesting my appearance at the office of internal affairs at city hall. When I arrived, there were three men in that room and they offered me a chair so that I had two of them in my back. The leader of that group stated that they had been authorized to handle the situation. And he began reading from a piece of paper.

"I have been authorized to handle this situation about your sudden discovered Austrian citizenship and to explain to you your legal situation from the GDR's point of view. The Ministry for Internal Affairs of the GDR has carefully investigated your situation and according to the available facts, led us to the following conclusion. Because of the fact that your mother was living at the territory of the German Democratic Republic at the moment of its founding, she became automatically and in accordance with the law citizen of the GDR. Although she left the GDR 1950 illegally, she did not lose her citizenship, because she returned 1956. Since she was GDR citizen when you were born you inherited GDR citizenship by birth. Hence you're a GDR citizen."

I had difficulty keeping my face as apathetic as possible, but I was close to exploding. And these guys, which I read later in the STASI files were STASI officers, were professional enough to recognize that.

"For reasons unknown to the Ministry of Internal Affairs, you had suddenly the impression to be an Austrian citizen in addition, and it seems that you somehow have been able to convince the Austrian government that you're an Austrian citizen because of your father."

I could barely keep my temper any longer and to create a kind of release for myself I asked, "I do get a copy of this statement, don't I?"

"No. And before you ask, it is not allowed to make notes of this discussion."

"You call this farce a discussion, you call my mother a liar, and me a charlatan, who mysteriously was able to bewitch the Austrian government to grant me Austrian citizenship, and don't even have the guts to give me a copy of this fabrication?" I threw out now angry enough to forget all fear.

To my surprise, he stayed calm. "Can I continue? You need to understand that the law of the GDR has priority over the laws of Austria, since your normal residence is here. That is actually according to international law. Based on that law, you have to apply for a passport of the GDR and a visa to travel to Austria. Since the responsible comrades at the government of the GDR are concerned you would not come back and leave your family behind so that the government of the GDR has to provide for them, the probability that such an application could be successful seems to be very small."

This was devastating.

"So, what you're saying is, as long as I live inside the GDR, I have no possibility to travel to Austria? No chance to meet my father, or have my father see his grandchildren?"

All the thoughts and plans we had made, me traveling to Austria and checking out the situation, getting a job and building up some decent assets so that the family could come and have a new start together were falling flat within seconds. As much as I tried not to let them find out about my feelings, they were professionals enough to notice. And they thought they had me cornered and could now cut me to pieces.

And that was the biggest mistake somebody made when confronting me with no choice. I'd not cave in, never! I was used to the situation that I had to swim against the stream, that was what I was doing all my life. And thanks to the great education in political history, I had learned that the leader of the underground German Communist Party during WWII Ernst Thälmann had a motto which I had made my own. And even though I wasn't a communist anymore, I still have that motto because it was very inspiring.

I will rather die upright standing, than living on my knees.

"We have to make you an offer, though, which we believe you can't deny," said one of the guys sitting behind me suddenly into my thoughts.

Anger began to rise again inside of me, and I turned around.

"If you have something to say to me, look at me!" I said and turned back to the guy who was in front of me all the time.

For a moment I saw the face of the guy turning mad, but that was only for a blink of the eye. Then he was looking friendly again.

"No reason to be angry—the comrade meant we would like to make you an offer. If you lay aside your Austrian citizenship, we will grand you the allowance to participate on the trial trips with the vessels you build."

The allowance was called a PM3 and was issued only to trustworthy people. This would mean approximately twenty-five percent salary increase per month.

"You got to be kidding me," was my immediate replay.

Again that short flush of anger changed his face for a microsecond or so.

"Wait, not so fast. We have more to offer. We will also give you a passport of the GDR that allows you to travel wherever you want."

In the meantime I had caught my countenance and could counter thinking straight.

"You really believe I'd walk over that bridge, too fragile to hold long enough to cross the water?

Which means the same as you think you can sell me a dog that doesn't hunt?

Do you really think I'm stupid enough not to know that this passport isn't worth the paper it is printed on because the visa to allow me to leave the GDR is the key? Who will guarantee for that the visa would or would not stamp into it? And when I lay aside my Austrian citizenship, I have nothing to barter for a visa anymore."

They tried to convince me that this would never happen; all three are talking at the same time. But all I needed to silence them was to remind them on the incident with Wolf Biermann, the East German singer-songwriter who was stripped of his citizenship while being in West Germany on an official tour. The official reasoning was that he had denounced the GDR by his disgraceful lyrics. There was silence in that room because they had no answers to that. With that I stood and was on my way out when the guy who was sitting behind the desk agitated asked me,

"What about the proposal with the GDR passport?"

"Let's face it, that wasn't really a proposal, that was a trap, and I'm too big to fall for the cheese," I answered, looking over my shoulder on my way out.

FREEDOM'S NIGHTMARE

When I came home that night, I was really disturbed. We had set so much hope into the ability to get me traveling to Austria, building a new starting base for our family, and all was wiped out with the findings of the investigators of the department of internal affairs.

And the most devastating thought was that I believed they were right. That it wasn't a construct of lies and half truths what the STASI had put together, considering the big black cloud that hung over the past of my mother. She had told us pieces of that history, one piece now and another piece, then when she was pressed to say something, but it was never a complete story. And as I would find out later many things just weren't true. That story about being part of a refugee track behind the Russian lines in 1945 crossing the Russian rear behind the frontline for about nine hundred kilometers north to south, from the coastline of the Baltic Sea into the hills of Bohemia, was it reality or a huge lie as so many things in our life?

And when I confronted her with the statements of the ministry of internal affairs about her, having a registered place of residence before 1949 and with that became a GDR citizen and therefore made me a GDR citizen too, she denied everything. Yet in the light of the statements the strange situation with me getting my first identification card made suddenly more sense than ever. After Christiane and I had carefully waged our chances in any direction, we decided to travel to the Austrian embassy and see what they had on ideas and possible situations with similar cases so we could get an advice.

We talked to the legal advisor at the embassy, but all he could say was that there wasn't an easy way and that the GDR government was correct considering my rights, the law of the country I had my place of residence had priority. He also told us that we weren't the only people being unable to exercise our rights as Austrian citizens. The Austrian embassy suspected a total of over eighteen thousand Austrians living in East Germany not knowing about it our having no chance like we, mainly as a result of the Second World War. I told him I could not just sit down and accept being imprisoned behind that wall pointing out the window where the east side of the Berlin Wall was clearly visible.

He tried to calm me down and insisted that I should not think about doing stupid things such as crossing the border illegally because I could

lose my life, but I never thought about that. So I said that I'll probably file for the allowance to leave this prison legally and I'd hope that
the Austrian embassy would support us. He, typical diplomatic, did not
deny that possibility directly, yet explained that there was really little the
embassy could do.

Finally we traveled back home. And the next day I wrote my application for permission to leave the GDR permanently to live with my family
in Austria. Again I did not use the mail boxes in our city, knowing that
there was a fishing order for mail with my address in both directions active,
and I sent it to all the government departments where I had send my
statement of Austrian citizenship. According to the East-German law the
responsible department had 6 weeks to give an intermediate notification.

The day after the letters were dropped at the mail boxes, I asked
Manfred Dumm for a meeting and explained to him that I had send the
application. He was shocked.

"Harald, you should not have informed me, because now I have to
inform HR of the company."

"I know that, but I also know that those who did not inform their company that they applied for leaving the GDR ended up to become unemployed within days, and I don't want to live on the street with two children."

"I've never heard such thing."

"I know, Manfred, because you're living in an illusory world, built by
communistic propaganda, written in trash papers you call news. You're living in a world of lies you consider the truth, because you don't know what
truth is, since you never read it."

"I promise you, you will not lose your job."

"I'm praying for that, Manfred."

He called HR at the same minute I closed his office door behind me, as
I could read later in the STASI file. I did not get fired and we had enough
work to do.

During one of my former visits at the embassy, I had also asked if they
could help to find my father since all the attempts to get an address or
phone number through the relatives of Christiane failed. They said they
would try, and now I had his address and a phone number in my hand. I
finally had discovered which one of the few public phone booths were so

connected that it was possible to call Austria direct without needing the long-distance connection board, which was controlled and monitored by the STASI. At noon time I went out of the shipyard to call the number in Vienna. The phone rang for several minutes and nobody answered.

The problem with a call to a foreign country from the booth was that the payment counted at the same second the foreign phone began to ring. I had coins for about ten minutes, and when they were gone, the connection broke. I thought that noon might be a bad time, nobody might be home. I changed another bunch of paper east marks into a pocket full of coins and went to the booth at night. Since Austria was in the same time zone as we were, I was sure I'd get someone on the phone this time. And really I did get an answer this time. The phone rang two or three times and then there was a voice. I said I'd like to talk to Rudolph Zieger and he said it's I.

For several seconds I lost my voice. I had no remembrance of his voice, none, zero. This was the first time in my life that I consciously heard the voice of my biological father. I was thirty-one years old at that moment.

I finally caught my voice.

"It's your son, Harald. I have not many coins left, and I need your help."

"Where are you, Harald? Where are you calling from?"

"I'm in East Germany, in Stralsund. I'm calling from a phone booth, and I need your help, because I want to get out of here out of this prison, and they won't let me go."

"I know some people at the Ministry of Foreign Affairs. I'll make some phone calls tomorrow. Don't call me on this number again, because of my wife. Here is another number you can call."

Then the connection broke.

For several days I went out of the shipyard at different times and tried to call him again, only the second phone number I had and later both numbers alternately, but I never got him on the phone again. Not knowing why I could not get him on the phone, I thought desperately about an alternative how I could contact him without alerting the STASI about that connection.

One Sunday, we were coming back from a trip to the island Rügen, when we had to stop behind a huge truck, and when I finally focused my thought on my environment, I realized that this was a truck from Austria. Like a bolt from the blue it hit my mind that there was an ability to get messages to and from Austria. Since I wasn't prepared in any way for an immediate action, I began to work on a plan.

I wrote a letter, and had my Austrian passport with me when I drove to that spot the next Sunday, where I knew that trucks coming from the island would have to stop when the railway crossing was closed. I knew that there were many trucks coming through on Sundays because the ferry from Trelleborg in Sweden ended in Saßnitz and for many trucks to Austria it was the shortest connection. In addition they could drive through East Germany on Sundays, while they had to stand still in West Germany, and these were the two reasons why they used this route.

I did not wait long, the railway crossing barrier closed and a few minutes later a truck with an Austrian license plate stopped. I jumped out of my car, looking again to all sides to make sure nobody was watching me, ran to the truck and knocked at the driver's door. He opened and I showed him me passport, told him that I was an Austrian and that I needed him to deliver a letter to my dad. He said "Not here. Follow me, outside of town is a large parking lot and I'll stop there and check my wheels." With that he closed the door, the barrier lifted and he drove away. I ran to my car and tried to catch up with him but lost him due to the traffic lights.

When I finally stopped at the parking lot alongside his truck, I could explain my situation.

"Oh, how I hate these communists," he said and then told me the story why that was the case.

"My brother-in-law was employed with the Voest Alpine Inc., and they built several facilities in East Germany over several years. He fell in love with a girl from that area, and they decided to get married. The communistic bureaucrats delayed the issuing of the approval that she was able to marry two times, so long that each time the validity of his certificate was expired and he needed a new one. While all that was going on over a period of three years, she got diagnosed with kidney failure and died. If he could have gotten her to Austria, she would have had a chance to survive. The only treatment under the Universal Health Care system in East Germany was kidney removal."

"That is a very sad story, and I understand you're bitter, but that's how they play here."

"Since his job in East Germany was done, and he was back, working in Austria, he needed a visa to get to her funeral. It was denied since he wasn't a relative. No, I'm not bitter. I'm mad as hell, and if I ever get a chance, these devils will pay for it."

I explained my situation, and told him he could read my letter if he wanted because I could understand that he might be in danger. He said that wasn't necessary, because I'd not had let it open when I thought it was dangerous. Then he said I should watch for him on Sundays at the Intershop at the ferry exit in Saßnitz. It might not be that he was there every Sunday, but his trips to Sweden were almost certainly regular. With that he wished me all the best and drove off.

The next Sunday he was there. Again very carefully we walked a few steps apart through the small bistro which was attached to the Intershop and he gave me a new phone number and told me that my father was well situated in Vienna, had a newly built house and a construction business. I was one happy man at that moment.

Having discovered a secure connection, even though with long delays, I was hopeful I'd be able to correspond with my father, and he could surely be helpful to get me out and to have a decent start in Austria. But I never got a connection with that new phone number and gave finally up wasting my money. For several weeks, Sunday after Sunday, we drove to Saßnitz and waited at the Intershop parking lot for the two ferries coming in on Sundays from Sweden, in vain. Although there were many trucks and several with Austrian license plates, our contact wasn't among them. Not knowing what happened, I did not wanted to risk anyone else's life or future and decided not to contact another truck driver again.

Many years later, already in Austria, we tried to improve our life by working with the Amway business for a while; we were at a large warehouse where Amway had its store, to pick up some goods.

I was waiting outside at my car for the forklift coming around the building when suddenly the driver jumping out of a truck appeared to look very familiar to me. I walked closer and called at him and when he turned around his face almost derailed. He walked towards me, grabbed my hand, and could barely fathom that it was me. Now East Germany did not exist at that time anymore and it wouldn't be a miracle, but it was a miracle that we should meet after so many years, and it could only happen on divine interference.

He said that he was sorry that he could not help me further on because his route through East Germany was cancelled and he was driving all over Western Europe after that last meeting we had in Saßnitz. I told him that we actually were in Vienna since 1985 and lived outside of Vienna. He gave me his address and said we should visit him, but for reasons I can't really remember we never did. God does really works in our lives in absolutely mysterious ways.

Since I did not tell anybody about the application to relocate to Austria, and my boss had no interest at all to talk about it, it stayed a secret. Yet I knew that I would like to get some of our belongings shipped to Austria when the allowance would finally come, and since we were sure it would come, I had to begin to prepare for it. All the radar and radio communication systems as well as the smaller winches for the GTS trawlers were supplied by the Russians. All of these systems came packed in nice solid wooden boxes. Some were really large and excellent to use for our stuff to pack. So, over the next couple of weeks I made sure that I got four of those cases, filled with several square meters of heavy duty plastic foil set aside for me.

At the same time one of my Trial Manager colleagues who was originally a machinery engineer and had traveled a board of GDR merchant ships had bought an old farm house and started to completely rebuild it. He had himself an incredible story to tell. His father was a medical doctor at the district hospital and one of the most renowned gynecologists in East Germany and president of the association of gynecologists of the GDR. His brother had studied medicine too and had become a recommended child orthopedist in East Germany. As such he was sent to Angola to train doctors at a children's hospital East Germany had equipped with instruments and systems.

When his two-year contract was over, there was no direct flight from Angola to East-Berlin. His flight back to East Germany was with a connection stop in Zurich, and he accidentally entered the wrong plane, landing with his family at the Frankfurt Main Airport instead of East-Berlin. My colleague was at this time on a merchant ship at the entrance port of the Suez channel when the message over radio came to escort him to the East-German embassy in Cairo, from where he was escorted by two STASI officers via Bucharest back to East-Berlin. His seaman's muster book was confiscated and he was sent to work at the shipyard in Stralsund. Only because of the distinguished position of his father was it that they had not to undergo all the hostile treatment other families had.

His wife's family had some other renowned personalities among their ranks, and one of them was a very well renowned architect. He had designed a very luxurious home out of that old farm house using an additional part of the large yard that came with it. Because of the almost unlimited connections of his father and the constant flow of West German money—his brother had easily found employment at one of the best orthopedic clinics in West Germany and felt guilt that his brother lost his job—neither construction material nor construction workers, usually Fridays till Mondays, were a problem.

And since he considered me a good friend, he asked me all the time if I would come with him when he was on tour for material. Here an example how that worked. His relative had designed a self-supporting stair from the first floor up to the attic were a large studio was to be built. The problem was that there was no hardwood for stairs available, not even to think about a complete hardwood stair.

One morning he came into the office, grabbed the phone and began to make phone calls, which were going like, "Hi, I'm Tom, the son of Dr. S., and my father told me you can help me get 15 square meters of oak wood." Then listening to the phone for a while he asked to get a name or a number again to write it down, and he would hang up and call the next person.

After several phone calls he finally had a person on the phone that had the wood, or at least would have it within the requested time. He would then ask if this person would be at the office at a certain time—the time we would need to get there. Then he'd hang up and say to me, "Let's go."

We drove to that person's office where he laid a folded piece of paper on the desk after he had the confirmation it was the person he had talked too over the phone. That piece of paper he said contained the dimensions of the wood he needed and that he would come up with the double information when the delivery was done. The person took the paper to check the availability. That meant to see if the amount of West Mark in the folded paper was the right equivalent for the required goods, considering the doubling of it at delivery. The person would then come back and either confirm the delivery or would say something like "Uh, there might be a problem because the last delivery has been cancelled." Tom would then know that he had to increase the payment and would pull out another folded piece of paper and would say if he could check if that wood would be available. The same procedure would then usually lead to a confirmation. This time the price was right.

Tom then paid the price for the oak wood in East German Marks, which was laughably low, I think it was less than 300 East Mark for the 15 square meters, which is roughly 150 square feet, and would get a delivery. I'd have never in a lifetime gotten 15 square meters of oak wood for a stair delivered to the carpenter who would immediately begin to produce the stairs.

Many times I witnessed how connections and foreign money made things possible and material appear that was officially impossible. Either it was clinker bricks for the free hanging, four-sided open firewood chimney, or one hundred bags of cement, or roofing tiles, or bathroom fixtures or whatever you needed to build a house, all those materials which were absolutely unavailable under normal circumstances showed up at the construction side of Tom as if it wasn't a big deal. And even more surprising, the teams of workers, well trained and educated in their trade, brick masons, plumbers, heating contractors, carpenters, electricians, you name it, he called and they were there. This wasn't amazing anymore; this was just short of a miracle. But it wasn't.

It was the extreme proof that the only valid law of economy did work because humanly created restriction such as regulations and laws were completely excluded from the market. The single most effective law of a free market showed its absolute functionality even inside a totally restricted and controlled communistic economy, or better because of that.

DEMAND and SUPPLY DETERMINE the PRICE! No question about what right do you have, how valuable you are to society, no question how much do you need it compared to others, no question how much do you deserve it more than others; no question whether or not it was evaluated by the several different agencies such as health, environment, farm law and I don't know what else.

All those regulations were nullified by the situation that the official currency wasn't worth the paper it was printed on. Somebody had a DEMAND for a specific good or service and others could offer it. If you were able to pay the fair market price, you could get everything you needed when you needed it and at the quality you paid for. And if anybody tried to screw somebody either with service or material, he was done, out of business, because the message that he did try to screw someone was around within minutes, even with a phone system based on the time before WWII. It was an economy inside an economy and everybody knew about it. Even though the STASI had a special department fighting this black market as it was called, they had little success. Only sometimes, when people got too greedy and their lifestyle was obviously in total contradiction of their official income, they got caught and sentenced to jail time.

One day I wanted to have a hundred percent proof that it was only the ability of Tom to bribe the people at the warehouse to get the stuff he needed. So I went in first and bagged with all kind of reasons but all I got was that the clerk finally and gracefully entered my name in that all-too-well-known book. Then Tom walked in and not even ten minutes later he came out with a piece of paper confirming the delivery of five tons of sand to his place the next day. All he paid was 10 West Mark to the clerk. And if you by chance run into an honest person in a warehouse dealing with rare goods people couldn't buy as needed, you would take the paper back and say something like, "Oh, I'm sorry, that's my money I did not know it's in that paper thanks for notifying me." But, honestly, I never experienced that in all the years I saw someone tried to buy stuff and had to use that trick, or Tom bought things using the currency of the workers class enemy. And the most incredible part of it was that all of these activities happened during working time, and most amazingly everybody knew about it and nobody said anything.

I was thinking about getting the wooden cases out of the shipyard and into my basement cage. For that I needed a piece of paper that confirmed that these cases weren't usable anymore and that I had paid the equivalent of value to the shipyard. I got that paper for signing off on a similar piece of paper for almost 60 meters of coaxial cable, which was almost unavailable on the street. We called it *"one hand washes the other,"* and there was actually a commercial created by the government to fight this kind of organized theft and that went like: "When one hand washes the other doesn't mean it is a clean action!" Those posters were hanging everywhere and most people even don't look at them, because they were too busy to try to find what they needed. With that piece of paper signed by the shipyards wood trash operating manager, I had no trouble to drive three times onto the shipyard area, load my trailer with a case and leave the shipyard through the heavily controlled main gate. The guards, all active police men, would check the paper, walk around the car, check the trunk as well as the trailer to make sure I did not have anything else loaded, and then let me pass. Nobody looked into the cases where I had the plastic foil needed to make the cases watertight since we did not know how we could ship them.

There was actually a very nice joke told at work at this time.

A guy comes to the main gate with a hand barrow filled with sawdust. The guard looks at the material pass where is written, Allowed to take a hand barrow of sawdust home every night," and since he is very suspicious he works with his both hands through the sawdust to see if there is something else hidden. He can't find anything and shaking his head he lets the guy go.

Next day, the guy with the hand barrow comes again, the hand barrow full of saw dust. Again, same procedure, nothing to find and the guard has to let him pass, but not without stating: "I know you're stealing something, I'm not sure yet what, but I'll get you." This goes on day by day, the guy comes with the hand barrow, the guard checks the sawdust, finds nothing and threatens the guy that he knows that he's stealing something, but has to let him go.

After several days, the guard can't take it any longer and says to the guy with the hand barrow: "Listen, I know you're stealing something. I can't figure out what and therefore I'll give you a pass on whatever it is you're stealing, but tell me what it is. It drives me crazy that I can't figure it out." The guy with the hand barrow of sawdust thinks for a moment and says then: "Hand barrows. Every single night I go out with a hand barrow full of sawdust and come back to work in the morning empty handed. I throw the sawdust into my garden and sell the hand barrow on the black market on the weekend."

That was as close to reality as it could be. Some comedians made another joke: "Why are the workers of the GDR lately going with a back-pack to work and not using the normal small briefcase any longer?" The answer is: "Erich Honnecker said at the 9. Central Party Convention: 'We can get much more out of our peoples' owned companies.'" And the whole "republic" was laughing for days. It was around the time when Tom bought his oak wood for the stairs that we got the answer from the state department of internal affairs, application denied. No reasoning just one sentence. We were devastated. Almost all night we were sitting, praying and talking about what to do now. We were almost so far as to travel to East Berlin, go to the embassy and sit there until they would let us go to Austria. But we knew that wasn't the way GOD would us have handled this situation. GOD can only support what is righteous and that would be not. But at least I could go to the embassy and ask for advice.

A couple of days later at the embassy all that they could do was encourage me and ask me not to despair. I went home and wrote another application to the state office for internal affairs to leave East Germany. And after several weeks the same answer came. Just one sentence saying something like, "Your application to legally relocate to Austria is denied." Again we were really devastated and we needed a lot of praying to stay in faith with our vision we thought that GOD was with us.

And again I traveled to Berlin to visit the embassy. You might think that I should know by now that they weren't really a help. I did know, yet it gave me some kind of strength to talk to those people. And there was another reason for doing that. We believed that the continuous personal contact with the embassy would somehow restrain the STASI from doing something stupid, such as arrest us. Later we would find out that this was actually true. This time I asked to get an appointment with the Ambassador. Unfortunately he wasn't in and his assistant checked his schedule and we agreed on a meeting some weeks later.

When I was on my way back to the subway to catch the train to Stralsund and walked down the street, I had to pass the American embassy in East Berlin, which was right at the corner. Suddenly I had the idea to test my bravery and to see what happened when I'd enter the American embassy. It wasn't just to make waves; I did have a real reason.

Waiting on the corner of the street right across the embassy, I watched the two policemen walking along the building from the left and the right side, crossing way in the middle and turning at the end of the building to walk back. After several passages of those two guys, I figured out that I was long inside the building before they even were able to get close to me when I started across the street at the same time when they reached the end of their walk. And that was it.

I walked fast, not running, and was through the main door in no time. And then I was stopped.

The next door, completely glass from ceiling to the floor, did not open. Only after the door behind me had completely closed did this one in front of me open. And I wasn't in the embassy yet. I was surrounded by glass from three sides and a window, I think to my left, where a Marine asked me what I wanted. I explained that I had an uncle in the United States and needed help to contact him. He opened the next glass door and there was a room to sit down and tables and all kind of information.

And here I read something about engineers which was part of a speech of Ronald Regan about the requirements of the century challenging the American industry. After a few minutes a man appeared.

"What is your name? What can I do for you? What brought you in our embassy?"

"My Uncle Harry immigrated to the United States in 1955 or so, and I'd like to go in touch with him."

The guy was very friendly and smiled. "How can we here at the embassy help you with that? I mean do you have a letter we need to forward?"

"Oh, no, I don't have his address. So what you really could help me with, is find my uncle."

He looked at me still with a smile on his face.

"What do you mean we should help you find his address? Do you have his phone number? With that we can find his address."

This guy is funny, I thought for a moment, and then considering his strong American accent, thought he may have misunderstood what I said.

"No, I have no phone number and no address, all I know is his name and that he immigrated to the US in 1955 or maybe 1956. With his name and when he came to your country, you must have some registration that he arrived. I saw that in movies."

"I understand, but that registration did take place in 1955 or 1956 or whenever your uncle arrived at the US. That's now almost thirty years ago, and we don't know where he moved after that."

"Wait, you're telling me that you don't know where a certain American lives? How can you find them when needed? That's insane, everybody moves around wherever and whenever, and the government has no clue where you live?"

"That's correct. It's not the government's business to know where a specific individual lives."

I was flattened. That was unbelievable. Living in a country where you did not think for a second that the government wouldn't know where you lived was incomprehensible for me.

"I'm sorry that we can't help you with that, but in case you get an address and need to contact him in a safe way, we will certainly try to help."

With that he escorted me to the exit, said good-bye, and I was back on the street.

I would not have Uncle Harry's address until 2003.

When I left the embassy I noticed immediately the hectic activities around me. Several people moved in a way which was typical for surveillance of people. Reading a newspaper without paying attention to the text but to the surrounding, sitting on a bank when everybody was hastily walking by and crossing the street at any time, I crossed until he recognized that I had discovered him.

Even that movement when he broke the contact was suspicious. And just a few minutes later I saw him about fifty yards behind me, talking to a uniformed policeman. The policeman then accelerated his walk and caught me just before I was about to round the corner.

He demanded my ID pass and I handed it over according to the law. He opened it and began loudly reading my personal data, including my birth date and residential address. When he handed it back to me I asked him if the STASI guy was not brave enough to check me by himself. He flushed and said no word but turned around and walked away.

As an engineer for radio communication systems I knew that he had pressed the sending button all the time and he realized that I knew it.

After arriving home, I wrote the next application and sent it in.

Certain Telegrams Travel Longer Than Others in a Communistic Country

Several weeks later we brought the children to their grandma which they loved and had real joy there for some days. Then we drove to Berlin, checked in at the hotel, and went to the embassy next morning to see the Austrian Ambassador.

When we arrived at the embassy, everybody was just astounded to see us. When we asked why, they asked if we did not receive the telegram.

"No, I did not get any telegram. When did you send it?" I said and it was now on me to be astounded.

They told us that the telegram was sent about four days ago and it was telling us that we should come on Thursday instead Tuesday because the Ambassador had another commitment which he could not move.

Normally a telegram would be delivered within two to three hours and we had no doubt that this telegram needed to be read by so many people all over East Germany from Berlin up to the guy at the internal affairs office in Stralsund, that it could take probably another year to get it delivered if at all.

When I explained that I could not come back on Thursday because I had to work and it was always a day-long trip to be there, they asked if we were willing to wait some hours and to keep the visit to maximum of twenty minutes. I confirmed and we set down and waited, which wasn't really that bad because they had all kinds of Austrian and West German journals and newspapers and so on and time was flying by. Then we were asked into the office of the Ambassador and a few minutes later he came in.

"I'm briefed about your situation, and I'm really sorry about the hardship you're going through."

"Mr. Ambassador, we have now applied three times for the allowance to leave East Germany legally. All applications have been denied, and we're actually very frustrated."

"You need to throw a stone into the water, so that it makes rings, and put a train on the rails to push things forward."

I should have known it, but I did not expect that the Ambassador, although a diplomat, would pull that stunt with us. He actually started his diplomatic twaddle we were so used to by the East German TV. While he was telling us all that diplomatic verbiage, I just stopped listening, and slowly a thought went through my mind, and my brain shifted into high gear.

"I'm really sorry that I can't help you much better, but try to get something rolling."

"Mr. Ambassador, you may have brought me to think about what I could try and that's a great help."

With that we were out, and he could run to his next important diplomatic meeting to achieve nothing.

Maybe that wasn't such a bad idea. I had my personal ID card at that time already totally filled with stamps about the extended validity, and that meant I needed a new personal ID card.

When we came home that time, the next day I went to the police department where the personal ID's were issued and filled out a form. At the line with the citizenship I wrote AUSTRIA and then placed the form at the basket were a clerk came from time to time and pick all of them up.

There were approximately twenty people in front of me, so I sat down and began reading the book I had with me. I wasn't even able to open the page where I was in my reading when the door of the office flew open and my name was called.

You should have seen the looks on the faces of the people sitting there probably for several hours and here this guy comes and within two minutes is called in. I went in that office with a guy, I believe it was a Lieutenant.

"What do you mean with Austrian at the line citizenship?"

"Because I'm an Austrian citizen and here is my certificate."

He looked at that then back at me and back at the certificate and after thinking about it for a minute he sent me out to wait.

After a while, I was reading in my book when I heard my name, a woman was there at the door, handing me my old personal ID card and said it was done and I could leave now.

I took the ID card and looked into it where the validity was noticed and what I saw made me laugh loudly. Across the whole page, filled with other stamps and remarks, was a stamp as long as the page was saying: "The validity of this ID card is extended" and then written by hand was *indefinite.* I guess this was the only personal ID card worldwide which was indefinitely valid. So much about making waves and putting a train on the rails.

Some months after that we received the denial of the third application and slowly it became an unbearable but realistic threat that we would never get the allowance to leave that largest prison on earth. I called the embassy this time, because I wasn't able to get vacation, and asked for another meeting with the Ambassador.

I got one for about six weeks later and Christiane and I drove there, leaving the children at her mother's again. The appointment was not moved this time but the embassy was like a bee house. That was all because the Austrian chancellor was about to visit East Germany officially shortly. Again we were asked into the office of the Ambassador and he came through another door right behind us.

"How is your situation?"

"We did receive an additional denial of the application for leaving this prison, and slowly I have the feeling that I should have agreed to the proposal of the STASI to lay aside my Austrian citizenship in exchange for an East German passport."

"You shouldn't say that. The citizenship of any nation is something really valid. Laying aside a citizenship in exchange for a short-term benefit is dishonorable to that nation."

"But, Mr. Ambassador, how long can a family like ours live in that uncertainty? Not knowing whether or not my children get a decent chance to build their own future because they get punished for their father?"

"I'm really sorry to hear that, but I'm definitely restricted in my abilities to help. If we would be in West Germany, I'd just grab the phone and call the Minister of Internal Affairs and the situation would be cleared in minutes."

"Dear Ambassador, if we lived in West Germany, we wouldn't need your help, we would just pack our stuff and go," I said to him, raising my voice in disbelief of what I had just heard. He looked at us, nodded several times and said, "You need to throw a stone into the water, making waves, and set a train on the rails too."

I don't know to this day, writing these lines, whether it was me at the edge of exploding or if it was him remembering that he had told us that verbiage a few months ago. He suddenly jumped out of his seat.

"Excuse me please I'll be right back," he said and went out of the office.

For almost half an hour we were completely alone in the office of the Austrian Ambassador in East Germany. I don't really know whether or not we could have done anything scary, but I'm pretty sure that we would have probably been able to call the White House in Washington or find all kind of strictly secret phone numbers on his rolodex or who knows what else. But we had both a decent education and knew that it didn't behoove us to do so.

Then he was back in the office.

"I have to apologize for leaving you alone for so long. But I had a long phone conversation with the Ministry of Foreign Affairs in Vienna. You may know that there is a state visit of the Chancellor scheduled for the official cutting the tape action for the new rolling mill, built by the Voest Alpine. This is a special opportunity for the Austrian government to exchange a list of specific asked favors and this time it is a list of so-called hardship cases of family reunion. It was agreed upon a list of ten families which would be accepted during the meeting of Honecker and the Chancellor. The phone call with the Minister of Foreign affairs was about to get the allowance to put you on this list. And the Minister confirmed that family Zieger could be added to the names on the list.

"I have to leave now because a lot of things are on my table, but the lawyer of the embassy will take care of you and make sure that you do all that is necessary."

The lawyer wasn't really unknown to me anymore since we had met several times before, and he was really happy to see us finally having a chance to get out. He dampened our excitement a little though.

"First of all, get used to the thought that it will not happen overnight."

"How long do we have to wait? Please give me a realistic time?"

"You are on number eight of the list out of ten. And you need to apply for the relocation to Austria again."

"Not again, I'm really tired of writing this stupid letters to a bunch of communists, who have a lot of fun denying it."

"It is really necessary. If you don't have a current, not denied application, they will say, 'Look, they don't really want to go—they don't even have an application open.'"

"Okay, I understand that it needs to be done."

He gave me the special wording I should use this time because of the list we were on.

With a lot of hope and joy we left the embassy. This time we were full of hope that it all would work out for good. We understood that it would take more time and we needed to be patient. I wrote for the fourth time an application to allow us to relocate to Austria and used the wording the lawyer told me. Several months later I was invited to a meeting with the head of the department of passport and registration, at the police station, because they were responsible for everything that had to do with residential place registration and passports as well as the ID cards. Not knowing what they wanted from me, I drove to the office direct from work still wearing my blue-colored work clothing.

I was asked into a conference room and placed at one of the small sides of the huge conference table. After a short time a police major appeared accompanied by a woman with the rank of a Lieutenant. Both took place at the opposite end of the table.

"We asked you to come to this meeting, because we're instructed to give you the decision about the application to get the allowance to relocate to Austria. This application had been denied."

"Did you fear that I would jump over the table and choke you? Was that the reason that you placed me at this end of the table or because you needed another officer with you?

Not waiting for any reaction I stood and left the room and the building. I was about to explode. What more could I possible do to get my family out of that prison and out of the influence of the indoctrination of the educational system that already was working on the effort to brainwash my son since he had almost a complete first school year finished. I cried out to God bagging for help or an idea and was totally devastated.

I lay awake almost all night. I was really tired the next day when I started work, and Manfred Dumm asked me if I felt sick. That was the solution. I'd be sick and drive to Berlin and talk to the people at the embassy. So I somewhat hesitantly confirmed that I did not feel well and said that two, three days would be enough to get well. He agreed and sent me home.

The next morning at 5:00 a.m. I was at the railway station to catch the train to Berlin. I was at the embassy at noon and had to wait because everybody was out for lunch. That was actually good because I had time to calm down reading newspapers and think what I'd complain about. When the lawyer, his name was Antony, arrived he asked me immediately in his office.

"I'm surprised to see you at the embassy."

"Yeah, me too. Yesterday I got the denial for the relocation application, and they did it verbally. Maybe they don't want me to have any proof in my hands when it gets dirty? They totally ignored the list and the Austrian Chancellor, so what other chance do we have to get outta here?"

"It's not as bad as you think. Already three families are gone to Austria, and you need a little more patience."

This confirmed at least that somebody worked on that list and we would be gone sometimes also. But it was hard to swallow that in almost six months only thirty families had moved out. That could mean another full year or more until we were on top of the list.

Not overly satisfied, I left the embassy, caught the train and was home late at night. Having four hours to think about the whole process and all the events since I had been confirmed as an Austrian citizen, a thought flashed through my mind, but I could not grab it. I knew instinctively that God had given me an idea but I could not fill it out. Having had not much sleep for about three days, I was still not really up to the work, but I couldn't stay home and chew on nothing.

Then suddenly it hit me. It was around ten in the morning when I could clearly formulate the idea which was circulating in my brain for several hours. I jumped on my bicycle and drove to the police station. There I found the door closed and recognized that it wasn't official office hours. I knocked the door several times and finally a pothole was opened and a policeman looked through telling me that there were no office hours that day. I told him that he would be in big trouble if he would not immediately tell his Major that I was standing here and needed five minutes to talk to him. About five minutes later the door was opened and I could enter. He guided me into the same conference room where I had been just a few days ago. He said that the major would be there shortly.

This was the case and when he set down on the other end of that huge table.

"What is it that you need to see me on a non-office day?"

Now it was on me to let out these unbelievable sentences I had formulated over the last several hours in my mind. And I began to throw it at him.

"I was at the Austrian embassy yesterday, as you may or may not know already. I had a long conversation with the Ambassador to inform him about the decision to deny the petition of the Chancellor of the Republic of Austria to allow my family to relocate to the country of my origin. The Ambassador reacted indignantly to the fact and assured me that the embassy would immediately create an official diplomatic note to the Minister of Foreign affairs of the GDR, expressing the indignation about the disregard of the petition of the Austrian chancellor. "

I could see that the expression on his face began to change, although it wasn't really clear in what direction. So I went on.

"I don't know whether or not the decision was made here in this building or wherever, and I don't know who was responsible for the decision to deny the petition, but I'm pretty sure that the result of the official diplomatic note of the Austrian Ambassador to the Minister of Foreign affairs of the GDR will be the total destruction of one or the other career."

He looked at me with the attempt to make a stone face, but I could clearly see a mixture of fear and unbelief.

"Are you threatening me?"

"No, not at all. All I try is to warn you that the Austrian embassy in Berlin is currently working on an official diplomatic note to the Minister for Foreign affairs expressing the indignation about the disregard of the petition of the Austrian chancellor. That's it, I just wanted to inform you, since I don't know who is responsible and I know only you of those who are working my case. You know whom you have to talk to." I stood and left the room, jumped on my bicycle and drove back to work. I felt so much better. I can still empathize that feeling.

The next day, around ten, the secretary of my boss called me and said she got a call from my wife and I should come home if I could as soon as possible. My boss wasn't in that day, so I just jumped into my car which I'd used that day and drove home. Christiane showed me a postcard sent by the police department with just one sentence on it.

"You're requested to report to the address above as soon as possible in person."

It was signed by that same major I had talked to the day before. When I arrived at the building, it was at official office hours, and there were many people sitting at the waiting area or standing around because there were never enough chairs. I looked around for a while not knowing which door to knock when a woman clothed with a work coat asked me if she could help me. I confirmed that she could, and showed her the postcard. She looked at it then at me and said follow me. At the office she placed a piece of paper in front of me together with a pencil and said:

"Note down what you need to do, your application for relocation to Austria has been approved."

I almost fell from the chair, but immediately caught my breath and began to make my notes.

Vienna Became a Town in West Germany and Friends Missed a Dinner

While writing down my notes, my mind was almost in flames running in high gear. All kind of thoughts shot through my mind, and I had difficulty staying focused on what she told me. She pushed a piece of paper over the table

"You have to collect all those signatures from all those institutions. When you have all of them, you have to come back to the police station to deposit that signature list. You will then have to go to the office of internal affairs of the city to get a piece of paper, which allows you to receive your passports. You will get the passports here at the police station with the valid visa to leave the GDR. Then you need to get the entrance visa for Austria. You have to leave the GDR within the limited time stated at the visa."

"How much time do I have to do all of that?"

"No time limit to that point when the passports with the visa are issued. From that point on, you have the time the visa officer determines."

When I looked up from my notes, I saw for the first time that she tried to be friendly or at least show a friendly impression on her face.

"But you better not take too much time to get those signatures and stamps, because things can change in a heartbeat."

I went out of the police station, still feeling as if I was caught in a cloud of fog, and drove home. When I had told Christiane every single detail we embraced each other, thanked the Lord and began to think about what to do first. Since I had no idea how much time the collection of those stamps would take, I decided not to go back to work and focus on that task.

Later that evening I drove to the apartment of Manfred Dumm and rang the bell. When he opened the door and saw me standing in front of him, he was surprised since I was not at work; he thought I was sick. I explained him that I'd not come back to work because my application was confirmed and I had a lot of administrative stuff to do. He understood and said under these circumstances he wouldn't expect me to work since my time in the country was limited anyway.

Next day we started the process of collecting stamps from institutions we didn't even know existed. At the same time we began to ask people we knew about stuff we had to sell if they were interested. The first institution we had to go to was the Central Bank of the GDR. No normal citizen of the country could have an account there, and with that we considered the order to get a confirmation from them that we did not owe them anything somewhat weird. But it was required and we needed that stamp and the signature.

When we entered the hall, there were several cashiers behind a high barrier, and we went to the first woman who became available. I explained why we were there and that we needed the stamp and a signature, and she said that she could help us with that. During the process of checking our names, even birth names against their records—still everything on paper—she asked where we would go and we said to Vienna, Austria. A smile flushed over her face, and she said that she would love to go there once in her life.

Then she bent herself over closer to us and whispered, "Do you know that you can transfer your money in Austrian Shilling to the official course of seven Shilling for one mark to Austria?" We were astounded. She said further, "I'll not stamp and sign that paper now, I'll open an account for you and you can pay every single mark you have into that account. A special agreement between the GDR and Austria guarantees that you get your money within maximum of twelve months. All you have to do when you arrive in Austria is to go to the National Bank and request a transfer."

We walked out of the banks as if we were in dreamland. This changed everything. Now we knew that we had to sell whatever we could to get a decent start in Austria. Don't get me wrong, we weren't rich even with all we could sell.

We had six different banks on that paper which I didn't know existed, nor would we ever have the ability to open an account. Christiane began to sort out clothing and stuff we wanted to get sent to Austria, and I was running from one bureaucrat to the other at the Stralsund customs to find out how I could send our stuff there. Since Stralsund was a harbor town and ships from Scandinavia came in several times a week, we had a well established harbor customs office. Finally I was able to talk to an officer who was willing to hear me out. I explained to him that I was in the process of collecting the stamps on that paper and he actually wanted to see it, not because he did not believe what I said, but because he had never seen one or met one who had it.

The reason was that the normal procedure was very different from what we experienced, and we were very thankful that God had guided us with that very gentle voice inside of us during the times of trial and tribulations.

Normally when you applied to get allowance to relocate it would have the final destination West Germany. More than 99 percent of all applications went that direction. It also created a lot of anger among those who had to work on these cases because they were one hundred percent communists and despised people who wanted to leave that prison they called the Worker Paradise. That led to all kind of harassments lasting as long as possible. Even to the last second those people had their feet on East-German ground.

We knew of people who had been virtually thrown out of their beds in the middle of the night, had time to clothe their children and themselves, and were then pushed into a transporter usually used to transport criminals to the prison. The transporter would drive directly to a border crossing between East Germany and West Germany and virtually thrown out of the country in the middle of the night, sparely clothed walking through no-man's land to freedom.

The STASI would then confiscate and sell all their belongings, keeping the money to finance the attack on the next family. And frankly, these were the harmless cases.

I met a man—one of the alcoholics I tried to convince to repent and find his way to GOD—who ended where he was because of an application for relocation to West Germany. As soon as he sent in the application, using the mail box at his home town, he was arrested by the STASI and questioned under inhumane conditions for several weeks. His family did not know where he was and police wouldn't answer their questions. When he was released he was immediately fired by his company. Although you couldn't be unemployed in East Germany, at least not officially, he was.

Since he could not provide for his family and was under constant pressure by the government institutions, his wife filed for divorce, and since he was an *asocial element* as it was officially called, she was divorced in an hour without him even present.

That was when he ultimately broke and he started to drown his grief in alcohol. I met a human wreck, and I could not find a way to open his mind for the hope Jesus has for even the horrible sinner. That was the way it usually went, and all thinkable variations in between. We were really under the hedge and protection of our Lord Jesus.

Back to the customs officer though. He was astounded to see all the institutions he said he had never heard of too. Then he instructed me how it could go. I had to write a list of all the goods I'd like to send to Austria, and I should be very detailed with that list, e.g., shirt for boy, blue, size six long sleeves, and for books, the title, the year printed, the issue number the year first issued, the author, how many pages and the ISBN number. Then I should send this list to the state customs office with the request to allow moving these goods to our new residential place and you need to give an address. That needed not to be the final destination; I couldn't have it at a forwarders warehouse or so. And then we had to wait. If it was approved, one of the officers would come to our apartment and check it and seal it. Then it was ready to be shipped.

Now the next part was to get the necessary documents to ship several wooden cases owned by a private person who was leaving worker's paradise for good by train. To send those by truck with the only existing forwarder of East Germany was out of any consideration.

It took me several days to find the right person at the railway station who handed me a stack of paper with several copies only after she had seen my stamp collection paper because she could not believe that I was given time to do all of this. In the mean time Christiane had most of the stuff we wanted to keep packed into three wooden cases I had brought months ago from the shipyard, not being really sure that we would ever be able to use them. Since we knew that we would get all our money transferred to Austria and that to an unbelievable course the exchange rate of one GDR mark to seven Austrian shilling was the same as the Deutsche Mark to the Austrian Shilling, we informed our relatives, mainly Christiane's sisters, but all we earned was mocking unbelief. They just did not believe that our money would be transferred since normally people would be robbed blank instead.

FREEDOM'S NIGHTMARE

And we began to sell furniture using the ability to talk to my colleagues since I knew where to find them at certain times even though I did not work any longer. Several of them came to our home and bought what they liked. We brought the stuff we could not sell to my sister in Saßnitz, who was still waiting for her application to be answered. Since the effort to write down all the different details for the book list as required would take several days, we decided not to do that and brought all of our books to my mother-in-law since she had enough space for storage.

Christiane had gotten a gift from her aunt in West Berlin, a small biscuit plate made at the famous porcelain manufacturer Meißen. Since the instructions from the custom listed explicit products from that manufacturer as precious and not allowed if it had a certain age, we went to the museum to get some expertise on that little piece of porcelain.

Although the Meißen porcelain manufacturer was in East Germany and they produced a lot of porcelain even for daily usage, it was a rarity and many East-German citizens had never seen a piece of it. The guy at the museum was at the first moment really excited to see a piece from that manufacturer because he thought it would be something really valuable. Maybe he considered it already confiscated by the custom and handed it over into the museum possession.

He brought a huge book, it was a catalogue with pictures and descriptions of all ever produced Meissen porcelain and checked first the specifications of the signature symbol, those famous two crossed blue swords. Their design, color and type of crossing were different for different centuries. With that he easily dated the plate into the 20th century. And within a few more minutes he was sure it was from the early 1950s and with that not considered historically valuable enough to be confiscated. He wrote a short statement and we could leave.

The confirmation letter from customs came, and we had a reason to enjoy bureaucratic stupidity as its best. Quote, "The confirmation for the export of our goods described the destiny of the goods as Vienna, West Germany (FDR)."

It seemed that none of these government bureaucrats was able to catch the idea that not everybody wanted to move to West Germany. There is no Vienna in West Germany, and Vienna is so clearly known as the capital of Austria throughout Europe that every little kid would know it.

Two days later, the local customs officer came to check our wooden cases and to make sure that we did not have somebody hidden in there or whatever they thought we may do. I had ordered a truck to transport the cases to the railway station, but I had to do that separately. The only forwarder was the government-owned company, and they were really slow in understanding that they should bring those from our place to the railway station.

But finally they got it and promised to be there at a certain time. As you may remember, our apartment was at the sixth floor—in American counting 7th floor—and there was no lift. But three of my colleagues had promised to help me to get the cases down because they were anything but light.

My colleagues came as agreed but not the truck. Knowing that delays were part of the system, we waited quite a while until my colleagues began to push because they needed to go back to work. I went down the stairs, jumped into my car and drove to the next phone booth. It took me several minutes, actually almost half an hour, until the responsible dispatcher was on the phone only to tell me that the truck was on its way and he had no clue why he was late and I should wait.

When I turned around the corner into our street I saw the truck just rounding the opposite end of the street corner. At first I was about to brake, turn around and try to catch him on the other side of the block, because I thought he missed the address. But then I saw my colleagues at the walkway. When I joined them they were actually angry at me, because they thought I missed the truck on purpose. So I had to explain what happened, and they told me that at the same moment I was out, the door the bell was ringing and the truck driver was at the door. So he must have taken the other way around the block in the same direction as he disappeared when I came back.

Nobody wanted to take any money for the help, and I thought it would be a great idea to invite all of them to a last dinner night at the most famous restaurant in Stralsund. Everybody was thrilled about a great meal on my check and with that they went back to work. We were almost done with the collection of those stamps and signatures, and when we checked our personal papers such as certificates, we realized that the only birth certificate for Christiane was in the family book with her mother. So I called the office for internal affairs at her birth place telling them we needed a separate certificate and that I'd come and pick it up. Next day I drove there and was back in the evening. The reason I'm writing about that is that all of these trips were a constant reason for concern because we were sure that the STASI was watching us constantly, which turned out to be true.

From many stories we had heard about, read partly in the news papers or knew from personal relationship, we knew that the STASI had the objective to try until the last minute to find a legal, internationally credible reason to convict people like us and to jail them if possible for an indefinite period. Every trip either by car or by public transportation was accompanied by a constant alert for the environment to recon immediately if there was something unusual, and with that to disappear at the spot, virtually to become invisible.

We knew from incidences that STASI officers in civil clothes would arrange a mass beating with the uniformed colleagues waiting behind the corner, and as soon as you were close enough they would just catch everybody and arrest them. Since you were in the midst of it, you would be sentenced within a few days to many years in jail for creating a public uproar. And that was just one trick they used. Others were accidents, thefts or false accusation. It was vital to be alert at any given time you were on the street.

Finally we had to sell our car. It wasn't a problem to find a buyer; to the contrary, we had to decide to whom we would sell it. Since cars were the rarest investment besides building a house, the market for used cars was enormous. New cars were so seldom, that it was a permanent theme in conversations. The first thing you do when you turned eighteen was walk into the nearest car registration agency office and register for a car. You'd fill out a form, and it was up to you to hold the information on that form current. Isn't that strange? Everything about your person, from your first cry as a newborn baby until your last breath, was automatically meticulously written down in that specific personal file called the *Personalakte*. And you had no knowledge what was in there, and the file would be wherever you were without requiring any activities from your site. But if you wanted to buy a car, waiting time ten to fifteen years, or a sail boat—I actually did—or things like that, it was your own responsibility to inform that specific office where you made your first application when things changed. And things changed in ten to fifteen years a lot, not just your address.

Then when everything went well, the registration office had your current address; you would one day find a postcard in your mail stating that your car was ready for you. Then there was an address of the place where to get it and a time and a date. It was explicitly mentioned that you should not call or try in any other way to contact the delivery personnel because that could automatically exclude you from receiving your car, since it was considered an attempt to bribe people. Not that those who worked at these delivery offices were not corrupt, that would be a human miracle given the luxury a car presented, but they wanted to be corrupt in their own kind and therefore they decided how that would run. When you arrived at that place with your card and a cashier check for the complete car price, you were asked to fill several other forms and to wait until your car was ready to be transferred to you. The filling of the forms was an opportunity to try to have a small influence about let's say the color, because they may have two or three different colored cars that day.

Since the type of the car, meaning either a Trabant or a Wartburg, the East-German made cars, or a Russian or Polish derivative of the Italian FIAT 124. or the Romanian derivative of the France Renault or the Czechoslovakian Skoda, that decision was already made when you filled out the first registration form. And you best not change that later in life because you'd changed your mind, or the reputation of a certain car was decreasing or something else, because that would start your waiting timer from zero.

Another change might have been possible, depends on how much real money you were able to invest in a mind-changing project, to get a 3-door instead of a 2-door Trabant or a 5-door instead of a 4-door Wartburg, always depending on if those were even available that specific day.

And that was pretty much your level of last-minute influence on what kind of car you would drive around after ten to fifteen years' waiting time, working overtime until the doctor sent you home, tried to squeeze every single pfennig out of helper work you could do on weekends and bagged around through your whole list of relatives to get the money together.

Because when you earn an average of 800 mark a month and the cost of living is about 600, with two children a little more and with school children even more, there wasn't much to get the money together. But it was possible over all the years so that you could finally put between twelve thousand for the lowest level Trabant and up to twenty-five thousand for the highest level Russian car on the desk of the delivery agent.

And then you'd live with this car for at least the next ten to twelve years until the next registration became current. And that wasn't less exciting than getting the car in the first place since car repair shops were as rare as the cars themselves and spare parts even more rare and again, your hard-earned money counted little when you needed a fix.

Based on those facts, used cars were worth more than new cars, especially with a well-maintained service book. If you had enough money, or better yet the right kind of money, you could find certain parking lots on weekends and would walk around cars where the left rear window was a gap open. You would without attracting attention investigate the car of your interest as good as possible parked at that spot and would then when you're really interested throw your proposal on a folded piece of paper through that gap at the side window. If your proposal found the appreciation of the owner he would contact you within the week and you could have a trial drive with him, and if everything was okay, the deal would be made. Or you'd be visited by two police officers in the evening because the car was a trap to catch people like you, since those were considered black market deals and were threatened with five to seven years in jail. All that needed to be considered when we thought about selling our two-year-old Skoda 120LS.

But as with all things during that time, we had the LORD watching us. One of the weekend brick masons at Tom's project was very interested in buying our car when we told them about the fact a few days after we had the allowance to leave.

Although Tom thought this guy wasn't able to pay the price, that brick mason showed up at our apartment a few days before we were at the point to sell it with a check in his hand and we couldn't say no. It was the usual market price considering the conditions, quality, and reputation of the car, approximately eight thousand Mark over the new price.

I could have gotten probably ten thousand over the new price and actually one of my former colleagues who had changed to another branch on the shipyard offered me that amount two days later, but I did not know what was really behind that and said no. It could have been a trap and the probability was huge because I'd later find out that he was an informant for the STASI, yet he was never used against me or my family.

This was just one other example of how the basic market law really works when artificial regulations are cut out. Supply and demand determine the price. A highly sophisticated world run by some control freaks which consider themselves the elite which knows exactly what is right and wrong destroys everything mankind has accomplished.

We had also bought a huge suitcase and had several other lager suitcases as well as one little one for each of the kids so that we could utilize the maximum number of suitcases on the plane.

We had now everything sold that was possible, but we still had some stuff we had agreed upon to give it to Christiane's sister. And now we made our last shopping tour, which was the travel agency. There was really only one. I asked how much the tickets from East Berlin to Vienna would be flying with the East-German airline Interflug. The woman behind the desk looked at me as if I'd just fallen down from a tree. After that first moment of unbelief, she asked me if I had the passports for every person who wanted to fly with the visa in them. I said that I didn't have them yet, but it should only be a question of days. She said that I could not get any information because that would require valid passports with visa.

I told her that I needed to know how much it was, because I'd have to lock my money into a special account and could not pay anything from it, neither could I get money back from it and I had to do that before I got the passports. Fearful, looking around and over her shoulder, she went through her books and wrote the price for the tickets for me, Christiane, Lennart, and Melanie on a piece of paper, which she put into a travel flyer of the city and handed it to me.

It wasn't cheap, and normally the average East-German citizen would have thought twice to use such a luxury. But first of all we had the money, since we had sold nearly all of our belongings, and secondly there weren't many East-Germans who were able to fly to Vienna. Calculating to have some cash at hand and the cost for the taxi we would need to get from Christiane's sister's home to the airport and her back home, we kept almost twice the monthly income in cash, and all other money was deposited to the GDR Staatsbank account.

We got our final stamp from that very friendly lady at that bank, and with that we had all we needed to go back to the police station. Don't forget, we had no car and had to use the public transportation system. And believe it or not, that enormous efficient and comfortable public transportation system the liberals are so crazy about, it doesn't exist. Oh, yes, if you're living in Berlin, or Colon, or Munich or even Dresden or Leipzig you might be able to go to any point in those cities without walking more than ten minutes.

But not outside of the large cities now, and not in East German before the collapse and the billions of Deutsch-Mark invested in the devastated infrastructure of the second largest technical museum in the world. And for sure not in Stralsund! Yes we had a public transportation busses driving from a central bus station through the different parts of the city, but it was so organized that the different quarters were not directly connected.

Let's say you wanted to go from quarter B to quarter F. You had to take the bus from B to the central bus station and then get the bus to quarter F. The usual interval was twenty minutes, and don't think for a moment that the busses were synchronized, meaning when a bus arrived two minutes after the scheduled time, your connection was gone and you waited twenty minutes.

No, there wasn't a nice restaurant or waiting room either, more like your greyhound station in downtown Cincinnati was eight years ago when I used the American legend.

But we had become used to it and we were together and had actually some fun with the kids. In the morning though, I was usually alone on those trips as far as Christiane's presence was not required, since Lennart still had school. When I arrived at the police station I presented the stamped paper, which had suffered somewhat during those weeks of collection tours, and I apologized for it. That actually yielded a smile for me and some nice words like nobody ever apologized for that and we have seen worse papers back.

She then handed me another piece of paper, and with that I had to go to the office of internal affairs and to lay down my East German citizenship. Then I would come back to her where she would have the East German passports with the visa ready. Before I could walk out she asked me about the Austrian visa, which would need to be in those passports too if I'd need them and how long it would take to get them.

Again this was absolutely unusual, and the only reason for that friendly treatment was probably based on the fact that we were on that list handed from one wrapper of the Austrian chancellor to the other wrapper of the East-German dictator.

Knowing that I could buy some time to wrap up all things as needed, and that I'd get my visas at the embassy within two minutes—even though I wouldn't need them—I said I was informed it would take a week. With that I was dismissed and walked the ten minutes to the office for internal affairs instead waiting for the bus.

The woman there was formal but not unfriendly and asked me first where my wife was. I said that she was home and she said she needed to be there with me because we would both have to sign separate papers for each of us. When I said that I'd be back in the afternoon she said that wouldn't work because office hours were only Wednesdays from 8 to 12. That meant hurry, or wait for another week to get the passports.

I ran down the stairs and on the market place for a taxi, and again I believe there was the hand of the Lord because you would normally not find a taxi in front of the city hall other than for marriage, and it wasn't Saturday. I jumped into the taxi and told him that he had my future in his foot and I had fifty east marks in my hand for him if he would make it to my address and the return in under thirty minutes. Running upstairs in six floors grabbing Melanie onto my arms and sending Lennart down the stairs was one uninterrupted movement.

When we were in the car I could tell Christiane why we had to hurry and the taxi driver was now even more inspired to break all records and speed limits. And he knew that he would get a warning for speed controls through taxi radio. We arrived at the office of internal affairs ten minutes before she closed the office.

We were instructed to write an affidavit that we voluntarily declared that we wanted to lay down our East German citizenship and I had to add that for my children. I looked at her.

"I understand that is the way to go for me and my children since we're Austrian citizens. But why would the East-German government lose a citizen and make my wife stateless since she could live in Austria as East German citizen without problems."

"Please Mr. Zieger, don't dispute with me about sense and nonsense of this ruling, just write the sentence on the paper if you want to go."

We did what we had to do, and when we were done, she handed us a certificate of release from East-German citizenship and said that we could get our passports with those certificates.

When we arrived back at the police station, the Lieutenant had our passports ready to be signed by us and the visa to leave the largest prison on earth for good was valid until July 10th. It was June 27th, which gave as plenty of time to get everything arranged.

From there we walked to the travel agency and the young woman who had given me the price for the ticket several days before smiled when I put the passports on the desk. It took about an hour till we had the tickets in hand, and with big smiles on our faces we walked out into the sunny afternoon on the old market of this historic city.

The next day I traveled to East Berlin to get the visa for Austria into the East German stateless passports and asked if the embassy would be able to contact my dad so he would pick us up from the airport. I gave them the flight data and they said they would inform the Ministerial for Foreign affairs to take care of that.

We had agreed with Christiane's sister, who lived with her family in a city right at the Elbe river about two hundred kilometers northwest of East Berlin, that they would come and pick us and the rest of our stuff up on Friday when Lennart had his last school day and would get his report. For Monday July 8th we had the tickets to Vienna.

I was very generous and wanted to say thank you to all of my former colleagues who had helped to get things done, and for that I send word out that we would love to invite several of those named to a dinner at the most famous restaurant in Stralsund. This restaurant was just recently opened in a very old, completely restored historical building. It was a former granary dating back to the Hanseatic League period when Stralsund was a very rich Hanseatic League city. And as it was with all restaurants when they were new, they were well visited, and we had to reserve a table in advance to be sure to get in there.

Unfortunately only one of my former colleagues really had the guts to come to the dinner and sit with us. He told us that the management, he avoided names, had strongly recommended not to conspire with a traitor who had betrayed the cause of the workers class, because that could have a deep impact in their personal file.

Friday we packed all morning to get the rest of the stuff into the small car and the trailer, and when Lennart came with his report for his first year, which was awesome, we left Stralsund. We arrived at the town late at night, and over the weekend were unpacking and moving stuff around, the work which kept us from becoming sentimental.

I have to confess that danger was limited to the women, all the in-laws and Christiane, because I had almost no room for thoughts about anything in East Germany.

Late at night on Saturday I got a telegram from the embassy that I needed to call them urgently. But it was too late to get anybody on the phone, so I decided to call them on Monday morning before we left for the airport.

When I called the embassy on Monday, they told me that they had received information from Austria that my father was not in the position to accommodate my family and that there had been made arrangements to get me accommodated for the first couple of days by the city of Vienna. Yet my father would be at the airport and bring us to the apartment.

We arrived at the airport Berlin Schönefeld with enough time to check all our baggage and have some time to spend with Christiane's sister. Yet it was impossible to get a table at the only restaurant and so we just stood at the terrace and watched some foreign airline planes but mostly Interflug take off.

Then it was time to go through the security check, and that was a drama.

Both children had stuffed animals, Lennart a cat and Melanie a dog. The security check required them to be put onto the belt to run through the x-ray, and it took some good words to convince both that the stuffed animals would come out just fine on the other side. We were then guided to a special waiting room, and after about twenty people or so had arrived, and the time was due, we were all loaded into a bus and driven to the airplane.

The airplane was parked at a separately secured area, fenced with at least fifteen feet and topped with three-foot barbed wires. The bus stopped at the gate and an officer of the border police entered the bus and checked again the passport and the visa of each passenger. He left the bus, the gate opened and we stopped at the plane.

When we entered the plane it smelled as if they had just set off several teargas grenades. And I was sure it was teargas, because the smell immediately located the information about the horrible experience with the training sessions with teargas during my boot camp time in my mind and brought it to the forefront. I was close to throwing up. We found our seats, and after several more minutes of security check the plane began to roll out of the security area onto the airport, the runway, and finally lifted off into Freedom.

Sachverhalt zum Material:

Am 02. 10. 1980 wurde durch die ZKG bekannt, daß ein Hinweis von
einem IM aus dem op. Gebiet vorliegt, nachdem ein Student, der
in der Fachrichtung Elektronik in Berlin studiert und im Hans-
Loch-Viertel wohnhaft war, bei der Volksmarine zur Zeit seinen
Dienst versieht. Dieser Student soll beabsichtigen, bei einer Aus-
fahrt mit einem Schiff die DDR illegal zu verlassen.

Die im Verantwortungsbereich der 1. Flottille eingeleiteten Sofort-
überprüfungen ergaben, daß der

Zieger, Harald
geb. am 11. 07. 1954 in Bünde/BRD

The message from the pastor who visited us from the
West German partner church to his STASI case officer
arrived a few months later at the STASI headquarter in
Berlin and initiated the OPK = operative individual
surveillance, a 24/ monitoring of my life for almost 4 years

in 1134 Berlin studiert hat. Während
des Studiums hatte er eine Nebenwohnung in 1136 Berlin, Hans-Loch-
Straße 261/7.
Der leibliche Vater des L. soll in Österreich leben. Ob Verbindun-
gen zu diesem bestehen, ist nicht bekannt.

The Message from the West German Spy set all in motion

FREEDOM DOESN'T MEAN YOU DECIDE

The First Shock in the Free World and the strange similarities

AFTER A FEW minutes in the air the smell wasn't that noticeable anymore, either it got reduced by the filter system or we just got used to it. The flight was uneventful, and after only a little over an hour the plane descended in its approach to the Vienna airport. We had told our children that we were moving to a new living place and that we would live there from now on. It was an incisive change in our as well as in their lives, and we knew that they had much more to fight with all that was changing so fast in their small world. To make it interesting we said that we would move to a country where there were mountains everywhere.

And that was something, since we had lived to this time at the coastline of the Baltic Sea and the highest elevation was approximately three hundred meters. Approaching the airport, the plane made a huge turn and all we could see was the large Vienna valley opening towards the Hungarian Lowlands. The mountains which border to the West were invisible from our seats. Lennart looked intensively for those huge mountains I had described many times over the last weeks and could not see them. Suddenly he began to cry and said sobbing, "There are no Mountains! I want to go back to Stralsund!" I was stunned and did not know what to say when suddenly the man on the other side of the aisle offered to look through the window on his side, because there he could see the mountains, although far away, but clear. And Lennart's face was one big smile.

All passengers were brought by bus to the terminal as it was usual at that time in Vienna, and we pulled out the East-German passports and walked through the pass and customs control in no time. We were just blown away to experience the easiness compared to all the checks and restrictions at the East-Berlin airport.

We had to wait a while until our many suitcases appeared on the baggage claim belt. As we walked out of the baggage claim area, which is contrary to the American airports a restricted area, there he was, my father whom I had never seen cognizant in my whole life, and in a few days I'd turn thirty-two.

He seemed not to have changed a bit compared to the photograph I had from the mid-50s, and that was the reason I recognized him immediately. He was there with his wife, and after being introduced to each other—no hugs and no kisses; we were foreigners-—he said that there was no chance to get the baggage into the small car they came with.

Taking the suitcase with the stuff we needed for the night, we left the other suitcases at the baggage registration, and my father said we would pick it up the next day. On the way to the accommodation, his wife was very friendly but also eager to here our story, and I have to say that over the next several months many people were very friendly to us, mainly to get the story about our release from communist East Germany told. My father said that he was surprised by the sudden call from the Ministry of Foreign Affairs on Friday and wasn't able to accommodate us. He had to pull some strings and got us accommodated at the homeless shelter of the city of Vienna. Now, that was something.

But we knew we had to expect some difficulties, because we knew we would have to start all over again, begin our lives from zero. On the way to the homeless shelter we stopped at a restaurant where ate eat and told the story of how we could get out of East Germany. Finally at around 7:00 p.m. we were at the shelter. The administration was led by a woman who could easily apply as a drill sergeant of the Marines. In a few words and with an extreme dialect so that we had difficulties to understand, we were instructed how to use the room, the restrooms and the showers. She led us to the room and disappeared after she handed me the key. The room was approximately ten by ten feet, had two bunk beds and a small table with two chairs. The window was barred and the whole room had a stench after fresh plastering. That stench was actually so intense that we had to open the window all the time we were in that room. Lucky enough, the window pointed to a small side street with almost no traffic.

Next morning, the administration helper took me in the car of the shelter to the Social Security office for the district. After waiting for an hour or so and filling out tons of forms, I got a total of 1,750 Austrian Shilling for the month of July. At this time 100 dollars was worth 1,999.00 Austrian shilling. The reason I know that to the point will become clear later. I did not get social welfare for Christiane because even though she was my wife, she wasn't an Austrian citizen, and with that she had no entitlement for social welfare.

Barely remembering the way the car had taken, I walked back to the homeless shelter; it was almost forty-five minutes to walk. When I arrived at the shelter, the administration office door was open and the woman called me in. After she learned that I had received the social welfare payments I had immediately to pay the fee for the room and partly energy, water and waste for the month of July. A total of 180 Austrian Shilling disappeared in a second. Christiane and the kids were in the room, and we decided to find the German embassy to get the passport situation started. Since East Germany had deprived our citizenship, and only the children got automatically the Austrian citizenship through me, Christiane was de facto stateless. Yet every German, no matter where, born or living, was, based on the West German constitution, a German citizen. All we had to do was to apply for her documents.

Using the public transportation system was another huge difference to everything we had seen in our life so far. Streetcars and subways were comfortable and departed almost every five minutes. Schedules and plans for those transportation lines were freely available and with reference to our limited financial basis we decided that God would forgive us if we did not pay for it.

And I have to confess that none of us was ever caught traveling without ticket during the time when we had no income. Later we bought regularly the monthly tickets and for the children a year ticket because that was easier for them to travel around. And I was caught when I once forgot to buy a new ticket.

We found the German embassy and were directed to another address just two streets around the corner to the visa office. Unfortunately it was vacation season, and the people there couldn't do much for Christiane besides handing her a pile of forms to fill out and come back.

On our way back to the shelter we decided that we would need to buy some groceries to be able to cook. Not knowing anything about the grocery store situation in Austria, we walked into the first shop we passed on our way.

Unknowingly it was the most expensive and most luxurious grocery shop at that time in Austria and belonged to the Julius Meindl chain.

The shock was overwhelming. We needed several minutes to master our astonishment.

We knew that there was everything possible to buy in a western grocery store compared to the East-Germans, but what was so amazing was the cleanliness and the meticulousness of how the different goods were presented. Everything was clean and looked like it was made for a TV show.

But it was real and people were there buying food, and finally we started to look at stuff we would like to buy and were shocked by the prices.

There were three reasons. First of all it was a pricy shop, secondly it was in a high income area, probably the second highest income area in Vienna because it was the Embassy district, and thirdly the exchange rate. One Deutsch Mark was more than seven Austrian shilling, and we were in addition used to the highly subsidized basic food prices from East Germany. There we paid 1.25 mark for a loaf of bread with 2 pounds, and here it was almost twenty shilling. We restricted ourselves to the necessary stuff and left that shop. Back at the shelter, I had just a few minutes to rest when my father arrived to pick me up to get the suitcases from the airport.

He had an old VW Bus and it was so loud that we could barely talk to each other without yelling. With that the conversation was brief and limited to the highlights about what to do first. He told me that his wife did not know about us children from his marriage with my mother and that he was in great trouble. That explained why I couldn't reach him on the phone after the first call.

During my visits at the embassy in East Berlin, I had developed a good connection to the cultural attaché because of the certification of my engineering degrees, and often we talked just about all the world and his brother. When I was there to get the visa he gave me a phone number and a name and said I should call this man immediately when I arrive in Vienna, because he would be able to help me at least somewhat to get started. Based on the first several hours of experience at the homeless shelter, we decided to put that on first priority. The next morning, Wednesday the tenth of July, I called that phone number, got the man on the phone and asked for a meeting. He agreed to see us that morning and we were on our way.

He was the general manager of an organization that helped young Austrians from the different districts who came to Vienna find apartments without having to pay the enormous down payments or at least put those on a payment plan. Again we had to tell our story and when we were done, he walked with us to the apartment office.

"Unfortunately, we have only a small two-room apartment available, and by law, we can't rent that to a family with two children."

"Do you think it is more according to the law to live in a single room with two children in a homeless shelter?"

That changed her mind. We got the key to have a look at it and when we came back, we signed the rental contract and could move in. The manager gave me an address where we could get used furniture with a specific form he filled and signed for us. I called my father and told him that I needed his help to move the luggage and he was absolutely stunned.

He came, and when we carried out our suitcases, the homeless shelter manager was not only stunned she was angry that we could find an apartment within two days. The money I had paid for the whole month though was gone. We loaded the suitcases on that VW Bus and the children travelled with Christiane to that apartment using public transportation.

At the furniture storage we found an old double sofa which could be converted into a bed and some chairs because the apartment had a double bed in the bedroom and a table and two chairs in the living room. The biggest problem was the energy. The Vienna energy supply company was owned and operated by the city and it was 100 percent unionized.

The rental office clerk had given us a phone number to call in the morning next day, because it was already after three when all that signing and form filling was done and nobody would pick the phone she said. I called next morning and got the woman on the phone who did the scheduling for that city district.

"I have the next schedule free for you on Monday morning, seven a.m."

"Wait a moment, I can't wait till Monday, I have two little children, and they need to eat. How can I cook for them without energy till Monday?"

"Go to the restaurant. Children love that." And with that, she hung up. I called my father.

"Hey, Dad. I just got off the phone with the energy department, and they told me the earliest schedule they have is Monday morning."

"Nothing new with these gangsters in Vienna. Call me back in fifteen minutes."

I waited fifteen minutes at the phone booth and called him again.

"Harald, I talked to that high ranking officer at the Ministry of Foreign Affairs. You know that guy who called me to pick you up from the airport? Here is his number. He'll take care of this issue, and you shall call him in about twenty minutes."

After twenty minutes I dialed the number, and after three or four rings, he picked up the phone and I introduced myself.

"Mr. Zieger, your energy will be turned on tomorrow morning at seven a.m. And if you ever think I can be helpful to you, call this number, and I'll see what I can do."

The problem with the system I learned this way, is the same as in East Germany: if you needed something, you needed to know somebody who knew somebody. Just with a different background. Here it was the extreme intersection of business and political power because of position. Since every single hand movement was regulated between the union and the city hall administration, which runs the show for nearly all services in Vienna, people are constantly busy checking out, if that what they in a first onset of activity would just go and do it. But they wouldn't move a finger until they found out that their job description allowed them to move the finger. And if that isn't the case they would just not move the finger and tell you: "It's not my job"! Only if somebody who was in a position to cause harm in such a way that they would get in trouble, asked for something, people in unionized companies would go out of their way to actually get things done.

And the absolute specialty of Austria was and partly still is the absolute obsession of the Austrians with the title somebody had. This guy at the Ministry of Foreign Affairs had the title of a Legationsrat (German for legation counselor). You had to be very high up on the power line, reporting direct to the Minister of Foreign Affairs, to get this title.

And I guarantee you when the manger of a Vienna city service gets a call and the voice on the other end says, "This is the secretary of legation counselor XYZ, the legation counselor would like to ask you a favor, and I connect you." And then that XYZ with the right accent and the specific tone says that he is a little concerned about the efficiency of the service this manager is leading, I guarantee you—even today—that manager stands behind his desk, and the only words he can bring out of his mouth is repeatedly. "*Jawohl Herr Legationsrat, Jawohl.*" (German for: Certainly, Mr. Legation Counselor, certainly).

Next morning at seven the energy department electricians came and switched on the power and one of them said that he thought that I must have some really good connections high-up because their schedule had been changed overnight which hadn't happened in over fifteen years.

A standard saying in Vienna was "Even if the Danube floats backwards it won't happen." The first couple of weeks were really hard, especially for Christiane and the children. She would go with the kids to the huge supermarket that was within walking distance and would buy whatever she could get at the lowest possible price.

The kids ate mainly fruits and vegetables with growing appetite—one week oranges as much as they could, next time bananas and then some other fruits. We got some cookware from my father wife and every day some more parts what we needed. All attempts to get a decent job lead from the government-controlled job services were useless. That job service at first denied to accept my graduate certificate but accepted the under-graduate certificate. With that they sent me to a hotel which was looking for an electrician on call. Since that was meant day and night, they wanted me to sleep at the hotel where they had rooms for service personnel in the attic.

My father told me to forget about those idiots and check the newspa-pers on weekends. So on Saturday, I went to the newspaper dealer which is called Tabaktrafik in Austria. It goes back to 1784 when the imperator signed the monopole for tobacco in to law. It was actually focused to give disabled veterans a stable income, and also widowers of nonredeemable officers a chance to survive. Although disabled persons are still preferred to get a Tabaktrafik business, everybody could apply. And those businesses were actually very profitable, especially at high frequented places.

I bought two of the most common newspapers I knew already from our visits to the embassy in East Berlin. Over the weekend I wrote a list of all those jobs I thought would fit my qualification and experience and prioritized them from A1 through C10.

Monday morning at eight, I was at the phone booth and began to make appointments, and when I had the week filled, I refreshed myself, took ten shillings in my pocket as an emergency coin and walked out the door. When I came home late in the evening, I had the ten shilling still in my pocket for the next day, ate a small dinner and we went to bed.

On the second day I almost got hired. A large and very renowned company was looking for an electrician and was willing to pay a decent wage. I filled the application at the HR office, and when the clerk asked for my phone number and I said I didn't have one yet, she said I should wait she will talk to the manager. A few minutes later the manager came out and invited me into his office.

He wanted to get the whole story, and when I was done telling a shortened version, he gave me the advice not to apply for a job below my qualification level. He said that he would hire me on the spot but he believes that wouldn't be right. When I asked why he explained that if I would take a job below my qualification either in Austria or even in West Germany, I'd never again get a job as a graduated engineer. I'd automatically disqualify myself. That was new to me and it reduced the number of possible jobs dramatically.

The next experience was with Brown-Bowery. When I had filled the application form the hiring manager asked me in his office and again as so many times over the years he wanted to know how I was able to get out of East Germany with my family. The he explained me that he had a job for me which was almost a perfect match with my experience. They had to install and test a large switch panel at a new power plant in Brazil and the needed a project manager for that. And then came the knock-out question. "How good is your English?" Practically zero at that time. When I left I had the feeling that he was even sorrier than I was that it did not work out. He gave me his business card and said that I could use him any time as reference and that was the greatest help I got so far.

Exactly four weeks after we entered Austria at the Vienna airport I got a job and that at a time when the economy was down and many people were unemployed and on welfare support. Everything was new and therefore it was a three-month-test period agreed.

The company was specializing in power station control systems, and my job was to design the desulfurization for the coal-fired power station. It was about three months before I was allowed to make the first line on paper. The whole company was like a freezer and the deputy head of the design team was a socialist.

He was a relatively good engineer but he had absolutely no clue about economics. All the desks were placed on the window side of the long rectangular room, and the drafting boards were on the other wall. The desks were so arranged at a certain angle that the head of the design office could virtually see every single person's hand. And from time to time he would call the name of one of the sixteen engineers to remind him that he wasn't on vacation. When he was out though, almost immediately heavy debates started in which several engineers tried to persuade the deputy that the socialized industry preceding the Voest Alpine a huge conglomerate of steel makers and mills and all kind of other manufacturing plants were permanently on the edge of bankruptcy and needed tax payer's money to be rescued.

He desperately denied that fact and argued that the socialized industry had a far more comprehensive objective than just to make disdainful profit. He reasoned that it was much more important to give people a job than to make money. For almost two months I did not share in these debates. But then a new guy came and he was seated right in front of me. Within a few days we became friends. He was partner in an engineering company and hired himself out to certain projects from time to time to stay in touch with technology.

And he knew my history, I guess from the HR manager of the company. The next time the debates about the money dissipation through the socialized industry and the use of that industry to provide secure employment for failed politicians by both parties started, he just dragged me into it. By directly addressing me he said that I'd probably be able to explain in detail how all of that would end if it not stopped soon. And I explained to the general amazement of all the left leaning engineers how life really is when the main focus lays on employment and profit is just not necessary.

When the three months' trial and learning time were over, I had designed the desulfurization system for a huge new coal-fired power station. When it was built downstairs at the workshop, I went there several times to talk with the professional who put everything together and they really appreciated that, saying that they were stunned that an engineer from the design department would come to their dirty hall. They had probably never seen a hall in East Germany. For me that was normal. I wanted to see what I had designed on the drafting board in original, operation and in function.

A week later I was invited to a meeting with the HR manager, and when I arrived the deputy design manager was there too, in his function as the union boss for the salaried employees. I was enjoined not to fraternize with the blue-collar workers, and my continuous political statements were not really appreciated. Although I had an answer on my tongue, I bit my lips and that was it. This was the signal for me to look into the newspapers on the weekends again. I realized that freedom in a country where people did not really appreciate being free and considered a pretended security, wasn't really worth much. Oh yes, you were free to go where you wanted and you could live and work where you could find your place, but Austria had over the years become a society of appeasers. Whenever a situation became tense, the public opinion would call for a compromise on both sides, and what came out was often the lowest possibility instead the correct solution. And the trade association actually promoted the lowest number of strike hours in all Europe. And they were proud about that. I learned that freedom did not always mean that you can decide and found out that real freedom must be something else.

Our wooden boxes from East Germany had arrived, and with that we had most of the stuff we needed to get the children and ourselves clothed and all the dishes and so on. One day when I came home, Christiane had a huge smile on her face. She put almost 2,000 Austrian Shillings on the table, and that was a lot of money. From my current income as a design engineer I had a net pay of roughly 9,000 Shillings after all the taxes and fees were consumed. That was almost 20 percent of my monthly income. She told me that she found that money under the door when she came out of the bedroom after cleaning, 200 dollars US to be exact. That's how I knew what the dollar was in shillings at that time.

So I was going on, continuing my journey for freedom, not knowing that the only place where you could find freedom was inside of yourself.

And it took me several more years to recognize that you can only have that freedom inside of yourself when you have Jesus with you in your heart.

Within a few days I had sent out several applications, and in November I was hired to lead the electronic drive systems department of a UK based corporations subsidiary in Vienna. When I had the interview with the CEO, I still did not speak English. So he said he would hire me under two conditions. First I had to learn English, and second I needed a new passport, because he did not want to risk sending me behind the iron curtain—where our main business was—with a passport issued in East-Berlin with no visa from East Germany in it. To the second condition I agreed immediately, saying neither did I.

But for the first condition I said that I couldn't afford to go to school. He said the payment wasn't my problem but the learning. I started the new job, and every single night after work from 5:00 p.m. till 10:00 p.m. I went to English class at a private institute. The class size and the teacher were fine-tuned to success. We were eight students, and on weekends we had language laboratory where we had four hours listening to tapes of native British speakers and had to answer questions in dialogues recorded on tapes. That was going on for eighteen months.

I was several times in the UK at headquarters and was pretty successfully in designing electronic-controlled frequency inverters solutions for several huge projects for customers in Austria and the eastern bloc countries. Our money arrived from East Germany, and daily life became easier and easier for Christiane and the children. Melanie began school in September too, and both had a short way to go through a nice little garden. We decided to use the largest portion of our money to make a down payment for a house we had seen to be built outside of Vienna, just twelve miles north of the inner city where my office was.

My colleagues, my secretary and my staff were all stunned that I'd put my money into a house instead of using it for vacation and travel to see Europe and enjoy what I had missed for so many years. They couldn't understand that we had different priorities, and one of those priorities was to give our children the best possible way to a high education and a secure and loving home.

Oh yes, we thought several times, especially during those first weeks and month of hardship and limitations, about going to the American embassy and applying for an immigration visa. I was sure that with our stateless passports from East Germany and under the administration of the great President Ronald Reagan, we wouldn't have had a problem to get the visa. But we were responsible parents.

We wanted the best for our children, and weighing up the conditions under which we would enter the United States, we considered ourselves a load to the American Society and thought that our children would face incredible difficulties to reach the objectives they could lacking the knowledge of the language.

Two years after we entered Austria and began a life in freedom moved into our new house. It was a great moment, and we lived there with short interruptions for twenty years.

I made another move and worked for a couple of years for the Unilever Corporation in Austria leading the Electrical Maintenance department of a huge chemical plant, finally ending up at the Vienna electronic manufacturing facility of Philips Electronics Austria. I began a complete new phase of my professional career with Philips Austria. Taking over the responsibility for the manufacturing and facility maintenance of a multi-billion-dollar manufacturing plant with five different divisions was a huge challenge. And I enjoyed it very much and for sure the paycheck and all the benefits which came with it. Within a few months I had several new friendly colleagues, who seemed to have been waiting for someone to take on the old hardened and inefficient structures.

But I also had several enemies, some of whom tried to blackmail me by creating incidents which in one case could even have cost lives. But I had the complete and unconditional backing of the general manager, and with that I worked tirelessly to improve the reliability of machines and processes.

The way was long and hard, and the implementation of certain instruments such as preventative maintenance and autonomous production process teams was under permanent attack of many people. One of my biggest enemies, and I mean that with regard to the weight his word at the top management as well as with regard to the power he had to bring the whole facility to a screechy hold, was the union boss of the blue-collar workers.

And I bring that example here to make clear what a devastating effect an overbearing power of a union has. The first confrontation was absolute unexpected. One of the mechanics came to me and asked for a wage increase. Now, he wasn't really one of the best, and although there wasn't much to complain about his work, there was no reason to increase his wage either. He told me that his girlfriend was pregnant and that he had to rent a larger apartment, and now with all the expenses they had and her not working, he needed just more money. I asked him what I could do for the problem that he had not enough money. And he said I could raise his hourly wage by five shilling, which was almost 8 percent of his current wage. I explained that I couldn't do it, and that I would not do it even if I was able.

He was baffled and said that never happened to him before. I told him that we had approximately fifty different problem zones in the area where he worked as a mechanic, which caused about 27 percent downtime, and if he would come with three suggestions to solve three of those problems, I would grant him a five shilling increase from today on. Then I dismissed him. The next time I saw him was when I had to sign his unemployment application several days later because he quit.

But other mechanics heard about what I told this guy and they came. Several of them realized projects which catapulted our machine reliability in certain areas by 10-15 percent. And I increased their wages backdated to the day when they made the suggestion for the improvement.

That was when the union boss whom I had not seen before called my secretary and told her I should come to his office. I told her to call him back and set up a meeting that would fit my schedule. She hesitated but finally went on. A few minutes later the union boss appeared in my office and yelled at me that I had to take that back and in the future when he wanted to see me I had better come.

I told him that I did not have time for politics but since he was here and I had to clarify the situation, he should accompany me to the general manager. At the general manager's office he blamed me that I had broken the very fine-spun collective agreement for the electronic industry and that he would be able to shut down this plant within the hour if I not take back the extra raise for those mechanics. It took me five minutes to convince the GM that I did what I was hired to do and then he sent me back to work.

Later I heard that it took him three hours to make the union boss to accept that workers are better when they get rewarded for achievements and not for time of employment. Did he understand that this was the right thing to do? I doubt it. One day I was just sitting down in my seat in an airplane to fly to a company which used a machine we were about to buy. I had in the mean time become the manager of the video tape manufacturing department in addition to being the maintenance manager. When I opened the newspaper and a shock hit me.

The Berlin Wall was open.

It was open in both directions, meaning people from East Germany could unhindered walk over to West Berlin. For several months we had followed with eagerness the development in East Germany. We had seen the almost endless columns of Trabant and Warburg cars driving from Hungry through Austria to West Germany. With eagerness we watched TV reports about the faster and faster downturn of the stability of the hated STASI-secured regime of embittered old men, whose dreams of a communistic united Germany fell apart under the increasing economic distress the people were not willing to endure any longer. And whenever I was asked if I believed the wall would fall as Ronald Reagan demanded from Gorbachev, my answer was always, "Only if Erich Honecker falls before." I knew that he and his cohorts would follow the Chinese example and a massacre was imminent in the same way as on the Tiananmen Square. But he was fallen and his successors had more feel for reality than he had and the wall was open.

FREEDOM'S NIGHTMARE

You Can't Trust a Bishop or a Lawyer Even When He Works for the Lutheran Church

After I was back from my business trip, we tried to get in touch with our relatives in East Germany but still there wasn't a chance to just call somebody and talk to them. And letters still needed several days, sometimes more than two weeks, to end in our mailbox.

But following the news, and thanks to satellite TV, we were able to see more than just the two to ten minutes reports the Austrian government-controlled TV reports broadcast about East Germany. And that was understandable since the bondage of the Austrians to countries such a Czechoslovakia, Hungry and Yugoslavia was much stronger due to common history for centuries until the end of the First World War. Satellite TV brought us a direct view on what came thick and fast when the poorly and by fear held together order in East Germany collapsed.

With the fear to be killed for having your own opinion gone, there was no holding anymore, and the will of the people to clean up the rotten system of oppression and to reunite Germany again was unstoppable.

Several new initiatives came to the light of public attention, and among those were an organization which was called the *Democratic Departure* which joined the debates at the "Round Table." The Round Table was formed after the political power of the SED was so damaged that they agreed into discussions how to prepare East Germany for the first real democratic elections. The Democratic Departure was founded immediately after the fall of the Berlin Wall and Wolfgang Schnur was elected chairman. When I saw the first reports about those meeting and discovered that Wolfgang Schnur was one of the leading members of the opposition, it began to evoke the years of fight for freedom again. I remembered that one Saturday and how he was troubled by the unbelievable development that people would rather live as stateless people with no rights than to be citizen of that GDR under a SED regime.

Then in March 1990, Wolfgang Schnur was the leader of the *Alliance for Germany* and had great chances to win the election for the Premier Minister at the first free election in East Germany when the news formally exploded in the media.

It turned out that Wolfgang Schnur was controlled by the STASI as the informant *Torsten* and had reported about several of his clients he had presented at the same time. He resigned and disappeared from the official news at least until the lawsuit against him ended with a one-year sentence.

It was a crazy time, and the STASI and their cohorts tried to hide whatever information they were possible to hide. The newly elected government of East Germany decided to break-up the Stasi but only after a huge uproar of the people demanded to stop their activities and bring justice to those who were victims of more than forty years of arbitrary arrests, torture and murder for political reasons.

Based on some rumors and the suspicion that the STASI had begun to destroy files and evidence of their decade-long oppression, people seized the STASI offices in several state capitals and demanded the destruction of the STASI structures.

The party the New Forum asked the people of Berlin to demonstrate in front of the STASI central headquarters in Berlin to ensure that the transfer of to the committees went well. But something went wrong and suddenly the masses began to require entrance to the building and finally broke through the gates and stormed it.

Till today there are many voices of those who knew the scenes behind the public news, who believe that this storming was a planned and well executed action of the STASI itself which used trained infiltrators to initiate the storming. At the same time behind the scenes inside the building basements a number of STASI officers were busy destroying hundreds of thousands of files and cleaning out safes with highly explosive documents about political and economical leaders from all over the world.

The newly elected East-German government had the dream to stabilize the GDR as a separate nation in the world and create a democratic society different from the FRG. But the people of Germany had a different idea about their future country. And in demonstrations all over the territory of East Germany, weekend after weekend was the slogan to hear: "Wir sind EIN VOLK!" (German for: "We are ONE PEOPLE!"), which was developed from the demonstration's main slogan just a year ago when the protestors against the communistic regime chanted: 'Wir sind DAS VOLK"! (German for: "We are THE PEOPLE!")

FREEDOM'S NIGHTMARE

That call for the union of the German people was finally accepted and the negotiations between the politicians of east and west started as the 2 + 4 Talks. After the allied victors of the Second World War agreed to the unification, the date was set for October 3, 1990, and was based on the implementation of the West German currency the Deutsch Mark in East Germany as the common currency for all Germans. A lot of different events, activities, fights and disputes accompanied the unification process and the contracts signed by all the involved parties from the United States through Great Brittan, France and Russia as the victorious powers of the second world war.

Many of these fights about property rights, unjustified condemnation under Russian military and occupational law as well as the compensation for the victims of the communistic regime ended in disgrace for the German judiciary and the rule of law.

On the other side of the aisle many of those who had helped to keep the communistic dictatorship alive for so many years won their fights to keep their extraordinary retirement payments the German government was obliged to pay.

That because of the wording of a hasty written unification contract duck-taped together within a few weeks with more than one thousand pages. That contract was signed and voted on within hours, not even read by the lawmakers who voted on it. Sounds somewhat familiar, doesn't it?

Many books were written about the process, and I'm not about to try to go deeper into this contemporary history here.

But we had a pretty good impression of what was going on in Germany during that time because we used the connections we had to try to build a business on the side with Amway. It turned out that even Amway organization was completely overwhelmed by the tide of the events and the speed with which it developed. And through that we spent many hours in that part of Germany where we once were hated traitors thrown out and ripped off of a citizenship that only a small percentage really wanted.

The most amazing thing though was in 1990, you could drive up the East-German highway from Dresden to Berlin at two hundred kilometers per hour, eighty was the speed limit, and you'd not see one single policeman on the street. If you ran into one by chance, he would almost apologize for being in your way. And yes we visited our family, both on my side and Christiane's, and met some old friends.

I still believe that the implementation of the Deutsch Mark and the immediate forced unification of Germany was the reason for the following beginning of the economic and monetary catastrophic development for whole Germany. The German economy never really recovered from all the corruption related to the privatization of the East German industry, the billions of Deutsch Marks and later Euros pumped into a totally devastated infrastructure and totally misguided financial regulations for private investments. From the first minute on, I had the opinion that it would take a whole generation if not two to erase the cradle to the grave accommodation mentality indoctrinated over forty years into the brains of East Germans. Only a small percentage were eager to go ways such as Christiane and I had chosen to go, expecting more from life than three meals a day and a warm apartment.

A Trip to Berlin Makes Us Feel the Icy Air of a Dictatorship Again

Part of the unification contract was the reappraisal of the STASI apparatus and their possible crimes against the people of East Germany. The newly founded government agency had a huge challenge in front of it. Millions of documents were spread out over the whole country at the state, district, and local STASI offices and several secret locations.

Millions of files had been destroyed, and experts believed that it would take decades and legions of people to put them back together to readable files. But despite of all those hindrances, the law requested the agency to let everybody who believed that there might be a file existing about them to apply for the possibility to look into the collected information and if possible to discover those who had reported to the STASI about their lives.

Millions of East Germans filed applications, and the agency swelled to a huge colossus for several years. Although we had actually a lot of different topics on our personal map, we filed an application and almost forgot about it.

Our general lives became more and more comforting. I earned good money in my job, and although I worked almost sixty hours a week and often spent some hours at the weekend at the plant because of some special activities going on, I thought we had a good family life. It took a specific development at the Austrian Lutheran Church General Synod to discover what a huge mistake that was. Based on the law in Austria both of our children had Sunday school at school. It was called *Religionsunterricht* (German for lessons in religion), and children were required to participate according to their religious orientation. It was part of the education, and the grades for that subject appeared on the year's reports.

Those who declared themselves atheist did not have to send their children to those curses. Most of the time a pastor or for the catholic children, a priest from a nearby church, would come into school to hold the lessons.

Not though the Muslims, because they despised the schools as satanic and sent their children to school only because otherwise they would end in jail because public school participation in Austria was mandatory. That changed in the nineties, and now it's only Germany where you go to jail if you refuse to expose your children to the government-controlled indoctrination.

Yes, Germany is again on the edge of becoming a dictatorial regime. This time it is the dictatorship of the political correctness, the denial of a German culture and the denial of a German identity.

But let's go back to Austria and the beginning 1990s. I was tied into my job as much as a human being can be.

I did not realize how far our children had walked away from Christianity and how far the Lutheran Church was away from the Bible until the press conference of the Austrian Lutheran bishop about the decision made at the General Synod. The General Synod had unanimously voted to allow those who openly practiced a homosexual lifestyle to participate in the Lord's Supper, the holy sacrament that celebrates the remembrance on our Lord Jesus.

That was too much. I sent a letter about my disagreement about this decision to the bishop and declared that I could no be longer a member of a church who spent more thoughts on how to appease the political correctness than to fight the growing immorality. A long search for a new spiritual home almost ended in a destruction of our family. Both our children became Buddhists and Christiane and I, mostly I, strayed to find a new spiritual home. I buried myself in work, founded my own business and accepted the management position for an electronic engineering company in Germany only to find out that God doesn't allow you to run away as long as you're doubting whether or not you're doing the right thing.

In the midst of all that searching and still living in Austria, we received the confirmation from the agency for the reappraisal of the STASI documents that our files had been found and completely prepared to be read at the central office in Berlin. Our appeal to get the files sent to us was denied, and with that we had no chance but to go there, that was in 1994.

When we entered that building in Berlin, the former headquarters of the most effective and inhumaned organization after the KGB of Russia, I felt a clip squeezing my heart together and making it difficult to breathe. It was as if the past would reach out to my body and try to destroy me now, since it could not do it years ago. After a few minutes waiting, a young woman asked us into her office where we had to get through some formalities to ensure we were the right persons to see those files. Then we were instructed about the rules and regulations during our visit, and when she was done with that, she added a statement which I barely listened to because so many thoughts were running through my mind.

She said that she worked for almost three years now at this agency and she couldn't imagine the amount of tragedy hidden in many of these documents for so many families, since she was born and raised in West Berlin. Because of that she said further, her daily work was filled with the tragedies of lives. But what she had seen when she was preparing our documents had shocked her so much that she almost decided to quit. She could not understand how human beings could create such an amount of documents and put so much effort into the attempt to destroy especially in our case a family for no other reason than the striving for freedom.

She guided us into room about 40 x 40 feet with 8 tables with chairs at each of them. Five or six of these tables were occupied, and we chose one on the other side of the wall where nobody seated at that time. It was silent in the room and only now and then you could hear a suppressed moan out of shock or anger about something the person had just read in his files.

Then the door to the room opened, and as it is human nature all heads turned towards the door. And in awe-stricken silence the heads of all the people in that room followed the cart where the folders containing our documents were loaded on. A total of ten binders, each four inches thick, were laying on that cart, and in an instant those words from that young woman about her shock flushed through my mind, now capturing the total meaning of it.

It took me a couple of seconds to catch my breath and try to find a way how to start. There were six binders focused on me and four binders focused on Christiane.

Although the number of files created based on my person outnumbered those on Christiane by many, her files went back to her childhood. She was not even considered an adult when the STASI began to collect information about her behavior and opinions. She had a Christian home where she grew up in and never made a secret out of it. Don't get me wrong, she was a very silent person, you could almost call her introverted, and she still is the silent part in our marriage.

But she would definitely not attend certain events and she did not join certain organizations, and she wouldn't say anything when her school class had lessons in political subjects. All of that was recorded, even back to her being second grader in school, when she had to stand up among the classmates to show that she was a Christian who did not believe that the great leader of the East-German communist party was worthy to be admired. And she was mocked for her belief in a non-historical fiction as the STASI wrote about Jesus. Her documents contained reports of her colleagues reporting about her wearing clothing from the West and receiving gifts from relatives in the West which was latest from the mid 70s on called *NichtSozialistisches Ausland* (None Socialistic Abroad [NSA]) or sometimes, especially in connection with goods, it was called NSW (German for: None Socialistic Economy). She read what her colleagues, who were sitting next to her during an eight-hour shift of radio operating, reported about her. Those colleagues as informative employees of the STASI wrote reports that she was wearing perfume which was definitely not produced in East Germany.

And it went so far that the STASI had instructed one of their assets they had in West Berlin to infiltrate the Lutheran Sisterhood of the Red Cross of West Berlin to collect information on Christiane's aunt who was a nurse past seventy years of age, specialized in intensive surgery assistance and intensive care. She was at this time already retired but worked mainly on weekends or during the night at the ICS to watch patients.

She used the money that she earned to buy stuff to support my mother-in-law with three little girls after their father took his heels and disappeared in West Germany. Many of those reports were clearly made out of pure envy about stuff Christiane got from her relatives in West Berlin and West Germany that they could not get their hands on.

But instead of saying, "Hello, how is it that people can have all that stuff, being Germans like we are, and we can't, what's wrong here?" they envied others and helped to destroy their lives so that they couldn't have it either. All that following the brainwashing instructions of an atheistic communistic system that denied any kind of differentiation between individuals. And for that they got 50 East marks, or sometimes when the report was worth digging into something where the leading officer smelled an opportunity to crown himself they got 100 East mark. Worth nothing else than several bottles of hard liquor they needed to deafen the guilty conscience.

Year after year reports were collected, and with the meticulousness of the proverbial German thoroughness sorted and conditioned to be used at that moment when the system finally caught her at a point where it could destroy her. It was stunning what effort the STASI had put into the permanent surveillance of a single, totally harmless person out of mere fear that her life could be an example for others.

Then I turned to my pile of folders while Christiane with tears in her eyes read about the despicable deceitfulness of people who surrounded her for many years. And those tears caught again my attention when a few minutes later she read that her own brother-in-law wrote reports about us to his leading officer at the STASI. The content of the dossiers which had my name on the files was even more unveiling. One had the code name *Electronic* and was started early October 1980. The second one had the code name *Zugvogel* (German for migratory bird). The four-inch binders containing the files for the *Electronic*, were based on a telex from the department foreign intelligence to the central database for potential illegal crossing of the border that somebody who studied electronics in Berlin lived during that time at the dormitory Hans-Loch-Strasse, was now working at the Navy base in Peenemunde was planning to highjack one of the vessels to illegally cross the border to West Germany.

The immediate following dragnet operation discovered only one possible person, and that was me. Within hours of that message from the so-called operative area, as West-Berlin and West Germany was called, the apparatus of the STASI began to shift into high gear.

It took me several years to come to a conclusion about who the messenger was who sent this message which started on one side an incredible intrusion into my family's lives. Because of the imprecise description of the objectives, the STASI wasn't sure what I was up to and wanted to make sure that they got everyone who was involved, which probably saved me from being arrested on the spot.

At first the Navy base STASI office was informed that I could be in the process of planning or already actively coordinating a massive escape including several people by utilizing a vessel of the Navy. Based on the result of the dragnet action, a so-called *Arbeitsgruppe Elektronik* (German for operation team Electronic) was formed and began to collect information about me personally as well as about my family, Christiane's family as well as colleagues and former classmates from the Institute of Technology and Telecommunications Berlin.

All sources of information available to the team were pulled and analyzed. The earliest report about me was from the year 1970 when I was checked out whether or not it could be allowed to send me to undergraduate school for becoming an electrical engineer on a fishing vessel. And writing these lines here today, I discovered another confirmation. The official notice of the East-German Ministry for Internal Affairs about my mother was probably more correct than I ever wanted to acknowledge. The statement that my mother lived in East Germany after the Second World War, moved to West Germany and came back and therefore was citizen of East Germany was mentioned in that first report from 1970. At this time the STASI had no reason to make up something like the citizenship of my mother. Because it wasn't the reason for that early report, it was about the background check of me whether or not I could be entrusted with an undergraduate study.

And then it went on and on, page after page of reports, intermediate reports, and conclusions about the next steps and how to get better and more detailed information about my current and daily life. Then there were hundreds of protocols on meetings debating activities about how to collect more data and to seal the case for an arrest. Suddenly the case got changed from status *KK,* which meant collection and analysis of data about a person, to the status OPK which meant Operative *Personen Kontrolle* (German for operative personnel observation), which meant total surveillance around the clock.

What did just happen to switch from collecting and analyzing information to watch that guy around the clock he might have something in mind we don't like? The picture of me standing in front of an exhibition booth at the International Fair in Leipzig came in to my mind. During that visit at the International Fair, I had two very interesting meetings with people of electronic companies from the western part of the world, following the theme of the fair being open to the world in a climate of mutual relationships.

Unfortunately the opinion of the STASI was that this wasn't determined for me, or any other citizen of the workers' paradise. Among others I met with an engineer from SGS Ates, later SGS Thomson and today's STMicroelectronics and we had an interesting discussion about the four bit, 4 MHz Z80 microprocessor they produced. And I met with the CEO of a West German corporation which was a dealer of electronic components and was a manufacturer of crystals needed for clock generators.

I would have tried to apologize to them, if I'd have had their addresses when we came to Austria, because the STASI actually initiated checks on both persons using their assets in Italy and West Germany, and all that because I tried to get some unavailable technical documentation about electronic.

Both of them left my business card on their tables when they got back to the hotel at the end of the day, and the cleaning team which was most of the time directly employed by the STASI found it. That raised the alarm level into orange, and it was obvious through the next several reports that the leading officers—by the way, the team leader had the rank of a Cornel and his deputy was a Major—desperately tried to find someone they could place as close as possible into my personal environment.

The description of that person was so detailed in the skills that they were probably scared to find one. Comprehensive understanding of microelectronics, radio transceiver systems, basic understanding of the Bible and the Lutheran belief system, as well as an authentic legend about himself, such were the requirements the team had worked out for an informant to be placed next to me.

And they almost succeeded, not with the qualification but with placing somebody next to me whom I trusted to a certain point. A young man from our village who happened to like to go fishing had children at the same age as ours, and that was the connection point.

We went fishing together, and at a relatively early point I felt I should not to increase the relationship. My only reason was I did not like him very much. And I'm pretty sure that divine intervention, that small voice in the back of your head when you're about to do something wrong, was in place here again to save me and my family from the enemy. Now I saw his reports signed with an alias.

They tried to convince the HA-I, abroad intelligence, to place one of their valuable sources from West Berlin or West Germany for some time into my environment because they believed I'd freely open to such a person and speak about my intentions and connections considering West Germany. And they had several meetings about that. But as I could see from the protocols and reports, the HAI was absolutely against such actions because they had no safe address in the *operative region* as they called it, which they were willing to risk to be discovered since they considered me dangerous to such an extent that I was able to discover the complot.

The whole paperwork began to show the abnormal ambition to find a way to get me arrested. The formal objective of the opening of the KK activities at the beginning, to find out who I was and what I had in mind, was gone. It was replaced by a conviction that I was guilty because I showed a disagreement with the official politics of that country and they despised me for that.

The next idea was to send me to another subsidiary of the company also at a Navy base where many more people worked for our company and the possibility to have an informant there or to be able to place an informant from outside with a legend into my range of work.

Now I understand why they suddenly wanted me to learn everything about acoustic systems, such as sonar, and sent me for three months to the state capital to work at the Navy base in Warnemünde. That didn't work out sufficiently, and since even the attempted infiltration and collection of intelligence at the two namely listed companies went south, they decided to bug our phone.

Now you need to know that the phone system and the technology outside the major cities such as Berlin, Dresden Leipzig and so on was at the level of 1945. In our village with about 800 residents only five phones existed. One was the phone of the major and the other four were actually one. It was something called quarter phones. When you used the phone, nobody else could use one of the other three phones, because it was busy and you got the busy signal. Since Christiane's grandfather had decided to become a member of the Agricultural collective under the condition to be a leader of the field operation, he got one of those quarter-phones installed. With that we had a phone in house, and when nobody else was talking or the wires weren't cut we could use it.

I went through countless transcripts of phone conversations I had with people I knew or family members, and it was almost saddening how many resources the system wasted to find out whether or not I was about to steal a Navy vessel and leave the workers' paradise illegally.

Then in November 1981 again, the alarm level was increased to orange and the STASI made a huge effort to secure the area around our house. Several photographs obviously made at night with highly sensitive film material are part of the documentation. Why that sudden activity again?

The STASI had arrested a courier from West Germany who was under suspicion of working for a group in West Germany which was actively smuggling people out of East Germany when the relatives in West Germany had enough money to pay for it. That group was named *The criminal Lampl Gang* after the master mind and organizer a Mr. Lampl. The information gathered from that person sounded as if I would be at the last steps of organizing a mass escape of about 30 to 50 people utilizing my possibilities at the Navy base in Peenemunde.

And again all their resources were thrown into the effort to find out who was behind me.

Since they could not discover what I really had in mind and there were no obvious activities, at least they thought I was able to hide them so extremely well that they could not catch me, they believed that there was much more than just my desire for freedom. It became more and more clear, reading through those endless numbers of pages, that the STASI thought that I was somehow the leader of a group of people who was related to the disappearance of East German highly educated engineers and scientists.

One protocol was written about the cuts out of newspapers my mother-in-law received regularly form her cousin in West Berlin. It was mainly gossip about royal families of Europe and some other general news trash. Two officers, decryption specialists, at the state central office of the STASI were working for several months on those cutouts to try to crack the code used to transfer messages in hidden text files of those newspaper cuts from the enemy to me.

Why am I writing all of this in such detail? As I said before, and I can't repeat it often enough, I smell the rotten breath of the beginning of oppressive tyranny a hundred miles against the wind. I lived it, and I hated it. And I see, hear, and smell that same rotten indication all over the increasing power of the United States government and the hundreds of unchecked and bar off any control acting agencies. Although the intention with the Patriot Act was completely different in its attempt to restrict evil people from doing harm to the American people again, that law contains in itself the first step into a totalitarian system to control every single aspect of the lives of the people and to undermine the Law of the Land the Constitution of the United States.

And even though I once believed that you can try to reform an evil turned, yet with the best intention installed totalitarian system, I learned the hard way that freedom once lost can only be won back with the blood of martyrs. And anyone who believes that the peaceful overturn of the dictatorial regime in East Germany brought freedom to the German people makes a huge mistake. The Germany of today, as free as it appears, is not a free country. You're again in a situation there as you are almost here that you can't say what you believe.

And newly created words such as Homophobic or Islamophobic are massively used by the politicians and mass media to silence any critics of immorality or inhumane behavior and terror.

The chapter with the operative personnel surveillance was finally closed when I was sent to report to the new work place—the shipyard in Stralsund. When I was done reading—it was actually kind of flying through—hundreds of pages of partly ridiculous assumptions and untenable accusations, that iron grip on my heart that I felt several times when an application to leave that prison East Germany was declined clipped my heart again.

And on it went with another two binders, and I thought that the worst was behind me and it couldn't get worse, but it did. Page after page I had to read the betrayal by people of our own blood, family, brother and best friends. Colleagues you fought for hours together to get problems solved to get the next ship supplied to the Russians so that the next thousand barrel of oil could flow through the *Trasse der Freundschaft* (German for pipeline of the friendship). That pipeline of the friendship had become a pipeline of no cash, no oil. Those colleagues wrote reports just to get another benefit or to denounce you poor, despicable. I had to read a list with names of former classmates at the Institute of Technology and Telecommunications in Berlin who were working for the STASI as informants and were considered to move one of them with a specific legend into my working field at the shipyard. I knew of one of my classmates being employed by the STASI since we knew he was delegated from there to get a graduate degree in communications.

But the others, not for a second did I consider one of them reporting on their classmates, yet they did. One of those was part of our study group sitting together with us four and preparing for the tests. Even today writing these lines my blood runs cold and I have difficulties to agree with myself having forgiven all of those who sinned against me. Yet at the same time I remember the greatest gift God gave us and specifically me, when he allowed me to recognize his grace for me to gain faith in Jesus Christ who died for me so that I'm forgiven. But I'm human, and it is difficult not to fall back from time to time and think about revenge. But those are only seconds and thoughts.

Report your Neighbor

The Realization of a Life Dream Appears to Become a Nightmare or Why So Many People Encouraged Me to Write This Book

Eventually, nearly exact twenty years later, the great dream became reality and we moved to the United States of America. Together with a friend of mine we founded a small company to penetrate a niche marked with the modern technologies and organizational requirements of a highly competitive manufacturing world.

We dreamed to come to the greatest country on God's earth because we believe it doesn't matter where you come from, who you are and what qualification you have. We believe it matters that you are willing to work hard, being self responsible and honest. We believe that the Family, innocent life and private property still is respected and friendship, humility and the free will to charity is the basis for the great success of the American people.

When we came to the United States twenty years after we thought we had stepped into freedom, I did immediately two things. I bought a book about the Constitution of the United States of America and I applied for membership to the NRA.

We believe that your Constitution—this unique document written as an outcry for freedom (the first book I bought when I came to the United States)—still guarantees the basic rights of freedom from a bone-crushing government. We believe that the first amendment guarantees your right to put God's first place in your life, no matter where you are, at home or in public, and we believe that your second amendment is based on the awareness of the founding fathers that the people need an instrument to defend their rights.

You may have noticed that I never wrote that we believe that your Constitution gave you the rights. The only thing the Constitution does is to *guarantee* that the government is prohibited from touching those rights.

The Declaration of Independence clearly states that there are *several rights given to mankind by God the Creator*. Not just those rights named in the Declaration of Independence, but all natural rights are given by God.

It should be undisputed that whenever you consider that something is given to you by man, or governments, it is at the hands of the same power to take that away at their will. Not even certain conditions will secure that you can keep those, because the same power that gives you those things can define and change the conditions. The best example was the situation with the East German officers offering me a passport. If you have no right to travel whenever and wherever you want, that piece of paper is worth nothing.

We love to stay here because we believe in the people of the United States; we believe that rationality and common sense will triumph over irresponsibility because Americans believe that you have to earn your living and not live from other people's earning.

All that appears to be thrown away for the short enjoyment of an easy life. It appears that all those who are in power or in control lost their mind and the focus on what made the United States of America the greatest nation on God's earth. This incredible country with a constitution which is second to none in the world where the society is built on self responsibility, encouragement to be active and realize your wildest dream of success.

The country—we believe—formed by the most brilliant minds of history, is based on the approval of the scripture that *with God everything is possible.*

But it did not take much time till we recognized it wasn't that country anymore, at least not as we believed to know it from all the great books written about the land of opportunities. The denial of a higher moral authority by removing God as this highest moral instance from the public life created a *men authority.* And consequentially that leads to the argument that men has the right to decide what is right and what is wrong. Over a long time the expressive intellectuals have begun to define what has to be accepted by the society as moral. Even if they themselves are anything but tolerant, they demand it from others. Slice by slice, dead, slow and gently the fundamentals of the success of the United States are chopped off.

When we decided to move to this country to build our version of an American Dream, I still had those pictures in my mind, formed at the time when I was sitting in that library many years ago reading the great books about the United States. I remember that when those pictures flashed through my mind, preparing our household for being shipped over here, I thought it is true: reading is really cinema in your mind.

And more and more, day by day, a little deeper we got the feeling that we were moving backwards in time. That the United States of America, that great nation of free people, is moving towards socialism in its most terrifying form. It's a form of bondage so hazy that most of the people who do not bother to be informed about the general picture of politics are not able to realize how far the fetters or the lack of political maturity and freedom has already infused their daily life.

But I have also discovered that knowledge about European history and culture is very marginal and among the hundreds of people in several different states and all kind of educational levels I met. There were only few who really know exact details. Mostly those were former members of the Armed Forces of the United States, brilliantly educated and devoted to serve and with a deep love in their hearts for their country.

But I also encountered that it is not just a lack of knowledge about Europe or other parts of the world. There is a horrifying deficit in knowledge about the most important documents of the United States, the Declaration of Independence, the Constitution and the Bill of Rights. And to add insult to the injury, even the knowledge about current political situation and the what, why, when, and where in the political arena is poorly developed. Please don't get me wrong here, I won't blame the average American, but I have to ask: how could that happen? How could a nation so intensively blessed by the grace of God with prosperity become so negligent to the decay of their society, the loss of their freedom and the chipping away piece by piece of their God-given rights?

Where was the outcry and the public outrage of all those who called themselves Christians (followers of Christ Jesus) when the Supreme Court misinterpreted the First Amendment in 1963? If the founders of this great nation would ever have thought for a millisecond that it would be possible that the Bible could be banned from the public life of education, they would have had written the First Amendment in a way that would assure the Bible would be part of education.

If they would have had the slightest suspicion that the people would become one day so disconnected with the affairs of their own nation that they would allow politicians to ignore the Constitution, they would have written a paragraph in the Constitution automatically nullifying any law granting powers to the federal government not listed in the Constitution. They really believed that a literate and somewhat educated people, with a lot of common sense as it was in their time, would not accept the complete annihilation of the meaning of the Tenth Amendment.

The American people are guilty of neglecting the huge responsibility God laid in their hands when he by divine intervention on several occasions secured the victory for the American people in the Revolutionary War.

The responsibility was to secure a safe country for all of those who were suppressed by a tyrannical government and to guarantee the exercise of freedom of religion.

The guilt lies at the politicians as well as at the Pastors, Reverends and Priests of the churches throughout the United States. Instead to call their congregations to speak out and deny following the road into bondage, *they sold Jesus for a tax exemption.*

The consequence of the ignorance of the ban of the Bible from public schools did not take long to happen. I believe that the 1968 student revolt was a precisely orchestrated attack on the moral basis of a Judeo-Christian society. With the ability to stir up the always rebellious youth, now to a large part never educated in the biblical principles of moral, integrity and what is right and what is wrong defined by the Creator, the progressives successfully built the basis for their next step of the destruction of the moral foundation of the United States.

The Supreme Court decision in Roe versus Wade was the next defining step towards the annihilation of any divinely inspired moral compass. It opened the door to million times mass-slaughter of innocent unborn life every single year since. Over a fifty million Americans have been slaughtered by those who consider the unborn baby a blob of flesh and determined the safest place for a baby—mother's womb—a slaughterhouse.

What followed was an endless chain of degeneration of morals and integrity, and many churches across the nation decided to stay silent. They were silent because there was this law requiring non-profit organization not to interfere with political issues. That is what I call the *sell-out* of Jesus Christ for a tax exemption.

Politicians who are worshipping God Almighty on Sunday in churches all over the country are worshipping the devil from Monday through Saturday. What else can you say to those who confirm Judges to the Supreme Court who definitely stated, and proved throughout their career that they are in total agreement with Roe versus Wade? And I do not make a difference between Republican, Democrat, left or right, top or bottom and whoever you would like to declare guilty.

I dare to blame each and every American! There have been those among us who have been so busy to improve our lifestyles by working as much and as hard as possible. Yet putting the food for the family on the table, paying the bills in time and saving some money for a better education of our children occupied us day by day so much, that we did not realize that the Universities of the United States had become a breeding bed for the next generation of socialistic stupefied and blinded parents.

And then there are those just doing the opposite and being not busy at all, making their living on the shoulder of others. And nobody recognized that the so-called *intellectuals* have taken over the country, step by step, the educational system first, then the mass media and finally the judiciary. You can read about it when you study the reams of books about the strategy and tactic of a bloodless revolution to implement communism worldwide. The American version was the *Rules for Radicals* written by Saul Alinsky (ISBN 0-394-44341-1) for those who don't have it yet. It was this strategy that ruined most of the European countries after the 1968 student revolts because the KGB in personal union with the East German State Security Police had infiltrated the student organizations and turned them into the instrument for the communistic world revolution—they called it the *march through the institutions.*

Europe today is the result of that strategy, and even here in the United States they are on the cusp of success. The educational system is broken because it is centralized, your social system is broken because it is centralized, and soon your health care system will be broke because it has been centralized. The only way to correct that is to reconstitute the Tenth Amendment of the constitution, yet the state politicians are not much better than the federal politicians, always on the run to grab more money from the pockets of those who are still working as hard as they can to provide for their family with no time to discover the lies of these corrupt gangsters in suits. Only to give the stolen money to those who don't work and have time to listen to the lies they get told. State politicians are bribed by federal tax payers' money to reduce the state independency even more.

How much freedom is left if a social worker has the power to take your children into state custody by obtaining a verbal court order, reasoning there are indications you may try to *flee the state?*

How much freedom is left if your child is *banned* from school for saying a silent prayer in the hallway of that school?

How much freedom is left if you can lose custody for your children because you decide that teaching homosexuality is acceptable human behavior collides your Christian beliefs? Because of that you take them out of school for those lessons, and you're now threatened with a lawsuit and jail time. How much of your freedom is left?

How much of your freedom is left when it becomes a crime to dig a hole in your backyard because you want to have a pond?

How much freedom is left when it becomes a crime when you decide to follow the demand of a growing number of people and sell the milk from your homestead as a raw product instead turning it into dead matter by pasteurizing it?

How much freedom is left if a government agency determines what you can do with your own property because at a distance of five miles runs a small creek?

How much freedom is left if police can arrest you because you're standing on public ground reading out loud verses from the Bible, the same book the president lays his right hand on to swear the oath of office?

How much freedom is left when police can storm your home in the middle of the night, stun you and your children only to find out they are at the wrong address and nobody cares about it?

You think that can't happen in the United States? You believe I'm talking about my experience of thirty-two years living under an oppressive regime in East Germany?

Think again. It happens right before your blinded eyes. Every single day your God-given rights, constitutionally guaranteed, are trampled on.

How much freedom is left if the police can decide that they have to ransack your home without a warrant signed by a judge and a federal court decides that your Fourth Amendment is not violated because the police officer believed he smelled marijuana yet he had a severe cold?

How much freedom is left when a federal court decides that your secured investments are less valuable then the unsecured promises of a phony retirement fund of the Union where never has single cent been paid?

What is the Constitution of the United States of America worth, and what does it really mean to a representative who answers the question of a journalist if the law they're about to pass is constitutional? Constitution? Are you kidding me?

When the current President announced his candidacy for the office of the President of the United States in February 2007, my wife and I watched the TV report about his speech in Springfield, Illinois, and we were shocked. Not by what he said, that all sounded pretty good for a normal, untrained ear. And for those who believed it is the way to go, it was good. But for us it was as if we were thrown back twenty-five years. The tone, the cadence, and the composition of the words sounded so familiar to us that we thought for a moment we would hear one of the East-German communist leaders holding a speech.

You can't really put it into words, but we were immediately alarmed. Given the devastating situation of the educational system and the clearly perceptible disconnection of a young generation from the reality of life, a life defined once as the American Dream, we understand that this man was able to hit the right strings especially among that generation.

Being raised in an environment where everybody gets a trophy for being there, not for being the best, where the minimalistic accomplishment is considered a *good job* and responsibility is transferred to others, they demand to get what they wanted, not what they deserved.

The promise to ensure these kinds of demanded entitlements was exactly what was so scary. We had experienced where the assurance of the supply of entitlements of an all-powerful government leads. As an engineer I try to bring it to a very easy-to-understand comparison. There is a law in physics which teaches that whenever you bring a high-energy level together with a low-energy level, the combined energy level will balance out at the lowest possible common energy level. The whole universe was created that way and the same is with a society.

You can't improve people's lives when you reduce the incentive to strive for being better than the average. There is no way to improve the moral standard of living by removing the moral standards and allowing every single person to create its own moral standard.

The power granted to an ever-increasing anonymous army of unprincipled bureaucrats by the Patriot Act scared the wits out of me. Why? Because it allows the government to gain a position above the law of the land, the Constitution of the United States.

When I talked to my American family about my concerns, all I earned was disbelief. "No, Harald" was the answer, "that's not a problem for me, because I have nothing to hide. Only those who want harm us and our way of life have to fear the Patriot Act" was the answer I got.

And even in that answer lays the reason to oppose such laws and why your founders wrote in the Declaration of Independence these words: "And for the support of this Declaration, with a firm reliance on the protection of divine Providence, we mutually pledge to each other our Lives, our Fortunes and our sacred Honor."

What if there comes a government that considers your thoughts, words, writings and activities as a threat to the existing power? *What if* an administration considers suddenly those who *cling to their Bible, guns and beliefs* as a threat to their administration? *What if* an administration decides that people who believe that there are *certain unalienable rights not granted by a government or a piece of paper, but endowed by their creator to mankind* are a threat to their power? *What if* an administration suddenly finds out that those who served in the armed forces and swore an oath to "Uphold and defend the Constitution of the United States against all enemies foreign and domestic" mean to keep that oath no matter what?

All the months during a very turbulent year 2008 I heard answers to those questions, which I asked whenever possible, indicating that nobody thought this was really possible in the United States. And because I knew that only a vigilant people with a lot of understanding was able to stop evil I started to speak out.

I spoke among small groups first, but more and more publicly at Tea Party rallies and Tea Party group meetings later. And it was at one such a rally when I had a flashback to a time in history when I was scared to death because of the political system I lived in at the time.

It was when I was invited to speak at the Cincinnati Tea Party event on Labor Day 2009 at the *Voice of America*. I remembered that night many years ago when the signature of the radio broadcast *Voice of America* boomed out of my transistor radio to drone through a silent night in a small town in a communistic-controlled country. *That memory was almost overwhelming because I'd never dreamed I would be standing on that same historical ground talking about what freedom means to me and what it will mean to your children when it is lost.* With all that on my mind and the continuous encouragement of friends, radio show hosts, and many people I never met personally, I decided that there might be a reason to write this book. During the years I've been here in the United States of America, I've experienced so more friendly, open-minded and warmhearted people than ever before in my life. I'm more deeply connected to this country than I ever believed possible just a few years ago.

FREEDOM'S NIGHTMARE

That might be because of the friendships we've experienced. But it can also be because of the knowledge I gained about this nation during the last years and that I strongly believe that the United States of America is the last hope on earth for a life of freedom and prosperity. This hope is about to be wiped out by changing from *Equality of Chance* to *Equality of Outcome.*

And my love for this country might also be based on my heritage, since I discovered just recently that my grandmother was born in the United States and my grandfather has been naturalized 1938.

The real reason why grandmother moved to Austria with my father and the two girls might be forever be a secret of history.

Yet it feels like an invisible string pulled all these years—from the time reading the books about the wide and endless waving grassland of the prairies and the bitter cold of the Alaskan winter nights, until I finally settled down in a country that despite all the restrictions and limitations is still the freest in the world.